Reading Russian Sou

M000280678

Reading Russian Sources is an accessible and comprehensive guide that introduces students to the wide range of sources that can be used to engage with Russian history from the early medieval to the late Soviet periods.

Divided into two parts, the book begins by considering approaches that can be taken towards the study of Russian history using primary sources. It then moves on to assess both textual and visual sources, including memoirs, autobiographies, journals, newspapers, art, maps, film and TV, enabling the reader to engage with and make sense of the burgeoning number of different sources and the ways they are used. Contributors illuminate key issues in the study of different areas of Russia's history through their analysis of source materials, exploring some of the major issues in using different source types and reflecting recent discoveries that are changing the field. In so doing, the book orientates students within the broader methodological and conceptual debates that are defining the field and shaping the way Russian history is studied.

Chronologically wide-ranging and supported by further reading, along with suggestions to help students guide their own enquiries, *Reading Russian Sources* is the ideal resource for any student undertaking research on Russian history.

George Gilbert is lecturer in modern Russian history at the University of Southampton, UK. As well as editing the present volume, his publications include *The Radical Right in Late Imperial Russia* (2016), and he has published in English and Russian on a variety of articles on different aspects of the social, cultural and political history of the late Imperial period.

The Routledge Guides to Using Historical Sources

How does the historian approach primary sources? How do interpretations differ? How can such sources be used to write history?

The *Routledge Guides to Using Historical Sources* series introduces students to different sources and illustrates how historians use them. Titles in the series offer a broad spectrum of primary sources and, using specific examples, examine the historical context of these sources and the different approaches that can be used to interpret them.

Reading Primary Sources
The Interpretation of Texts from Nineteenth and Twentieth Century History
Edited by Miriam Dobson and Benjamin Ziemann

History Beyond the Text
A Student's Guide to Approaching Alternative Sources
Edited by Sarah Barber and Corinna Peniston-Bird

Understanding Medieval Primary Sources
Using Historical Sources to Discover Medieval Europe
Edited by Joel Rosenthal

Memory and History
Understanding Memory as Source and Subject
Edited by Joan Tumblety

Understanding Early Modern Primary Sources
Edited by Laura Sangha and Jonathan Willis

Sources and Methods in Indigenous Studies
Edited by Chris Andersen and Jean M. O'Brien

Sources and Methods in Histories of Colonialism
Approaching the Imperial Archive
Edited by Kirsty Reid and Fiona Paisley

History and Material Culture
A Student's Guide to Approaching Alternative Sources, 2nd Edition
Edited by Karen Harvey

Reading Russian Sources
A Student's Guide to Text and Visual Sources from Russian History
Edited by George Gilbert

For more information about this series, please visit: www.routledge.com/ Routledge-Guides-to-Using-Historical-Sources/book-series/RGHS

Reading Russian Sources

A Student's Guide to Text and Visual Sources
from Russian History

Edited by George Gilbert

Routledge
Taylor & Francis Group

LONDON AND NEW YORK

First published 2020
by Routledge
2 Park Square, Milton Park, Abingdon, Oxon OX14 4RN

and by Routledge
52 Vanderbilt Avenue, New York, NY 10017

Routledge is an imprint of the Taylor & Francis Group, an informa business

British Library Cataloguing-in-Publication Data
A catalogue record for this book is available from the British Library

Library of Congress Cataloging-in-Publication Data
Names: Gilbert, George, editor.
Title: Reading Russian sources : a student's guide to text and visual sources from Russian history / edited by George Gilbert.
Description: Abingdon, Oxon : Routledge, 2020. | Series: Routledge guides to using historical sources | Includes bibliographical references and index.
Identifiers: LCCN 2019045062 (print) | LCCN 2019045063 (ebook) |
ISBN 9780815394969 (hbk) | ISBN 9780815394976 (pbk) |
ISBN 9781351184175 (ebk)
Subjects: LCSH: Russia–History–Sources–Study and teaching (Higher) |
Soviet Union–History–Sources–Study and teaching (Higher) | Diplomatics–
Russia. | Diplomatics–Soviet Union.
Classification: LCC DK3.R43 2020 (print) | LCC DK3 (ebook) |
DDC 947.0072–dc23
LC record available at https://lccn.loc.gov/2019045062
LC ebook record available at https://lccn.loc.gov/2019045063

ISBN: 978-0-8153-9496-9 (hbk)
ISBN: 978-0-8153-9497-6 (pbk)
ISBN: 978-1-351-18417-5 (ebk)

Typeset in Times New Roman
by Swales & Willis, Exeter, Devon, UK

Contents

List of illustrations

List of contributors

The list of publications cited below is to illustrate research interests; they are not comprehensive.

Courtney Doucette is Assistant Professor of History at the State University of New York at Oswego. Her research focuses on the cultural and social vectors of reform, the history of the Soviet press, and the forms of popular participation in politics in the late Soviet period.

George Gilbert is Lecturer in Modern Russian History at the University of Southampton. Editor of the present volume, his publications include *The Radical Right in Late Imperial Russia* (2016), and articles on aspects of the social, cultural and political history of the late Imperial period.

Dan Healey is Professor of Modern Russian History at St Antony's College, University of Oxford. He is the author of *Russian Homophobia from Stalin to Sochi* (2018) and *Homosexual Desire in Revolutionary Russia: The Regulation of Sexual and Gender Dissent* (2001), and writes on Soviet medicine, sexualities and gender history.

Jeremy Hicks is Professor of Russian Culture and Film at Queen Mary University of London, teaching courses on Russian film, literature and translation. His publications include: *Dziga Vertov: Defining Documentary Film* (2007) and *First Films of the Holocaust: Soviet Cinema and the Genocide of the Jews, 1938–46* (2012), and he has also published various articles on Russian and Soviet film, literature and journalism, including frequent reviews on contemporary Russian documentaries for Kinokultura.com. His most recent work is entitled *The Victory Banner: Cinema, Ritual and Repetition in Russia's Memory of World War Two*.

Sarah Hudspith is Associate Professor of Russian at the University of Leeds. She specializes in Russian literature from the nineteenth to twenty-first centuries. She is co-editor of *Russian Culture in the Age of Globalization* (2019) and author of *Dostoevsky and the Idea of Russianness* (2004), as well as articles on Tolstoy, contemporary women writers, narrative, humour, and the city.

Dakota Irvin is a Visiting Lecturer in Russian and East European History at the University of North Carolina at Chapel Hill. His articles have been published in *Revolutionary Russia* and *Vestnik Sankt-Peterburgskogo universiteta*, and he contributed a chapter to *The Fate of the Bolshevik Revolution* (2020).

Jennifer Keating is Assistant Professor of Modern East European History at University College Dublin. She is a historian of the Russian empire in the late nineteenth and early twentieth centuries, using environmental history as a middle ground from which to explore the idea and practice of imperialism. Focusing primarily on the geographical edges of the state at moments of imperial expansion and collapse, she is currently completing a book manuscript on environmental dimensions of empire building on Russia's southern frontier in Central Asia, 1881–1916.

Claire Le Foll is Associate Professor of East European Jewish History and Culture in the Parkes Institute at the University of Southampton. She is the author of *L'école artistique de Vitebsk (1897–1923): Eveil et rayonnement autour de Pen, Chagall et Malevitch* (2002), *La Biélorussie dans l'histoire et l'imaginaire des Juifs de l'empire russe (1772–1905)* (2017), as well as numerous articles in English, French and Russian on the history and culture of Jews in Belorussia.

Claire Shaw is Associate Professor in the History of Modern Russia at the University of Warwick. Her research focuses on the history of disability and the body under Soviet socialism. She is the author of *Deaf in the USSR: Marginality, Community, and Soviet Identity, 1917–1991* (2017), and *Stalin (All You Need to Know)* (2018).

Katy Turton is a Visiting Research Fellow at Queen's University, Belfast. Author of *A Family Affair? The Role of Family Networks in the Russian Revolutionary Movement* (2018), she specializes in the history of women's involvement in the Russian Revolution.

Pavel Vasilyev is Senior Lecturer at National Research University Higher School of Economics in St Petersburg. He defended his doctoral dissertation on drug abuse and drug policy in early Soviet Russia at the St Petersburg Institute of History of the Russian Academy of Sciences in October 2013. His recent publications include articles in *Historical Research, Rechtsgeschichte – Legal History, The Journal of Social Policy Studies* and *Vestnik of Saint-Petersburg University, History*.

Mark Vincent is an Associate Tutor at the University of East Anglia. His main research interests focus on criminality in the Balkans and former Soviet Union. His publications include *Criminal Subculture in the Gulag: Prisoner Society in Stalin's Labour Camps* (2020) and a number of different articles on various aspects of crime and penality in the early Soviet state.

Peter Waldron is Professor of Modern History at the University of East Anglia. His books include *Radical Russia: Art, Culture and Revolution* (2017), *Russia of the Tsars* (2011), *Governing Tsarist Russia* (2007), *Between Two Revolutions: Stolypin and the Politics of Renewal in Russia* (1998), and *The End of Imperial Russia, 1855–1917* (1997).

Monica White is Associate Professor of Russian and Slavonic Studies at the University of Nottingham. She is a co-editor of *Byzantium and the Viking World* (2016) and author of *Military Saints in Byzantium and Rus, 900–1200* (2013), as well as articles about a wide range of topics pertaining to the medieval Orthodox world.

Andy Willimott is Lecturer in Modern History and Fellow of the Institute for Humanities & Social Sciences at Queen Mary University of London. His publications include *Living the Revolution: Urban Communes and Soviet Socialism, 1917–1931* (2017) – winner of the Alexander Nove Prize – and *Rethinking the Russian Revolution as Historical Divide* (2018).

Acknowledgements

First and foremost, I am grateful to all of the authors in this volume for writing their chapters, the care and commitment they have put into them, and patience during the editorial process. These high-quality essays present innovative readings of source materials that should challenge and excite students, and illustrate the manifold approaches one can take when reading sources. Some authors mentioned to me how their chapters were tricky to write, and students would do well to consider that even for experts immersed in the scrutiny of sources discussing their findings is not always a straightforward process.

I would also like to thank those who were approached to write a chapter but for a variety of personal and professional reasons had to decline. Several passed on helpful suggestions about who to approach in the wake of not being able to provide a contribution themselves, and so their expertise has aided the compilation of this collection of essays. A number of colleagues read drafts of chapters, providing comments and queries for authors, and I wish to thank those people too – several are mentioned in the notes to various contributions.

At the University of Southampton, a number of people have had input into the volume. Discussions at an early stage with François Soyer (now at the University of New England in Australia) and David Brown provided useful insights into shaping the volume. Particular thanks to Joan Tumblety, editor of an excellent volume in this series, *Memory and History: Understanding Memory as Source and Subject*, who generously shared her ideas and plans for that book and the resulting discussion which helped shape this volume.

Another group to thank is the editorial staff at Routledge. I would like to thank Eve Setch and Laura Pilsworth who invited me to put together the current volume, a challenge I accepted immediately due to my view, based on my own teaching experiences, that there is a genuine gap in the field for such a resource. Eve together with Zoe Thomson – a most careful and diligent editorial assistant – have shown great enthusiasm for the project and responded in a timely manner to my queries. I am grateful for their editorial encouragement, which has helped move the project along at a reasonable pace. No less than five readers reviewed the book's proposal: size constraints mean that I have not been able to respond in depth to all of their constructive criticisms, or include all the source types suggested, but I have sought to answer several of their most substantive points, and I hope this effort has improved the final volume. A time-consuming element of the project was seeking various permissions, especially image rights: thanks to those people who allowed various images and materials to be reproduced in this book. Thanks also to Jonathan Clark and Rob Collins, who kindly offered to proof-read the manuscript at different stages.

Working on an edited collection has shown to me the positive aspects of collaborative scholarship, all the more so when united around a shared desire to produce genuinely innovative work. The past researches of the many people cited herein as well as those immediately working on the volume are testament to this. Many students, colleagues and friends have contributed in ways that are perhaps less directly discernible but no less relevant: my thanks to them.

George Gilbert
September 2019

List of abbreviations

Names and organizations

FSB	Federal Security Service
NKVD	People's Commissariat of Internal Affairs
OGPU	Joint State Political Directorate

Archives

GARF	State Archive of the Russian Federation
RGADA	Russian State Archive of Ancient Documents
RGAE	Russian State Economic Archive
RGAKFD	Russian State Archive of Film and Photo Documents
RGALI	Russian State Archive for Literature and Art
RGANI	Russian State Archive of Contemporary History
RGASPI	Russian State Archive for Socio-Political History
RGIA	Russian State Historical Archive
RGVA	Russian State Military Archive
RGVIA	Russian State Military History Archive
TsDOOSO	Centre for the Documentation of Social Organizations of Sverdlovsk Oblast
f.	fond (collection)
op.	opis (inventory)
d.	dela (file)
l. [ll.]	list [listy] (sheet) [sheets]

A note on names, translations and dates

Throughout the text the widely recognized Library of Congress system has been used for transliteration; but, there is always an element of personal preference to this process. One exception is concerning widely familiar names, so we have 'Trotsky' instead of 'Trotskii', and 'Dostoevsky' instead of 'Dostoevskii'. Another is in the footnotes and bibliographies when a given work or author's name has been published differently. Document titles have been transliterated in the footnotes, though all dates have been translated into English.

Most contributors have used Russian-language originals of sources that contain Ukrainian names, so for consistency's sake I have used 'Kiev' and 'Odessa' rather than 'Kyiv' and 'Odesa'.

Another fun element of studying Russian history is frequent name changes. Place names in Russia have been rendered in the officially recognized form of the day – so, St Petersburg and Petrograd refer to the same location, but change depending on the year in question.

Dates before February 1918 are given in accordance with the Julian calendar, thirteen days behind the Gregorian (Western) calendar in the twentieth century. Dates thereafter follow the Gregorian calendar.

Introduction: reading Russian sources

George Gilbert

An enigma, a threat to Western power, the policeman of Europe, a cradle of culture and civilization: all of these words and phrases, and many more, have been used to describe Russia, a country that attracts ceaseless interest from a variety of audiences; but, closer analysis of its history shows Russia defies easy descriptions, continually resisting popular attempts to label and mislabel it. To understand the country and get closer to a deeper understanding of the land, its peoples and its rich and often dramatic history we need to go beyond clichés. One way of doing this can be to examine the sources that have shaped the understanding of those who have explored Russia's history, reconstructing the history of the country from the bottom up through selective analysis of different source materials. As part of the successful and user-friendly *Routledge Guides to Historical Sources* series, this book seeks to meet such a need in providing assessment of sources that have underpinned our understanding of Russian history. In doing so, the volume strives to be innovative in its approach. Though focused on exploration of source materials and containing remarks of a general nature, there is much fresh research contained within the pages of this book. Whilst exploring sources it attempts to introduce students to key problems and issues in the study of Russian history.

The present volume includes analyses of different types of source materials and approaches to the study of varied periods in the Russian past. The chapters have been contributed by a range of people at different stages of their academic careers from the international academic community, and mostly but not wholly by people who are historians by training. Whilst seeking to acquaint students with possible approaches towards the study of Russian history, it strives to maintain a clear vision. This book is not a guide to the practical issues of using archival repositories in Russia or post-Soviet states: there are good resources for those.[1] Nor is it a source reader, of which a great many are now available on a variety of periods and topics.[2] Instead, it explores methodological problems in using different types of sources, considering these as a point of departure for thinking about Russian history. In doing so it invites the reader to discover new ways of thinking about the Russian context, considering a variety of problems and perspectives in interpretations of source material and, therefore, of Russian history. The sources that appear within the chapters are based on a mixture of English translations and Russian-language originals, explored in fifteen original contributions.

The book is designed to appeal to a mixture of audiences and demographics. The primary audience is imagined to be undergraduate and postgraduate students at universities, but it should also be useful for doctoral students undertaking the initial stages of their research, or possibly advanced school students studying Russian history before entry into university. The remarks in the book should also appeal to those generally interested in Russian history – readers who have likely come across various secondary works on Russian history but who might not yet have considered the problems of using primary source materials of different types in depth. The inclusion of a broad range of materials in this book speaks to such varied demographics. An unavoidable point is how the Russian language impacts upon our understanding of such materials. It is assumed that many of those using the volume will not have advanced Russian language skills, which has been reflected in the selection of the materials, the style of the contributions and suggestions for further reading in each chapter. Even so, advanced (or even quite limited) linguistic skills will always help us go beyond the obvious points of any source, so contributors have been encouraged to engage with issues of language, which will necessarily confront any student of Russian history, including those confined purely to English-language sources or translations. Those with advanced linguistic skills might still consider the methodological and conceptual approaches outlined within the book, and several chapters engage with issues of using archival materials mostly in the original Russian. So, though the reader of this book might not know Russian, the book encourages them to think seriously about language and the issues that will pose to their study of Russian history.

Though designed to be user-friendly and accessible, the volume does not (and should not) shy away from difficult questions in the interpretations of such materials. Tumultuous and, in some chapters, emotional and difficult events are described therein. Students should continually be alert to the fact that study of Russian history can involve challenging materials as well as politically, socially and emotionally complex issues. On the other hand, some events and materials remind one that many of the problems and cares of people in Russia, even in its most apparently dramatic historical moments, are much the same as those for other people across time and space, including in largely peaceful times; popular behaviours can be surprising and provocative, but they can also be typical and mundane – sometimes both. Considering such a range of perspectives and behaviours, one can only conclude that good history is usually complex.

Sources in the Russian context

Before we begin: what do we mean by 'Russia?' Is it a place? An idea? A set of peoples? A territory? A nation? This volume uses Russia in the deceptively simple sense meaning a country, but – to complicate matters – depending on the period in question we would not always recognize this as the territory of modern Russia we see on a map today. We refer to the federation that first emerged in the time of Kievan Rus, subsequently became a centralized Russian state during the tsardom of Muscovy, then, the largest state in the Russian empire as proclaimed by tsar

Peter the Great after 1721 and, following the fall of this empire in 1917, the largest republic within the Soviet Union (sometimes known informally as Soviet Russia) that lasted until 1991.[3] The majority of the sources featured within this volume emerge within these contexts. Yet, any student of Russian history should realize that scrutiny of many sources will also involve those emerging outside of Russia. Complex processes of migration, rural and urban change, population displacement, conflict, centre/periphery tensions (and many others) saw large numbers of people flow between Russia and the surrounding states throughout history, complicating this understanding of what we mean by 'Russian'.[4] There are important points to be made about the often complicated relationships between Russian and non-Russian peoples within Rus, tsardom, the Russian empire and the Soviet Union. Even when analysing texts and visual sources that originate within Russia itself, one must bear in mind these relationships, given the complex ways in which they impinge upon our understanding and interpretation of the sources at our disposal.

Many authors touch upon the relationships between Russians and non-Russians, in sometimes surprising ways. These include assessment of non-Russian sources, but also important questions concerning identity, territory, empire and power (to name a few) that emerge when exploring sources emerging within the Russian context. Questions concerning Russia's shifting relations with surrounding nations, including countries like Ukraine and Belarus, feature within this volume. Several chapters explore sources emerging within the Russian empire (1721–1917), a complex and multivalent entity which contained within it a quite remarkable diversity of peoples. Within Russia itself, at every stage of our timeframe, there was huge variety and complexity. Chapters often touch upon materials from Moscow and St Petersburg, but sources included go beyond this geography: for instance, Irvin's chapter on surveillance reports largely focuses on materials drawn from primary (in this case archival) sources consulted in the city of Ekaterinburg. Study of Imperial Russia necessarily involves considering demographics, language and national and/or ethnic identities when exploring materials originating from this context. Other chapters consider the relationship between Russia and the wider world, including not only Eastern and Central Europe but countries further afield like the United States. Transnational connections are an emerging area of interest that contributors take note of, and much quality literature is emerging in this area.[5] Remarks often refer to the production end of sources, including those published in languages other than Russian, but also their dissemination and reception once the source has been released. On the latter point, we might consider how non-Russian audiences might have different ways of seeing materials that initially appeared in Russia. The historian must be alert to a variety of possible perspectives.

Given our aim of exploring Russia through sources, it seems sensible to provide a few remarks on the peculiarities of Russian history. Most books in the *Routledge Guides to Historical Sources* series take a different approach to this one, which is a work of area studies, rather than a study of sources from a particular chronological period, or different types of textual or non-textual materials. Like any country Russia has its own a peculiar history, with a variety of social, cultural, economic, political and other processes contributing to the formation of the country we see today. Beyond this rather obvious point there are, I believe, additional motivations for creating such a volume with Russia as its primary frame.

First, there is the issue of historical context and how that impinges upon our understandings of the sources themselves. If we take, say, a memoir, diary, autobiography or TV series, we need to place these in the context of Russia's own historical development. This includes urgent and transformational processes: territorial acquisition, often on a vast scale, wars both inside and outside of Russia's borders, revolutions of different types and at different times, and civil war(s). These events all had their own implications, which affect the content, style and presentation of such sources. One should also be alert to arguments over periodization and how this affects our understanding of Russian history: for example, do the Russian revolutions of 1917 emerge most clearly and significantly when we look in depth at key events from within the revolutionary year itself, or instead as part of a longer-term process: in Peter Holquist's neat and influential phrasing, a 'continuum of crisis' that spanned war, revolution and civil war from 1914 to 1921.[6]

Second, a key lens for interpreting Russia has been provided by the profound impact that ideologies of different types have had on the country. This certainly has greatly influenced how people have written about the history of Russia. Perhaps nothing has had broader ramifications than the revolutions of 1917 and their impact in both the short and long term. In his beginner's guide to the Russian Revolution, Abraham Ascher cites a professor's quip: 'If you tell me what a person's view of 1917 is, I can most probably divine [their] political views on all major contemporary issues'.[7] Several authors in this book mention the so-called 'totalitarian' model, a central analytical frame for understanding Soviet Russia in the Western hemisphere following the Second World War. Influenced by a negative view of Marxism and Communism, this scholarly frame has left an indelible impression on historical writing: to one significant writer, the Soviet Union was a 'tragedy' offering only lessons in what is to be avoided.[8] But, at the other end of the political spectrum, the Soviet project generated a number of contemporary sympathizers in America, Europe, Asia, Latin America and Africa. For many observers, it offered a plausible alternative to the capitalist model of development for much of the twentieth century. Decades later, long after the collapse of the Soviet Union, the Russian Revolution continues to generate intense interest from the politically engaged. Some contemporary accounts still lean towards sympathetic portrayals of the lead actors, like Vladimir Lenin.[9] Long before the revolutions of 1917, ideology had a strong impact in Russia: it shaped both the actions and practice (praxis) of the revolutionary movement during the nineteenth century, and, in the same period, the identity of the conservative Russian state – a vision of nationalism uniting Russian Orthodoxy and autocracy that holds an appeal for many today, both inside and outside of Russia.

Third, ideology connects to diverse and personal ways of exploring the Russian past, and can be usefully married with other approaches, such as the turn towards social and cultural history. Looking at the lives of the people of Russia can breathe new life into often desiccated debates regarding official and non-official ideologies, complicating our understanding of ideology and the lives of the people of the country that we are studying. With respect to social history, influential work has shown how one's view of Russian or Soviet power – including its cultural norms and values – can shift in the mind over years, months, days or even hours.[10] Scholarship has explored how people of all types actively wrote themselves into the revolutionary project, often borrowing the language and discourse of the regime to present themselves as Soviet citizens. Influential scholarship has explored processes of self-fashioning and self-understanding amongst Russian and Soviet citizens: did people in 1930s Soviet Russia, in Stephen Kotkin's phrase, come to 'speak Bolshevik'?[11] The impact of such work is clear from a number of contributions here, and can usefully challenge the 'totalitarian' model of how ideology functioned in Russia and the Soviet Union. In this reading, we might shift the conceptual lens away from exploring the doctrines of the state, ruling party or leader towards individual and often shifting and contingent identities, and the interplay of social and political factors located at the interstices of human experiences. Sophisticated work such as Sarah Davies's study of popular opinion under Stalin – analytically informed and supported by a firm grounding in the primary sources of the period – has explored the behaviour of people at a variety of levels and from different walks of life, trends continued by contributors to the present volume in their own research.[12]

Fourth, we must not overlook how the state often played a key interrogative and coercive function for much of the period under review, which necessarily impacts upon the sources we are exploring. Two clear examples of this are demonstrated by processes of surveillance and censorship.[13] Several contributors address the question of how even slight or partial modification of a source by a particular branch of the Russian state's infrastructure or bureaucracy affects the way we read it. If a newspaper is censored, or if a letter has been perlustrated (meaning intercepted and possibly edited) then important processes of mediation have occurred. This affects the content of what we are reading, and hence we must be aware of filters that have been applied to the source material that we are looking at.[14] In both late Imperial and Soviet Russia the state was often keen to use practices concerning some form of surveillance or editing, though its ability to enforce these varied depending on the period in question. In Richard Pipes's view, late Imperial Russia might have been heading 'towards the police state', but it did not have the practical wherewithal or ideological coherence to put its plans into action.[15]

Fifthly and finally, the peculiarity of technological development in Russia impacts upon our understanding of the materials consulted in this volume. When certain technologies became prevalent in Russia transformed the popular impact of several of the source types featured within these pages – taking one example, witness how advances in print technology contributed to a press boom in the late Imperial period, especially at the outset of the twentieth century. The expansion of the press, both official and non-official, had marked impacts upon political processes as well as the construction of individual identities of different types, based on estate (*soslovie*), class, social, ethnic, sexual, national or religious categories. In addition, as well as impacting upon what types of sources can be produced, technology also affects how sources can be curated and stored, which naturally affects the types of documents that we can consult as historians.

Organization and scope

This volume is comprised of a series of chapters covering different time periods and a wide variety of source materials. Three chapters at the outset of the volume are dedicated to approaches and periodization, whilst the remaining twelve focus on varieties of sources. This might seem like many, but a few caveats are needed: much of interest has not been included in the present volume. Certain types of archival sources which make intriguing reading for the scholar of Russia with access and the skill set to interrogate them have not been included – for instance, court files.[16] There is also no chapter on oral history, an innovative and intriguing way of doing history that offers exciting research pathways in a variety of ways.[17] In pre-revolutionary Russia especially, oral reports on important news could precede the printed text. Another point to consider regarding oral history relates to variation in the cultures of Russia's peoples. Some peoples within the Russian empire recorded their lives and stories primarily through oral means well into the twentieth century: to cite one example, the Chuvash peoples (a Turkic ethnic group native to a region from the Volga to Siberia) primarily communicated in this way, with written sources only becoming plentiful from 1900 to 1910.[18] In spite of such omissions, at least some of which would have been included in a longer volume, there is a logic and coherence to what has been included below.

The book is designed to be both useful and accessible, which has been reflected in the choice of materials. I have also attempted to reflect major debates in the study of Russian history by selecting materials that have proven influential to some of these debates. Related to both points, the volume is designed primarily for use either in a classroom environment or as a supplement for the student's own studies. The variety of materials included tends towards those encountered by students who have started to read seriously around Russian history but have perhaps not yet fully considered important methodological, conceptual and technical problems in using different varieties of primary source material. Many examples of source types in this volume can be found in translation, with more examples likely to appear in the future. This includes two chapters on memoirs, one of which is a more specialized assessment of prison literature, and contributions on diaries, autobiography and novels. The book includes assessments of both textual and non-textual sources, the latter of which can be watched or experienced by those with basic or non-existent Russian language skills provided that appropriate and accurate captions, translations or subtitles are provided. So, there are chapters on art, film and TV and maps.

Conversely, some of the source types can typically be encountered only in specialist repositories in Russia and former Soviet states. Such collections are therefore only going to be seen by those with advanced Russian-language skills and privileged access. However, archival research is the mainstay of many scholars, yielding many of the field's most important discoveries, and all students of Russian history should be alert to this vital feature of research culture. Two examples of sources included here that are usually encountered in archives are letters and surveillance reports. 'Letters' is a broad genre that can be split into different sub-categories, like petitions and denunciations, and, allowing for this feature, many examples are accessible to the scholar with no or limited archival access. In contrast, relatively few examples of surveillance reports are available in translation. Both letters and surveillance reports are well worth further scrutiny, as they often provide core source materials for secondary studies.[19] They have proven influential on how historians think about scholarship: consider for instance the research of both Matthew E. Lenoe and Sheila Fitzpatrick, in which letter-writing itself becomes the focus of scholarly enquiry.[20]

On the other hand, many types of sources in this volume can be readily found in abridged or complete form in document collections, and, increasingly, within online collections of primary sources. This includes the press in both the late Imperial and Soviet periods. Though huge gaps remain, increasing proportions of the press have been digitized.[21] Together, this choice of sources varies the methodologies and concepts in the chapters themselves, enhancing the intellectual interest of the collection, and, it is hoped, expanding the readership of the volume.

A goal has been to address a variety of different types of materials including both texts and visual sources. The latter can be highly useful in a classroom environment, often proving very teachable as sources – film clips and propaganda posters can make strong impressions on students of Russian history.[22] Furthermore, visual sources provoke a different kind of intellectual enquiry that readers should be alert to: as the chapters by Keating, Le Foll and Hicks all note, questions we might ask of visual sources can overlap with those for texts – these might concern production and reception – but others are quite distinct to the type of visual source under assessment: for instance, the technical problems of certain types of artistic production, or the regulation of film via censorship.[23] There has been an attempt to create space for sources that can provoke innovative readings of the material; in one chapter, Vincent explores the semiotic meanings of tattoos in the Russian prison system.

A few remarks are needed on the chronological frame of the book. The general remit has been to provide a broad chronology. Certain periods are given relatively scant exploration, but it has been an aim to include one thorough assessment of source materials from an earlier period in history: such materials are explored in White's chapter on early medieval sources (starting c. 900). Other chapters span the late early modern period to 'modern' (early 1990s) Russia. The majority of these chapters deal with the nineteenth and twentieth centuries. Whilst five contributions primarily explore source materials selected from the Russian empire, nine chapters assess materials from the Soviet period (1917–91). Broadly speaking this reflects the current state of the field, with more scholars engaged in research on the Soviet era than on any other period in Russian history. This broad chronology can invite us to think seriously about the technical problems of using sources from different periods: this can include their (re-)production, technological aspects and availability. It can also provoke us to consider context, and processes of continuity and change occurring between different historical periods: Rus, the Russian empire and the Soviet past.

Reflecting the mixed backgrounds of the contributors, the sources and approaches in this book represent a variety of voices. This is not merely to reflect current fashions: perspectives must be considered as they always affect the historian's craft. Vasilyev's chapter on positionality engages with such issues in the most overt way, encouraging students to consider the twin problems of 'positioning' and 'positionality' in the study of Russian history. Like several other chapters, Vasilyev's contribution includes the study of marginal groups, in this case structured around the methodological and historiographical problems of studying late Imperial drug policies and communities impacted by drug abuse. As a partly personal account, the chapter invites us to consider how someone from the Russian educational system considers prevailing trends in Western historiography; in contrast, other chapters are the products of contributors working in various European and North American contexts.

Thinking thematically, social history is a key interest of the volume, and in using this text students will encounter a diverse range of voices through the source record that has been scrutinized. There has been a thorough attempt to think beyond the class-based discourses that originally shaped Russian studies in an earlier period and include a broader range of identities, some of which have been rarely or only recently explored in the study of Russian history – though of course class identities can and do intersect with these newer frames. Thus, chapters on source types include extensive analysis of homosexuality (Healey), the deaf community in the Soviet Union (Shaw) and prisoners in the Soviet penal system (Vincent).[24] Varied male and female perspectives have had a huge influence on the scholarly literature surrounding a vast range of topics in Russian history. Whilst Turton's chapter is the one to most overtly engage with women's history through a thoroughgoing examination of the works of Aleksandra Kollontai, the related though distinct category of gender is a key area of enquiry, with most chapters making reference to gendered perspectives within their analyses.[25] Nationality is a recurrent theme of many chapters; in contrast, more could be said on race as a specific and particular category of analysis in the Russian context.[26]

As described above, politics and political practices have indelibly shaped study of the Russian and Soviet pasts. Some chapters focus more overtly on the politics of the Russian and Soviet states, and how these impact upon our understanding of the source traces that they have left behind. This is readily apparent in Waldron's chapter, which explores questions concerning the availability of source material. Doucette's exploration of late Soviet letters also addresses such questions, though in a markedly different way: her careful analysis encourages us to think about the practices of the Soviet state (what did they keep, and why) and also the concerns of citizens at an everyday level, which were reflected in the letters they wrote in to major newspapers. Conversely, a good number of chapters focus closely on what might be broadly conceived of as 'culture', including ideas, systems and behaviours, but also semiotics, symbols and codes. Chapters by Hudspith, Willimott, Le Foll, Gilbert and Hicks all explore the role of culture as a historical phenomenon, exploring a range of areas in how culture can help us understand Russian history. This can include state-building and the state's own use of propaganda, but, if the source record allows for it, the reception of different forms of culture amongst mixed audiences, which might include subversive readings of the state's cultural products.[27]

Though the chapters are individually interesting and challenging, ultimately the goal has been to provoke further exploration of research pathways that have proven influential in the study of Russian history. Essays address tried and tested frameworks such as political, social and cultural history, as well as themes like politics and power, gender, marginality, culture-building and citizens' self-understanding. Some chapters incorporate assessment of Russia's provinces: Irvin and Hicks are among those to consider questions concerning centre and periphery.[28] Reflecting my own perspective as editor, I have encouraged contributors to engage with recent, innovative readings of different types of sources, both in their assessments and in the notes.

Problems of interpretation

At the outset of the volume, it is only the editor's intention to make a few brief, contextually-driven remarks on Russia relating to the exploration of different types of source materials. Individual chapters carry their own methodological and historiographical assessments, with the below comments only generally applicable to chapters in this book and source assessment.

An immediate issue is accessibility. This might involve the closing, opening and in some cases closing (again) of archives in Russia itself: rich repositories of knowledge and meaning that provide many of the documents that subsequently find themselves interpreted in secondary texts or translated as standalone works. Chapters by Waldron and White, among others, address a basic challenge: what can we get hold of? Even for those not at the cutting edge of archival research, knowledge of what is out there now and what is likely to become available soon impacts upon what we can say about Russia. The challenges of source availability are manifold: they might be primarily political, in the sense that a particular source is considered too sensitive to release. For instance, many secret police files of a more recent era are still closed to researchers (classified) within the Russian Federation; intriguingly, the same (or similar) files can sometimes be available in the archives of former Soviet states, for instance Ukraine.[29] In other cases, challenges are more technical, concerning, for example, the marked deterioration of sources over time; these might have been damaged by climate changes, transport, or simply be badly stored. This is most to the fore with sources from earlier periods of history, but source materials from the more recent past might also have deteriorated, and so the originals may be unavailable to consult for the researcher. Indeed, it is an unusual researcher of Russia who has never come across at least some deeply desired material said to be 'in restoration' and therefore off-limits. More positively, increasing amounts of material are available online: these include many secondary texts (including extracts), and collections of different types of primary sources, presented in well-organized, scholarly websites and curated by specialists on the period, often with enlightening commentary. Supporting materials can include podcasts which might consist of interviews with specialists, as well as blogs and comment.[30]

Having (perhaps) found our sources, other questions might occur to us, chiefly concerning the veracity of such materials, and whether we can place our trust in what we have found. Echoing the style of many of the below contributions, the student should adopt a questioning approach here. Questions might include: are our sources accurate? Are they reliable? Do the sources provide us with a truthful picture of the 'reality' of the past? More negatively, if we feel sources are not accurate, have they been falsified? What is unreliable as a result of deliberation? Could other errors be more incidental? Several chapters engage with themes of accuracy and reliability (including those by Shaw, Hudspith, Turton, Healey and Keating), adopting a critical approach towards their sources.

The sociologist Jean Baudrillard in *Simulacra and Simulation* commented that we live in a world of more and more information, and less and less meaning. Given the plethora of materials we are likely to encounter, we need to think carefully about what is most useful for us: what sources should be urgently consulted, what are potentially useful, and what can be discarded. Several contributors engage with the issue of whether sources are representative or 'telling' (e.g., Gilbert, Le Foll, Willimott), using materials telling us about an idea, person or event. It could be that these are somehow representative of a trend, movement, idea or period, or, conversely, that the author/creator was a figure of particular and historical importance. In the context of scrutiny of maps from the Imperial period, Keating sagely notes that such maps can function as privileged or 'value-laden' sources, providing multiple insights at once, in part due to the multiple actors involved in their compilation and then dissemination. The creation, distribution and display of maps means they have multiple functions for the historians, providing varied clues as to the dissemination of power in society.

Conversely, we should be aware of the limitations of any group of sources: this does not mean not using them, but just that we should proceed with caution. In this regard, Irvin's chapter on surveillance reports (*svodki*) highlights many possible pitfalls of using this source type. Of these reports, said to monitor the 'mood of the population', we might consider issues pertaining to accessibility, reliability, whether they are a true 'representation' of the population, and changing political prerogatives. Such surveillance records are useful for many historians, but they cannot be taken at face value. These insights also pertain to other types of sources, including different genres of texts. Siobhán Hearne's astute reading of denunciations and defence letters with respect to prostitution offered in the leading area-studies journal *Kritika* cites repositories in the Russian State Historical Archive in St Petersburg and the Latvian State Historical Archive in Riga. Hearne notes how a selection of petitions and letters on this subject provide useful insights into 'attitudes towards sexuality and morality', though whilst using a diverse source record she notes that we must be aware of important variations in geography, demographics and cultural attitudes (to name a few) that shape the sources at our disposal. Furthermore, the fragmented nature of this source record – and obviously not everyone wrote, let alone kept letters – makes it impossible to say whether the corpus examined is truly representative. An additional challenge in this case is we do not have a complete picture of what the authorities kept. But, given the plethora of insights such sources can yield, and the fact many such collections have been hitherto completely untapped by researchers, such explorations are well worth conducting for the scholar.[31]

Using a combination of types of materials can provide a useful way of extracting more meaning from the source record, and tell us more about an event, idea or person than the use of only one type of source. Consider, for instance, a surveillance report curated by the Russian police which notes numbers at a demonstration in the late Imperial period and any subversive activity. This source can be used in conjunction with, say, a newspaper report, to consider what the respective texts say about the demonstration, though one must look closely at the dates and/or context to check that they are in fact describing the same event.[32] The newspaper column might provide a lively and personal opinion, but should be scrutinized to see if details like the number of people in the crowd as cited in the report – in other words, the facts reported in another source – are corroborated here. By using two source types, we might form a more complex but also nuanced picture of contemporary interpretations, as well as the facts of the case. Related to this, voices from the source record can interact with one another, sometimes in surprising ways. In a fascinating recent study of humour under Stalinism, Jonathan Waterlow uses the metaphor of cross-hatching to describe the 'often unconscious mixing of official and unofficial discourses, values and assumptions' that permeated the Soviet 1930s. He adopts this technique in order to shift interpretation 'away from images of head-on collisions and clashes between the official and the unofficial, between state ideology and ordinary people's lived realities'. In his reading, unofficial and official discourses as well as spoken and unspoken assumptions actively informed one another rather than cancelling each other out.[33] This metaphor of cross-hatching can be usefully applied to approaches in the present volume. Though the chapters in this book sometimes treat different source materials and perspectives in isolation, we must note in reality the use of different types of sources is often a complex affair, with materials and, therefore, the voices that resonate within the source record having mutual influence on one another.

Notes

1 For this, see the guide by Samantha Sherry, Jonathan Waterlow and Andy Willimott (eds.), *Using Archives and Libraries in the Former Soviet Union, v.2.0* (BASEES-Open Access, 2013); on the 1930s specifically see Sheila Fitzpatrick and Lynne Viola (eds.), *A Researcher's Guide to Sources on Soviet Social History in the 1930s* (Abingdon: Routledge, 1990).

2 Examples include Basil Dmytryshyn, *Medieval Russia: A Source Book, 850–1700*, 3rd ed. (Gulf Breeze, FL: Academic International Press, 2000); Gregory L. Freeze (ed.), *From Supplication to Revolution: A Documentary Social History of Imperial Russia* (New York and Oxford: Oxford University Press, 1988); Michael C. Hickey (ed.), *Competing Voices from the Russian Revolution* (Oxford: Greenwood, 2011); Lewis Siegelbaum and Andrei Sokolov (eds.), *Stalinism as a Way of Life* (New Haven, CT and London: Yale University Press, 2004); J. Arch Getty and Oleg V. Naumov (eds.), *The Road to*

Terror: Stalin and the Self-Destruction of the Bolsheviks, 1932–1939 (New Haven, CT and London: Yale University Press, 1999); Edward Acton and Tom Stableford (eds.), *The Soviet Union: A Documentary History*, 2 vols. (Exeter: Exeter University Press, 2005 and 2007).

3 On changing conceptions of Russian identities, see Geoffrey Hosking, *Russia and the Russians: A History* (London: Allen Lane, 2001); for the Imperial period specifically, see Hosking's *Russia: People and Empire, 1552–1917* (Cambridge, MA: Harvard University Press, 1997) and Andreas Kappeler, *The Russian Empire: A Multiethnic History*, trans. Alfred Clayton (London: Routledge, 2001); on the early Soviet period, a leading study is Terry Martin, *The Affirmative Action Empire: Nations and Nationalism in the Soviet Union, 1923–1939* (Ithaca, NY and London: Cornell University Press, 2001).

4 A useful collection exploring such themes is John Randolph and Eugene M. Avrutin (eds.), *Russia in Motion: Cultures of Human Mobility since 1850* (Chicago, IL: University of Illinois Press, 2012).

5 One recent example pertaining to the (presently) under-scrutinized late Imperial period is Faith Hillis, 'The "Franco-Russian Marseillaise": International Exchange and the Making of Antiliberal Politics in Fin de Siècle France', *Journal of Modern History*, 89 (2017), pp. 39–78.

6 An example of the former trend is Alexander Rabinowitch, *Prelude to Revolution: The Petrograd Bolsheviks and the July 1917 Uprising* (Bloomington, IN: Indiana University Press, 1968); conversely, we might note the influence of works like Peter Holquist, *Making War, Forging Revolution: Russia's Continuum of Crisis, 1914–1921* (Cambridge, MA: Harvard University Press, 2002), and Mark D. Steinberg, *The Russian Revolution, 1905–1921* (Oxford: Oxford University Press, 2017).

7 Abraham Ascher, *The Russian Revolution: A Beginner's Guide* (London: Oneworld, 2014), p. xi.

8 Martin Malia, *The Soviet Tragedy: A History of Socialism in Russia, 1917–1991* (New York: The Free Press); other examples of this trend are Orlando Figes, *A People's Tragedy: The Russian Revolution 1891–1924* (London: Pimlico, 1996); Richard Pipes, *The Russian Revolution, 1899–1919* (London: Harvill, 1990).

9 China Miéville, *October: The Story of the Russian Revolution* (London: Verso, 2017).

10 Sheila Fitzpatrick, *Tear Off the Masks! Identity and Imposture in Twentieth-Century Russia* (Princeton, NJ: Princeton University Press, 2005); David L. Hoffman, *Stalinist Values: The Cultural Norms of Soviet Modernity, 1917–1941* (Ithaca, NY and London: Cornell University Press, 2003).

11 The phrase is the title of the fifth chapter in Stephen Kotkin, *Magnetic Mountain: Stalinism as a Civilization* (Berkeley and Los Angeles, CA: University of California Press); on subjectivity in Soviet Russia, see Sean Guillory, 'The Shattered Self of Komsomol Civil War Memoirs', *Slavic Review*, 71 (2012), pp. 546–65; Choi Chatterjee and Karen Petrone, 'Models of Selfhood and Subjectivity: The Soviet Case in Historical Perspective', *Slavic Review*, 67 (2008), pp. 967–86; Igal Halfin, 'From Darkness to Light: Student Communist Autobiography during NEP', *Jahrbücher für Geschichte Osteuropas*, 45 (1997), pp. 210–36; Jochen Hellbeck, 'Working, Struggling, Becoming: Stalin-Era Autobiographical Texts', *Russian Review*, 60 (2001), pp. 340–59.

12 Sarah Davies, *Popular Opinion in Stalin's Russia: Terror, Propaganda and Dissent, 1934–1941* (Cambridge: Cambridge University Press, 1997). Regarding this work, see Dakota Irvin's comments in his chapter.

13 Censorship in late Imperial Russia is explored in Caspar Ferenczi, 'Freedom of the Press under the Old Regime, 1905–1914', in Olga Crisp and Linda Edmondson (eds.), *Civil Rights in Imperial Russia* (Oxford: Clarendon Press, 1989), pp. 191–214; Benjamin Rigberg, 'The Efficacy of Tsarist Censorship Operations, 1894–1917', *Jahrbücher für Geschichte Osteuropas*, 14 (1966), pp. 327–46; Charles Ruud, *Fighting Words: Imperial Censorship and the Russian Press, 1804–1906* (Toronto: University of Toronto Press,

1982); on the Soviet period, see Valeria D. Stelmakh, 'Reading in the Context of Censorship in the Soviet Union', *Libraries & Culture*, 36 (2001), pp. 143–51; Peter Kenez, *Cinema and Soviet Society: From the Revolution to the Death of Stalin* (London: I. B. Tauris, 2001); Herman Ermolaev, *Censorship in Soviet Literature (1917–1991)* (Boston, MA: Rowman & Littlefield, 1997).

14 Jonathan W. Daly, 'Perlustration in Imperial Russia', *Kritika*, 17 (2016), pp. 466–74; see also the remarks by Doucette in her chapter on Soviet letters below.

15 Richard Pipes, *Russia under the Old Regime* (Harmondsworth: Penguin, 1974).

16 An insightful analysis of this source pertaining to the Russian context is Claudia Verhoeven, 'Court Files', in Miriam Dobson, and Benjamin Ziemann (eds.), *Reading Primary Sources: The Interpretation of Texts from Nineteenth- and Twentieth-Century History* (London: Routledge, 2008), pp. 91–105.

17 See Corinna M. Peniston-Bird, 'Oral History: The Sound of Memory', in Sarah Barber and Corinna M. Peniston-Bird (eds.), *History beyond the Text. A Student's Guide to Approaching Alternative Sources* (London: Routledge, 2009), pp. 105–21.

18 Alison Kolosova, 'Chuvash Understandings of *Sobornost'* amidst Church Conflicts of the Early 1920s', paper delivered at workshop, 'Conflict and Concord in Russian History', Ural Federal University in Ekaterinburg, 4 September 2019. I am grateful to Dr Kolosova for alerting me to this important point.

19 Key studies that make heavy use of surveillance reports are Jonathan Daly, *Autocracy under Siege: Security Police and Opposition in Russia, 1866–1905* (DeKalb, IL: Northern Illinois University Press, 1998), idem., *The Watchful State: Security Police and Opposition in Russia, 1906–1917* (DeKalb, IL: Northern Illinois University Press, 2004); and Iain Lauchlan, *Russian Hide-and-Seek: The Tsarist Secret Police in St Petersburg, 1906–1914* (Helsinki: Suomalaisen kirjallisuuden seura, 2002).

20 Matthew E. Lenoe, 'Letter-Writing and the State: Reader Correspondence with Newspapers as a Source for Early Soviet History', *Cahiers du Monde russe*, 40 (1999), pp. 139–69; Sheila Fitzpatrick, 'Supplicants and Citizens: Public Letter Writing in Soviet Russia in the 1930s', *Slavic Review*, 55 (1995), pp. 78–105; see also remarks by Doucette in her chapter.

21 On the press see work of Louise McReynolds, *The News under Russia's Old Regime: The Development of a Mass-Circulation Press* (Princeton, NJ: Princeton University Press, 1990); idem., *Murder Most Russian: True Crime and Punishment in Late Imperial Russia* (Ithaca, NY: Cornell University Press, 2012); also, Joan Neuberger, *Hooliganism. Crime, Culture and Power in St. Petersburg, 1900–1914* (London: University of California Press, 1993); on the press and the revolutions of 1917, see Steinberg, *Russian Revolution, and Richard Stites, Revolutionary Dreams: Utopian Vision and Experimental Life in the Russian Revolution* (Oxford: Oxford University Press, 1989). A recent study of experimental life in the early Soviet period that draws heavily on the early Soviet press is Andy Willimott, *Living the Revolution: Urban Communes and Soviet Socialism, 1917–1932* (Oxford: Oxford University Press, 2017); see also Willimott's remarks in his chapter.

22 See for example Victoria E. Bonnell, *Iconography of Power: Soviet Political Posters under Lenin and Stalin* (Berkeley, CA: University of California Press, 1997); Peter Kenez, *The Birth of the Propaganda State: Soviet Methods of Mass Mobilization, 1917–1929* (Cambridge: Cambridge University Press, 1985); David Brandenberger, *Propaganda State in Crisis: Soviet Ideology, Indoctrination, and Terror under Stalin, 1927–1941* (New Haven, CT and London: Yale University Press, 2011).

23 Several chapters on non-textual sources are offered in Barber and Peniston-Bird (eds.), *History Beyond the Text*; see also Karen Harvey (ed.), *History and Material Culture: A Student's Guide to Using Alternative Sources*, 2nd ed. (London: Routledge, 2018).

24 Pages of first-rate literature could be cited here; this note will only include a few recent works on communities and identities featured in this volume. On homosexuality, see

Dan Healey, *Homosexual Desire in Revolutionary Russia: The Regulation of Sexual and Gender Dissent* (Chicago, IL and London: The University of Chicago Press, 2001); Ira Roldugina, 'Rannesovetskaia gomoseksual'naia subkul'tura: Istoriia odnoi fotografii', *Teatr*, 16 (2014), pp. 188–91; idem., '"Pochemu my takie liudi?" Rannesovetskie gomoseksualy ot pervogo litsa: novye istochniki po istorii gomoseksual'nykh identichnostei v Rossii', *Ab Imperio*, 2 (2016), pp. 183–216. Prostitution is examined in Siobhán Hearne, 'The "Black Spot" on the Crimea: Venereal Diseases in the Black Sea Fleet in the 1920s', *Social History*, 42 (2017), pp. 181–204. Soviet deafness is explored in Claire L. Shaw, *Deaf in the USSR: Marginality, Community, and Soviet Identity, 1917–1991* (Ithaca, NY: Cornell University Press, 2017); see also the remarks her chapter.

25 Students should note the rich collections of primary sources on this theme. On Imperial Russia, see Robin Bisha, Jehanne M. Gheith, Christine Holden and William G. Wagner (eds.), *Russian Women, 1698–1917: Experience and Expression* (Bloomington, IN: Indiana University Press, 2002); for the early Soviet period, see Sheila Fitzpatrick and Yuri Slezkine (eds.), *In the Shadow of Revolution: Life Stories of Russian Women: From 1917 to the Second World War* (Princeton, NJ: Princeton University Press, 2000).

26 An interesting contribution on anthropology in the late Imperial and early Soviet periods which includes analysis of race as a specific category is Marina Mogilner, *Homo Imperii: A History of Physical Anthropology in Russia* (Lincoln, NE: University of Nebraska Press, 2013); see also the recent work by Brendan McGeever, *Antisemitism and the Russian Revolution* (Cambridge: Cambridge University Press, 2019).

27 On the late Imperial period see Jeffrey Brooks, *When Russia Learned to Read: Literacy and Popular Culture, 1861–1917* (Princeton, NJ: Princeton University Press, 1985); on culture and resistance in Stalin's Russia, see the essays in Lynne Viola (ed.), *Contending with Stalinism. Soviet Power and Popular Resistance in the 1930s* (Ithaca, NY and London: Cornell University Press, 2002).

28 Relating to the revolutionary period, see Sarah Badcock, *Politics and the People in Revolutionary Russia: A Provincial History*, updated edition (Cambridge: Cambridge University Press, 2011).

29 Polly Corrigan, 'Political Police Archives in Ukraine and Georgia: A Research Note', *Europe-Asia Studies*, 71 (2019), pp. 1–15.

30 The list of good websites is forever multiplying: two I draw on frequently in my own teaching are Sean's Russia Blog (Sean Guillory). <http://seansrussiablog.org> (accessed 17 June 2019); and Seventeen Moments in Soviet History. <http://soviethistory.msu.edu> (accessed 17 June 2019).

31 Siobhán Hearne, 'To Denounce or Defend? Public Participation in the Policing of Prostitution in Late Imperial Russia', *Kritika*, 19 (2018), pp. 717–44 (p. 720).

32 Two works that adopt this approach are Robert Weinberg, *The Revolution of 1905 in Odessa: Blood on the Steps* (Bloomington, IN: Indiana University Press, 1993); Laura Engelstein, *Moscow, 1905: Working-Class Organization and Political Conflict* (Stanford, CA: Stanford University Press, 1982).

33 Jonathan Waterlow, *It's Only a Joke, Comrade! Humour, Trust and Everyday Life under Stalin* (Oxford, 2018), p. 6.

Further reading

Acton, Edward, and Tom Stableford (eds.), *The Soviet Union. A Documentary History*, 2 vols. (Exeter: Exeter University Press, 2005 and 2007).

Chatterjee, Choi, et al. (eds.), *Everyday Life in Russia Past and Present* (Bloomington, IN: Indiana University Press, 2014).

Dmytryshyn, Basil, *Medieval Russia: A Source Book, 850–1700*, 3rd ed. (Gulf Breeze, FL: Academic International Press, 2000).

Fitzpatrick, Sheila, and Lynne Viola (eds.), *A Researcher's Guide to Sources on Soviet Social History in the 1930s* (Abingdon: Routledge, 1990).

Freeze, Gregory L. (ed.), *From Supplication to Revolution: A Documentary Social History of Imperial Russia* (New York and Oxford: Oxford University Press, 1988).

Garros, Veronique, Natalia Korenevskaya and Thomas Lahusen (eds.), *Intimacy and Terror: Soviet Diaries of the 1930s* (New York: New Press, 1995).

Hickey, Michael C. (ed.), *Competing Voices from the Russian Revolution* (Oxford: Greenwood, 2011).

Perrie, Maureen, et al. (eds.), *The Cambridge History of Russia*, 3 vols. (Cambridge: Cambridge University Press, 2006).

Sherry, Samantha, Jonathan Waterlow and Andy Willimott (eds.), *Using Archives and Libraries in the Former Soviet Union, v.2.0* (BASEES-Open Access, 2013).

Steinberg, Mark D. (ed.), *Voices of Revolution, 1917*, documents translated by Marian Schwartz (London and New Haven, CT: Yale University Press, 2001).

Part I
Contexts and approaches

1   Early medieval sources[1]

Monica White

The East Slavs entered the historical record relatively late.[2] Little is known about them before the tenth century, but archaeological evidence supports the scattered textual references to tribes living in remote northern forests, surviving by hunting, gathering and subsistence agriculture. Sustained contact with the wider world was precipitated by outside forces; in particular, the long-distance trade routes which began crossing through Eastern Europe in the mid-eighth century. The people to the north-west, known in English as Vikings and in Greek and Slavonic sources as Varangians, were desperate to obtain luxury goods from the distant Byzantine empire and Abbasid caliphate: in particular silk, spices, jewellery, and silver. The Varangians' route to the southern markets took them across the Baltic Sea to the forests of Eastern Europe, where they gathered commodities for trade, including fur, slaves, wax, and honey, and shipped them south along the river system. As this trade intensified over the course of the ninth century, many Varangians established permanent settlements in what is now north-western Russia. By the early tenth century, they were settling in the mid-Dnieper region, between the resource-rich forests of the north and the markets of the south. One of these settlements, Kiev, became the base of a princely family which came to dominate the corridor between the Baltic and Black Seas. The members of this family are known to modern scholars as the Riurikids, after Riurik, their legendary Varangian progenitor. In order to consolidate their power, the Riurikids founded new settlements for defence and trade, improved systems for tribute collection, and flirted with organized religion. The regent Olga was baptized in the 950s, followed in c. 988 by her grandson Vladimir, whose actions established Eastern-rite Christianity as the official religion of the realm. The Riurikids' support of the Church helped them maintain their grip on power, as did their 'collateral' succession system, in which every son had equal status and the right to rule a city. Younger brothers rotated up through smaller to larger cities in their patrimony as their older brothers died off and the next generation rotated in. Although this arrangement became exceedingly complex after a few generations and caused frequent squabbles, it was an effective way to keep a large and sparsely populated territory under the control of a single family. With a strong incentive to found new towns to accommodate the growing clan, the Riurikids expanded their territory steadily through the eleventh and twelfth centuries, forming the state known as Rus. This term, which can also function as an adjective, originally referred to the Varangians who made their home in Eastern Europe.[3] The phrase 'medieval Russia' should be avoided, both because it is inaccurate and because of contemporary political sensitivities, since Rus is the common heritage of Russia, Ukraine and Belarus. By the same token, the main language spoken in Rus was not Old Russian but Old East Slavonic, which is attested in a number of dialects.[4]

In addition to lively contacts with Byzantium and the kingdoms of Western Europe, the princes of Rus maintained close ties with the peoples of the western steppe. Relations between these groups and various branches of the clan were complex, encompassing trade, mercenary service and warfare in a constantly evolving web of alliances. This delicate balance of power was shattered by the Mongols, who conquered Rus and many of its neighbours between 1237 and 1241. The Mongols imposed various obligations on their subjects, in particular the requirement that each prince obtain a patent to rule his city from the Mongol khan in Sarai, the capital of the region of the Mongol empire known as the Golden Horde. Because the Mongols knew and cared little about local succession customs, they tended to promote princes whom they trusted ahead of those with a legitimate claim to a city according to the rules of collateral succession. Low-ranking princes could thus get ahead more quickly by ingratiating themselves with the khan than by engaging in traditional princely politics. The princes of Moscow were the ultimate winners in this process, gradually dispossessing the other princely families over the course of the fourteenth and fifteenth centuries. I have therefore chosen as the notional end point of this chapter the death of prince Iurii Danilovich of Moscow in 1325 (although the dates of many medieval sources are approximate at best). Known to history as the progenitor of the powerful grand princes and early tsars, he was in fact one among several princes in his generation who were roughly equally matched. Thereafter, however, the balance of power began slowly but surely to shift in Moscow's favour, ushering in a new era in the history of the East Slavs.

Given the constraints of the present volume, it would be impossible to provide a survey, even in broad outline, of all of the types of sources which were produced in Rus over more than five centuries following the first appearance of the Varangians in Eastern Europe. Instead, this chapter will attempt to convey some sense of their diversity by presenting three categories of sources which were produced in different media and for different purposes. Birchbark documents were the text messages of their day: short, casual notes written by and for a relatively broad cross-section of the public on cheap and widely available material. Chronicles were the opposite: lengthy, formal historical narratives often commissioned by a local prince and composed by monks on expensive parchment. Non-written sources are also crucial to understanding a society in which literacy was restricted, and archaeological materials from Rus offer rich insights into its society and culture. Lead seals, which reveal much information about social and religious practices, will be explored in detail.

The discovery of the first birchbark documents in 1951 caused a sensation, and it would not be an exaggeration to say that these modest texts have radically changed scholars' understanding of Rus society.[5] They came to light during archaeological excavations in Novgorod, now a small provincial city in north-western Russia, but for many centuries the northern capital of Rus and a prosperous centre of trade.[6]

The poor, anaerobic soil which made medieval Novgorod vulnerable to famine had the unexpected benefit of preserving organic materials. This feature has made it a beacon for archaeologists, who continue to organize digs in the city every summer. Among many other rare items, including clothing, leather shoes and wooden toys, archaeologists were astonished to discover strips of birchbark inscribed with Cyrillic writing. The corpus has grown steadily over more than six decades since the first document was unearthed and, at the time of writing, numbers over 1,200 individual items (Figure 1.1).[7] For ease of reference, each birchbark is given a number based on the order in which it was excavated, preceded by an abbreviation indicating the city in which it was found (N. for Novgorod, Smol. for Smolensk, St. R. for Staraia Russa, etc.). Only a small number of birchbarks, some 3 per cent of the total, have been found outside of Novgorod and its dependencies. However, it is clear that birchbark writing was a widespread phenomenon since the authors of many documents excavated in Novgorod refer to sending their messages from other cities. Novgorod's over-representation in the corpus is the result of its unique combination of anaerobic soil and intensive archaeological excavations.[8] The current number of birchbarks is, no doubt, only a fraction of the total preserved, and much less of those originally produced, and there is every reason to expect discoveries to continue at a steady pace. In such a rapidly expanding field, at least some aspects of any summary will inevitably become outdated. Nevertheless, the availability of new tools for the study of birchbarks and the recent appearance of ground-breaking research in the field makes this a particularly exciting time to explore them.

Although no two birchbarks contain the same message, certain patterns in their content have emerged. Most take the form of correspondence, and often have named senders and recipients. Most are, however, fragmentary, whether as a result of accidental or deliberate damage (often, seemingly, to preserve confidentiality). Of those which can be deciphered in whole or in part, the majority concern what might broadly be described as business and legal affairs: buying and selling goods,

Figure 1.1 Drevnerusskie berestianye gramoty, Gramota no. 9.

http://gramoty.ru/birchbark/document/show/novgorod/9/ (accessed 19 February 2019).

commissions for services, managing property, making and paying back loans, and so on. However, numerous other topics are represented, from marriage proposals to intelligence reports to children's writing exercises to prayers.[9] In the early years of scholarship about birchbarks, the breadth and mundanity of their subject matter caused much excited speculation about mass lay literacy. Closer analysis of a larger number of texts has revealed that many, but not all, concern the affairs of the elite. It now seems reasonable to assume that a large cross-section of people had some recourse to birchbark writing, although it was much more widespread at the higher levels of society.[10]

None of the texts includes dates, but the archaeological features of Novgorod allow many of them to be placed within twenty-year intervals.[11] This has shown that birchbarks are among the earliest surviving examples of East Slavonic writing, with the oldest known specimens dating from the 1030s – that is, within the first generation of the systematic introduction of writing following the official conversion to Christianity in the late 980s.[12] Birchbark writing increased steadily until about 1200, when domestic and international upheaval, followed by the Mongol invasion and famine, caused a steep decline in the number of texts produced. Thereafter the numbers increased again, although they did not return to their twelfth-century peak before disappearing entirely in the fifteenth century.[13]

One of the attractions of the medium of birchbark was its accessibility: it was a freely available material which could be easily inscribed with a stylus. By contrast, parchment was extremely expensive and paper was not widely available until the fifteenth century (in fact, the increasing availability of paper was one of the reasons for the decline of birchbark writing).[14] However, birchbark's ease of use for medieval writers does not imply ease of interpretation for modern scholars. The documents are often illegible due to damage, but even complete texts are difficult to read. They were written without spaces between words, usually by people who were not professional scribes, and often in the Novgorodian dialect, which differed significantly from standard Old East Slavonic. Even when the words of a text can be deciphered, their meaning is often mysterious. This is because most birchbarks had a pragmatic purpose, such as conveying urgent news, commands or changes to plans. The fact that they were unceremoniously discarded in the mud indicates that they were not intended to be read outside of their immediate context. It is thus understandable that they omit most or all of the context which would be necessary to gain a full understanding of the situation. In this respect, they are more similar to nineteenth-century telegrams or modern text messages than to formal business or personal letters.

Consider the following birchbark, N439, from 1200 to 1220, which is fairly typical of business-related messages:

> [+ From Moise]j [to] Spirko. If Matej hasn't taken the batch (of wax) from you, ship it to me with Prus; I've sold off the tin and lead and all the wrought wares. I no longer have to go to Suzdal. Of the wax, 3 batches have been bought. You have to come here. Ship some tin – about four lots, about two sheets of the red (copper) – and pay the money immediately.[15]

The abrupt, straightforward tone indicates that the sender and recipient shared a general understanding of their affairs, but needed to clarify certain details. As Jos Schaeken observes, Moisej must have been the proprietor of a business who was travelling out of town and wanted his associate, Spirko, to visit him and send some goods. Moisej's brief message gives us a snapshot of the workings of these long-distance merchants on the eve of the Mongol invasion: the wares they traded and in what amounts, and one of the cities they regularly visited. On the other hand, there is a great deal we do not know: Moisej's location, whether he traded in any other products, why he decided not to go to Suzdal, how much money Spirko needed to pay and to whom, and so on.

Despite such lacunae, the decipherment of the birchbarks by archaeologists, linguists and historians has increased our understanding of many aspects of Rus society. For example, of the birchbarks with named senders and/or recipients, Schaeken calculates that 'dozens' were written by or addressed to women, providing rare evidence for their daily lives and concerns.[16] Before the discovery of these documents, such information was gleaned largely from the civil law codes of Rus. These compilations, which were expanded and revised multiple times over the course of the eleventh and twelfth centuries, contain a great deal of information about Rus society, but are necessarily abstract and generic. They inform us, for instance, that women could own and manage property in their own name, and that provision for widows and unmarried daughters had to be made upon the death of a male head of household.[17] Birchbarks confirm this evidence: many of those written by or to women concern the same type of business affairs as described in other documents, showing that women frequently engaged in such activities. But birchbarks also reveal some of the consequences of women's economic activity which could not be inferred from the laws. As Eve Levin points out, despite having some financial autonomy, women were always dependent on men to a greater or lesser extent. She cites the example of birchbark N531, from 1200 to 1220, in which a woman named Anna pleads with her brother to act on her behalf after a business deal has gone badly wrong and her husband has shamed her and thrown her out of the house.[18]

Birchbarks also complement the law codes in shedding light on more intimate aspects of women's lives. Marriages in Rus tended to be arranged by the parents, and two birchbarks illustrate negotiations between parents and matchmakers (N731, from 1160 to 1180 and N955, from 1140 to 1160). However, N377, from 1280 to 1300, contains an unsentimental marriage proposal directly to a woman, without the mediation of a matchmaker: 'From Mikita to Malanija. Marry me. I want you, and you me. And Ignat Moiseev is witness to that. And in property [...]'. Violation of the laws about women's dowries, which were supposed to remain their property, is also attested, as in N9, from 1160 to 1180: 'From Gostjata to Vasil'. What (my) father gave me and (my) relatives gave [i.e. my dowry], that is with him. Now, taking a new wife, he won't give me anything. Having struck hands (in a new marriage contract), he has sent me away and has taken another. Please come!' Following the death of the parents, brothers were supposed to provide for their unmarried sisters (normally by arranging a marriage), and N49, from 1410 to 1420, illustrates a woman's reliance on her natal family in widowhood as well: 'A bow from Nastas'ja to my lords, to my brothers. My Boris is dead. How, lords, will you care for me and my children?'[19] Whereas the law codes give us an idealized and generalized view of how society was supposed to operate, these and many other birchbarks shed light on the strategies people actually employed for dealing with difficult situations, providing an unrivalled source for everyday life.

For those who read Russian, Ianin's *Ia poslal tebe berestu...* is an ideal introduction to the history and study of birchbarks.[20] Aimed at a general readership, the volume is richly illustrated and includes a wealth of analysis and anecdotes by a prominent scholar who led the Novgorod excavations for many decades. The documents themselves have been published in diplomatic editions since shortly after their discovery in the ongoing series *Novgorodskie gramoty na bereste* (*Novgorod Documents on Birchbark*), currently in its twelfth volume, which includes the discoveries through 2015. They are also particularly suitable for electronic presentation because their number is constantly growing, and readings are occasionally reinterpreted on the basis of new linguistic and palaeographic insights. The project *Birchbark Literacy from Medieval Rus: Contents and Contexts*, led by Jos Schaeken, has produced a comprehensive website (www.gramoty.ru) which includes maps, multi-lingual bibliographies and a searchable list of most birchbarks discovered to date. Each numbered document links to an image of the original, plus a transcription and translation into modern Russian. Although scholarship in English about the birchbarks is not abundant, it is growing steadily. A welcome new addition is Schaeken's *Voices on Birchbark: Everyday Communication in Medieval Russia*, which provides an excellent scholarly overview of the subject with numerous tables, maps, illustrations and a full bibliography.

Compared to birchbarks, the study of chronicles might seem relatively straight-forward. Instead of fragmentary communiqués excavated from the mud which contain fleeting references to the affairs of a random assortment of otherwise unknown people, these are formal historical compositions about the deeds of churchmen and rulers, presented chronologically in a tidy manuscript. The Rus were prolific chronicle writers and relatively large numbers of these documents survive, shedding light on everything from trade agreements to battles to the conversion to Christianity. Since chronicles were often commissioned by princes, who had the means to pay for scribes and parchment, they tend to emphasize the deeds of that group, while also reflecting the interests of their monastic authors. Thus, if the birchbarks give a 'bottom up' view of Rus society, chronicles are much more 'top down'.

Yet the polished presentation of the chronicles belies various problems of interpretation, and there are many technical difficulties with which researchers must contend. For example, most chronicles use an annalistic format, with yearly entries describing local and international events, but this system is far from straightforward. The Rus used a calendar imported from Byzantium which counted the years not from the birth of Christ but from the creation of the world, generally reckoned to have occurred in what we would designate 5508 BC. The year started in either March or September, but it is not always clear which system an individual scribe is using. Scholars must also have a basic knowledge of different scribal hands and the multiple abbreviations used to conserve parchment, as well as the types of ambiguities and mistakes which can occur in texts written before the advent of standardized orthography and moveable type. Modern critical editions of chronicles can simplify matters by giving normalized readings, textual variants found in various manuscripts, and dates according to the Gregorian calendar. Even so, it is important to be aware of the complexities of the original text: for example, if an argument hinges on an event happening in a particular year, one must be certain whether the chronicler is using the ultra-March or ultra-September system.

Another difficulty is that chronicles are not the products of single authors who wrote their works from beginning to end, in the manner of modern historians. Rather, they were compiled over many years from diverse and often obscure sources of uncertain reliability by usually anonymous scribes. Traces of the process of compilation can sometimes be discerned, as when a chronicle reproduces a passage from another known text (e.g., a Byzantine chronicle), a scribe signals an insertion, or the narrative abruptly changes tone, but such obvious signs are rare. Moreover, related chronicle texts were often compiled and rewritten by multiple independent authors over several generations, resulting in complex family trees of texts whose interrelations are extraordinarily difficult to unpick. Compounding this uncertainty is the fact that all extant chronicles which cover the early medieval period survive in manuscripts which are significantly younger, and it is usually impossible to reconstruct how a chronicle acquired its surviving form. Does the extant manuscript faithfully reproduce writings from centuries earlier, or did one or more scribes of intermediate manuscripts editorialize, make historically inaccurate insertions, or delete information which was not flattering to a certain prince or his ancestors? Such questions are often impossible to answer definitively, although this does not stop them from being debated by scholars. In any case, those who work with the chronicles must bear these uncertainties in mind. It is advisable to consult as many witnesses of a given text as possible, ideally in original manuscripts as well as modern editions.

No text illustrates the challenges of chronicle studies better than the *Povest' vremennykh let* (hereafter PVL; usually translated as *The Primary Chronicle* or *The Tale of Bygone Years*), which forms the core of most of the chronicles which have come down to us. It was probably compiled in the early twelfth century in Kiev,[21] and provides the oldest surviving native account of many key episodes in the history of Rus: the arrival of the Varangians, the foundation of various cities, the deeds of the early Riurikids, the acceptance of Eastern-rite Christianity and the development thereafter of princely politics and international relations. Additionally, an extended prologue narrates the pre-history of the Slavs starting with their descent from Noah's son Japheth, incorporating anecdotes from ancient and biblical history and ethnography which happened to be known to the compilers.

The PVL no longer exists as a stand-alone document, but was incorporated into a number of later compilations which continue its historical narrative. The oldest of these, known as the Laurentian text, was copied by the monk Lavrentii for a prince of Suzdal in 1377 and focuses on the history of north-eastern Rus. Complementing that is the Hypatian text, compiled in 1425 and discovered in the monastery of St Hypatius in Kostroma, which mainly discusses events in the south-west.[22] Three other, somewhat younger, manuscripts also contain early witnesses of the PVL, and its content overlaps to some extent with another family of early chronicles from Novgorod.[23] Although all of the witnesses of the PVL follow a similar basic narrative structure, they are inconsistent with each other in many details, and a great deal of scholarship has been devoted to determining which version of various passages is closest to the original.[24] Another vexed problem, that of the hypothetical prototype of the PVL known as the *Nachal'nyi svod* (primary compilation), is too complex to be discussed in this chapter, but a summary of the debate can be found in Cross and Sherbowitz-Wetzor, and Sean Griffin's *The Liturgical Past in Byzantium and Early Rus*.[25]

Problems of reconstruction aside, the surviving versions of the PVL show that its compilers drew on a wide variety of sources to form their narrative, in addition to recording the events of their own day. The range of the source material is impressive and includes copied or lightly adapted versions of everything from biblical apocrypha and liturgical texts to Byzantine historical writings to orally transmitted legends. Although this diversity provides much narrative interest, it means that the trustworthiness of the PVL is not consistent and must be assessed separately for each episode. Without doubt, a number of passages do provide valuable information about a time and place which is otherwise poorly documented. The entries for 907, 912, 945 and 971, for example, include the texts of peace and trade agreements between Rus envoys and the Byzantine leadership which were ratified following Rus attacks on Constantinople.[26] Many details, such as the large number of personal names of the signatories and the practical nature of the content, mean that there is no serious doubt about the authenticity of these documents, which shed light on the conduct of trade and international affairs, as well as the spread of Christianity among the Rus.

Other passages in the PVL must be interpreted more cautiously, such as the regent Olga's embassy to Constantinople.[27] In its entry for 955, the PVL claims that the princess was baptized there, and that her beauty caught the eye of her baptismal sponsor, the emperor Constantine VII. In order to stave off his advances, she had to remind him of the prohibition against romantic relationships between god-parents and god-children. This anecdote is not found in Constantine's own account of the embassy in his handbook of imperial ceremonial, which also omits the baptism.[28] The Byzantine historian John Skylitzes does mention the baptism, although he wrote his account about a century after the event.[29] This is only one of many examples of the fact that supplementary, and often contradictory, information about events described in the PVL can be found in sources in different languages, and researchers must make an effort to consult as many of them as possible. Interspersed with such historical, or at least historically based, accounts are entirely fictional narratives, such as that of Olga's revenge. Following the murder of her husband Igor by the tribe of the Derevlians in 945, Olga is said to have exacted a terrible vengeance by burying one group of emissaries alive, smothering another group in a bathhouse, massacring 5,000 of the tribe in their capital city, and finally burning the city to the ground.[30] This story was clearly added for entertainment value and can usefully be compared with certain episodes in the Norse sagas, but should not be interpreted historically.[31]

Another remarkable component of the PVL is the *Pouchenie* (Instruction) of Vladimir Monomakh, a great-great-great grandson of Olga who ruled Kiev from 1113 until his death in 1125.[32] There is no serious doubt among scholars about the authenticity of this text, in large part because of the amount of detail it contains about the prince's life. Vladimir states that he composed the testament near the end of his life for the benefit of his children, who were, like him, active in Rus politics. In a vivid narrative, he recounts numerous hunts and military campaigns against other princes and the steppe-dwelling tribe of the Cumans (also known as the Polovtsy) over the course of some fifty years, concluding, 'Among all my campaigns, there are eighty-three long ones, and I do not count the minor adventures.'[33] The account provides much valuable information for historians seeking to understand the intricacies of twelfth-century politics, as well as numerous personal and place names which are otherwise unknown. However, the *Pouchenie* is not just a list of battles, but also a rare insight into the mind of a prominent layperson. Although princes frequently commissioned chronicles and other works, which thus reflect their interests, there are very few examples of works which they actually composed. The *Pouchenie* shows its author to have been deeply concerned with Christian values. More than half of the text is devoted to meditations on Scripture, prayers addressed to Christ and the Mother of God, and admonitions to his children to live upstanding lives and support the Church. Vladimir also provides examples from his own conduct to inspire his readers:

> In war and at the hunt, by night and by day, in heat and in cold, I did whatever my servant had to do, and gave myself no rest. [...] I did not allow the mighty to distress the common peasant or the poverty-stricken widow, and interested myself in the church administration and service.[34]

In addition to its value as an historical source, the *Pouchenie* also provides insights into the process of chronicle compilation. Although there is no separate manuscript of the text, it was clearly not written as a dated chronicle entry, like most of the material in the PVL, but was originally an independent composition. It is found only in the Laurentian text, which means that it was not part of the original PVL compiled in the early twelfth century, but was inserted into a later copy which was almost certainly compiled after Monomakh's death. The testament appears, together with a letter from Monomakh to his rival Oleg Sviatoslavich, following the entry for 1096 – most likely the date of the letter, but certainly not that of the *Pouchenie*, which refers to its author as elderly. Apparently, then, when the compiler of the manuscript included the letter in the material for 1096, he decided to add another work by the same author for good measure, despite the fact that it was completely unrelated to the events of that year and was written two decades or more later. By doing so, he saved a composition which would otherwise have been lost. These clues, and many others like them, show something of the eclectic and unpredictable work of the scribes who compiled the PVL and other chronicles.

Serious study and publication of the chronicles began in the eighteenth century, but the standard modern editions are published in the *Polnoe sobranie russkikh letopisei* (*Complete Collection of Rus Chronicles*). Work on this project began in the mid-nineteenth century and is not yet complete, although all chronicles from the early medieval period have been published, sometimes in multiple editions. These volumes are generally of a high standard, providing variant manuscript readings and indexes, and many are available electronically through the website of the Russian State Library (www.rsl.ru). In addition to the Laurentian text of the PVL, translations into English include Mitchell and Forbes (1914) and Heinrich (1977).[35]

The discussion above has explored two types of written sources from Rus which served very different purposes: casual personal communications versus formal historical compositions. The bookmen of Rus produced many other genres of writing which could also have been productively studied in an introduction of this sort, including (among others) hagiography, law codes, sermons, epic poetry and pilgrims' narratives.[36] Important as these are, however, it is also vital for historians of this period to acquire some familiarity with material sources (including artistic, architectural and archaeological items). They are, firstly, crucial to understanding a society in which literacy was much more restricted than in later centuries. Although the birchbarks show that reading and writing were not the exclusive preserve of the clergy and secular elite, there were certainly many people who never or very rarely engaged with the written word. Material sources are often the best means of gaining insight into their lives, since descriptions of these groups by others can be oversimplified and stereotyped. Secondly, the mass destruction of Eastern European cultural heritage in medieval and more recent times means that written sources from Rus are not plentiful. The archival riches enjoyed by modernists, and even Western European medievalists, are simply not available. Relying solely on written sources is thus particularly limiting for the study of Rus, since much information about diverse topics can be gleaned from alternatives. Although archaeological research on Rus is only beginning to be published in English, Androshchuk's *Vikings in the East: Essays on Contacts along the Road to Byzantium*, Brisbane, Makarov and Nosov's *The Archaeology of Medieval Novgorod in its Wider Context: A Study of Centre/Periphery Relations* and Ivakin, Khrapunov and Seibt's *Byzantine and Rus' Seals* provide helpful introductions.[37]

The diversity of Rus archaeology is impressive, encompassing everything from craft production to burial practices to trade, in both urban and rural contexts. Although any of these topics would make an informative introduction to the subject, the study of lead seals (sigillography or *sfragistika* in Russian) was chosen for its broad relevance and accessibility to non-specialists. Seals demonstrate how material sources can enhance our understanding of the processes and context of writing, providing a wealth of information about document production, as well as onomastics (the study of names) and iconography. These objects consisted of a unique two-sided image and/or inscription which identified the sender of a document and served as a mark of authenticity. They were made from lead discs with a hollow channel running through the middle. After a string was threaded through the channel and attached to the document, the disc was impressed with an engraved pliers-like tool. This conferred the desired image on the disc and crushed the channel, securing the document. Valentin Ianin, who published definitive editions of the seals discovered through 1998, identified a number of types belonging to various social groups which account for the majority of seals, although a significant number cannot be assigned to a type because they are damaged or indecipherable. As with birchbarks, people from Novgorod are over-represented in the corpus of lead seals thanks to the extensive excavations which have taken place there. However, the durability of lead means that the distribution of seals is more even than that of birchbarks, and hundreds have been found across the territory of Rus.

Because of the effort and expense required to produce seals, their very existence shows that the documents to which they were attached conveyed important information, and hence needed authentication. Similar efforts can be seen with the birchbarks, many of which also conveyed sensitive messages: although attaching a lead seal to this lightweight medium would not have been feasible, some writers seem to have attempted to ensure confidentiality by using coded symbols, omitting personal names, or even instructing addressees to tear up messages upon receipt.[38] Thus, in all likelihood, many of the documents to which seals were affixed were related to the administrative, legal and governmental affairs of princes, prominent churchmen and civic officials. Although the vast majority of these documents have been lost – only 7–8 per cent of known seals from Rus are still attached to documents – the existence of the seals still provides hints about the volume of official correspondence and record-keeping.[39]

Seals can, moreover, provide information about the conventions governing the choice of patron saints among the secular elite, and hence their religious practices more generally, a subject for which few other sources exist. The Riurikids' naming conventions followed certain strict rules.[40] Princes were known by their given names and patronymics, but usually received two given names: a traditional clan name (e.g., Vladimir, Sviatoslav, Iaropolk) and a baptismal name in honour of a saint. A prince could thus be known by up to four names – his own clan and baptismal names and those of his father – adding another layer of complexity to their sprawling family tree. The chronicles and other written sources usually (but not always) refer to princes only by their clan names, which obscures important information about the veneration of saints. Seals, however, can provide insight into these questions: many princes favoured a design which featured a portrait of their own patron saint on the obverse (front), and an inscription, self-portrait, or portrait of their father's patron saint on the reverse (back). By pooling information from written sources, seals attached to documents with known authors, and lone seals, scholars can fill in lacunae in the genealogy of the Riurikids and recover information about the favoured patron saints of the clan. Seals show, for example,

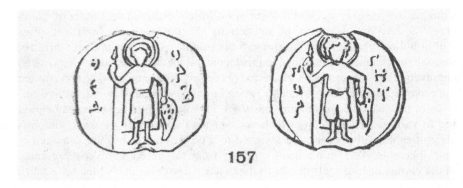

Figure 1.2 Seal of Mstislav Iurevich depicting Saints Theodore and George (mid-twelfth century)

Reproduced with permission of Valentin Yanin and Petr Gajdukov, Moscow State University.

that princes' saintly namesakes came from a select group: the 104 decipherable types of princely seals published by Valentin Ianin feature only 38 saints, 20 of whom appear only once or twice. The four chief military saints (George, Demetrios, Theodore Teron and Theodore Stratelates) account for over a quarter of the depictions and their popularity is matched only by John the Baptist, the Archangel Michael and Basil the Great (Figure 1.2). This indicates that, in their choice of names, the parents of young princes were not restricted by the ecclesiastical calendar, which commemorated at least one male saint on most days of the year. More important were considerations of prestige and, in many cases, military prowess.[41]

Seals also illustrate the adaptation of Byzantine cultural practices in Rus. For example, many Byzantine seals (although not imperial ones) feature the Greek inscription 'Lord, help your servant x'. Examples of such seals evidently made their way to Rus and appealed to some of the early Riurikids, who used these inscriptions on their own seals. Other types of Greek inscriptions are also found on Rus princely seals, including a number which use the Byzantine title 'archon' to describe their owners.[42] Practicality was clearly not the primary concern behind these inscriptions. If few people in Rus could have read East Slavonic inscriptions, no one besides a handful of clergy (including, presumably, the princes themselves) could have read Greek ones, particularly given the abbreviations needed to make the inscriptions fit on the surfaces of the seals. Instead, the use of Greek writing was meant to convey the owners' sophistication and piety, as well as their connections (whether real or imaginary) with the powerful Byzantine empire. This broader message was unlikely to have been lost on the recipients of the documents, even if the exact meaning of the Greek was.

Byzantine conventions were undoubtedly prestigious, but portraits of saints on seals tell a somewhat different story. All but two of the saints who were depicted on seals in this period were imported from Byzantium.[43] In a number of cases, however, the portraits of Byzantine saints on Rus seals depart significantly from all known styles in Byzantine iconography. For example, the seal of a Novgorod mayor (*posadnik*) from the mid-twelfth century depicts the emperor Constantine the Great seated on a throne and holding a spear and shield, a portrait type which does not exist in Byzantine art.[44] The military saint Demetrios, whose Byzantine iconography also does not include that pose, is nevertheless depicted in a similar manner on a slightly later seal belonging to the prince Vsevolod Iurevich.[45] These saints were widely venerated in Byzantium and Rus, and many aspects of their cults were identical in both places. For the purposes of personal identification, however, it was apparently acceptable to change their established iconography, showing nuances of their cults which are not apparent in most other media.

Because it is rarely taught in the English-speaking world, the history of early Rus can seem at best inaccessible and at worst irrelevant. Until recently, a lack of materials for non-specialists did little to change this situation. As the volume and quality of traditional and online resources grow, however, it is becoming increasingly feasible to study this important period in the history of the East Slavs. In addition to being fascinating in its own right, Rus is crucial to gaining a nuanced understanding of the subsequent history and politics of Eastern Europe, from the Slavophile–Westernizer debates of the nineteenth century to Russia's annexation of Crimea. Many of the deep-seated cultural anxieties which played a role in these and other episodes are obscure to Western observers who are not familiar with the relevant historical background, much as the sensitivities about devolution in the UK are incomprehensible to many in other parts of the world. Medieval sources cannot, of course, be used simply as a decryption device. As with all historical sources, using them requires an appreciation for what they can and cannot tell us. As this chapter has shown, researchers must approach them critically and with the necessary background knowledge to use them appropriately. Thus prepared, early medieval sources can provide a wealth of information relevant to all periods in Eastern European history.

Notes

1 I would like to express my thanks to a number of colleagues who generously assisted me with the preparation of this chapter. Jos Schaeken kindly sent the page proofs of his book a few months prior to its publication. Judith Jesch and Fjodor Uspenskij provided references about the Norse sagas, and Sean Griffin sent relevant draft chapters of his forthcoming book. Alexei Gippius, Jos Schaeken and Petr Gajdukov kindly allowed me to reproduce the images used in this article. I am very grateful for their help.

2 Detailed studies of the history summarized below can be found in Simon Franklin and Jonathan Shepard, *The Emergence of Rus 750–1200* (London: Longman, 1996); and Janet Martin, *Medieval Russia 980–1584*, 2nd ed. (Cambridge: Cambridge University Press, 2007).

3 Compare the origin of the name England from the Angles, who began invading Roman Britain in the fifth century.

4 When written in Cyrillic, the term Rus is spelled with a soft sign (Русь) denoting palatalization of the final consonant, which in transliteration is rendered as an apostrophe (*Rus'*). However, since Rus is used as an English word in its own right, it seems unnecessary to indicate a palatalized 's' sound which does not exist. This is my preference, but a range of practices can be found in English-language scholarship.

5 Valentin L. Ianin, *Ia poslal tebe berestu...*, 3rd ed. (Moscow: Iazyki russkoi kul'tury, 1998), pp. 29–31.

6 This city on the Volkhov river, properly known as Novgorod the Great or Novgorod Velikii, should not be confused with Lower or Nizhnii Novgorod on the confluence of the Volga and Oka rivers.
7 Jos Schaeken, *Voices on Birchbark: Everyday Communication in Medieval Russia* (Leiden: Brill, 2019), p. 18.
8 Ibid., pp. 18–24.
9 Simon Franklin, *Writing, Society and Culture in Early Rus, c. 950–1300* (Cambridge: Cambridge University Press, 2002), pp. 35–45; Schaeken, *Voices*, p. 57.
10 Eve Levin, 'Novgorod Birchbark Documents: The Evidence for Literacy in Medieval Russia', in Charles L. Redman (ed.), *Medieval Archaeology: Papers of the Seventeenth Annual Conference of the Center for Medieval and Early Renaissance Studies* (Binghamton, NY: Medieval and Renaissance Texts and Studies, 1989); Schaeken, *Voices*, pp. 38–40.
11 Ibid., p. 27.
12 Aleksej Gippius, 'Birchbark Literacy and the Rise of Written Communication in Early Rus', in Kristel Zilmer and Judith Jesch (eds.), *Epigraphic Literacy and Christian Identity: Modes of Written Discourse in the Newly Christian European North* (Turnhout: Brepols, 2012), p. 230.
13 Schaeken, *Voices*, pp. 28–30.
14 Ibid., p. 30.
15 Ibid., pp. 59–60.
16 Ibid., p. 40.
17 Daniel H. Kaiser, *The Laws of Rus': Tenth to Fifteenth Centuries* (Salt Lake City, UT: Charles Schlacks, Jr., Publisher, 1992), pp. 30–2, 38–9. The law codes are a complex subject in their own right which cannot be studied separately in this chapter. The references here are to the 'Expanded Redaction' of the *Rus Law* (*Russkaia Pravda*), which Daniel Kaiser argues was compiled in the 1140s but continued to be used for several centuries thereafter: Kaiser, *The Laws of Rus'*, p. xviii.
18 Eve Levin, 'Women and Property in Medieval Novgorod: Dependence and Independence', *Russian History/Histoire Russe*, 10 (1983), pp. 154–69 (pp. 160–9). Eve Levin has used this birchbark and a number of others as the basis of a fictional but historically plausible reconstruction of Anna's life, which provides a fascinating introduction to the subject of women in Rus. See Eve Levin, 'Anna, a Woman of Novgorod', in Donald Ostrowski and Christian Raffensperger (eds.), *Portraits of Medieval Eastern Europe, 900–1400* (Oxford: Routledge, 2018).
19 Schaeken, *Voices*, pp. 95–6, 98–9, 102–3.
20 Ianin, *Ia poslal tebe berestu…*.
21 Donald Ostrowski (ed.), *The Pověst' vremennykh lět: An Interlinear Collation and Paradosis*, vol. 1 (Cambridge, MA: Harvard University Press, 2003), p. xvii.
22 Samuel Hazzard Cross and Olgerd P. Sherbowitz-Wetzor (eds.), *The Russian Primary Chronicle Laurentian Text* (Cambridge, MA: The Mediaeval Academy of America, 1953), p. 4.
23 Ostrowski (ed.), *The Pověst' vremennykh lět*, vol. 1, pp. xix–xxi, xxxix.
24 The most comprehensive attempt to date to reconstruct the text of the PVL can be found in Ostrowski (ed.), *The Pověst' vremennykh lět*. For an English translation of the Laurentian text only, see Cross and Sherbowitz-Wetzor, *Russian Primary Chronicle*. In the following discussion, references will be given to both versions.
25 Ibid., pp. 13–19; Sean Griffin, *The Liturgical Past in Byzantium and Early Rus* (Cambridge: Cambridge University Press, 2019).
26 Cross and Sherbowitz-Wetzor, *Russian Primary Chronicle*, pp. 64–8, 73–7, 89–90; Ostrowski (ed.), *The Pověst' vremennykh lět*, vol. 1, pp. 31, 10–32, 1; 32, 24–37, 28; 46, 11–53, 29; 72, 18–73,19.
27 Cross and Sherbowitz-Wetzor, *Russian Primary Chronicle*, p. 82; Ostrowski (ed.), *The Pověst' vremennykh lět*, vol. 1, pp. 60, 25–61, 22.

28 Constantine VII Porphyrogennetos, *The Book of Ceremonies*, vol. 2, trans. A. Moffatt and M. Tall (Canberra: Australian Association for Byzantine Studies, 2012), pp. 594–8.
29 John Skylitzes, *A Synopsis of Byzantine History, 811–1057*, trans. J. Wortley (Cambridge: Cambridge University Press, 2010), p. 231.
30 Cross and Sherbowitz-Wetzor, *Russian Primary Chronicle*, pp. 78–81; Ostrowski (ed.), *The Povest' vremennykh lĕt*, vol. 1, pp. 55, 10–60, 1.
31 See for example Hermann Pálsson and Paul Edwards (trans.), *Eyrbyggja Saga* (London: Penguin, 1989), p. 79; Snorri Sturluson and Lee M. Hollander (trans.), *Heimskringla: History of the Kings of Norway* (Austin, TX: University of Texas Press, 1964), p. 582.
32 Cross and Sherbowitz-Wetzor, *Russian Primary Chronicle*, pp. 206–15.
33 Ibid., p. 214.
34 Ibid., p. 215.
35 Robert Mitchell and Nevill Forbes (eds.), *The Chronicle of Novgorod, 1016–1471* (London: Offices of the Society, 1914); Lisa Heinrich, 'The Kievan Chronicle: A Translation and Commentary', unpublished thesis (Vanderbilt University, 1977).
36 Anthologies of Rus literature in English translation include Basil Dmytryshyn, *Medieval Russia: A Source Book, 850–1700*, 3rd ed. (Gulf Breeze, FL: Academic International Press, 2000); Serge A. Zenkovsky, *Medieval Russia's Epics, Chronicles and Tales*, 2nd ed. (New York, NY: Meridian, 1973). See also the series *Harvard Library of Early Ukrainian Literature: English Translations*.
37 Fedir Androshchuk, *Vikings in the East: Essays on Contacts along the Road to Byzantium* (Uppsala: Acta Universitatis Upsaliensis, 2013); Mark A. Brisbane, Nikolaj Makarov and Evegenij Nosov, *The Archaeology of Medieval Novgorod in its Wider Context: A Study of Centre/Periphery Relations* (Oxford: Oxbow, 2012); Hlib Ivakin, Nikita Khrapunov and Werner Seibt, *Byzantine and Rus' Seals* (Kiev: The Sheremetievs' Family Museum of Historical and Cultural Rarities, 2015).
38 Schaeken, *Voices*, pp. 73, 128–30.
39 Valentin L. Ianin, *Aktovye pechati drevnei Rusi X–XV vv.*, vol. 1 (Moscow: Nauka 1970), p. 5.
40 A. Litvina and F. Uspenskii, *Vybor imeni u russkikh kniazei v X–XVI vv.: dinasticheskaia istoriia skvoz' prizmu antroponimiki* (Moscow: Indrik, 2006).
41 Monica White, *Military Saints in Byzantium and Rus, 900–1200* (Cambridge: Cambridge University Press, 2013), pp. 113–15.
42 Ianin, *Aktovye pechati*, vol. 1, pp. 14–33.
43 The exceptions were the Rus princes Boris and Gleb, who were murdered in 1015 and soon attracted a cult following.
44 Ianin, *Aktovye pechati*, vol. 1, p. 225; Monica White, 'Veneration of St. Constantine in Pre-Mongol Rus', in Dragiš Bojović (ed.), *Saint Emperor Constantine and Christianity* (Niš: The Centre of Church Studies, 2013), p. 357.
45 Ianin, *Aktovye pechati*, vol. 1, p. 208; White, *Military Saints*, pp. 185–6.

Further reading

Androshchuk, Fedir, *Vikings in the East: Essays on Contacts along the Road to Byzantium* (Uppsala: Acta Universitatis Upsaliensis, 2013).
Cross, Samuel Hazzard, and Olgerd P. Sherbowitz-Wetzor (eds.), *The Russian Primary Chronicle: Laurentian Text* (Cambridge, MA: The Mediaeval Academy of America, 1953).
Dmytryshyn, Basil, *Medieval Russia: A Source Book, 850–1700*, 3rd ed. (Gulf Breeze, FL: Academic International Press, 2000).
Franklin, Simon, *Writing, Society and Culture in Early Rus, c. 950–1300* (Cambridge: Cambridge University Press, 2002).

Franklin, Simon, and Jonathan Shepard, *The Emergence of Rus 750–1200* (London: Longman, 1996).

Gippius, Aleksej, 'Birchbark Literacy and the Rise of Written Communication in Early Rus', in Kristel Zilmer and Judith Jesch (eds.), *Epigraphic Literacy and Christian Identity: Modes of Written Discourse in the Newly Christian European North* (Turnhout: Brepols, 2012), pp. 225–50.

Ianin, Valentin L., *Ia poslal tebe berestu…*, 3rd ed. (Moscow: Iazyki russkoi kul'tury, 1998).

Levin, Eve, 'Women and Property in Medieval Novgorod: Dependence and Independence', *Russian History/Histoire Russe*, 10 (1983), pp. 154–69.

———, 'Novgorod Birchbark Documents: The Evidence for Literacy in Medieval Russia', in Charles L. Redman (ed.), *Medieval Archaeology: Papers of the Seventeenth Annual Conference of the Center for Medieval and Early Renaissance Studies* (Binghamton, NY: Medieval & Renaissance Texts & Studies, 1989), pp. 127–37.

Martin, Janet, *Medieval Russia 980–1584*, 2nd ed. (Cambridge: Cambridge University Press, 2007).

Ostrowski, Donald, and Christian Raffensperger (eds.), *Portraits of Medieval Eastern Europe, 900–1400* (Oxford: Routledge, 2018).

Schaeken, Jos, *Voices on Birchbark: Everyday Communication in Medieval Russia* (Leiden: Brill, 2019).

Zenkovsky, Serge A., *Medieval Russia's Epics, Chronicles and Tales* (New York, NY: Meridian, 1974).

2 Primary sources and the history of modern Russia

Peter Waldron

In 1866 the Imperial Russian Historical Society was founded, receiving imperial approval for its charter from Tsar Alexander II and installing Prince Petr Viazemskii, a member of the State Council, as its first president. The founders of the society were drawn from Russia's social and political elite, including Count Dmitrii Tolstoi – the Minister of Education and Chief Procurator of the Holy Synod, Konstantin Zlobin, the Director of the State Archives and Alexander Polovtsov, a member of the Senate and future adviser to Tsar Alexander III. The society proclaimed that its aim was to 'collect, edit and disseminate … materials and documents relating to Russia's national history'[1] and over the next half-century, it played a central role in publishing primary sources on the history of Russia, producing 148 volumes of materials, along with a 25-volume biographical dictionary of Russia. At a time when the historical profession was small and access to archives was only available to a select few, the thousands of pages of documents published by the society were an invaluable source that made primary materials available to a wide audience.

The Provisional Government that replaced the Romanov regime at the beginning of March 1917 wanted to demonstrate that it had rejected the Tsarist state's arbitrary approach to governing and to law. Within a few days of taking power, it established an investigatory commission to look into the actions of former ministers and senior Tsarist officials and determine the extent of illegal actions they had committed with the intention that its investigations would be published in full as historical record. The chairman of the commission, the lawyer N. K. Murav'ev, declared that 'there were whole [Tsarist] government institutions that committed crimes every single day. In one entire institution – the Ministry of Internal Affairs – no senior official could carry out their duties without breaking the law'.[2] The commission took testimonies during the spring and summer of 1917 from former Tsarist officials, but the Bolshevik revolution intervened before publication could take place and it was only in the mid-1920s that the Soviet regime produced seven large volumes containing the materials produced by the commission.

The Bolshevik regime that came to power in the October revolution of 1917 demonstrated considerable initial enthusiasm for bringing historical materials into the public domain. Within weeks of the revolution, the new regime published material from the archives of the Imperial Ministry of Foreign Affairs containing the 'secret treaties' that the Tsarist state had concluded with other powers. Seven volumes of documents appeared between December 1917 and February 1918, causing considerable embarrassment to other governments and suggesting that the Bolsheviks had a much more open attitude to access to official sources.[3] The pre-revolutionary tradition of publishing sources was continued with the establishment of the journal *Krasnyi Arkhiv* (Red Archive) by the Bolshevik historian Mikhail Pokrovskii.[4] Between 1922 and 1941, the journal published 106 volumes of materials drawn largely from state archives dealing with both the pre- and post-revolutionary history of Russia. The rationale for the journal's work showed a different emphasis to that of the Imperial Historical Society: 'it aimed steadfastly ... at bringing out new material that would enrich historical science; at the same time, it aspired to ensure the trustworthiness of its publications, making use of historiographic methods of accuracy and authenticity'.[5] Both *Krasnyi Arkhiv* and the Imperial Russian Historical Society's document collections represented invaluable resources for historians, providing materials that were otherwise wholly inaccessible.

Neither the Tsarist nor the Bolshevik approach to enabling access to primary sources was primarily motivated by altruism or a desire to throw open the doors of dusty archives and allow unfettered access to the treasures and secrets that they contained. The Imperial Historical Society's volumes are often dry and concentrate on administrative and political materials, while the Bolsheviks' publication of the 'secret treaties' and the volumes of *Krasnyi Arkhiv* was motivated by a powerful desire to legitimize the new Soviet regime by discrediting the old order and showing the deep-seated roots of revolutionary politics inside Russia. The second volume of *Krasnyi Arkhiv*, for example, contained materials dealing with the history of Russia's working class, letters by the novelist Dostoevsky written while he had been imprisoned in the late 1840s for his part in a revolutionary conspiracy, as well as a letter from the future Kaiser Wilhelm to Tsar Alexander III in 1884. History was never neutral for the Soviet regime and it remained intent on carefully selecting the nature of the materials that it placed in the public domain.

Even while the civil war was raging in the years immediately after 1917, the Bolsheviks were busy establishing a nationwide system of archives, drawing together materials that had been held in a variety of government and private collections before 1917. The State Archive of the Russian Republic was founded in 1920 as the central repository for historical records, and over the next decade it was divided into more manageable units. While the voluminous records of the Tsarist regime were located in Petrograd – St Petersburg's name from 1914 – the move of the capital to Moscow early in 1918 meant that the new Bolshevik state's documents would be concentrated there. In 1925, with Petrograd having been renamed Leningrad in honour of the Soviet state's first leader, the Leningrad Central State Historical Archive was brought into being to act as the Soviet state's main repository for pre-1917 archival materials, with Soviet-era documents remaining in Moscow. In 1931 the Moscow archive was renamed the Central Archive of the October Revolution to recognize explicitly its role in preserving materials relating to the post-1917 state, and a significant quantity of records held in Leningrad that related to pre-1917 political parties and to the imperial family were transferred to the Moscow archive.

The Soviet state was prepared to shuffle historical records between archives to suit its own particular conception of Russia's history, and it was more interested in the formal institutional structures of archives than it was in making their contents freely available for historical research.

History was vital to the Soviet regime: it had built its own legitimacy on a version of Russia's past that was deeply contentious and it was intent on preventing access to archival documents that could be used to challenge the Soviet orthodoxy. Between 1938 and 1960, Soviet archives were under the jurisdiction of the state security service and the continuing ethos of the archival administration, even after archives gained their own administrative autonomy directly under the Soviet Council of Ministers, was that the materials preserved in archives had to be carefully guarded from untoward inspection. Much of the archival material relating to the post-1917 history of the Soviet Union itself was closed to researchers, or else was only accessible to well-trusted members of the Soviet historical profession who could be relied upon to utilize documents in ways that supported the state's own interpretation of the past. The Soviet state wanted to maintain close control over access to archives: researchers had to present a recommendation from their place of study or employer before they were allowed to consult archival materials, and they were restricted to working with documents that related to the topic that they had identified when first seeking archival access. Tsarist history was almost as equally contentious for the Soviet regime and access to material relating to the pre-revolutionary period was also tightly controlled. Documents that could suggest that there could have been an alternative path of development for Russia that would have avoided the 1917 revolutions were kept under especially close restrictions, but very wide classes of material were locked away from scrutiny. Foreign policy and military affairs – even reaching back into the eighteenth century – were particularly difficult areas for archival access, partly because the archives dealing with these topics remained closely linked to the relevant Soviet ministries, rather than coming under the control of the overall national archive administration.

Soviet scholars were well aware of the context in which they were studying history and of the limitations this placed on their access to archives. Even had they succeeded in seeing documents that cast doubt on the broad Soviet conception of history, censorship would have ensured that they would not be able to publish work that took a contrary view.[6] Foreign scholars were viewed with the deepest suspicion by Soviet archive directors but, increasingly from the 1960s onwards, both graduate students and established academics took advantage of improved cultural links between the Soviet Union and Western states to spend time in the USSR studying the history of Russia and the USSR. While Soviet archivists often found the presence of foreign scholars to be disconcerting, the overarching cultural policy of the Soviet government meant that they had to provide foreign scholars with access to materials. Foreign scholars were not constrained by the Soviet approach to history and were, of course, able to publish their work outside the USSR, but could find themselves condemned as 'bourgeois falsifiers of history' by the Soviet regime or, as Sheila Fitzpatrick – one of the leading Western historians of the USSR – was branded in the Soviet press in 1966, a 'cheap anti-Communist scribbler'.[7]

The ideological pressures faced by Soviet historians to conform to the Marxist-Leninist straitjacket in their approach to the past meant that, for some, the most appealing way for them to work as professional historians was to concentrate on the publication of collections of primary source materials and to focus on the particular problems faced by historians in dealing with primary sources. A whole sub-discipline of the Soviet historical profession became devoted to *istochnikovedenie*, the study of sources as a generic topic, and it was a significant part of the curriculum for students of history. Soviet historians wrote extensively on the utility of source materials and the methodological approach to take in utilising different types of sources, with a 1973 textbook for university students containing 32 separate chapters dealing with different varieties of sources, including a piece entitled 'The works of K. Marx, F. Engels and V. I. Lenin as historical sources for the history of the USSR'.[8] Stemming from this methodological concern with sources, large numbers of collections of carefully edited and annotated documents were produced by Soviet historians. They included such monumental works as the five-volume edition published to mark the fiftieth anniversary of the 1905 revolution,[9] and the many collections devoted to regional studies, providing materials focussed on clearly defined areas.[10] While confining themselves to working with primary sources did not mean that Soviet historians could completely avoid the ideological frameworks which constrained historical analysis and debate, producing extensive and well-annotated collections of documents could provide a more neutral way for historians to approach the study of the Russian and Soviet pasts. There were, of course, major limitations even in dealing with sources: significant topics remained entirely closed to research and discussion so that, for example, the horrors of Stalinism were never a subject of historical research in the pre-Gorbachev Soviet Union. The publication of very substantial numbers of edited primary sources could not compensate for the severe limitations placed on access to archives by the Soviet regime, but this type of publication did give some insight into the richness of the materials held in the USSR's huge archival collections and did provide valuable materials that made the study of Soviet history more feasible.

The Soviet Union laid great stress on its success in ensuring that its entire population was literate and that Soviet citizens had access to books. Public libraries were an important part of the Soviet drive to improve literacy rates and to inculcate high educational standards in a population which had, until 1917, been deprived of access to universal schooling, but very few books were on open shelves in Soviet libraries, with the great majority held in closed stacks requiring specific requests for access. A second layer of screening prevented the public from gaining access to books that were regarded as subversive or otherwise representing a threat: such works were kept them in special stacks (*spetskhran*) and were available only to a tiny number of readers. The Lenin Library, the national library of the Soviet Union in Moscow, held more than quarter of a million books, half a million editions of periodicals and more than two million newspapers in these special stacks with only some 4,000 readers permitted to access them.[11] Browsing the shelves was barely possible in Soviet libraries, and the same practice held sway in bookshops, with most books shelved behind counters and needing a request to a salesperson before a prospective purchaser could even handle a volume. The difficulty of access to books in bookshops was especially frustrating, since the Soviet Union operated a rigorous system of censorship of every type of publication – books, magazines and newspapers – before they could be sold to the public. Every book on sale in a Soviet bookshop had already been through a detailed process of review to ensure that its contents were acceptable to the regime, while foreign-published works were treated with extreme caution by the Soviet state and were barely available. This level of control over access to historical sources and writing showed the importance the state attached to history as a means of justifying its own existence, since it based its own legitimacy on a historical process through which capitalism had come to its inevitable collapse and had been supplanted by Bolshevik socialism.

The USSR did not, however, hold a monopoly on primary sources available for the study of its history. The revolutions of 1917 resulted in a substantial wave of emigration from the new Soviet state, with some three million people leaving and settling across the world. The émigrés included large numbers of the Russian political and social elite and some of them were able to take important collections of documents with them when they left. The new Czechoslovak republic was an important destination for Russian émigrés and Prague became an important centre for Russian historians and lawyers in the early 1920s. The Czech government promoted the establishment of a Russian university which provided a home for scholars such as the historian Alexander Kizevetter and the lawyer Pavel Novgorodtsev, and in 1923 émigrés established the Russian Historical Archive Abroad in Prague. Financed initially by the Czech government, the archive was intended to collect materials relating to the Russian revolution and it encouraged Russians who had emigrated to deposit any materials they possessed with the Prague archive. The repository acquired significant collections relating to the Russia radicals Alexander Herzen and Petr Lavrov, together with a wide variety of documents relating to the Civil War, and its appeal to émigrés to donate materials resulted in the archive gaining a collection of more than 800 unpublished memoirs reflecting the experience of Russians who had gone into exile after 1917.[12] The liberation of Prague by the Red Army in 1945 meant that the archive faced a very different fate: in December 1945 the majority of its documentary holdings were donated to the Soviet Union by the Czech government and despatched to Moscow. During the 1950s its materials were dispersed across more than 30 national and regional archives in the Soviet Union. Some libraries and archives outside Russia took advantage of the availability of materials in often financially stressed émigré hands to purchase documents and books, sometimes resulting in important source materials finding a home in improbable locations. During the 1920s and 1930s, through the guidance of the Russian historian Archibald Cary Coolidge, the Harvard Law Library acquired more than 5,000 items relating to pre-Soviet Russia, including the rare printed minutes of the Tsarist Council of Ministers after 1906. Libraries and archives were also able to acquire materials from people who had been expelled from the Soviet Union: in 1940 Harvard University bought the archive that Leon Trotsky had accumulated and brought with him to Mexico, signing the contract just before Trotsky was assassinated by one of Stalin's agents.[13] Some Soviet archival materials came into other hands by accident: Nazi troops captured the Soviet city of Smolensk in July 1941 as they stormed eastwards and seized control of the regional Communist Party archive which the Soviet authorities had been unable to evacuate in the face of the Nazi advance. At the end of the war, the Smolensk archive came into the hands of the Americans and eventually ended up in the USA's National Archive in Washington, the materials forming the basis for Merle Fainsod's 1958 book *Smolensk under Soviet Rule*, the archival sources providing unrivalled insight into the day-to-day government of the USSR.[14]

The nature of the sources available for the study of the history of Russia and the Soviet Union had a profound impact on the nature of historical writing while the Soviet regime remained in power. The historical profession inside the Soviet Union was very closely controlled, with the mechanisms of censorship and restrictive access to archives and libraries determining the types of history that could be written. Ideology played a central role in shaping Soviet historical research and writing, with Marxism–Leninism emphasising wider economic and social forces in the making of both past and present. History was class-based, and Soviet historians devoted much effort to discussing the role of working people in Russia and, especially, their role in bringing about revolution. The peasantry too were the subject of substantial research, aimed at demonstrating their innate revolutionary qualities and sympathies with Russia's nascent working class. Other groups in pre-revolutionary Russian society – the middle class, nobility and the church – were treated in much less detail by Soviet historians and their role in Russia's past was analysed overwhelmingly in terms of the ways in which they attempted to frustrate the march of Russia's working people and peasantry towards revolution. The roots of the 1917 revolution were a central concern for Soviet history, and every hint of rebellion in Tsarist Russia was subjected to minutely detailed discussion and analysis, as the Soviet state sought to establish its own pedigree as a legitimate government. Even the Decembrist revolt of 1825, an attempt at a coup d'état by privileged military officers on the death of Tsar Alexander I, was lauded by Soviet historians for its attempt to launch a 'manifesto to the Russian people', aimed at overthrowing the feudal and serf-owing structures of the early nineteenth-century Russian state.[15] There was a powerful need to establish the innate revolutionary qualities of the Russian people, and even individuals and movements that had the most tenuous connection to radicalism were enlisted in the service of the historical path that lead towards the Bolshevik revolution of 1917.

This approach meant that there were significant *lacunae* in the way in which Soviet historians approached Russian history: the ideological emphasis on economic and social forces as playing the determinant role in the historical process meant that individuals received much less attention. Historical biography suffered particularly from this approach. Archival collections relating to prominent individuals in Tsarist Russia and the USSR were often difficult to access, and Soviet historians understood that attempts to work on the lives of important political figures in pre-1917 Russia would be doomed to failure and, worse, would blight their careers in the future. Whilst biography established itself as one of the key genres in Western historical writing during the twentieth century, the Soviet Union largely shunned serious biography as a historical tool. Russia's tsars were never the subject of serious biographical studies by Soviet historians, and the same held true for ministers and establishment political figures. Soviet political figures were treated hagiographically or else, in the case of the men and women who had fallen from favour, ignored completely and their part in the historical record erased. Soviet publishers went as far as airbrushing figures such as Trotsky and Nikolai Bukharin, both executed by Stalin's regime, from photographs from the 1920s when they had been a key part of the Soviet leadership.

Utilising a wide variety of memoirs, letters and diaries to construct a biography of a monarch or politician was a skill that was not part of the Soviet historical tradition and the ways in which Soviet archives were organized militated against such an approach. All archives in the USSR came under the control of the Main Archive Administration, a body responsible to the Soviet Council of Ministers from 1960, and this ensured a uniformity in archival organization and structures that was unknown in the West. The system laid down by the national Soviet archival administration concentrated on organising archival materials following institutional structures, rarely incorporating materials relating to individuals into those frameworks. Personal archival collections were usually treated as entirely separate from the institutionally focussed collections that represented the majority of Soviet historical archives, so that while the great bulk of materials relating to the pre-1917 Tsarist government was held at the Central State Historical Archive in St Petersburg, many collections concentrating on prominent individuals, including the Romanov family, were located in Moscow at the Central State Archive of the October Revolution. Neither did Soviet history embrace the revolution in historical research and writing in the West in the 1960s that brought social and cultural history to the forefront of historical enquiry. The ideological straitjacket of Marxism–Leninism precluded any other intellectual framework for conceptualising the study of the past in the Soviet Union, while the rigid structures of Soviet archives and their concentration on institutions and the structures of society and government made it difficult to break away from that approach. The Soviet Union contained almost no archives outside this official structure, so that different approaches to the collection and accessibility of source materials were extremely difficult to accomplish. Archives focussing on feminism, or the lived experience of working people, or on the lives of people with different ethnicities, simply did not – and could not – exist in the Soviet Union. The stifling uniformity of the Soviet approach to intellectual life, and to society more generally, meant that innovative approaches to the study of the past were unlikely ever to emerge in the pre-Gorbachev USSR. Deprived of the opportunity to develop source collections in directions that strayed from Soviet orthodoxy, historians in the USSR were rigidly constrained in their work.

The very tight controls exerted by the Soviet regime on the availability of source materials had a profound effect on the ways in which the history of Russia and the USSR could be written outside the confines of the Soviet Union itself. Between 1950 and 1978, the British historian E. H. Carr published his 14-volume *History of Soviet Russia.*[16] By far the most detailed and lengthy work on Soviet history written in the West, Carr's monumental series of books were written without him carrying out any work in Soviet archives. Carr was able to use materials in the United States, including the Trotsky archives in the Houghton Library at Harvard, but Soviet archives themselves were closed to him – and, until the 1960s, to any other Western historian wanting to study Soviet history. Carr therefore had to base his books largely on printed sources, including the officially sanctioned statistical information produced by the Soviet regime. The nature of the source material that was available to Carr played an important part in determining the way in which he structured his account of Soviet history: lacking material that could give real insight into the politics of the Soviet Union, Carr placed very great emphasis on the process of economic development. He used *Socialism in One Country* and *Foundations of a Planned Economy* as titles for the books that took up most of his series, suggesting that it was economics rather than anything else that dominated Soviet history. While there continued to be little access to a wider range of sources on Soviet history, Carr's approach to Soviet history could gain currency and, especially during the 1950s and 1960s, when there was no alternative set of source material available, his account was widely read.

By the mid-1960s, however, foreign scholars were beginning to gain access to Soviet archives and were able to place their own interpretations on the materials held in Moscow and Leningrad. Sheila Fitzpatrick's description of how she worked within the deeply restrictive atmosphere of Soviet archives to produce an analysis of the early Soviet Commissariat of Enlightenment and Lunacharskii, its first head, demonstrates how scholars from outside the Soviet Union could utilize their training and different approach to write history that was very different from Carr's work.[17] But even with some access to Soviet archives, and with inquisitive and diligent Western graduate students using their skill to ferret out material that the Soviet archival authorities would have preferred to remain hidden in the depths of the stacks in Moscow and Leningrad, the types of history that could be written – even by foreign scholars – still had limitations. Deprived of proper access to archive catalogues and indexes, foreign scholars needed to make use of existing published Soviet historical writing as a proxy guide to available archival materials and were then heavily dependent on the conscientiousness and goodwill of Soviet archivists to locate appropriate source materials. Even though foreign historians studying Soviet history had been exposed to the radical changes in historical thinking in the West during the 1960s and beyond, the limitations of Soviet archival practice still made it difficult to engage with the social and cultural history of Russia and the USSR in the same depth as was feasible in Western Europe and North America.

Stalin's dictatorship ended with his death in 1953 and, while the Soviet leadership that succeeded him drew back from the terror and violence that had characterized his regime, there was no consistent relaxation of policy to allow for a more nuanced view of the Russian and Soviet past. The stagnant years of Brezhnev's leadership during the 1960s and 1970s paved the way for the accession to power in 1985 of Mikhail Gorbachev, the youngest Soviet leader since the 1920s, who recognized that the USSR required radical reform if it was to thrive. For the new leader, an essential component of his policy of *perestroika* was openness – *glasnost'* – with the Soviet people about the condition of the USSR and what he was trying to achieve. Explaining the role of the Soviet Union's history in producing the parlous conditions in which it found itself by the 1980s was an essential element of Gorbachev's policies and, by the first months of 1988, Soviet journals and newspapers were filled with revelations about the Soviet past. Gorbachev wrote that 'freedom of speech made it possible to … turn directly to the people' but he recognized that 'none of the trends of glasnost … produced such a psychological shock as the restoration of a reliable, rather than a mythological, idealized and romanticized history of the Soviet period'.[18] Almost no topic was immune from examination, with the political struggles of the 1920s and the nature of Stalin's ensuing regime subject to particular scrutiny. This commitment to *glasnost'* included much wider access to the materials held inside Soviet archives and, as the Soviet Union stumbled towards its eventual demise in 1991, more and more materials were opened for examination. Archivists themselves were prominent in calling for more openness in access to materials and, while discussions were progressing about a new law to govern the USSR's archives, a group proposed that materials in state archives should be opened for consultation after thirty years and that the new law should apply not just to state archives, but also to the records of the Communist Party, the Soviet Union's real locus of power. No conclusion, however, had been reached on a new archive law before the USSR collapsed at the end of 1991.

Gorbachev's emphasis on openness had implications not just for the domestic history and politics of the Soviet Union, but also for its wider international relations. In 1989, the Soviet government published for the first time the secret protocols to the Molotov–Ribbentrop pact of August 1939 between the USSR and Nazi Germany which had paved the way for the Second World War and had allowed the USSR to occupy the independent Baltic states. Gorbachev also renewed investigations into the Katyn massacre of 1940 when thousands of Polish officers were killed by the Soviet Union: after four years work, archive staff ensured that Gorbachev was shown a file kept in a special archive containing the Communist Party Politburo's resolution, signed by Stalin and his colleagues, ordering the execution of the Poles.[19] This process of greater access to archival sources did not mean, however, that the Soviet archives were thrown wholly open to the public. Instead, archive directors and their political masters took decisions selectively to release documents that had previously been kept closed – often in the special stacks – for publication or else to allow accredited researchers to consult them.

The materials that were released into public view were, however, sufficiently dramatic to undermine the foundations of the Soviet regime that had ruled since 1917. For the first time, Stalin's terror was able to be openly discussed with details of its real horror and extent published. The verdicts reached against Soviet leaders at the show trials of the 1930s were overturned and figures such as Nikolai Bukharin were posthumously cleared of the supposed crimes for which they had been convicted and executed. The real extent of the USSR's wartime casualties was revealed, after four decades of official statements hugely underestimating the true scale of the losses suffered by the Soviet people. The nature of the forced

collectivization of agriculture after 1928, with its legacy of famine and deportations, was brought into the open. History ceased to be a subject of purely academic
interest for the Soviet people, as genuine sources – hidden from view for decades –
were published. As R. W. Davies writes, 'in the course of 1987 and 1988, tens of
millions of Soviet citizens became passionately involved in studying their country's
past, and in rethinking the principles and practice of Soviet socialism'.[20] This first
glimpse into the real Soviet past – which was to be magnified in the 1990s once the
USSR had collapsed – held immense personal resonance for millions of the Soviet
people. For the first time, they were able to begin to understand the history of their
own families, and to learn what had happened to people who had simply disappeared during the 1930s and about whose fate it had then been impossible – and
dangerous – to enquire. Openness about the Soviet past held a much wider significance for the state as a whole: the legitimacy of the regime was built on a depiction
of the history of the USSR since the revolution of October 1917 that had deliberately concealed much of the reality of the Soviet experience. As Soviet media
began to publish more and more material that revealed the nature of the USSR's
past – and especially Stalin's dictatorship – the foundations on which the Soviet
Union had been constructed began to crumble. The violence and arbitrariness with
which almost every section of the Soviet population had been treated under Stalin –
whether it was the peasantry during collectivization, non-Russian nationalities who
had been subjected to deportations, or the millions who had been executed or sent
to the Gulag – was made public for the first time in the late 1980s and helped to
destroy the faith of many Soviet people in the fundamentals of the system in which
they lived. Even the most sacrosanct of Soviet experiences – the Great Patriotic
War of 1941–45 – was not exempt, as it became clear that the number of deaths
suffered by the Soviet people was far higher than the regime had acknowledged
during the forty years since the end of the war. As Gorbachev's policies produced
economic calamity for the Soviet people, and the USSR's status as an imperial
superpower was being splintered, the unveiling of the realities of the USSR's history helped to fatally undermine the Soviet state.

The attempted coup by hardline members of the regime in August 1991 severely
undermined the authority of Gorbachev and the Communist Party, leading to the
break up of the Soviet state into its fifteen separate constituent republics at the end
of 1991. Boris Yeltsin's accession to power in Russia – by far the largest of the
post-Soviet states – overturned the dominant role of the Communist Party and Yeltsin turned on the organization of which he had been a leading member and sought
to use material from both party and state archives to advance his own political
position at home and internationally. During a visit to South Korea in 1994, Yeltsin
gave copies of archival documents that showed the central role of North Korea in
starting the Korean War in 1950 to his South Korean hosts, while in the run-up to
the presidential elections of June 1996, Yeltsin announced plans for the writing of
a 'New History of the Russian State', utilising materials from the archives, at the
same time appearing with the Orthodox Church patriarch to lay the foundation
stone for a new cathedral in Moscow.[21] During the 1990s, Russia's archives were
frequently chaotic, with inconsistent approaches to the release of materials and

numerous instances of corruption as the authority of the Russian state failed to match the control exerted by the Soviet regime. But very large amounts of archival material did emerge into the public domain and restrictions on access loosened, albeit with some sets of archival material – notably those in the Presidential Archive and the archive of the Foreign Ministry – remaining extremely difficult for researchers to penetrate.

This archival revolution that took place as the USSR collapsed changed not only the content of the history that could be written about Russia and the Soviet Union, but it radically affected the fundamental nature of the approaches that both Russian and foreign historians could take to the past. The constraints imposed by Marxism–Leninism disappeared from the academic study of history, so that Russian historians no longer had to conform to the rigid restriction of the Soviet ideological approach. As a result, they could analyse the past in ways that were inconceivable during the Soviet period: social and cultural history, in particular, began to gain a hold in Russian historical writing, as did biographical studies. Making the transition to new ways of thinking posed a substantial challenge for some Russian historians and the older generation of scholars, in particular, found it more difficult to make the transition to a new approach. But the best historians, who had often kept as closely engaged as possible with the wider international innovations in historical writing, were able to utilize the newly available archives to best advantage and produce very valuable studies of the Soviet and Russian past.[22] The Soviet tradition of producing high quality editions of primary sources stood historians in good stead as they gained access to archival materials that had been closed to researchers for decades. With its first volume appearing in 1997, the series *Rossiia XX vek. Dokumenty* (Twentieth Century Russia. Documents) has published more than 70 major collections of archive materials, including volumes on every period of Soviet history. Materials dealing with the 1930s and 1940s make up a significant proportion of the series, with volumes dealing with Stalin's deportations of national minorities and the terror providing insight into topics that had previously been completely closed to historical enquiry.[23] This series, and others, built on the long-standing Russian and Soviet tradition of publishing major collections of carefully edited primary sources brought often controversial and disturbing material into the public domain.

Access to archives became less restrictive in the 1990s for foreign researchers too, for the first time gaining access to the full catalogues and indexes of Russia's archives and no longer segregated from Russian researchers and made to work in separate reading rooms. Foreign scholars were also able to study in archives in Russia's provincial cities and towns, access to which had been unthinkable before the Gorbachev era.[24] This had a major impact on the nature of the history that foreign scholars could write: while they had been confined to working in the archives of the central government and its institutions in Moscow and Leningrad, their main focus had been on national politics and economics. Provincial Russia had remained closed to foreign scholars so that, even when they did address provincial events and issues, it was the metropolitan perspective that guided analysis. But opening up provincial archives to foreign scholars had a dramatic impact on the approach that they could take to the history of Russia and the Soviet Union. Highly original studies focussed on regional issues and movements have been produced, with scholars able to illuminate national questions through analysing the perspective of the millions of people who lived outside the two great cities of Moscow and St Petersburg. Work on the revolution of 1917 and its aftermath in Saratov,[25] the role of the peasantry in the province of Viatka during the revolution[26] and the the revolutionary experience in the Volga provinces of Nizhegorod and Kazan[27] have each cast light on hitherto unexplored areas of the history of revolutionary Russia. Russian historians have long produced doctoral dissertations based on provincial sources, but the dramatic changes in the overall framework of historical study in post-Soviet Russia have enabled work on topics that could never be the subject of proper research in the Soviet Union. Opposition to the Bolsheviks in the years after 1917 was a topic that Soviet historians could only approach in strictly ideological terms, and the Bolsheviks' opponents had been consistently demonized in historical writing.[28] But the opening of archives has transformed this area of historical understanding, allowing detailed analysis of widespread provincial opposition to the Bolshevik regime in the years after 1917.[29] The history of Russia and the Soviet Union has been rebalanced away from the metropolitan-centred focus that had dominated historical writing for decades to a much more varied set of approaches that recognize the significance of the provincial experience in constructing real national history.

The splintering of the USSR into fifteen separate republics in 1991 provided the opportunity for further innovation in the study of the history of the former Russian Empire and the Soviet Union. Each capital of a Soviet republic possessed its own national archive which mirrored the structures of the Soviet state's central archives in Moscow and Leningrad and it had been part of Soviet archival practice to disperse materials connected with the constituent parts of the USSR to repositories in each of the republics. The abrupt removal of Moscow's authority over the non-Russian republics that gained their independence as the USSR collapsed provided significant opportunities for widening access to archival sources and bringing new views of the history of the non-Russian republics to the fore. These new approaches were especially evident in the three Baltic states – Estonia, Latvia and Lithuania – which had been forcibly annexed by the Soviet Union in 1940. The Estonian State Archive has carried out careful and detailed work on the records they hold to identify the number and identities of the people arrested and deported by the Soviet authorities during the 1940s as they tightened their grip on Estonia. As a result, the Estonian organization Memento has published a dozen substantial volumes listing the names of the victims and setting out the nature of the source materials on which their research has been based.[30] In Ukraine, the Central State Archive has been opened to researchers and, alongside this, the Ukrainian archives of the Soviet-era security service – the KGB – have been opened for research. While corresponding documents in Moscow remain firmly guarded and away from any form of public scrutiny, the materials available in Kiev provide exceptional insight into Soviet internal security policy and its wider implications.[31]

The nature and significance of primary sources has formed an integral part of the study of the history of Russia for more than a century and a half. The dramatic changes to the regimes that have presided over the the USSR and the Russian Empire, and their sharply differing attitudes to archives and the past, have shaped the nature and content of the histories that could be written, whether in Russia itself or outside its borders. The vicissitudes that Russian and Soviet historians have endured did help develop a fine tradition of editing and publishing primary sources, even during the darkest days of Stalin's dictatorship, so that when attitudes to the past became more open during the 1980s, historians were able to utilize their skills to bring documents illuminating previously closed issues into the public domain. The history of Russia and the Soviet Union provides the opportunity for reflection on the relationship between primary sources and the writing of history: past and present have been inextricably linked as politics and history have intertwined.

Notes

1 *Sbornik Imperatorskogo Russkogo Istoricheskogo Obshchestva*, vol. 1 (St Petersburg: Tipografiia Transhelia, 1867), p. 10.

2 P. E. Shchegolev (ed.), *Padenie tsarskogo rezhima. Stenograficheskie otchety doprosov i pokazanii, dannykh v 1917 g. v Chrezvychainoi Sledstvennoi Komissii Vremennogo Pravitel'stva*, vol. 1 (Leningrad: Gosudarstvennoe izdatel'stvo, 1924), p. 7.

3 *Sbornik sekretnykh dokumentov arkhiva byvshego Ministerstva Inostrannykh Del*, 7 vols. (Petrograd: Tipografiia Komissariata po Inostrannym Delam, 1917–18).

4 See George M. Enteem, *The Soviet-Scholar Bureaucrat. M.N. Pokrovskii and the Society of Marxist Historians* (University Park, PA: Pennsylvannia University Press, 1978).

5 N. Bel'chikov, 'Kratkii obzor dokumentov, o publikovannykh v "Krasnym arkhive"', *Krasnyi Arkhiv*, 100 (1940), p. 35.

6 See R. Sh. Ganelin, *Sovetskie istoriki: o chem oni govorili mezhdu soboi* (St Petersburg: Nestor-Istoriia, 2004) for an enlightening insight into the Soviet historical profession.

7 Sheila Fitzpatrick, *A Spy in the Archives. A Memoir of Cold War Russia* (London: I. B. Tauris, 2013), p. 47. *Protiv burzhuaznykh fal'sifikatorov istorii i politiki KPSS* (Moscow: Politizdat, 1970) is a typical example of the attitudes displayed to Western historians.

8 I. D. Koval'chenko (ed.), *Istochnikovedenie istorii SSSR* (Moscow: Izdatel'stvo 'Vyshaia shkola', 1973).

9 *Revoliutsiia 1905–1907 gg. v Rossii, dokumenty i materialy*, 5 vols. (Moscow: Izdatel'stvo Akademii Nauk, 1955–61).

10 For example, *Rabochii klass Urala v gody voiny i revoliutsii v dokumentakh i materialiakh*, 2 vols. (Sverdlovsk: Uralprofsovet, 1927).

11 R. W. Davies, *Soviet History in the Yeltsin Era* (Basingstoke: Macmillan, 1997), p. 87.

12 Marc Raeff, *Russia Abroad. A Cultural History of the Russian Emigration, 1919–1939* (New York, NY: Oxford University Press, 1990), pp. 68–9; George Fischer, 'The Russian Archive in Prague', *American Slavic and East European Review*, 8 (1949), pp. 289–95.

13 Jean van Heijenoort, 'The History of Trotsky's Papers', *Harvard Library Bulletin*, 28 (1980), pp. 291–8.

14 Patricia Kennedy Grimsted, *The Odyssey of the Smolensk Archive. Plundered Communist Records for the Service of Anti-Communism* (Carl Beck Papers in Russian & East European Studies, 1201, University of Pittsburgh, PA: Pittsburgh, 1995); Merle Fainsod, *How Russia is Ruled* (Cambridge, MA: Harvard University Press, 1953). In 2002 the archive was returned to Russia.

15 M. V. Nechkina, *Dvizhenie Dekabristov*, 2 vols. (Moscow: Akademiia nauk SSSR, 1955), is the standard Soviet work.

16 E. H. Carr, *History of Soviet Russia*, 14 vols. (London: Macmillan, 1950–78).

17 Fitzpatrick, *Spy*, pp. 168–212.
18 Mikhail Gorbachev, *Memoirs* (London: Doubleday, 1996), pp. 203, 210.
19 Ibid., pp. 480–1.
20 R. W. Davies, *Soviet History in the Gorbachev Revolution* (Macmillan: Basingstoke, 1989), p. vii.
21 Kathryn Weathersby, 'Korea 1949–50. To Attack, or Not to Attack? Stalin, Kim Il Sung, and the Prelude to War', *Cold War International History Project Bulletin*, 5 (1995), pp. 1–9.
22 For example, Boris Kolonitskii, *Tragicheskaia erotika: Obrazy imperatoskoi sem'i v gody Pervyi mirovoi voiny* (Moscow: Novoe literaturnoe obozrenie, 2010).
23 *Stalinskie deportatsii 1928–1953* (Moscow: MFD, 2005); *Lubianka. Stalin i Glavnoe upravlenie gosbezopasnosti NKVD* (Moscow: MFD 2004).
24 See Donald J. Raleigh, 'Doing Soviet History: The Impact of the Archival Revolution', *Russian Review*, 61 (2002), pp. 16–24.
25 Donald J. Raleigh, *Experiencing Russia's Civil War Politics, Society, and Revolutionary Culture in Saratov, 1917–1922* (Princeton, NJ: Princeton University Press, 2002).
26 Aaron Retish, *Russia's Peasants in Revolution and Civil War: Citizenship, Identity, and the Creation of the Soviet State, 1914–1922* (Cambridge: Cambridge University Press, 2008).
27 Sarah Badcock, *Politics and the People in Revolutionary Russia. A Provincial History* (Cambridge: Cambridge University Press, 2011).
28 For example, M. S. Kedrov, *Bez bol'shevistkogo rukovodstva* (Leningrad: Krasnaia gazeta, 1930).
29 Liudmila Novikova, *Provintsial'naia 'kontrerevoliutsiia': Beloe dvizhenie i Grazhdanskaia voina na russkom Severe, 1917–1920* (Moscow: Novoe literaturnoe obozrenie, 2011).
30 See, for example, *Repressed Persons Records. Küüditamine Eestist Venemaale, 1949, Deportation from Estonia to Russia*, book 5, vol. 2 (Tallinn: Eesti Memento Liit, 1999).
31 See, for example, Jonathan Waterlow, *It's Only a Joke, Comrade! Humour, Trust and Everyday Life under Stalin* (Oxford, 2018).

Further reading

Acton, Edward, and Tom Stableford, *The Soviet Union. A Documentary History*, 2 vols. (Exeter: Exeter University Press, 2005 and 2007).
Bidlack, Richard, and Nikita Lomagin, *The Leningrad Blockade 1941-1944. A New Documentary History from the Soviet Archives* (New Haven, CT: Yale University Press, 2013).
Daly, Jonathan, and Leonid Trofimov, *Russia in War and Revolution, 1914–1922. A Documentary History* (Cambridge, MA: Hackett, 2009).
Fitzpatrick, Sheila, *A Spy in the Archives* (London: I. B. Tauris, 2013).
Fitzpatrick, Sheila, and Yuri Slezkine, *In the Shadow of Revolution: Life Stories of Russian Women from 1917 to the Second World War* (Princeton, NJ: Princeton University Press, 2000).
Getty, J. Arch, and Oleg V. Naumov (eds.), *The Road to Terror. Stalin and the Self-Destruction of the Bolsheviks, 1932–1939* (New Haven, CT: Yale University Press, 2008).
McCauley, Martin, and Peter Waldron (eds.), *From Octobrists to Bolsheviks* (London: Edward Arnold, 1984).
Sakwa, Richard (ed.), *The Rise and Fall of the Soviet Union 1917–1991* (London: Routledge, 1999).
Siegelbaum, Lewis, Andrei Sokolov and Sergei Zhuravlev (eds.), *Stalinism as a Way of Life A Narrative in Documents.* (New Haven, CT: Yale University Press, 2004).

3 The power of positionality?

Researching Russian history from the margins

Pavel Vasilyev

On the evening of 8 October 2015, Zhanna S. was supposed to celebrate her 24th birthday. Having given birth to her first baby just a few months before, she did not intend to organize anything large – just a small family gathering. Still, there were some preparations to be made and, being immersed in them, she did not immediately notice when her husband, Artem, failed to arrive back home in time from his shift in his temporary job as a taxi driver. Now he did not return her calls, and, after a couple of hours of frustrating waiting, the anxiety grew bigger and bigger. The party was definitely spoiled – but it was only the beginning of the story.

Worried relatives were finally able to locate Artem's whereabouts by the end of the evening. It turned out that he had been apprehended by the police while trying to re-sell a small dose of a popular synthetic drug. As he himself explained later, he decided to do it to get some extra cash to be able to get his wife a present for her birthday. When Artem's relatives rushed to get him out of the police precinct, they were met with a 'business proposal' from one of the officials who doodled an enigmatic '*million*' on a piece of paper. That meant that the police were willing to turn a blind eye on the case in exchange for an exorbitant sum of 1,000,000 rubles (roughly 16,000 US dollars).[1] The family was unable to raise this amount of money in a short time and Artem had to face trial. Given his earlier suspended sentence for a similar incident, the prospects did not look too promising – and, indeed, after a few months of unsuccessful litigation, he was sentenced to four years in prison. In July 2018, having served half of his sentence, Artem was finally released on parole and was reunited with his family.

The reason I know about this incident in so much detail is that Artem is a brother of my then-girlfriend, Polina, and on the evening of 8 October 2015 I was staying in their apartment in south-western St Petersburg during one of my research trips to the city as a postdoctoral fellow at the Center for the History of Emotions in Berlin. The reason why I am telling this story here is a bit more complex. In a nutshell, it has to do with the perceived connection between a researcher and the 'subjects' of their research. The cruel irony of fate on that evening back in 2015 was that one the primary foci of my archival research in St Petersburg was the history of drugs and drug policy in nineteenth- and twentieth-century Russia. Moreover, I came to occupy an increasingly critical position on both the effectiveness and necessity of the government policing of the drug market, and often used my academic publications and presentations to express these unpopular views. At the same time, Artem's imprisonment suddenly served as a powerful visceral reminder about the high rates of drug related incarceration, widespread police corruption and the precarity of male urban employment – all of the concerns that inform and influence both my academic scholarship and political position.

This chapter builds on my previous work on the history of marginalized social groups, such as users of psychoactive drugs, female criminal offenders and Gulag prisoners.[2] Taking the notion of 'positionality' as the point of departure, it traverses some of the methodological and ethical issues arising from my experience in writing and publishing on such sensitive topics in the Russian context. The chapter discusses how the personal experience of growing up in a troubled working-class neighbourhood on the outskirts of St Petersburg and having close friends and relatives in prison provided the author with a sense of connection to these seemingly marginal historical actors and the ability to empathize with their stories. At the same time, it warns of possible dangers of over-emphasizing this 'connection'.

Building on the work of Rita Charon, the chapter argues for an increased attention towards ethical issues while researching vulnerable populations and extends her argument to historical scholarship on Russia. In particular, it discusses the implications of this approach for the non-consensual use of primary sources and data. The chapter closes with reflections on how to reconcile this imperative with the drive to give oppressed people their voice in history and the use of ethically appropriate terms in historical writing.

A sense of connection

I grew up in a crowded four-generation *khrushchyovka* (low-cost, concrete-panelled apartment buildings from the 1960s) in a no-name neighbourhood on the outskirts of St Petersburg, even further south-west than Polina. Such areas – not unlike banlieues in France or council estates in the United Kingdom – are often associated with high unemployment rates, prevalence of crime and drug abuse and general urban decline. Throughout the 1990s and the early 2000s, the streets of the neighbourhood were perceived as quite dangerous, and it was not uncommon to encounter someone sporting a gun or using a syringe for intravenous drug injections. Jobs were scarce and low-paid, and by comparison a career in crime certainly looked very attractive. Our own apartment was robbed twice during that period.

Due primarily to my parents' huge intellectual and financial investments in my education, I was able to 'escape' the troubled neighbourhood of my birth and to pursue an academic career internationally that has led me to a prestigious postdoctoral fellowship at the Polonsky Academy in Jerusalem. At the same time, I have never ceased to nurture and cultivate my sense of connection to the place where I grew up and to the people who are living there. My parents and my grandmother are still living in the same *khrushchyovka* apartment, and I visit the neighbourhood quite often. I actually like the area a lot now, and I find its leafy exterior and the original, late Soviet modernist design very appealing to a historian's eye.

As I was climbing up the stairs of the academia ivory tower, however, I also became increasingly aware of the precarity and financial insecurity of academic employment in the neoliberal era – as well as the fact that everything that I write now comes from a privileged and potentially influential position. I want to believe that these concerns have also been reflected in the scholarly work on the history of marginalized communities in Russia that remains the main focus of my academic research. In the following, I wish to use the notion of 'positionality' to examine this perceived connection and to highlight both the productive and the more problematic aspects of it. In doing so, I provide a historical perspective on dealing with ethical issues in research on health and illness through the case study of the history of drugs – an inherently interdisciplinary and ethically problematic field.

Towards the ethics of researching vulnerable populations

Rita Charon has recently argued for an increased attention towards ethical and narrative issues in health research.[3] In particular, she is very critical of the non-consensual use of sources and data that were produced in a setting where one side is *a priori* dominant and the other subaltern (such as in a physician's office or a police precinct).[4] What implications, then, does this observation have for historical research that often deals with primary sources produced in such settings and in most cases by definition cannot obtain the permission of the respective actors? Can we reconcile this ethical imperative with the drive to give these oppressed people their voice in history?

To a large degree, my analysis in this chapter is informed by Eileen Pittaway, Linda Bartolomei and Richard Hugman's article on the ethics of research with vulnerable populations.[5] I find this work especially valuable, since it provides practical guidance to researchers that is often lacking in other publications. However, their article is aimed at social scientists (primarily in the area of social work) and by definition does not account for the specificities of *historical* research. I have therefore engaged in dialogue with Pittaway, Bartolomei and Hugman, and have attempted to translate their practical guide into historical terms.

I want to start with a paradoxical question. Social scientists mention the ethics of academic research involving human subjects passingly, almost as something taken for granted.[6] But does *historical* research really involve human subjects? In some sense, yes, but in most cases, they are certainly not alive anymore. Thus, it becomes difficult to discuss the issues of agency and capacity that are so closely linked to a new ethical vision of research participants.[7] In fact, the key issue of consent is impossible to obtain for historians. Pittaway, Bartolomei and Hugman also make a very important observation that 'informed consent' is context-specific:

> When I go into a horrendous [refugee] camp situation as a white researcher, the people are so desperate for any form of assistance they would agree to anything just on the off-chance that I might be able to assist. It makes asking for permission to interview them or take photographs a farce…What does 'informed consent' mean in an isolated refugee camp with security problems and no proper interpreters?[8]

Moreover, the authors state that the overall goal of their research is to 'add value to the lives of the people they are researching'.[9] In another instance, it is stated that research ethics 'should be extended to promoting the interests and well-being of extremely vulnerable research subjects'.[10] It can in itself be a problematic claim, but how is this different (or even possible) in history?

Pittaway, Bartolomei and Hugman list a number of concerns that vulnerable populations can have about research collaboration.[11] The most important reservations deal with confidentiality and security, which, I believe, are less important in historical research and are unlikely to be a concern.[12] Security can also be linked to the fact that these vulnerable populations are often engaged in or affected by illegal activities.[13] It is certainly true in the case of the history of drugs, and the early Soviet drug addicts were also very likely to be involved in petty crime, stealing, prostitution, and alcohol abuse (the latter is included here in the list of illegal or controversial activities as vodka was prohibited in Russia in 1914–25).[14] However, I believe that this will hardly be a concern for historians, and the moral and ethical dilemmas associated with the experience of learning about the 'crime'[15] will be alleviated by the fact that it happened around 100 years ago and the period of proscription has long expired (that is, when the understanding of the crime has not changed and it is still included in the Penal Code).

There is also a number of concerns that, I believe, are specific to a particular context that the authors study (refugee groups) or are irrelevant for historical research – false expectations of assistance from researchers, lack of feedback from research, fear of backlash from the government, distrust of researchers who 'fly in and fly out' of conflict zones, the potential for retraumatization, and the inability of many researchers to cope with the absolute horror of the experience of research participants[16] (I admit that the latter might be a concern for *some* historians, but it is certainly an exception rather than the rule).

According to Pittaway, Bartolomei and Hugman, 'the principle of reciprocity suggests that the risks and costs associated with participation in research can be offset by the delivery of direct, tangible benefits to those who participate'.[17] I agree with this statement in principle, but I think that it further suggests that if there are no (or very few) risks, it is perfectly legitimate to provide no (or a very small amount of) benefits. Accordingly, since confidentiality or security are unlikely to be concerns for historical actors, we can ignore the inescapable impossibility to improve their lives, give them control of the materials we collected, or lobby for a political change (all of these are the solutions that Pittaway, Bartolomei and Hugman propose).[18]

There is, however, a number of concerns in the list that at least seem to be more applicable to historical research. These include exploitation by previous researchers, class and ethnic distrust, and lack of consultation about recommendations and strategies – concerns that can probably be united under the 'stealing stories' label. While it is not possible to fully address these concerns, due to the impossibility of gaining consent from historical subjects or consulting them about possible research and publication strategies, I propose that we can still think of a solution through a kind of experiment.

The problem of ethnic distrust or 'going as a white researcher'[19] has special relevance for historians writing about drugs in the Russian empire and the Soviet Union, since the most important region for the production and consumption of opiates and cannabis, Central Asia, was also imbued with numerous and complex colonial power relationships. This was partially reflected in the work done by the researchers coming from the region,[20] and 'going as a white researcher' is certainly more challenging, since I can bring with me strong colonial stereotypes and misinterpret many local phenomena. Moreover, while Pittaway, Bartolomei and Hugman only mention class and ethnic/cultural distrust,[21] I believe it is possible to broaden the argument and add gender, age, sexuality and disability to the list.

It is certainly difficult to tell whether vulnerable historical subjects would have felt distrust towards historians as researchers, since this has to be constructed retrospectively. There is also an important time factor at play here: how would they have felt not just about any researcher studying them (this is a difficult question *per se*), but about some researcher telling their stories much later on? One way to approach this dilemma is to pay more attention to the reactions of the vulnerable populations of the past to their contemporary researchers (provided this is recorded in some of these texts).

For an example, consider the case with Ernst Joël's informative and influential handbook on addiction that was speedily translated into Russian only a couple of years after the original German publication.[22] Joël explicitly criticized the (apparently common) treatment of drug users as 'physically and morally defective' and stated that the addicts were totally discouraged by the 'rude, acrimonious and often cynical tone' of the physicians who seemed to focus on blaming the patient and not on discovering the true cause of the disease.[23] Moreover, he further suggested that the success of the treatment ultimately depended on establishing a strong patient–doctor relationship, which includes, *inter alia*, playing checkers and cards together.[24]

Accordingly, it may be possible to gather some information retrospectively. I, however, propose a more radical way to deal with the issues of distrust and exploitation. We can get a certain amount of information by asking the vulnerable subjects today the question posed above (i.e., 'How would you feel about some researcher writing about you in future years?'). This is where I rely on my perceived sense of connection and try to use both my personal experience and the conversations with my friends and relatives to improve and adjust my research agenda. I understand, of course, that a contemporary perspective could not be simply transferred to the early Soviet drug addicts, but the results of this experiment could produce new ways of thinking about vulnerability, exploitation, and the time factor. In a certain way, it would also assure that researchers 'listen' to vulnerable populations and ask for their ideas and solutions – a practice that Pittaway, Bartolomei and Hugman found to be extremely attractive and rewarding for their research participants.[25]

This practice would answer to the authors' call to include 'justice, recognition, self-determination, voice and agency',[26] empower the vulnerable subjects and assure the use of ethically appropriate terms. However, historians can also give a voice to the (formerly) oppressed communities and empower them by providing a rare opportunity for them to tell their story on their own terms.[27] A good example of this (complemented by numerous quotations and the use of visual images from the archives) is provided in Ira Roldugina's recent publications on the infamous Petrograd gay trial of 1922.[28] Roldugina shows how 'some of the detained perceived an unexpected encounter with the authorities as a chance to present their identity to the authorities and, possibly, legitimize it'.[29] I, too, try to include the testimonies of early Soviet drug addicts in my writing and publishing on the sensitive topics as drug history and drug policy.[30]

I am now married to Polina, and Artem is officially my *shurin*, or, as they say it in English, 'brother-in-law'. In conclusion to this chapter, I would like to reflect on the entirely accidental (yet serendipitously instructive) connection between the English word for a wife's brother and the Russian phrase that is often used to describe a professional criminal (*vor v zakone*, or, literally, 'thief-in-law'). When I was teaching English in St Petersburg in the early 2010s to make some money to support me through graduate school, I would often use this cheeky example to make the students memorize the names for the relatives acquired by the means of marriage. Drawing the connection between the often-hated in-laws and the shady world of criminality would usually provoke a good laugh in the audience and I think it also worked well for the purposes of instruction.

I do not think anymore that this pun is that funny, but I have now found a new meaning in this connection. As the Russian saying goes, *ot sumy da ot tiur'my ne zarekaisia* ['Never say never to poverty and prison'], and, indeed, Artem's prison experience reminded me of the visceral reality and widespread prevalence of incarceration in the country. Significantly, this incident was totally devoid of any political context and thus brought me in touch with the realities of persecution and imprisonment beyond the point of view of much-publicized political cases such as the ones of Mikhail Khodorkovskii, Oleg Navalnyi or Pussy Riot.

The latter case was actually quite instructive in helping me to make sense of my new situation. For the members of the Pussy Riot collective, their experience of incarceration meant, among other things, that they were now linked to the penitentiary system 'by the ties of blood'.[31] Straight after their release from prison in December 2013, Nadezhda Tolokonnikova and Mariia Alekhina announced the establishment of *Mediazona*, a Non-Governmental Organization (NGO) and a media outlet devoted to the issues of prison reform and the rights of all prisoners (not only 'politicals').[32] I now feel that in a certain sense I, too, am tied to the Russian penitentiary system (if only by the ties of marriage), and I will make every effort to make this visible and impactful in my own research on the history of crime, criminal law and punishment in modern Russia. While I do not recommend to anyone going through the experience of having close relatives in prison, I do think that in this particular case it at least made me a more engaged, a more empathetic and a more reflective academic – all qualities that I believe should lie at the cornerstone of any humane scholarship.

Notes

1 On 'ransoms' in connection to drug crimes in contemporary Russia, see the study conducted by the Andrei Ryl'kov Foundation. <http://rylkov-fond.org/files/2017/11/tsena-svobody.pdf> (accessed 1 August 2018).
2 Pavel Vasilyev, 'Drug Addiction and the Practice of Public Health in Late Imperial and Early Soviet Russia', *Vestnik of Saint Petersburg University, History,* 63 (2018), pp. 1100–19; idem., 'Sex and Drugs and Revolutionary Justice: Negotiating "Female Criminality" in the Early Soviet Courtroom', *Journal of Social Policy Studies,* 16 (2018), pp. 341–54; idem., and Gian Marco Vidor, 'Prisoners: Experiencing the Criminal 'Other',' in Benno Gammerl, Philipp Nielsen and Margrit Pernau (eds.), *Encounters with Emotions: Negotiating Cultural Differences Since Early Modernity* (New York, NY: Berghahn Books, 2019), pp. 184–206.
3 Rita Charon, *Narrative Medicine: Honoring the Stories of Illness* (New York, NY, and Oxford: Oxford University Press, 2006). See also Rita Charon and Marta Montello (eds.), *Stories Matter: The Role of Narrative in Medical Ethics* (New York, NY, and London: Routledge, 2002).
4 Cf., for example, Charon's remarks at the conference '"Attentive Writers": Healthcare, Authorship, and Authority', Medical Humanities Research Centre, University of Glasgow, UK, 23–25 August 2013.
5 Eileen Pittaway, Linda Bartolomei and Richard Hugman, '"Stop Stealing Our Stories": The Ethics of Research With Vulnerable Populations', *Journal of Human Rights Practice,* 2 (2010), pp. 229–51 (on the lack of practical guidance, see p. 232).
6 Pittaway, Bartolomei and Hugman, 'Ethics of Research', p. 231.
7 Ibid., p. 236.
8 Ibid., p. 234.
9 Ibid., p. 231.
10 Ibid., pp. 241–2.
11 Ibid., p. 236. On confidentiality and security, respectively, see also pp. 234 and 232.
12 I admit that in a small number of cases revealing a historical fact about a certain figure may harm the reputation of the living relatives of this person or even put them in danger. However, this is still more likely to happen with the members of the political elite and other famous individuals. I believe that the descendants of early Soviet drug addicts and their social surroundings probably will not read my academic publications – and even if they do, they will not necessarily associate these historical actors with their long-deceased relatives.
13 Pittaway, Bartolomei and Hugman, 'Ethics of Research', p. 235.
14 Mikhail V. Shkarovskii, 'Leningradskaia prostitutsiia i bor'ba s nei v 1920-e gody', In *Nevskii Arkhiv: Istoriko-kraevedcheskii sb.,* Issue 1 (Moscow, 1993), pp. 394–5; Nataliia B. Lebina and M. V. Shkarovskii, *Prostitutsiia v Peterburge: (40-e gg. XIX v. – 40-e gg. XX v.)* (Moscow: Progress-Akademiia, 1994), pp. 69, 90; N. B. Lebina, *Povsednevnaia Zhizn' Sovetskogo Goroda: Normyianomalii: 1920–1930* (St Petersburg: Neva: Letnii Sad, 1999), p. 31; Vadim I. Musaev, *Prestupnost' v Petrograde v 1917–1921 gg. i bor'ba s nei* (St Petersburg: Dmitrii Bulanin, 2001), p. 180; Pavel A. Vasilyev, 'War, Revolution, and Drugs: 'Democratization' of Drug Addiction and the Evolution of Drug Policy in Russia, 1914–1924', in Adele Lindenmeyr, Christopher Read and Peter Waldron (eds.), *Russia's Home Front in War and Revolution 1914–1922, Book 2: The Experience of War and Revolution* (Bloomington, IN: Slavica Publishers, 2016), pp. 411–30.
15 In many cases, the knowledge about the crime will come from a legal source (such as an investigatory report or court proceedings), and the dilemma about informing the authorities will naturally disappear.
16 Pittaway, Bartolomei and Hugman, 'Ethics of Research', p. 236.

17 Ibid., p. 234.
18 Ibid., pp. 237–8.
19 Ibid., p. 234.
20 Alisher Latypov, 'Central Asian Tabibs in Post-Soviet Archives: Healing, Spying, Struggling, and "Exploiting"', *Wellcome History*, 43 (2010), pp. 8–9; idem., 'Healers and Psychiatrists: The Transformation of Mental Health Care in Tajikistan', *Transcultural Psychiatry*, 47 (2010), pp. 419–51; idem., 'The Soviet Doctor and the Treatment of Drug Addiction: "A Difficult and Most Ungracious Task"', *Harm Reduction Journal*, 8 (2011).
21 Pittaway, Bartolomei and Hugman, 'Ethics of Research', p. 236.
22 Ernst Joël, *Lechenie Narkomanii. Alkogolizm. Morfinizm. Kokainizm* (Khar'kov: Nauchnaia mysl', 1930). The original German publication is Joël, *Die Behandlung Der Giftsuchten. Alkoholismus, Morphinismus, Kokainismus usw* (Leipzig: Georg Thieme, 1928).
23 Joël, *Lechenie narkomanii*, p. 55. Consider also other statements by Joël and his long-time collaborator Fritz Fränkel: 'Addiction is a disease, not a crime' (Joël, Die and Fritz Fränkel, *Der Cocainismus: Ein Beitrag Zur Geschichte und Psychopathologie Der Rauschgifte* (Berlin: Julius Springer, 1924), p. 24, or 'The addict is not a delinquent, but a patient' (Joël, Die and Fritz Fränkel, 'Zur Verhütung und Behandlung der Giftsuchten', *Klinische Wochenschrift*, 4 (1925), p. 1718).
24 Joël, *Lechenie narkomanii*, p. 70.
25 Pittaway, Bartolomei and Hugman, 'Ethics of Research', p. 240. I recognize, of course, that this is also only an approximation.
26 Ibid., p. 243.
27 I admit that it can be difficult to reconcile 'giving a voice' with something like a Butlerian critique implying that voice and subjectivity are socially constructed and only what is socially permitted can be said: Judith Butler, *Psychic Life of Power: Theories in Subjection* (Stanford, CA: Stanford University Press, 1997); Butler, *Giving an Account of Oneself* (New York, NY: Fordham University Press, 2005). This is probably something that Charon would criticize as well. However, I strongly believe that the benefits of giving a voice to the otherwise silent historical community outweigh any possible risks and skepticisms (precisely because the amount of such evidence available is usually very limited).
28 Ira Roldugina, 'Rannesovetskaia gomoseksual'naia subkul'tura: Istoriia odnoi fotografii', *Teatr*, 16 (2014), pp. 188–91; idem., '"Pochemu my takie liudi?" Rannesovetskie gomoseksualy ot pervogo litsa: Novye istochniki po istorii gomoseksual'nykh identichnostei v Rossii', *Ab Imperio*, 2 (2016), pp. 183–216. For more on homosexuality in early Soviet Russia and the 1922 trial, see Laura Engelstein, 'Combined Underdevelopment: Discipline and the Law in Imperial and Soviet Russia', *American Historical Review*, 98, (1993), pp. 338–53 (pp. 350–1); Dan Healey, *Homosexual Desire in Revolutionary Russia: The Regulation of Sexual and Gender Dissent* (Chicago, IL and London: The University of Chicago Press, 2001).
29 Roldugina, 'Rannesovetskaia gomoseksual'naia subkul'tura', p. 190.
30 Pavel A. Vasilyev, 'Prodavtsy kokaina pered narodnym sudom: Delo Lokotnikova i Briantseva 1921 g.', paper presented at the 'Malen'kii i bol'shoi chelovek v leningradskoi povsednevnosti' conference, S. M. Kirov Museum, St Petersburg, 8 November 2013; idem., 'Revolutionary Conscience, Remorse and Resentment: Emotions and Early Soviet Criminal Law, 1917–1922', *Historical Research*, 90 (2017), pp. 125–32; idem., 'Sex and Drugs and Revolutionary Justice: Negotiating "Female Criminality" in the Early Soviet Courtroom', *The Journal of Social Policy Studies*, 16 (2018), pp. 341–54.
31 'Tolokonnikovu iz Pussy Riot osvobodili vsled za Alekhinoi' [Pussy Riot's Tolokonnikova released shortly after Alekhina], BBC Russian, 23 December 2013. <www.bbc.co.uk/russian/russia/2013/12/131223_pussy_riot_tolokonnikova_release.shtml> (accessed 1 August 2018).
32 Mediazona. <https://zona.media/> (accessed 1 August 2018).

Further reading

Charon, Rita, *Narrative Medicine: Honoring the Stories of Illness* (New York, NY, and Oxford: Oxford University Press, 2006).

Charon, Rita, and Marta Montello (eds.), *Stories Matter: The Role of Narrative in Medical Ethics* (New York, NY, and London: Routledge, 2002).

Engelstein, Laura, 'Combined Underdevelopment: Discipline and the Law in Imperial and Soviet Russia', *American Historical Review*, 98, (1993), pp. 338–53.

Healey, Dan, *Homosexual Desire in Revolutionary Russia: The Regulation of Sexual and Gender Dissent* (Chicago, IL and London: The University of Chicago Press, 2001).

Latypov, Alisher, 'Central Asian Tabibs in Post-Soviet Archives: Healing, Spying, Struggling, and 'Exploiting'', *Wellcome History*, 43 (2010a), pp. 8–9.

_____, 'Healers and Psychiatrists: The Transformation of Mental Health Care in Tajikistan', *Transcultural Psychiatry*, 47 (2010b), pp. 419–51.

_____, 'The Soviet Doctor and the Treatment of Drug Addiction: "A Difficult and Most Ungracious Task"', *Harm Reduction Journal*, 8 (2011).

Pittaway, Eileen, Linda Bartolomei and Richard Hugman, '"Stop Stealing Our Stories": The Ethics of Research With Vulnerable Populations', *Journal of Human Rights Practice*, 2 (2010), pp. 229–51.

Vasilyev, Pavel A., 'War, Revolution, and Drugs: 'Democratization' of Drug Addiction and the Evolution of Drug Policy in Russia, 1914–1924', in Adele Lindenmeyr, Christopher Read and Peter Waldron (eds.), *Russia's Home Front in War and Revolution 1914–1922, Book 2: The Experience of War and Revolution* (Bloomington, IN: Slavica Publishers, 2016), pp. 411–30.

_____, 'Sex and Drugs and Revolutionary Justice: Negotiating 'Female Criminality' in the Early Soviet Courtroom', *The Journal of Social Policy Studies*, 16 (2018), pp. 341–54.

Part II
Varieties of sources and their interpretation

4 Imperial maps

Jennifer Keating

During the reign of Catherine the Great, a general land survey was instituted to map in detail the lands and estates of European Russia. In her instructions to the Cadastral Commission responsible for the geographical survey and collection of relevant materials, the Empress directed that

> all wastelands, rivers, streams and other natural boundaries that go by indecent names, especially those of the private parts, should in the survey books be recorded under other names, either excluding their former names or with a few letters added for decency.[1]

Thus it was that a slew of places, settlements and natural features received new names, almost overnight. The episode, beyond exposing polite sensitivities, alludes to some of the challenges of working with maps as historical sources. Do maps accurately represent territory? Or does territory come to represent what is inscribed on the map? How should we interpret cartographic materials: as scientifically objective sources used to chart geographical knowledge, or as objects of power, subject to the whim of their creator? Such questions take on additional pertinence in Imperial Russia, where maps were for the most part a carefully controlled medium. Closely regulated by the state both in production and circulation, they were privileged documents associated most often with the practice of imperial rule, implicated in territorial expansion, exploration, surveillance and the juridical process. Despite the secrecy that often surrounded their production, maps are a particularly rich source for historians of Imperial Russia. As materials that fuse scientific, geographic and ethnographic knowledge, maps can be read as inscriptions of power, identity and social attitudes, giving them, when analysed critically, the capacity to inform our understanding of some of the fundamental social, political and economic questions that span Russia's imperial history.

The institutions and evolution of cartography in Imperial Russia

As two-dimensional visual representations of terrestrial or maritime space, maps provide ready access to contemporary knowledge of territory, terrain and resources. Varying in scale, representing anything from an empire to a village, a sea to a forest, they are used most commonly to depict natural features (relief, climate, geology) and political geographies (international borders, administrative divisions). Besides fixing the location of settlements, topography and political borders, maps have a multiplicity of other purposes, including town planning and surveys of property, recording demography and rainfall, or plotting trade routes and maritime navigation. Schematic maps, often overlaid onto topographical cartography, provide graphic description of networks such as waterways, railways, roads and more besides.

Such sources are increasingly accessible to researchers working on the history of Imperial Russia. Within Russia, virtually all major archives from the Russian State Archive of Ancient Documents (RGADA) to the Russian State Military History Archive (RGVIA) contain a mass of cartographic material, supplemented by significant holdings in, amongst others, the collections of the Russian Geographic Society and the Academy of Sciences. In addition, the map departments of the National Library of Russia and the Russian State Library hold a wealth of material in loose-leaf and atlas form. Both libraries have also undertaken extensive digitisation of their cartographic collections, while a number of historical GIS projects, such as the Harvard *Imperiia* collaboration, have also made high-resolution cartographic material available online, often with multiple overlays.[2] This said, despite relative ease of access, maps can be problematic sources on a practical level. Some knowledge of Russian is essential to decipher place names, inscriptions, titles and so forth. Material can be difficult to work with, so large as to require specialist map tables, and often in poor condition, or filed with minimal descriptive notes to aid the researcher. There is also the matter of less 'official' maps: those produced without state sanction or not intended for popular circulation. Traces of such maps, including hastily drawn sketches of directions, routes and property, litter archival and personal records, but are far more difficult to locate and have survived in more haphazard fashion than those preserved in state archives or published in atlases or the illustrated press. Nevertheless, as will be explored below, all make for fascinating sources that reward the careful enquirer.

Imperial Russian mapping has its roots in the cartography of Muscovy, a distinctive genre associated with the 'sketch' (*chertezh*) style. As the Muscovite state grew and its territory expanded, maps became increasingly necessary instruments, used to chart new frontier zones, to identify populations liable for tribute levies, and for various other administrative and juridical purposes. Unacquainted with the method of rigorous mathematical survey practised in the West, Muscovite cartographers produced maps that were visually idiosyncratic: drawn to no particular scale, with neither grid lines nor linear measurements, and with varying orientations, these maps were 'more fanciful than informative' and very often took waterways – the chief means of travel and navigation – as their focus.[3] The most famous exponent of the Muscovite tradition, Semen Remezov, working in the late seventeenth and early eighteenth centuries, produced a wonderfully rich body of cartographical work, much of which was commissioned by the Siberian Chancellery, including his *Sketchbook* (1699–1701) and *Chorographic sketchbook* (1697–1711).[4] While the conventions of these maps may appear unusual to the modern eye, their striking beauty belied the fact that, as the seventeenth century drew to a close, the rapid proliferation of such materials provided a bedrock of surprisingly accurate geographical knowledge of Russia's borders, major settlements and topographical features.

It was the Petrine era, however, that marked a watershed in Russian cartography. Whereas maps in the Muscovite tradition were immediately recognisable by their pictorial, colourful, naïve style, the introduction of Western astronomy, navigation and surveying practices under Peter the Great reshaped the fundamentals of cartography, bringing Russian maps into closer alignment with those produced by Swedish and Dutch cartographers. Of notable influence was the new Naval Academy in St Petersburg, Moscow's School of Mathematics and Navigation, and the Academy of Sciences, which trained surveyors and geodesists to work using astrolabes and theodolites, facilitating the production of Russia's first maps 'constructed on a scientific base'.[5] Unlike traditional *chertezhi*, these new maps were almost always oriented to the north, were calculated using fixed astronomical points, and were standardised in geometric form by a series of 'Instructions', issued from 1720 onwards to inform the creation and systematisation of a fresh set of maps of the expanding empire, including the 1734 'General Map', overseen by I. Kirilov at the Senate. Under V. N. Tatishchev and, later, M. V. Lomonosov, head of the Geographical Department at the Academy of Sciences, a budding corps of surveyors produced increasingly precise maps on both local and imperial scales – including the first full atlas of the Russian empire in 1745 – using a combination of mathematical survey and anecdotal information relayed by local inhabitants and imperial explorers.

From the reign of Catherine the Great onwards, mapping became a vital undertaking in almost all state departments, many of which created their own drawing offices. This rapidly diversifying practice took both military and civilian form. In 1765, the creation of the Cadastral Commission marked the beginning of a hugely ambitious project to survey in detail the lands of European Russia, a task that took until the mid-1840s to complete, and which, via the office of the General Land Survey, produced over 600,000 maps on *uezd* and *guberniia* scale.[6] Away from civilian branches of the state, the parallel creation of the General Staff (1763) marked the gradual shift of responsibility for official cartography away from the Senate and the Academy of Sciences towards the military. The Academy's Geographical Department was absorbed into the Private Map Depot in 1800, and by 1812 a Military Topographic Depot within the General Staff (re-formed in 1866 into a new military-topographic service), proceeded to reinvigorate the ongoing mapping of state territory with ambitious projects to chart new borderlands, including Finland and Poland, in previously unknown detail.

The final major phase in the history of tsarist cartography arrived in 1845 with the foundation of the Imperial Russian Geographical Society. Working at first to improve the maps produced by Catherine's Cadastral Commission with the goal a 'universal, multi-purpose topographical map intended to meet the needs of a broad range of users', the society took the lead in bringing together the work of civilian land surveyors and military topographers, resulting in maps of ever greater precision and standardisation.[7] Efforts to update obsolete work continued, with new regions of the empire including the Amur valley and Central Asia mapped in detail for the first time in tandem with IRGO expeditions, and existing territories around the Black Sea, Crimea and the Caspian Sea rendered with new accuracy. This depth of knowledge in turn enabled the development of thematic cartography as the nineteenth century progressed, with a flurry of new surveys of state forests, population density, drainage basins, transport infrastructure, mineral resources, soil composition and so forth. Such studies – either loose leaf maps or detailed composite atlases – were very often commissioned by individual offices of the state, and in part reflected efforts to develop the imperial economy. The 1842 'Industrial map of the European part of Russia', for instance, compiled by the Ministry of Finance, made use of statistics on trade, taxation, mining and agricultural productivity to superimpose on the geography of Russia economic zones, ports, custom posts, docks and trade fairs,[8] and was indicative of the state's increasingly sophisticated familiarity with its populations and resources. From the 1860s onwards, such was the refined knowledge of Russia's territorial complexity that the General Staff was able to produce one-inch-to-one-verst scale maps, versions of which remained in use until the early Soviet period.[9]

Throughout this period, it must be remembered that there was little in the way of private map-making. The state dominated the production and circulation of maps and atlases, with cartography first under the firm control of the Senate and the Academy of Sciences, and later of the General Staff, government departments, and the Imperial Russian Geographical Society. The materials themselves remained for the most part unpublished, stored in local and central government archives. Thus, the overwhelming majority of maps – those with a scale larger than 1:1,000,000 – were available only to those permitted by the state, with the information contained within their pages, from administrative boundaries to the natural features of new frontier zones, highly privileged and judged to be potentially subversive in the wrong hands. Yet despite the continued secrecy that shrouded mapping practice, as the nineteenth century progressed cartography began to permeate popular culture, thus broadening the contours of Russia's map-world. Such material very often lacked detail (given the sheer size of the empire, even a large one-sheet map of Russia had to be drawn to a scale as small as 1:8,600,000), and in many cases bore scant resemblance to official cartography. Nevertheless, such sources remain an important sub-genre of Russian mapping, all the more significant precisely *because* cartography remained a restricted medium closely allied to state interests.

The gradual diffusion of map-related imagery was aided in part by the creation of the private cartographic company of A. A. Il'in in 1859 (a business that depended on cooperative ventures with the state), and underpinned to a larger extent by the growth of the popular press and rising literacy rates in the wake of the Great Reforms. Maps mingled with reportage in newspapers, first as inserts, and then as half-tone technology improved to allow for higher quality images, directly on the pages of the press. Sketch maps illustrating the Russo-Turkish war appeared in supplements of *Golos* (*Voice*), while *Russkoe slovo* (*The Russian Word*) featured maps to inform commentary on the Russo-Japanese war, and *Peterburgskii listok*

(*The Petersburg Sheet*) printed 'crude' maps to accompany accounts of Alexander II's assassination in 1881.[10] Meanwhile, cartography was a frequent feature in the illustrated press, including *Niva* (*Cornfield*), founded in 1870, *Vokrug sveta* (*Around the World*), and *Ogonek* (*Light*), which by 1914 boasted a circulation of some 700,000.[11] Beyond the obvious arena of the press, maps appeared in more diffuse settings within the burgeoning world of popular culture: used for instance to introduce readers to the geography of Russia and the wider world in travel guides, textbooks, school wall maps, and at national exhibitions. Mass-produced playing cards and adverts often contained simply-sketched line maps, while schematic diagrams of Russia's railway network, medical points and major towns were important components of resettlement handbooks, printed in their hundreds of thousands for peasants migrating from European Russia to Siberia, Central Asia and the Far East.[12] While we know relatively little about the ways in which these maps were read or understood within the context of popular culture, the increasing exposure of the Russian population to cartographic imagery cannot have failed to increase what Kivelson describes as their 'map-mindedness', itself an important qualification to the suggestion that mapping remained a state domain, beyond the reach of the population at large.[13]

Map reading as historical practice

This rich world of Russian mapping has traditionally been used as colourful illustration to scholarly works, as an aid to the study of unfamiliar geographies, or to inform research on the development of Russian cartographic practice. More recently, however, maps have become objects of study in their own right in works that range far beyond the history of cartography. In part aided by greater access to archives since 1991, and in part reflective of spatial and imperial 'turns' in the writing of Russian history, maps are now vital sources in a variety of studies focusing on imperial expansion, rulership, questions of identity, and the transmission of knowledge.[14] This diversification of use is firmly rooted in the conceptualisation, largely developed beyond the specific sphere of Russian history, that as a form of communication and representation, maps serve both practical *and* ideological purposes: a means to locate settlements, resources, routes and territorial borders, but also a vehicle to reflect and disseminate particular worldviews and political subjectivities.[15] As J. B. Harley and others have demonstrated, if we deconstruct a map, examining it critically rather than as a scientific form of knowledge, we discover that maps are just as much representations of power as they are of territory. Beneath the 'surface layer of standard objectivity', lie the norms, values and desires of their creators, deployed on the map face to define and control social and political relationships.[16] Such hidden intentions are often tremendously potent given the authority invested in the map as an impartial source of knowledge.

Maps in other words, served not just those who wished to chart, explore and travel across territory in a physical sense, but were also an 'essential tool of rulers', used to reinforce – and potentially subvert – established social and political hierarchies.[17] In an imperial context for instance, mapping could be used to denote what land was owned by whom: a powerful instrument in the hands of those who sought to control territory and to exclude others from legal ownership and use of land. Map-making was a key means by which the annexation or occupation of territory could be legitimised, while the survey of these lands produced rationales for states to manage and exploit local resources, along with the ethnographic ordering, and even erasure, of imperial populations. Thus maps produced by the state privileged the eye of the state, generating knowledge about land and populations that could be deployed to best advantage the imperial centre in its relations with foreign powers and in internal matters of governance.

Building on Harley's work, a lively body of research proceeds to suggest that as maps can be 'vehicles of power, symbolic of the establishment of authority', it is vital to read them 'in critical fashion and not as wholly objective artefacts displaying geographical knowledge'.[18] In this sense, maps have to be approached with 'healthy skepticism': just like any other historical source, they too are 'authored collections of information', and therefore must be considered to carry similar projections, biases and interests, and thus should be subject to interrogation.[19] What does a map purport to show? What truth claims does the source make and reinforce? Who produced the map, and for what purpose? Who might have had access to it? What work is the source doing, beyond the surface representation of territory? What can we make of the construction of the map – the use of colour, typography, shading, decorative elements, labelling, text, the placement on the page? Further, the specifics of the Russian context must also be taken into account. Although maps may appear relatively straightforward to read, this is not always the case. Muscovite maps can look decidedly odd to the modern viewer, often oriented to the south, thus resulting in sketches with the Arctic at the bottom of the map, or drawn according to multiple perspectives, resulting in images that could be understood from any angle. One must also consider that the format and circulation of most maps were subject to restriction: detailed, large-scale material was largely confined to state institutions, while more popular forms of cartography in the press were subject to the imperial censor.

Above all, context is critical when interpreting sources such as these that lie on the boundary between the visual and the textual, and scholars have found multiple fruitful ways to incorporate maps into research on the tsarist era. Approaching cartography firstly as a form of communication and a source of graphic knowledge, maps can provide important insights into the extent of, and limits to, Russian awareness of territory. A comparison of maps from across the seventeenth and eighteenth centuries for instance, reveals quite clearly how contemporary geographical knowledge developed. Early modern maps contained multiple errors, mis-drawn coastlines, mis-placed natural features and settlements, symptomatic of little-explored frontiers and a dearth of information about neighbouring states. Gradually, however, informed by increased contact with and travel to borderlands and external territories, maps became more precise: the details of China's coastline for example, became more accurate as expeditions to the east returned data about settlements, trade and river routes, and natural features along the Sino-Siberian frontier.[20] Meanwhile as the eighteenth century progressed, exploration in the

Pacific, North America and Russia's northern and eastern coastlines produced a host of new maps and atlases, along with the first charts to accurately map maritime spaces, particularly the Caspian and Baltic Seas.[21] With the involvement of the Admiralty, river systems were mapped in detail in the 1760s and 1770s, providing new charts of the Don, Volga, Oka, Neva and Moskva. Exploring the growing detail and accuracy of maps thus attests to the state's increasing knowledge of its expanding territory, resources and people.

Further, the development of mapping from the time of Peter the Great illuminates one facet of the broader adoption and adaption of technological and artistic models from Western Europe during Russia's 'century of apprenticeship'.[22] Likewise, maps have been used as evidence to trace the ways in which information circulated within and beyond political borders: Kivelson, for instance, charts how irrespective of the strictures of the state, there were in fact 'considerable flows of cartographic information and communication in early modern Russia'.[23] Illicit copying, smuggling, and the transfer of information between Europe and Russia reveal not simply the dynamics of knowledge circulation, but also point to the value attributed to the map by contemporaries. Copies of Remezov's maps and of the Godunov map (1666–7) were coveted by foreigners as 'tactical assets, objects of forbidden desire', and escaped the porous secrecy of the state to form part of a network of communications and information circulation that spanned the European continent and beyond.[24]

Second, framing maps as inscriptions of power and identity, as Harley would have us do, reveals that these materials did not simply record existing understandings of bounded territory, but also actively produced this knowledge. The applications of this 'scientific' information were multifarious. In the sphere of empire, exploration and geographical expeditions were essential components of the extension of imperial rule, with maps a vital medium used to confirm shifting imperial borders.[25] In the early nineteenth century, for instance, state mapping of Finland, Poland and Russia's North American possessions reinforced imperial knowledge of, and sovereignty over, land. The production of maps detailing these border regions served not just to increase state awareness of the economic and political potential of new additions to empire, but actively worked to bolster sovereignty over territory. If a map showed Poland within the borders of the Russian empire, then it seemed only logical that Poland *was* a part of the Russian empire.[26] Thus the mapping of new borderlands at all points of the compass produced territory as reality and, crucially, rendered conquered land as sovereign Russian space. Conversely, maps could further aid the assimilation of territory by what they did not show: 'empty' land, or land from which indigenous ethnic groups had been cartographically erased, was visually and legally appropriable. In this sense, maps contributed to the delineation and maintenance of Russia's 'geography of power': instrumental in the physical and discursive absorption of new territories into the empire, the ordering of their populations and plotting of their resources, and the imposition of the landscape of political administration.[27]

Beyond exposing some of the mechanics by which new territory was assimilated into the empire, maps also shed light on the workings of the state, and the ways in which hierarchies of social relations were sustained. Cadastral surveys, for instance, furnished landowners with greater knowledge of their estates, allowing them to settle boundary disputes, and to more accurately assess the number of serfs within their domain. In this sense, recourse to surveying and the consultation of maps most often sustained 'the economic [and social] interests of the ruling class'.[28] In a similar vein, awareness of topography and demography reinforced the state's claims to, and exploitation of, its human and natural resources right across its territory. Sunderland has suggested that the development of territorial sovereignty came to be a defining feature of Russian rule in the eighteenth century, with surveying, mapping and counting essential practices that strengthened the ever greater active management – or encroachment – of the state on its territory.[29] This desire to 'know' the empire via description and mapping reached its apogee in the nineteenth century, when the gradual transition to an industrialising economy was underpinned by diffuse state activities to map forests, waterways, minerals, canals and railways. Knowledge of the location and extent of such assets in turn enabled the state to more efficiently cultivate resources, identify economic zones, and designate sites with deficits of infrastructure or with potential to be developed. Maps were thus of great relevance not just at moments of imperial expansion, but also in the day-to-day maintenance of social and economic administration.

Moreover, cartography lends illumination to contradictory currents within the upper echelons of state and society. The renowned chemist Mendeleev called for an urgent re-thinking of geography at the turn of the twentieth century as he strove to 'remap Russian imperial territory as a modern rational space that could serve as a framework for the nation's balanced, self-sufficient economic, social and cultural modernisation'.[30] Observing the impact of mass migration, industrialisation and new transport networks, the chemist proposed that the Russian state move to properly integrate new population centres, nodes of production and supplies of raw materials, taking into account that recent demographic and economic changes had most likely shifted the empire's 'centre of gravity'. Doing so, he suggested a radical new cartographic projection, laid out vertically to stress Russia's Eurasian character and to enable the viewer 'better to apprehend the extent and unity of Russian space, its regional structure and the interrelationships between natural features, administrative divisions and major points of settlement'.[31] Although the idea gained little traction, Mendeleev's maps provide access to contemporary debates surrounding the modernisation of Russia in the late Imperial period, pointing to powerful lobbies for scientific rationalism and social integration within and beyond state circles.[32]

Maps, of course, did not always serve the state, despite the latter's attempt to monopolise cartographic production. As Seegel has suggested, maps were central to laying claims to contested borderlands, both by the imperial centre *and* by nation builders in these regions.[33] In Poland, Ukraine and Lithuania, maps were vital tools of legitimation, supplying 'rational' evidence of visions of territory that differed radically from those propagated in St Petersburg. Post-partition, Polish cartographers, for instance, continued to map a country that according to Russian records of the region no longer existed.[34] Here, we find projections of ownership embedded in the mapping of land, with cartography part of the construction of national identity in opposition to imperial rule. Maps had no less importance in local affairs across Russia. In her study of seventeenth-century cartography, Valerie Kivelson eloquently explored the ways in which mapping not only occupied a pivotal role in state-building by advancing the strategic interests of the state vis-à-vis expansion, tribute collection and administrative efficacy, but at the same time also spoke to localised understandings of the law and legal practices, particularly in relation to property disputes, along with contemporary perceptions of community, religion, and subjecthood.[35] Such connections between identity, culture, the local and the national have also recently been taken up in studies of Russia's regions.[36] As the nineteenth century progressed, increasingly detailed knowledge of particular regions, coupled with the relative decentralisation of some forms of administration such as taxation that emerged from Alexander II's Great Reforms, resulted in the strengthening of provincial authority and identity. As a counterpoint to the increasing sophistication with which the imperial state wielded cartography, maps had an important part to play in this process, as land surveys multiplied following the 1864 *zemstvo* reform. In Nizhnii Novgorod province, cadastral mapping to chart local topography and economic conditions became part of a broader tussle between the centre and provinces over the control of information, allowing local institutions such as the *zemstvo* to use the newly generated knowledge to by-pass central administration. Cartography thus lay at 'the intersection of state efforts to know its territory and local initiative',[37] with the mapping of soil, forests, watersheds and landownership a crucial instrument in the ongoing process of province-building by local elites.

Research such as this points to the role that maps played in generating and sustaining imperial, national and local identities. Indeed, examining the worldviews and imaginaries that are embedded in maps has been a profitable line of enquiry within the history of cartography for many years. Here, the form of the map merits close examination: the vast quantity of material produced by Catherine's Cadastral Commission, for instance, mapped localities in large scale, framing the geography with elaborate cartouches that depicted scenes from local folklore, ethnographic scenes, urban regalia, local flora, fauna, and economic symbols such as fish, forests or rye. In this way, maps could be used to 'fix' components of regional identity, blended with the symbolism of empire, most often the imperial crown and eagle. At the opposite end of the spectrum, the map as a two-dimensional expression of the nation found very different form in the commercial advertising scene that exploded at the end of the nineteenth century. An advert for Kalinkin beer, for instance, showed a woman in traditional Russian dress and an outsize bottle of beer standing on a globe.[38] The sky, lit by sunlight, was filled by a schematic map of Russia, reminiscent of railway maps, with urban points from Kiev and Odessa to Samara and Baku connected by black lines, and Moscow and Petersburg picked out in larger font. This type of map bore little relation to the precise detail of state-sponsored cartography, yet fulfilled similar imaginative functions: in this case binding together a community within the wider culture of print. Modern material culture such as this could be used to present the image of a unified nation 'made one through universal consumption', and thus contributes meaningfully to the broader study of national identity in Russia, particularly in the nineteenth century.[39]

An example: The *Map of Russia and Her Tribes*

Such examples give a flavour of some of the research directions that have been pursued in recent years using cartographic material, but moving from the general to the specific, how exactly might one go about exploring a source in more detail? Take as an example the famous *Map of Russia and Her Tribes*, printed in St Petersburg in 1866.[40] This is a relatively large map, over one metre square, drawn up by N. A. Terebenev, a member of the Academy of Artists in the Ministry of the Imperial Court.[41] Oriented in portrait, it features at the centre a map of European Russia, below which sits a smaller-scale map of Asiatic Russia. Inset at the division between the two is a plan of St Petersburg to the left, and a plan of Moscow to the right. Twenty-one vignettes surround the maps, each depicting a scene with four to six examples of named 'tribes', with the strip of images broken by a large coat of arms of the Russian empire at the top centre. Meanwhile at the corners of the main map block, sandwiched between the cartography and the pictorial border, are four smaller coats of arms: clockwise from top left, those of the Kingdom of Poland, the Grand Duchy of Finland, and the cities of Moscow and St Petersburg. What are we to make of this map, with little contextualising information? How might we go about reading this as a source?

Consider first the appearance of the map. Large, rich in colour and decorative flourishes, and with both pictorial and cartographic elements, this is evidently material intended for display, perhaps at an exhibition. Both the geographical overview of the empire and the accompanying labelled scenes seem pedagogical rather than designed to relay precise information: although the maps are accurate, at such a small scale they only record major settlements, rivers, mountains and coastlines, along with administrative divisions. Similarly, the inset plans of Moscow and Petersburg give an impression of the overall layout of the cities, but little detail besides. The sheet is intended, in other words, to provide an overview of the empire in relatively simplified form. Note also the arrangement of the material: the division of the map blocks between European Russia, which occupies the more prominent position, and Asiatic Russia, drawn to a smaller scale and located below, reflect of course the practicalities of representing a vast territory on a single sheet of paper, yet at the same time, very much confirm the existence of two Russias: one the European heartland, the other an Asiatic periphery.

Consider also the date of production. This source captures the empire at a period of expansion. At this moment, Russian America was still a sizable presence on the map of Asiatic Russia, skewing the projection to the right (the colony would be sold to the United States in 1867). Meanwhile on the mainland, the newly annexed regions along the Amur and Ussuri rivers are recorded in pink, and the current Russian gains in Central Asia along the Syr-Dar'ia river in

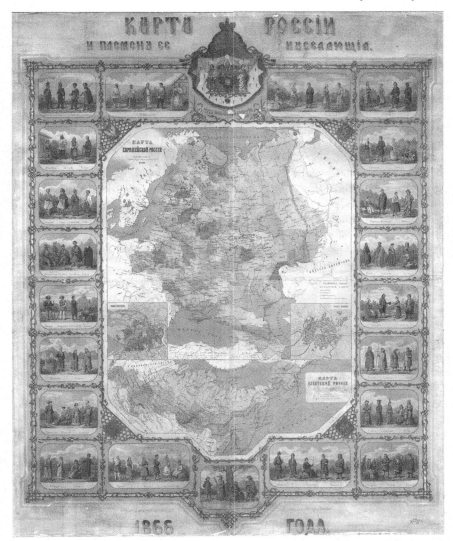

Figure 4.1 N. A. Terebenev, *Map of Russia and Her Tribes*, 1866, collection of the National Library of Russia, St Petersburg (К 3-Росс 2/112).

green (interestingly Tashkent falls beyond the boundary of the empire, despite its capture in 1865, testament perhaps to the length of time taken to produce this richly illustrated work). Thus the source makes concrete the new borders of the empire: symbolically extending sovereignty in pastel shades to regions that would formerly have fallen in the uncoloured part of the map was part of the process of assimilating new territory. Line and colour were also deployed to confirm *existing* territory. Again, the date of production is relevant: in the aftermath of the 1863 Polish revolt, cartography was one means by which currents of political separatism could be quashed, on paper at least, both by drawn confirmation of Russia's international borders, and the inclusion of the Kingdom of Poland's coat of arms. We also see superimposed on topography the Russian railway network, including lines already open, being built and planned. Much as in the Kalinkin beer advert, the black lines serve to visually draw together the territory of the empire, and allude also to the projected expansion of Russia's economic infrastructure in years to come.

Turning to the pictorial border, we find scenes that are striking in convention and composition, and bear clear relation to ethnographic work of this period produced in Russia and beyond.[42] This imagery was used to describe and classify ethnic groups, in turn producing 'types': pictorial or textual descriptions (stereotypes) of an individual who represented a named group. As has been explored by a number of scholars, this typing, or profiling, was itself clearly the product of a power relationship, most usually a way by which imperial actors could institute a hierarchy of 'us' and 'them', often further delineated by the settled status of a group (nomadic or semi-nomadic groups, of which Russia possessed many, were seen as lagging further behind the 'civilisational' development path than sedentary groups). In turn, this typing played a part in the state designation of a group's legal status and obligations. On this map, the ordering of the scenes is particularly telling. Along the top of the sheet, either side of the imperial crest, are Cossacks, Great Russians, Little Russians, Belorussians and Poles. At the very bottom of the page come Giliaks, Tungus, Aleuts, Chukchi. Between top and bottom, in descending order are Latvians, German colonists, Jews, Estonians, Finns, Samoeds, Buriats, Kirgiz to the right, and Bulgars, Greeks, Armenians, Chechens, Georgians, Bashkirs, Ostiaks, Tatars, Bukharans to the left.[43] Thus the border offers a prime example of taxonomic sorting, with those considered Slavs, and to a large extent the Orthodox 'faithful', closest to the imperial crown, those considered to be nomadic 'tribes' at the base of the hierarchy, and a descending order of assorted ethnicities displayed between. Note also that there is no mention of Ukrainians as a distinct group, only 'Little Russians'. In this sense, conveniently eliding Ukrainians into a larger Russian body served to erase the existence of a separate Ukrainian nation, at a time when the empire faced rising national discontent in its western borderlands.[44]

Thus although we know relatively little about the immediate production or use of this source, analysis of the map's components allows us to draw more far-reaching conclusions than simply suggesting that this is a colourful geographic map of the empire as it existed in 1866. Rather, the combination of ethnographic and geographic mapping produces a sheet that is in essence an allegory of empire. Inscribed on the map's surface is the image, both cartographic and pictorial, of Russia as a multi-ethnic empire, but one built on clear hierarchies of centre, periphery and ethnicity. By fusing together the human and topographical landscapes of empire, the map is a visual inscription of sovereignty that reveals some of the political ideals at the heart of the Great Reform era.

Conclusion

Maps then are never neutral or value-free, but rather, value-laden, and it is this quality that makes cartography a particularly practicable medium for historians. Rendered in ever-greater precision as the imperial period progressed, and now accessible in an abundance of institutions in Russia and beyond, maps speak to the accumulation of technical and geographical knowledge about the tsarist empire. Such seemingly objective forms of information should, however, be subject to the same level of historical scrutiny that would be extended to other visual and textual sources, and it is only when carefully contextualised that the true work that maps do comes into focus. In the Russian case, it is essential to acknowledge the close relationship between autocracy and cartography in the imperial period: mapping served primarily the civilian and military interests of the state, but it need not be viewed as exclusively a tool of central power. Rather, maps yield a multitude of valuable perspectives on the ways in which spatial, social and environmental complexities of Russia were understood and utilised by contemporaries; sovereignty, empire and administration were upheld; and local, regional and national identities were constructed.

Notes

1 Alexey Postnikov, *Russia in Maps: A History of the Geographical Study and Cartography of the Country* (Moscow: Nash dom, 1996), p. 51.

2 For the impressive Harvard Project, see: <https://worldmap.harvard.edu/maps/russianempire>. At the National Library of Russia, almost 5000 maps and atlases have been digitised and can be found here: <http://primo.nlr.ru/primo-explore/collectionDiscovery?vid=07NLR_VU1&collectionId=dgtcol19&lang=ru_RU>. A useful English-language site for digitised Russian cartography relating to Siberia and the Far East can be found at <http://frontiers.loc.gov/intldl/mtfhtml/mfsplash.html>.

3 Valerie Kivelson, 'Early Mapping: The Tsardom in Manuscript', in Simon Franklin and Katia Bowers (eds.), *Information and Empire: Mechanisms of Communication in Russia, 1600–1850* (Cambridge: OpenBook Publishers, 2017), p. 23. See also Leo Bagrov, *A History of Russian Cartography up to 1800* (Wolfe Island, Ontario: Walker Press, 1975), pp. 1–93 and Valerie Kivelson, *Cartographies of Tsardom: The Land and Its Meanings in Seventeenth-Century Russia* (Ithaca, NY: Cornell University Press, 2006).

4 A large number of plates, and incisive analysis, can be found in Kivelson, *Cartographies of Tsardom*, p. 133 onwards. Harvard's Houghton Library has digitised the *Chorographic Sketchbook*, which can be found here: <https://iiif.lib.harvard.edu/manifests/view/drs:18273155$1i>.

5 Leonid Goldenberg and Aleksey Postnikov, 'Development of Mapping Methods in Russia in the Eighteenth Century', *Imago Mundi*, 37 (1985), p. 63. For more on this 'scientific turn', see James R. Gibson, *Essays on the History of Russian Cartography, 16th to 19th centuries* (Toronto: University of Toronto Press, 1975), and more recently, Aleksei Golubinskii, 'New Technology and the Mapping of Empire: The Adoption of the Atrolabe', in Franklin and Bowers, *Information and Empire*, pp. 59–74.

6 Golubinskii, 'New technology and the mapping of empire', p. 61. *Uezd* and *guberniia* were administrative subdivisions of the Russian empire.

7 Postnikov, *Russia in Maps*, p. 100.

8 Ibid., p. 140.

9 See for instance I. A. Strelbitskii's 'Special Map of European Russia', commissioned in 1865, as one such map that became a template for later renderings, with such finely-honed detail as to show all settlements that exceeded five households. For more on Strelbitskii, see F. A. Chernyayeva, 'I. A. Strelbitsky – The Foremost Russian Cartographer of the 19th Century', *Canadian Cartographer*, 11 (1974), pp. 99–106.

10 Louise McReynolds, *The News Under Russia's Old Regime: The Development of a Mass-Circulation Press* (Princeton, NJ: Princeton University Press, 1991), pp. 83, 94, 186.

11 Jeffrey Brooks, *When Russia Learned to Read: Literacy and Popular Literature, 1861–1917* (Princeton, NJ: Princeton University Press, 1985), p. 115.

12 See for instance V. P. Semenov-Tian-Shanskii (ed.), *Rossiia: Polnoe geograficheskoe opisanie nashego otechestva* (Petersburg: A. F. Devrien, 1899–1914); *Pereselenie za Ural v 1912 godu* (Petersburg: Slovo, 1912); *Novaia natsional'naia i podrobnaia geografiia Rossiiskoi imperii*, St Petersburg, 1856 [card set].

13 Kivelson, *Cartographies of Tsardom*, p. 27.

14 On the increasing interest in Russia's spatial history, see Mark Bassin, Christopher Ely and Melissa K. Stockdale (eds.), *Space, Place and Power in Modern Russia: Issues in the New Spatial History* (DeKalb, IL: Northern Illinois University Press, 2010); Jane Burbank, Mark von Hagen and Anatolyi Remnev (eds.), *Russian Empire: Space, People, Power, 1700–1930* (Bloomington, IN: Indiana University Press, 2007); Jeremy Smith (ed.), *Beyond the Limits: The Concept of Space in Russian History and Culture* (Helsinki: SHS, 1999); Sanna Turoma and Maxim Waldstein (eds.), *Empire De/Centered: New Spatial Histories of Russia and the Soviet Union* (Burlington, IN: Ashgate, 2013). For useful surveys of Russian spatial history, see Nick Baron, 'New Spatial Histories of Twentieth-Century Russia', *Jahrbücher für Geschichte Osteuropas*, 55 (2007), pp. 374–400; Malte Rolf, 'Importing the "Spatial Turn" to Russia: Recent Studies on the Spatialization of Russian History', *Kritika*, 11 (2010), pp. 359–80.

15 This literature on the uses of cartography is vast. Some useful starting points include James R. Akerman (ed.), *The Imperial Map: Cartography and the Mastery of Empire* (Chicago, IL: University of Chicago Press, 2009); Benedict Anderson, *Imagined Communities: Reflections on the Origin and Spread of Nationalism* (London: Verso, 2006), pp. 163–86; Jeremy Black, *Maps and History: Constructing Images of the Past* (New Haven, CA: Yale University Press, 1997); Denis Cosgrove, *Geography and Vision: Seeing, Imagining and Representing the World* (London: I. B. Tauris, 2008); Martin Dodge, Rob Kitchen and Chris Perkins (eds.), *Rethinking Maps* (Abingdon: Routledge, 2009); J. B. Harley, 'Deconstructing the Map', *Cartographica*, 26 (1989), pp. 1–20; Mark S. Monmonier, *How to Lie with Maps* (Chicago, IL: University of Chicago Press, 2018).

16 Harley, 'Deconstructing the Map', p. 8.

17 Patricia Seed and John M. MacKenzie, 'Cartography and Empire', in John M. MacKenzie (ed.), *The Encyclopedia of Empire*, vol. 1 (Chichester: Wiley Blackwell, 2016), p. 426.

18 Seed and MacKenzie, 'Cartography and Empire', p. 435.

19 Momonier, *How to Lie*, p. 2.

20 Marina Tolmacheva, 'The Early Russian Exploration and Mapping of the Chinese Frontier', *Cahiers du monde russe*, 41 (2000), pp. 45–50.

21 Bagrov, *History of Russian Cartography*, pp. 157–73; Aleksey Postnikov and Marvin Falk, *Exploring and Mapping Alaska: The Russian America Era, 1741–1867* (Fairbanks, AK: University of Alaska Press, 2015).

22 See Golubinskii, 'New Technology and the Mapping of Empire'.

23 Kivelson, 'Early Mapping', p. 24.

24 Ibid., p. 57.

25 See the discussions of cartography in, amongst others, Mark Bassin, *Imperial Visions: Nationalist Imagination and Geographical Expansion in the Russian Far East, 1840–1865* (Cambridge: Cambridge University Press, 1999); Ryan Tucker Jones, *Empire of Extinction: Russians and the North Pacific's Strange Beasts of the Sea, 1741–1867*

(New York, NY: Oxford University Press, 2014); Kelly O'Neill, *Claiming Crimea: A History of Catherine the Great's Southern Empire* (New Haven, CA: Yale University Press, 2018).

26 Larry Wolff, *Inventing Eastern Europe: The Map of Civilisation on the Mind of the Enlightenment* (Stanford, CA: Stanford University Press, 1994), chapter 4. See also Aleksey Postnikov, 'Contact and Conflict: Russian Mapping of Finland and the Development of Russian Cartography in the 18th and Early 19th Centuries', *Fennia*, 171 (1993), pp. 63–98.

27 Anatolyi Remnev, 'Siberia and the Russian Far East in the Imperial Geography of Power', in Burbank, von Hagen and Remnev, *Russian Empire*, pp. 425–54.

28 Goldenberg and Postnikov, 'Development of Mapping Methods', p. 71.

29 Willard Sunderland, 'Imperial Space: Territorial Thought and Practice in the Eighteenth Century', in Burbank, von Hagen and Remnev, *Russian Empire*, pp. 34–66.

30 Nick Baron, 'The Mapping of Illiberal Modernity: Spatial Science, Ideology and the State in Early Twentieth-Century Russia', in Turoma and Waldstein (eds.), *Empire De/Centered*, p. 106. On changing ideas of regional space connected to demography and economics, see also Leonid Gorizontov, 'The "Great Circle" of Interior Russia: Representations of the Imperial Center in the Nineteenth and Early Twentieth Centuries', in Burbank, von Hagen and Remnev (eds.), *Russian Empire*, particularly pp. 87–90, and Nailya Tagirova, 'Mapping the Empire's Economic Regions from the Nineteenth to the Early Twentieth Century', in Burbank, von Hagen and Remnev (eds.), *Russian Empire*, pp. 125–38.

31 Baron, 'The Mapping of Illiberal Modernity', p. 113.

32 Mendeleev was a close acquaintance – until 1905 at least – of Sergei Witte, Minister of Finance 1892–1903.

33 Steven Seegel, *Mapping Europe's Borderlands: Russian Cartography in the Age of Empire* (Chicago, IL: University of Chicago Press, 2012).

34 For a related discussion on the relevance of cartography to another minority group within the empire, see Adeeb Khalid, *The Politics of Muslim Cultural Reform: Jadidism in Central Asia* (Berkeley, CA: University of California Press, 1998).

35 Kivelson, *Cartographies of Tsardom*.

36 Catherine Evtuhov, *Portrait of a Russian Province: Economy, Society and Civilization in Nineteenth-Century Nizhnii Novgorod* (Pittsburgh, PA: University of Pittsburgh Press, 2011), chapter 8.

37 Evtuhov, *Portrait of a Russian Province*, p. 166.

38 'Kalinkin pivo-medovarennoe tovarishchetsvo', 1905. See also an earlier version of the same advert, published in 1903, complete with an inset map.

39 Sally West, 'The Material Promised Land: Advertising's Modern Agenda in Late Imperial Russia', *Russian Review*, 57 (1998), p. 354.

40 State Historical Museum, Moscow, inventory number GO-8197. A high resolution version can be found on the website of the National Library of Russia: <http://leb.nlr.ru/fullpage/330838>.

41 Terebenev's personal file can be found in the Russian State Historical Archive (RGIA), f. 789, op. 14, d. 9.

42 Seegel, *Mapping Europe's Borderlands*, pp. 126–7. See also Jeffrey Brooks, 'The Russian Nation Imagined: The Peoples of Russia as seen in Popular Imagery, 1860s–1890s', *Journal of Social History*, 43 (2010), pp. 535–57; Nicholas B. Dirks (ed.), *Colonialism and Culture* (Ann Arbor, MI: University of Michigan Press, 1992); Ilya Gerasimov, Jan Kusber and Alexander Semyonov (eds.), *Empire Speaks Out: Languages of Rationalization and Self-Description in the Russian Empire* (Leiden: Brill, 2009).

43 This is not a complete list, but representative of the general division and location of the scenes. Overall, the map contains 58 labelled 'ethnicities'.

44 This was a fairly common occurrence in material displayed at geographical exhibitions and in exhibition catalogues. See Seegel, *Mapping Europe's Borderlands*, p. 214.

Further reading

Akerman, James R., *The Imperial Map: Cartography and the Mastery of Empire* (Chicago, IL: University of Chicago Press, 2007).

Black, Jeremy, *Maps and History: Constructing Images of the Past* (New Haven, CA: Yale University Press, 1997).

Burbank, Jane, Mark von Hagen and Anatolyi Remnev (eds.), *Russian Empire: Space, People, Power, 1700-1930* (Bloomington, IN: Indiana University Press, 2007).

Cosgrove, Denis, *Geography and Vision: Seeing, Imagining and Representing the World* (London: I. B. Tauris, 2008).

Evtuhov, Catherine, *Portrait of a Russian Province: Economy, Society and Civilization in Nineteenth-Century Nizhnii Novgorod* (Pittsburgh, PA: University of Pittsburgh Press, 2011).

Franklin, Simon, and Katia Bowers (eds.), *Information and Empire: Mechanisms of Communication in Russia, 1600-1850* (Cambridge: OpenBook Publishers, 2017).

Goldenberg, Leonid, and Aleksey Postnikov, 'Development of Mapping Methods in Russia in the Eighteenth Century', *Imago Mundi*, 37 (1985), pp. 63–80.

Harley, J. B., 'Deconstructing the Map', *Cartographica*, 26 (1989), pp. 1–20.

Kivelson, Valerie, *Cartographies of Tsardom: The Land and its Meanings in Seventeenth-Century Russia*, (Ithaca, NY: Cornell University Press, 2006).

Monmonier, Mark S., *How to Lie with Maps* (Chicago, IL: University of Chicago Press, 2018).

Postnikov, Aleksey, 'Contact and Conflict: Russian mapping of Finland and the Development of Russian Cartography in the 18th and early 19th centuries', *Fennia*, 171 (1993), pp. 63–98.

_____, *Russia in Maps: A History of the Geographical Study and Cartography of the Country* (Moscow: Nash dom, 1996).

Seegel, Steven, *Mapping Europe's Borderlands: Russian Cartography in the Age of Empire* (Chicago, IL: University of Chicago Press, 2012).

5 "It's only a story"

What value are novels as a historical source?[1]

Sarah Hudspith

In this chapter I will make a case for the benefits of using novels as a historical source, using the Russian nineteenth-century realist novel as an example. I wish to focus on the realist novel so as to problematize the notion of mimesis, which was once held to be the 'common ground' of history and literature.[2] In literary studies, realism and mimesis are closely related terms. Mimesis can be understood as imitation or reproduction, and thus in both historical and literary terms it speaks to notions of verisimilitude: that which is plausible and/or verifiable, in relation to truth. It is at the foundation of the literary category of realism, which was derived from the same category in fine art, not only denoting a lifelike representation but also marking a shift in subject matter from the mythological or biblical to real life. I will outline the complexities of literary realism in order to draw to the historian's attention the issues that must be considered when approaching novels as a historical source. I will highlight that from the nineteenth century onwards, the path taken by the literary and historical disciplines in Russia is somewhat different from Western Europe; the demands and challenges placed on realism in Russia were informed by the unique circumstances of Russia's historical and cultural development. An understanding of this situation should inform any consideration of Russian novels as historical sources. I intend to model appropriate methodologies for doing so in my analysis of Leo Tolstoy's *Anna Karenina*, specifically, its controversial final part.

Realism in history and literature

According to Western scholarship, the disciplinary distinction between history and literature became established in the nineteenth century as a consequence of the European Enlightenment. With a growing focus on empiricist notions of truth and scientific method came a move away from practices in common with *belles-lettres*; this was most prominently exemplified in Leopold von Ranke's rejection of the historical novel as practised by Walter Scott. However, the second half of the twentieth century has seen a re-evaluation of the rigidity of this distinction, supported by postmodern theory. Postmodernist thinkers such as Michel Foucault identified history as a narrative that is constructed and told in much the same way as a work of literature, thus emphasizing the fundamental artifice of historical narrative. Foucault analysed the relationship between discourse and power, point-ing to repressed narratives of marginalized groups which overlapped and undercut dominant narratives, thus problematizing our understanding of historical truth.[3] In a similar vein, Michel de Certeau examined the struggle of historiography to deter-mine that which is verifiably 'real'. De Certeau argued that historiography justified its assertion of what is 'real' by positioning it against what can be said to be 'false'. Fiction was one such 'false' discourse in opposition to which history defined itself. But, acknowledging that 'fictitious' discourse may be closer to the real than objec-tive discourse, he identified the task facing historians as to 'grant legitimacy to the fiction that haunts the field of historiography'.[4] In the USA, historian Hayden White's seminal *Metahistory: The Historical Imagination in Nineteenth-Century Europe* (1973) became the landmark text for those scholars perceiving benefits and opportunities in the more fluid disciplinary boundaries and the rapprochement between history and literature that postmodernism offered.

Nevertheless, the postmodernist approach to history is by no means universally accepted. Indeed, Benjamin Ziemann and Miriam Dobson describe the ongoing 'debate between postmodernists and the defenders of a "realist" conception of historical research' as a controversy at 'fever-pitch'.[5] Here, the term *realism*, when indicating a literary category, presents the potential to act as a red herring in assessing the validity of novels as a historical source, unless approached with a sufficiently nuanced understanding. Julia Reid has identified some of the common pitfalls associated with realism in relation to the study of literature for historical purposes. In her analysis, historians may be tempted into simplistic assumptions that realist novels offer unmediated, documentary evidence which straightfor-wardly complements traditional historical accounts, and thus they may fail to take sufficient account of the status of novels as works of the imagination, that is, as fiction. On the other hand, she also notes that in their attempts to argue for an understanding of history as a constructed narrative, postmodernist historians such as White misrepresent and dismiss realist novels as crudely and un-self-consciously mimetic.[6] Reid provides a useful overview of the debates surrounding realism in European literature, and indeed as she points out, it behoves the his-torian to be aware that the 'blurred boundaries between realism and fictionality, objectivity and subjectivity, empiricism and theory, and fact and fiction' have been as keenly interrogated in literary studies as in the discipline of history: the literary category of realism is complex and often elusive.[7]

Likewise, Reid outlines the changing trends through the twentieth century in relation to the status of literature as a historical source, ranging from scepticism and formalist ahistoricism,[8] to naïve assumptions about novels as illustrative of their time that overlook the sense of fiction as a constructed reality.[9] It may be stat-ing the obvious to say that these trends all point to a concern, shared between the disciplines of history and literary studies, for humanity's need to identify the real, and whether the real is relative or absolute. I am not a historian; it is not for me to adjudicate on the question of the extent to which the discipline of history should be concerned with establishing causation, and doubtless my argument in favour of using novels will not appeal to some. Nevertheless, I maintain that the meaning that can be garnered from fiction is generated by two forces in productive tension. On the one hand, fiction constructs *imaginary* worlds, however relatable to lived experience those worlds may be. On the other hand, the writing and publishing of a literary text can be considered in terms of being a historical event, and even if only in this respect, it is anchored in a form of verifiable *reality*, evidenced by documentary sources such as early drafts, the author's notes, diaries and letters commenting on the novel. With due caution towards the trap of intentional fallacy, these paratextual materials can be understood as voices in dialogue with the published work. Similarly, information on the reception of the work, such as reviews, data relating to print runs and sales figures both at the original time of publication and subsequently, and the canonical (or otherwise) acceptance of the text, indicate the changing meaning of the text over time and add further to the dialogue. Thus, the fictional text itself exists as one point in a network, which constantly negotiates between the imaginary world of the novel and the worlds with which that novel has come into contact. In these terms, we can begin to understand the postmodern notion of meaning arising out of the confrontation of different discourses.

Realism and the role of the writer in Russia

The disciplinary genealogies and interrelationships between literature and history played out in Russia in a different way from Western Europe, and contribute to the richness and complexity of Russian novels as historical sources. The divergence of history as a discipline away from *belles-lettres*, philosophy and rhetoric did not take hold in the nineteenth century in the same way as in the West; this was in large part thanks to the prestigious status of writers, and to the weighty subjects with which they were expected to engage. The nineteenth century was a time in which Russia subjected its relation to the rest of the world to intense scrutiny. This scrutiny was oriented towards Russia's historical trajectory, particularly by comparison with Western Europe, and expressed predominantly through the medium of literature. Questions were asked about whether Russia's historical and cultural development was unique, and were hotly debated by intellectuals of various political leanings and professions (writers of fiction and poetry, historians, philosophers and literary critics) in the pages of the thick monthly journals read by the educated classes. These debates were, of course, subject to state censorship and conducted under threat of repression, the severity of which fluctuated over the century depending on the stance of each successive Tsar; nevertheless, the sense of urgency to understand Russia's past, present and future led to professional writers being cast as critical friends. They attracted prestige as people qualified to comment with 'moral seriousness' on the 'accursed questions' of the human condition in Russia because they ran the risk of incurring state displeasure in order to contribute to the debates.[10] Thus, as writers of literature were expected to engage with these thorny questions, their mode of expression came under focus as the nineteenth century progressed. The prominent and influential literary critic Vissarion Belinsky proclaimed writers to be '[Russia's] only leaders, its protectors and saviours from the darkness of autocracy, orthodoxy and nationality'[11] and demanded that their art portray reality.

As the realist novel began to dominate European nineteenth-century literature thanks to the success of Dickens, Eliot, Balzac and others, in Russia the call for art to be socially engaged led to an increasingly politically inflected understanding of mimesis, with some high-profile radical thinkers such as Nikolai Chernyshevsky, Nikolai Dobroliubov and Dmitri Pisarev going so far as to prioritize what was useful to society over what was artistically accomplished.

Whilst these views are at the extreme end of the spectrum, the extent to which attention to artistic matters might impact on the moral engagement of a text remained a central concern. For example, Fyodor Dostoevsky tried to refocus the discussion by emphasizing the limitations of a realism in which the social imperative to reflect and comment on reality led to a crude and unsophisticated mimetic depiction. Whilst agreeing that literature should play an essential part in guiding and developing society, he defended literature's aesthetic qualities as the only means of communicating socially engaged content: works that prioritized a message over artistic form would be ineffective, whilst those that were artistically accomplished would be enduringly and universally relevant.[12] In relation to this, he advocated and indeed practised in his own works a broader understanding of realism than a narrowly utilitarian mimesis.

Dostoevsky's argument highlights the particular suitability of the genre of the novel for achieving this synergy of medium and message. Malcolm Jones explains why the novel was found to be the most conducive form for the role accorded to literature in nineteenth-century Russia:

> The novel was capable, as Bakhtin has famously argued, of absorbing all other genres. [...] Imaginative fiction could be manipulated in all sorts of ways unavailable to more direct forms of discourse and, above all, it was capable of relating, as no other medium could, broad social, political, philosophical and religious questions to the existential experience of the individual through the medium of narrative, thus facilitating entry to these questions at a variety of levels.[13]

What is important here is that it is precisely the fictionality of a novel that allows it to achieve the status of authoritative discourse, not simply its serious subject matter. To be sure, in a culture where censorship is in force, fiction can be a device that mitigates the threat posed by the discussion of difficult subjects by situating them in an imaginary realm ('it's only a story'); but there is more at play here. It is the sense of the reality of the world of the novel, as constructed by its literary (imaginative, figurative) language, generating meaning at the point at which it encounters non-fictional discourses.

Until now, I have focused on the nineteenth century, so as to demonstrate the foundations of literature's significance in Russia, and because my example for analysis will be taken from this period. A few words should be said about the Soviet era that dominated the twentieth century, in the context of my discussion of literature as an authoritative discourse, and of the understanding of realism. The Soviet state's attempts to mould the status of writers and literature to its own purposes ultimately did not disrupt Russia's tradition of turning to literature as 'the principal source of [its] national identity and cultural mythology',[14] even as visual forms such as cinema and propaganda posters were harnessed to disseminate Soviet doctrine to a wider audience. Stalin's 1932 epithet for writers – 'engineers of the human soul'[15] – may be contrasted with the 1965 assertion of poet and moderate critic of the Soviet regime Evgeny Evtushenko: 'A poet in Russia is more than a poet'.[16] These statements both confirm that the notion of the authority and responsibility conferred upon literary artists in Russia circulated between discourses of different political and ideological tenor.

The Soviet era also generated the concept of Socialist Realism, which became the official aesthetic theory and method in the arts, and which was defined in terms that resonate with the radical utilitarian demands placed on mimesis by the likes of Chernyshevsky, Dobroliubov and Pisarev in the previous century:

> Socialist Realism, being the basic method of Soviet literature and literary criticism, demands from the artist the truthful, historically concrete depiction of reality in its revolutionary development. At the same time, truthfulness and historical concreteness of the historical depiction of reality must be combined with the task of ideologically remolding and educating the working people in the spirit of socialism.[17]

However, the fact that this form of realism is ideologically inflected with the priorities of Soviet doctrine should not lead to a reductive perception of Socialist Realist novels that ignores their status as constructing, rather than representing, reality (if anything, the aspirational nature of Socialist Realism emphasizes this constructive element). Instead, Socialist Realism should be seen as a node in the network of the circulation of discourses. As Katerina Clark asserts in her study *The Soviet Novel: History as Ritual*:

> Still, 'politics' or 'ideology' should not be identified as some monolithic entity with which literature has interacted. Not only has the process of interaction been dialectical rather than a one-way street, but the 'extraliterary' pole of the dialectic has been made up of several distinct components, each of which has in turn interacted with the others – and again, dialectically.[18]

To return to the discipline of history, the status of literature as authoritative discourse has led to a greater proximity between the literary and historical disciplines in Russia than in the West. Consequently, there is a lasting tradition that the Russian public's historical consciousness is derived in large part from artistic works. Sigurd Shmidt notes, 'For most people […] great works of fiction and art supply the basic sources of the specific historical information *that they retain in their minds* [my italics]'.[19] In other words, the most memorable discourses are those narrated by artists. Similarly, Andrew Wachtel points out that contrary to the teachings of von Ranke in the West, in Russia historians were not seen as a greater authority than writers of literature. This allowed for a continuous flow of discourse between the literary and historical disciplines, which Wachtel terms 'intergeneric dialogue'.[20] The result was 'an implicit recognition that historical truth cannot be achieved through any one perspective, no matter how convincingly presented'.[21] My purpose in examining this fluidity of disciplinary boundaries is not to suggest that Russian writers are accomplished historians (though this case can be made in some instances[22]), but to demonstrate that Russia has an established tradition of embracing within its historical practice modes of enquiry which are not oriented towards the empirically verifiable as understood in the West. Thus, using literary sources to enhance the study of Russian history is a method that is appropriate to its subject and will bring the historian closer to how the Russians themselves perceive their history.

Tolstoy's *Anna Karenina* as a historical source

To demonstrate some of these issues in action, I intend to use Leo Tolstoy's novel *Anna Karenina* as a case study, focusing particularly on its eighth and final part which is set in the context of the so-called Eastern Question – the question of how Russia should support the Orthodox Slav peoples rebelling against the Ottoman Empire – leading to the Russo-Turkish War of 1877. In the context of Russian literature as an authoritative discourse, I will explore the question of why *Anna Karenina* did not shape the prevailing discourse on Russia's relationship with other Slavic nations in the same way that Tolstoy's earlier magnum opus, *War and Peace*, impacted on the discourse of Russian national identity. I will consider how the novel interacted with the discourses of ethnicity and empire and examine the part played by its status as a fictional text, in order to draw conclusions about the relation between discourse and power.

   Anna Karenina was Tolstoy's second major novel and may be contrasted with *War and Peace* in a number of ways relevant to this discussion. *War and Peace* dealt with the Napoleonic Wars, an important period of Russia's recent history; not only that, but it represented Tolstoy's own commentary on the nature of history as a discipline in that it was intended as a demonstration of the suitability of narrative fiction for capturing the discourse excluded by the prevailing 'great men' school of historiography of the time. *War and Peace* exemplifies Hayden White's assertion that

> historical discourse wages everything on the true, while fictional discourse is interested in the real [...]. A simply true account of the world based on what the documentary record permits one to talk about what happened in it at particular times and places can provide knowledge of only a very small portion of what "reality" consists of.[23]

War and Peace was published between 1863 and 1869, at the height of the Russian state's efforts to build a more unified national community, following such momentous events in the development of Russian national identity as defeat in the Crimean War of 1853–56 and the Emancipation of the Serfs in 1861. Its success cemented

Tolstoy's reputation as the leading literary figure of his time, a fact which may be measured in terms of the honoraria paid by publishers to writers: Tolstoy was able to command the highest honorarium of 500 rubles a signature.[24] The novel played a significant part in shaping the discourse of nation-building by cultivating a patriotic emotional response to the events of 1812 and the Battle of Borodino especially, such that the 1812 conflict with Napoleon became known as the Patriotic War. Its impact has lasted into the twentieth and twenty-first centuries, with Stalin ordering the mass reprinting of the 1812 sections during the Second World War for the purpose of spreading patriotic fervour; and it is frequently invoked as a shorthand to rebuke world leaders perceived as unaware of their hubris.[25]

Anna Karenina had no such impact on the discourse surrounding the Eastern Question and the Russo-Turkish War at the time of its publication, and in general it is remembered for other reasons than its contribution on this subject. The events in question enter into the novel only in Part Eight, after the suicide of the eponymous protagonist. Part Eight focuses on the ongoing tribulations of the novel's other central character, Konstantin Levin, who is contrasted with Anna in that he remains within the social conventions of the family unit, but who nonetheless faces struggles as intense as Anna's to find meaning and satisfaction in life. The current events enter into the text via Levin's half-brother, Sergei Koznyshev. Koznyshev, a dilettante scholar, has thrown himself into the work of the volunteer movement in support of the Orthodox Slavs in order to distract himself from the failure of his book. At the start of Part Eight, Koznyshev and a mutual friend, the professor Katavasov, are on their way to visit Levin in the country, and on their train journey they encounter volunteers heading for Serbia, amongst whom is Anna's devastated lover Vronsky, as well as fundraisers and supporters. On their arrival at Levin's estate, the family and friends discuss their different attitudes to the conflict and Russia's role in it. The main opposing positions are taken by Koznyshev, who celebrates the volunteer movement as a populist expression of brotherhood and solidarity and therefore as morally unassailable, and Levin, who expresses doubts in the concept of the will of the people, especially when used as a justification for war.

In this way, the backdrop of the Eastern Question offers a plot resolution for Vronsky and serves as one stage in Levin's continuous process of self-examination through providing a subject for debate. The views expressed by Levin in his lack of sympathy for the measures being taken against the Turks (despite his sympathy for the suffering Slavs), and the ironic portrayals of the volunteers encountered on the train, are markers against which Tolstoy indicates his moral priorities. Barbara Lönnqvist asserts that the use of contemporary events allowed for a greater grounding in realism, so that Tolstoy's characters 'stepped out of fiction and started mingling with the readers'.[26] But more significantly, says Lönnqvist, the conflict serves as 'a litmus paper that allows Tolstoy once again to test the life philosophy of his characters, to analyse their motives and actions, and most important, to dig into the origins of their convictions'.[27] In this respect, the reference to the conflict in the Balkans demonstrates that Tolstoy did not see his novel ending with his protagonist's suicide or the final part as a mere epilogue: Part Eight was an important part of the trajectory of Levin, whose story carries as much weight as Anna's.

However, problems arose with the publication of Part Eight. It was common practice for novels to be serialized in a monthly journal before being published in book form; *Anna Karenina* was being serialized in *Russkii vestnik* (*The Russian Herald*), its first instalments appearing in 1875 and continuing intermittently through 1876 and the first few months of 1877. Part Eight was due to appear in the May 1877 issue of the journal. At this time, the public outcry over the Turkish treatment of Orthodox Slavs had led Alexander II to declare war on Turkey the previous month, and the May 1877 issue of *Russkii vestnik* was devoted to articles celebrating Russia's history of fighting Turkey on behalf of Orthodox Christians. The negative stance towards the volunteer movement expressed in Part Eight of *Anna Karenina*, as Tatiana Kuzmic indicates, would have made a poor fit with the rest of the May 1877 issue[28] and the journal editor Mikhail Katkov asked Tolstoy to tone down the more politically inflected passages. Tolstoy refused, and withdrew the text from publication in *Russkii vestnik*, choosing instead to publish the ending of his novel himself as a separate booklet that came out in July 1877. In response to Tolstoy's refusal to make the changes he had requested, Katkov in turn published an ill-tempered announcement in the May 1877 issue, dismissively summarizing the remainder of the novel, which he judged as 'for all intents and purposes' over with the death of Anna.[29] This act scandalized Tolstoy, who considered publishing a riposte in a competing journal, but who ultimately appears to have decided that the final instalment would speak for itself. Despite his annoyance at Katkov's request to revise his text, Tolstoy did in fact make a number of subtle changes to Part Eight before publishing it as a separate booklet. Lönnqvist describes these changes thus: 'Thoughts and statements of the *author* were transferred to the *characters*. Opinions were spread out and a many-voicedness appeared.'[30] In other words, Tolstoy mediated the ideological aspects of Part Eight through recourse to artistic strategies that emphasize the text's status as a work of fiction.

The quarrel over the publication of Part Eight illustrates a number of points about discourse and power which are also explored thematically in the text itself. The relationship between journals, their editors and authors is negotiated as part of the power dynamic of literature as authoritative discourse. Tolstoy's interaction with the journals that published his work reveals the complexities of this dynamic. William Mills Todd III demonstrates that authors related to the process of serialization and engaged with the journal editors in different ways, depending on factors such as their status in the literary hierarchy, their financial circumstances and their attitude towards the literary profession. He argues that Tolstoy viewed the serialization of his novels as a draft for the final book version and made a number of revisions before that version was published; consequently his attitude towards serialization was quite casual.[31] Tolstoy also had other interests and occupations that competed for his attention with fiction writing, an activity that he often worried was self-indulgent and elitist. Thus the serialization of *Anna Karenina* was driven by his own timetable rather than that of the publisher or the journal's readership, stretching over three years, with long interruptions each year from early summer to December while he turned his attention to the management of his country estate.[32] It is perhaps not surprising, therefore, that despite the prestige Tolstoy now enjoyed following the success of *War and Peace*, he may have tested Katkov's patience.

At the same time, the history of the serialization of *Anna Karenina* marks developments in Tolstoy's understanding of the intersection of discourse and power. This is exemplified firstly in his growing doubts that the practice of *belles-lettres* did anything more than perpetuate the values of the ruling elite, and secondly in his concern for the way that public opinion was conceptualized and manipulated by the press. One of the reasons Tolstoy felt conflicted about the value of writing novels was his awareness that he was writing for a small, educated elite, once estimated by his fellow writer Dostoevsky to be just one five-hundredth of the population.[33] In the several years that had elapsed between the success of *War and Peace* and the publication of *Anna Karenina*, Tolstoy had become interested in education and literacy, and had pursued a series of projects writing and publishing shorter, edifying stories for a newly literate readership. These endeavours had caused him to reflect upon the realist style that he had mastered in *War and Peace* and problematize it through irony and parody in the works written for his new audience. Thus, for example, Caryl Emerson designates his 1872 short story 'The Prisoner of the Caucasus' 'a parodic undoing of his own novelistic style that marks his decisive break with the intelligentsia of his time'.[34]

If Tolstoy had made a 'decisive break' with the audience for whom he had written *War and Peace*, it is not surprising that the return to novel writing was fraught with contradictory emotions. His letters from the time of working on *Anna Karenina* testify to his difficult relationship with his work, declaring that he hated it and that it was 'tedious and banal'.[35] In Part Eight, Tolstoy offers an ironic portrayal of the intellectual elite through the character of Koznyshev and his ill-fated book. The opening chapter informs us that Koznyshev has spent six years of his life writing a work that bears the comically cumbersome title *Sketch of a Survey of the Principles and Forms of Government in Europe and Russia*. Prior to its publication in book form, sections of the text had been published in periodicals – a move that Koznyshev views as advance publicity – but he is disappointed to find that in spite of this, his book receives virtually no attention. After what Koznyshev considers to be an improperly long silence, just one review appears in a serious publication, and he is appalled to read its contents.

A close reading of this first chapter reveals, through the account of Koznyshev's book, Tolstoy's own ambivalent relationship with the literary industry. We learn that Koznyshev had made 'the most conscientious revision'[36] to his text between serializing sections of it and bringing it out in book form, and still it sank almost without trace. This is likely a self-parody, since Tolstoy himself was prone to reworking his drafts numerous times; but it may also work as a dig at Katkov in the ironic description of the ultimately fruitless revisions as 'most conscientious'. Further, Tolstoy satirizes the profession of scholarly criticism, firstly by prefacing the review of the book with Koznyshev's low opinion of the critic, so that the reader sees the ironic meaning of the narrator's assertion that 'In spite of his absolute contempt for the writer, Koznyshev prepared to read his review with the greatest respect'.[37] Secondly, Tolstoy has Koznyshev dismiss the flaws the critic identifies in his book as words taken out of context: 'it was too evident that they had been picked out deliberately';[38] instead he decides that the reviewer's motivation for the demolition job is revenge for a social slight: 'And remembering that when they had met he had corrected the young man in some word he had used that betrayed ignorance, Koznyshev hit upon what was behind the article.'[39] By doing this, Tolstoy comments on the vanity and petty concerns that abounded in the elite circles for which he was writing, and perhaps expresses some of his frustrations in relation to the writing process of *Anna Karenina* and the milieu from which he was becoming increasingly distanced.

Furthermore, the disputed section goes on to explore Tolstoy's growing anxieties regarding the power of the media over public opinion. Tolstoy viewed newspapers and journals as a persuasive force that shaped, rather than gave voice to, public opinion and so he was increasingly concerned that this force was therefore a source of interference in living an authentic, moral life.[40] According to Kuzmic, the role of the press in generating public interest in the Eastern Question was 'unprecedented'.[41] Tolstoy's opinion on this matter is expressed in a number of places in Part Eight, where the narrator undermines Koznyshev's insistence on a groundswell of public support for action in the Balkans by drawing attention to the character's own awareness of the press's exaggerations and headline-grabbing tactics. Additionally, Levin's father-in-law dismisses the news coverage as a cacophony of croaking frogs drowning out all other voices.[42] It is possible that the author's frustration with Katkov may in part be attributed to the fact that he had intended to air his misgivings about newspapers and journals in the very medium that concerned him, so as to offer a counterbalance to the prevailing narrative. As Reid says, 'serial fiction was more obviously engaged with the "real" world of non-fictional discourses, in the shape of the adjacent articles',[43] and the dispute over Part Eight prevented Tolstoy from adding his dissenting voice on both the Russo-Turkish War and the role of the press to *Russkii vestnik's* conversation.

The issues of public opinion and the will of the people are interrogated by Levin in Part Eight, and thereby Tolstoy's novel engages with discourses of Slavic identity and Russia's imperial aspirations in the Balkans. Koznyshev bases his concept of the will of the people on the idea of a collective consciousness derived from a shared ethnicity and religion: '"There is still a racial memory among the people of Orthodox Christians groaning under the yoke of the 'infidel Musulman'. The people have heard of the sufferings of their brethren and have spoken."'[44] Levin, on the other hand, finds that personal experience does not bear this out: '"That may be," said Levin evasively, "only I don't see it. I'm one of the people myself, and I don't feel it."'[45] He also exposes the othering of the Turks in his half-brother's celebration of the alleged nobility of the volunteers' self-sacrifice: '"But it's not a question of sacrificing themselves only, but of killing Turks," observed Levin timidly.'[46]

The attentive reader will notice that Levin's speech is qualified by adverbs that suggest his lack of confidence in his ability to make his point persuasively. The passage recounting the family discussion on the Eastern Question draws to a close with Levin giving up trying to argue with his half-brother and their friend the professor.

Koznyshev and Katavazov are typical representatives of the elite intelligentsia, of whose power over the discourses of Russian society Tolstoy was increasingly mistrustful. Rather than have Levin debate successfully with them, Tolstoy's novelistic technique is firstly to undermine Koznyshev through the ironic portrayal of him as a dilettante in the opening chapter of Part Eight, and then to contrast the contentions of the masters with the serene voice of one of the servants waiting on them. Levin turns to this servant as a representative of the people on behalf of whom Koznyshev claims to speak, seeking his view. The servant's response illustrates the lack of connection between the discourse of the ruling class and the ordinary people, as well as the propensity for this discourse to be imposed: '"Why should we bother our heads? Alexander Nikolayevich our Emperor has thought about it for us, as he always does. He knows best …"'[47] Just as he demonstrated in *War and Peace* that the traditional discourse of historians was not sufficient to capture history, so the novelistic form of *Anna Karenina*, exemplified in the imaginary scenario of Levin and Koznyshev, allows Tolstoy to show that the prevailing discourse of the intelligentsia was not sufficient to define such a thing as the will of the people.

The reception of *Anna Karenina*

Nevertheless, in spite of the way that *Anna Karenina* engaged the discourses of the time on the subject of Slavic identity, it did not become part of the national narrative in the same way that *War and Peace* did. To be sure, on this occasion, Tolstoy's views were at greater variance with the spirit of the time; all the same, given his status and the overall success of *Anna Karenina*, it is intriguing why this aspect of the novel was not more influential in contemporary debates. To my mind, there are a number of possible explanations. Firstly, I would argue that the quarrel with Katkov, and Katkov's subsequent dismissive summary of the novel's ending, which appeared in print before Part Eight did, plays a significant part here. Katkov's privileging of Anna's storyline over Levin's is a reading of the text that has endured to the present day, evidenced, as Kuzmic points out, by the focus of the numerous screen adaptations of *Anna Karenina*.[48] And in all fairness, the very title of the novel invites this interpretation and does nothing to alert the reader to Tolstoy's conception of the novel as the story of Anna and Levin in equal measure, as an exploration of the idea of family life. This idea is encapsulated in the novel's famous opening line: 'All happy families are alike, but an unhappy family is unhappy after its own fashion';[49] and Tolstoy's wife Sofya records her husband identifying family as the novel's 'main basic idea' in her diary for 3 March 1877.[50]

The weight of Katkov's voice in shaping the reception of the text is paralleled by the authority of the literary establishment in general. Although the reading public were, by all accounts, enthusiastic, according to A. V. Knowles, the more negative critical reception was coloured by 'an especially acrimonious period' in the rivalries and polemics between the monthly journals, as well as by critics' impatience with the intermittent serialization.[51] Knowles argues that the political positions espoused by different journals led the reviewers to find what they wanted to see in the novel and to use this as an opportunity to lock horns with their rivals.[52] The reviews that he surveys cover the spectrum of ideological stances and take Tolstoy to task for, variously, a defence of the old aristocracy, a failure to represent emerging classes, a lack of engagement with contemporary concerns and a narrow preoccupation with personal, sexual and family relations, although they are united in their praise for Tolstoy's style and artistic talent. Interestingly, none of the reviews he discusses appears to focus on Tolstoy's contribution to the Eastern Question. Knowles makes the point that the critical reception reveals much about literary critics' conception of the role of literature in society, owing to their judgement of *Anna Karenina* according to non-literary criteria, in other words 'political, sociological, and ethical viewpoints'.[53]

Such treatment is particularly evident in the response of Tolstoy's fellow artist, Dostoevsky, who unlike the reviewers cited by Knowles, focused in depth on Part Eight in his response to the novel. Dostoevsky shared many views with the Slavophiles and Pan-Slavists whose imperial ideal of a united Orthodox Christian brotherhood led by Russia was a contributing rationale in the war with Turkey. Dostoevsky had been writing on these themes in relation to the Eastern Question in his own monthly publication, *A Writer's Diary*. Having read Part Eight of *Anna Karenina*, he was immediately moved to devote two of the three sections of his combined July and August 1877 issue of *A Writer's Diary* to railing against Levin's position. What is of note here is not so much Dostoevsky's support for the Slavic cause, or his antipathy towards Levin, but that his palpable outrage at Part Eight stems from the extra-literary authority that until that point he had accorded to *Anna Karenina* as an example of outstanding literature. For him, the novel is 'a *fact* of special importance [my italics]'.[54] He writes:

> The book at once took on, in my eyes, the dimensions of a fact that could give Europe an answer on our behalf, that long-sought-after fact we could show to Europe. [...] *Anna Karenina* is perfection as a work of art [...] and [...] the novel's idea also contains something of ours, something truly *our own*, namely that very thing which constitutes our distinctiveness from the European world, the thing which constitutes our 'new word', or at least its beginnings [...].[55]

We can see from Dostoevsky's comments on *Anna Karenina* that he believed he had found in Tolstoy's novel the kind of symbiosis of artistry and content he had called for in the previous decade, such that it demonstrated something essentially Russian and at the same time something of universal value, hence his assessment of it as a 'fact of special importance'. At the same time he anticipated the criticism that it would be nonsensical to attribute so much importance to a work of fiction:

> Of course, people will howl and scoff that this is only a work of literature, some sort of novel, and that it's absurd to exaggerate this way and go off to Europe carrying only a novel. [...] I know very well that this is still only a novel [...]; if the Russian genius could give birth to this *fact*, then it is not doomed to impotence and can create [...].[56]

This passage of *A Writer's Diary* typifies the Russian understanding of literature in the ostensibly oxymoronic notion of *Anna Karenina* as both fact and fiction: the fictionality of a text does not in any way lessen its truthfulness or its authority, but is in fact organically bound to it.

Now, however, Dostoevsky's reaction to Part Eight of *Anna Karenina* reveals an inconsistency in his views. It seems the novel's harmony only exists insofar as Dostoevsky agrees with the position of the protagonists. He begins his polemic with repeated insistences that he understands Levin is a fictional character and should not be taken as a straightforward mouthpiece for Tolstoy's personal convictions. These insistences demonstrate that Dostoevsky as an artist had to admit that Levin's views on the Eastern Question were consistent with his character development and thus appropriate to novelistic priorities. Nevertheless, he cannot bring himself to accept them on this basis and reconcile them to his hitherto glowing opinion of the text. He laments: '[…] even though very much of what the author expresses through Levin evidently concerns only Levin himself as an artistically depicted character, I still did not expect this from such an author!'[57] After many pages, he concludes, 'People like the author of *Anna Karenina* are the teachers of society, our teachers, while we are merely their pupils. So what is it, then, that they are teaching us?'[58] Dostoevsky does not consider such elements of the text as the ironic portrayal of Koznyshev; he appears to assess Tolstoy's realism simplistically and thus to judge the novel by non-literary criteria. It is not clear how influential Dostoevsky's reading of the text was on the overall impact of Part Eight; nevertheless, he was reaching the pinnacle of his career and was soon to be lauded as the voice of the Russian literary establishment at the Pushkin celebrations of 1880, whereas Tolstoy thenceforward increasingly occupied the position of outsider and iconoclast. Thus it is reasonable to suggest that Dostoevsky's view did shape the reception of the text. One may also draw the inference that in the power dynamic of the Russian nineteenth-century literary industry, Tolstoy's status as top-ranking author in the hierarchy of publishing honoraria did not carry sufficient weight to allow his novel to challenge the dominant discourse effectively.

Conclusion

Through the example of *Anna Karenina* I have outlined the significance of artistic literature's contribution to the narratives of nineteenth-century Russia. I have shown how *Anna Karenina* as a novel is situated in the circulation of discourses on ethnic identity and empire. The historical event of the publication of its final part should be understood not only in relation to the contemporary events it references, but also in the context of a close reading of the text which identifies its novelistic strategies. I have argued that readings such as Dostoevsky's, which focus on a straightforward identification of the content as a direct intervention of the author, rather than as part of a constructed reality, ignore the concept of the novel as a medium that demonstrates the limitations of purely non-fictional discourses. The novelistic form of *Anna Karenina* is precisely what exposes those narratives marginalized by the dominant narrative of Russia as righteous defender of oppressed Slavic brethren.

Thus, I have shown that even though the novel did not have an impact on Russian perceptions of this period in history, in the way that *War and Peace* did in relation to 1812, a reading of it as a novel offers a more inclusive understanding of the Eastern Question. For the student of Russian history, a sensitive appreciation of the possibilities of fiction offers a fruitful expansion of horizons.

Notes

1 I am grateful to Richard Hibbitt for his valuable feedback on a draft of this chapter.
2 Lionel Gossman, *Between History and Literature* (Cambridge, MA: Harvard University Press, 1990), pp. 230–1.
3 See for example Michel Foucault, 'Sur les façons d'écrire l'histoire', in Daniel Defert and François Ewald (eds.), *Dits et écrits 1954–1988*, vol. 1 (Paris: Gallimard, 1994), p. 598; see also 'Truth and Power' in Paul Rabinow (ed.), *The Foucault Reader* (London: Penguin, 1991), p. 56.
4 Michel de Certeau, 'History: Science and Fiction' in *Heterologies: Discourse on the Other* (Minneapolis, MN: University of Minnesota Press, 1986), pp. 199–221 (p. 219).
5 Benjamin Ziemann and Miriam Dobson, 'Introduction', in Benjamin Ziemann and Miriam Dobson (eds.), *Reading Primary Sources: The Interpretation of Texts from Nineteenth- and Twentieth-Century History*, (Abingdon: Routledge, 2009), p. 1.
6 Julia Reid, 'Novels', in Benjamin Ziemann and Miriam Dobson (eds.), *Reading Primary Sources: The Interpretation of Texts from Nineteenth- and Twentieth-Century History* (Abingdon: Routledge, 2009), pp. 159–74, especially pp. 159–63.
7 Ibid., p. 159.
8 Formalist theorists of literature held the view that the meaning of literature does not derive from its external context, but is generated from close textual analysis independent of the author and his/her milieu. Formalism focuses on poetic language and structural features of the text; it was the prevalent school of literary criticism in Europe and the USA from roughly the 1920s to the 1970s.
9 Reid, 'Novels', pp. 162–4.
10 Malcolm V. Jones, 'Introduction', in Malcolm V. Jones and Robin Feuer Miller (eds.), *The Cambridge Companion to the Classic Russian Novel* (Cambridge: Cambridge University Press, 1998), pp. 1–17 (p. 5).
11 V. Belinsky, 'Letter to Gogol' trans. unknown, 1948. <www.marxists.org/subject/art/lit_crit/works/belinsky/gogol.htm> (accessed 06 November 2018).
12 F. M. Dostoevsky, 'Mr – bov and the Question of Art' in D. Magarshack (ed.), *Dostoevsky's Occasional Writings*, (New York, NY: Random House, 1963), pp. 86–137.
13 Jones, 'Introduction', p. 2.
14 David Bethea, 'Literature', in Nicholas Rzhevsky (ed.), *The Cambridge Companion to Modern Russian Culture* (Cambridge: Cambridge University Press), pp. 169–212 (p. 169).
15 Made during his address to a gathering of writers at the house of the novelist Maxim Gorky in October 1932. Helen Rappaport, *Joseph Stalin: A Biographical Companion* (Santa Barbara, CA: ABC-CLIO), p. 81.
16 Evgeny Evtushenko, *Bratskaia GES* (Moscow: Sovetskii pisatel', 1967), p. 69.
17 *Literaturnaia Gazeta*, 3 September 1934, cited in Bethea, p. 203.
18 Katerina Clark, *The Soviet Novel: History as Ritual*, 3rd ed. (Bloomington, IN: Indiana University Press, 2000), p. 8.
19 Sigurd Shmidt, 'Great Works of Literature as a Source of Historical Knowledge', *Russian Studies in History* 47 (2008), pp. 14–29 (p. 14).
20 Andrew Wachtel, *An Obsession with History: Russian Writers Confront the Past* (Stanford, CA: Stanford University Press, 1994), pp. 17–18.

21 Ibid., p. 12.
22 For example, Nikolai Karamzin, a writer of poetry and prose fiction, was appointed imperial historiographer in 1803 and his 12-volume *History of the Russian State* (1818–29) became enormously influential.
23 Hayden White, 'Introduction: Historical Fiction, Fictional History and Historical Reality', *Rethinking History* 9 (2005), pp. 147–57 (p. 147).
24 William Mills Todd III, 'Dostoevsky and Tolstoy: the Professionalization of Literature and Serialized Fiction,' *Dostoevsky Studies, New Series*, 15 (2011), pp. 29–36 (p. 32). A 'signature' referred to the printer's sheet of paper which would be folded and bound into the publication. One signature would produce sixteen pages.
25 See for example Ben Bagdikian, 'Perhaps Saddam Read Tolstoy and Bush's People Didn't', *Countercurrents.org*, 2003 <www.countercurrents.org/iraq-bagdikian041203.htm> (accessed 6 November 2018); Michael Emerson, 'How Tolstoy Might Have Portrayed the Legacies of Yanukovich and Putin', *Euractiv*, 2014. <www.euractiv.com/section/global-europe/opinion/how-tolstoy-might-have-portrayed-the-legacies-of-yanukovich-and-putin/> (accessed 6 November 2018).
26 Barbara Lönnqvist, 'The Role of the Serbian War in *Anna Karenina*', *Tolstoy Studies Journal*, 17 (2005), pp. 35–42 (p. 41).
27 Ibid., p. 36.
28 Tatiana Kuzmic, 'Serbia: Vronskii's last love. Reading *Anna Karenina* in the Context of Empire', *Toronto Slavic Quarterly*, 43 (2013), pp. 40–66 (p. 40).
29 Cited in Lönnqvist, 'The Role of the Serbian War in *Anna Karenina*', p. 35.
30 Ibid., p. 36.
31 Todd, 'Dostoevsky and Tolstoy', pp. 32–3.
32 See ibid., pp. 34–5 for a table detailing the timeline of the serialization of *Anna Karenina*.
33 Ibid., pp. 29–30.
34 Caryl Emerson, 'Pushkin and Tolstoy,' in Juras T. Ryfa (ed.), *Collected Essays in Honor of the Bicentennial of Alexander Pushkin's Birth* (New York, NY: Mellen, 2000), p. 28.
35 Letter to N. N. Strakhov, '25 August 1875', in A. A. Donskov (ed.), *Leo Tolstoy and Nikolaj Strakhov: Complete Correspondence*, vol. 1 (Ottawa: Slavic Research Group at the University of Ottawa, 2003), p. 215.
36 Leo Tolstoy, *Anna Karenin*, trans. Rosemary Edmonds (Harmondsworth: Penguin, 1987), p. 803.
37 Ibid., p. 804.
38 Ibid., p. 804.
39 Ibid., p. 804.
40 Lönnqvist, 'The Role of the Serbian War in *Anna Karenina*', p. 40.
41 Kuzmic, 'Vronskii's last love', p. 44.
42 Tolstoy, *Anna Karenin*, pp. 805, 843.
43 Reid, 'Novels', p. 161.
44 Tolstoy, *Anna Karenin*, p. 841.
45 Ibid., p. 841.
46 Ibid., pp. 844–5.
47 Ibid., p. 842.
48 Kuzmic, 'Vronskii's last love', p. 41.
49 Tolstoy, *Anna Karenin*, p. 13.
50 Cited in Barbara Lönnqvist, 'Anna Karenina', in Donna Tussing Orwin (ed.), *The Cambridge Companion to Tolstoy* (Cambridge: Cambridge University Press, 2002), p. 80.
51 A. V. Knowles, 'Russian Views of Anna Karenina, 1875–1878,' *Slavic and East European Journal*, 32 (1978), pp. 301–12 (p. 303).
52 Ibid., p. 303.
53 Ibid., pp. 309–10.

54 Fyodor Dostoevsky, *A Writer's Diary, vol. 2: 1877–1881*, trans. by Kenneth Lantz (London: Quartet, 1995), p. 1067.
55 Ibid., pp. 1067–9.
56 Ibid., p. 1068.
57 Ibid., p. 1062.
58 Ibid., p. 1099.

Further reading

Bethea, David, 'Literature', in Nicholas Rzhevsky (ed.), *The Cambridge Companion to Modern Russian Culture* (Cambridge: Cambridge University Press, 2012), pp. 169–212.

de Certeau, Michel, 'History: Science and Fiction' in Michel de Certeau (ed.), *Heterologies: Discourse on the Other* (Minneapolis: University of Minnesota Press, 1986), pp. 199–221.

Gossman, Lionel, *Between History and Literature* (Cambridge, MA: Harvard University Press, 1990).

Gutting, Gary, *Foucault. A Very Short Introduction* (Oxford: Oxford University Press, 2005).

Jones, Malcolm V., 'Introduction', in Malcolm V. Jones and Robin Feuer Miller (eds.), *The Cambridge Companion to the Classic Russian Novel* (Cambridge: Cambridge University Press, 1998), pp. 1–17.

Poggioli, Renato, 'Realism in Russia', *Comparative Literature*, 3 (1951), pp. 253–67.

Reid, Julia, 'Novels', in Benjamin Ziemann and Miriam Dobson (eds.), *Reading Primary Sources: The Interpretation of Texts from Nineteenth- and Twentieth-Century History* (Abingdon: Routledge, 2009), pp. 159–74.

Shmidt, Sigurd, 'Great Works of Literature as a Source of Historical Knowledge', *Russian Studies in History*, 47 (2008), pp. 14–29.

Wachtel, Andrew, *An Obsession with History: Russian Writers Confront the Past* (Stanford, CA: Stanford University Press, 1994).

White, Hayden, 'Introduction: Historical Fiction, Fictional History, and Historical Reality', *Rethinking History*, 9 (2005), pp. 147–57.

6   The late Imperial press[1]

George Gilbert

Introduction

What can we learn from using the Russian press[2] as a source? Take one example from the popular newspaper *Malen'kaia gazeta* (*Little Gazette*) in 1914, when one columnist offered reflections on urban life in late Imperial Russia: 'there is no deeper abyss than the sidewalk on the streets of a big city'.[3] In just one line we learn something about the preoccupations of this journalist, a little of the wider social context, and a hint of the power relations in Russian society. Some consequences of urbanization in the Russian empire are unveiled through this negative view of the city (an 'abyss'), whilst also giving us a sense of the vast scale of urban life. If we were to look at different editions of this newspaper alongside other contemporary publications, we would see that fears of the city were rife in the contemporary press, to the extent that it became something of a cliché. The visions constructed in the press show prevailing attitudes at the time, wider social forces and, when read critically, they can show us how power was constructed and disseminated in society.

In search of the press

The press as a source provides us with several lines of enquiry concerning any historical era. A newspaper, for instance, is a text, a chronicle of events and a record of an era. It provides a series of interpretations, illustrations and debates within its pages. Newspapers provide us with snap opinions – they put the 'new' in 'news' – but they are also complex institutions, with financial backing reflecting the interests of those who own them.[4] Though we will see what is in the news by reading a newspaper, the opinions offered are never unmediated, and so the press cannot provide an objective account of a period; as Anthony Smith has argued, 'journalism was the art of structuring reality, rather than recording it'.[5] Furthermore, whilst newspapers provide a point of view, an editorial line has the capacity to shift. As well as provide for their readership, newspapers shape and influence society through selecting the content to appear in their pages and thus a demonstration of particular interests.

Newspapers are topical accounts and frequently illustrative and telling sources, but scholars need to be mindful of the practical issues of using newspapers,

including unreliable evidence, false witnesses, or the personal preferences of journalists or editors. Conversely, many journalists were serious about their profession,
seeing themselves as moral witnesses of the age, providing accounts of the major
issues of the day as well as, in other cases, sensational stories to sell papers. With
the caveat that newspapers cannot provide us with a direct line to what the totality
of 'the people' thought, they can show the preoccupations of specific individuals, interest groups and social classes of a time and place. For example, Mark D.
Steinberg has shown how newspapers reflected and informed passionate debate on
workers' rights during the revolutions of both 1905 and 1917, with debates about
words like 'freedom' and 'democracy' unfolding across the pages of a newly liber-
ated press.[6] Newspapers are also useful from a social standpoint: the press has been
used to find clues to the development of lower-class cultures, and its diversification
in the last few decades of Romanov rule meant press organs came to reflect the
views of diverse groups, including both workers and women during the revolutions
of 1917.[7]

As serious scholarship of late Imperial Russia took off in the West, archival
access remained inconsistent. Even in later decades certain topics, especially those
concerning the internal history of the Soviet Union after 1917, remained difficult
to access. Newspapers functioned as a vital resource for researchers throughout
this period, providing facts and interpretations of the past sometimes unavailable
through other types of source. Even when other sources are plentiful, newspapers
can corroborate other types of evidence. Moreover, inter-textuality can be demonstrated by reference to other newspapers, journals and events, and therefore present
a deeper texture of a historical period. For instance, though archival holdings on
the revolution of 1917 are more widely available and known about than in previous
decades, newspapers can provide a feel of the period as they provide a picture of
everyday life and change through daily reporting on major (and minor) events.
Looking at papers throughout the revolutionary year shows a variety of perspectives, including most famously from political groups driving the events, but also
from more marginalized social forces, which has, overall, added to our understanding of the period. Sometimes collections of newspapers covering key events or
phases in history are aggregated in the form of document collections, making for
easy access.[8]

One does not have to travel to libraries or archives to get a taste of the variety
and interest of the press. Advances in technology have made original newspaper
sources widely available. Many examples of the newspaper as a complete text
are available for the reader, and for those with Russian, these collections form
a valuable resource. Increasingly there are advanced online resources collecting
hundreds of titles from both the national and regional press. There are still many
options in using papers for those without any Russian language skills: in one
volume from a prominent series of primary source collections, translations of
readers' letters sent to the newspapers *Novaia zhizn'* (*New life*) and *Rabotnitsa*
(*Working Woman*) during May 1917 are published in full, illustrating concerns of
a factory worker and a reader who self-identifies as an 'honest woman'.[9] Though
selective, publications such as the *Current Digest of the Soviet Press* provide

English-language translations for those without Russian. The late Imperial press is an important part of the source record of Russian history, with various textbooks, scholarly monographs and journal articles using newspaper comment to inform their analyses.

In Russia, newspapers first appeared in the 1720s, greatly facilitated by the foundation of the Russian Academy of Sciences in 1725. *Sankt-Peterburgskie vedomosti* (*The Saint Petersburg Messenger*), Russia's first newspaper, first appeared in 1727, and in 1756 *Moskovskie vedomosti* (*The Moscow News*) appeared with the foundation of Moscow University, and both of these publications lasted until the revolutions of 1917.[10] During the nineteenth century, the government took a more hands-on role in controlling the developing press through censorship and creating their own press organs. Several ministries founded their own newspapers: these included the Ministry of War, which founded *Russkii invalid* (*Russian Veteran*) after the conflict with Napoleon, and the Ministry of Internal Affairs, which produced *Severnaia pochta* (*Northern Post*) from 1809.[11] Entirely separate was the development of the commercial press, which hugely expanded from the Great Reform era of the 1860s. The number of daily and non-daily newspapers being published in St Petersburg was 29 in 1860; this had expanded to 89 by 1909, and 104 dailies were published by 1913. For Moscow, the number of both dailies and non-dailies stood at 11 in 1860, 43 in 1891, 63 in 1909, and 70 for just dailies in 1912.[12] Not only were there far more newspapers to choose from than before, but individual titles sold on a huge scale, with some of these designed for a mass audience with their mixture of news, scandal, comment and interest. *Peterburgskii listok* (*Petersburg News Sheet*) had daily street sales of 1,000 in 1867 and 2,200 in 1880; but, by 1905, it was selling nearly ten million copies every day on Russia's streets, and close to 24 million by 1915.[13] The daily newspaper *Novoe vremia* (*New Time*) published in St Petersburg which tended to focus primarily on news and politics had daily street sales of 4,000 in 1880, but over five million by 1905 and over six million by 1915.[14] This development applied to other more seriously-minded titles, and I. D. Sytin's daily *Russkoe slovo* (*Russian Word*) had a circulation of 759,000 in 1916.[15] The press boom also spread to provincial Russia, with different regions of the Russian empire acquiring their own press organs throughout the late Imperial period. In 1908 there were 602 Russian-language newspapers in the empire; by 1915, this had increased to 715.[16] The impact of these publications, with generally smaller print runs and a focus on local issues, was typically felt most acutely in the area of publication; conversely, major newspapers based in Moscow and St Petersburg were read in both the provinces and their city of publication. Print runs (if available) can give us a good sense of the size of the readership of any paper, but we should be mindful too of patterns of communal reading for many titles, which demonstrates an audience beyond the circulation figures. People could share and read out a single copy of a newspaper, suggesting a wider scope than we might otherwise envisage.

As the press expanded its content became increasingly diverse and specialized. Publications reported on national and international news, political, social and cultural issues, and presented reviews and calendars. These discussed what happened in Russia and elsewhere, framing stories around selected viewpoints and debates. Newspapers could also publish important documents: this included the 1905 October Manifesto and records of meetings of the parliament (State Duma), which had been established in 1906. One significant liberal newspaper, Pavel Miliukov's *Rech'* (*Speech*), commended for its political reporting, published the full text of the Fundamental Laws on 11 April 1906, reportedly before some ministers had had a chance to read it for themselves.[17] There was also the so-called 'thick journal', a Russian institution which first appeared in the nineteenth century. Unlike newspapers which sought to chronicle events for a fact-minded audience, the editorial and debate was most central to these publications. Broadly speaking these journals were split between liberal and conservative editorials, including articles by prominent members of literary society discussing many of the most important issues of the day: an example of the former was the well-known *Vestnik Evropy* (*The Herald of Europe*), and *Russkii vestnik* (*The Russian Messenger*), which was a typically more conservative publication.[18] Their content was divided between journalism (reviews of current affairs, discussion of political, social and cultural issues, reviews, calendars, debates) and literary publications (poetry, drama, short stories, serializations of novels, including translations). The thick journal's evolution occurred alongside that of the newspaper; together, the press played a major role in the development of the national conversation: like significant newspapers these journals reflected upon the influence of Western trends and ideas.[19]

In the case of some radical newspapers and journals appearing at the start of the twentieth century like *Iskra* (*The Spark*), the newspaper itself was an important node of organization for the group connected to it: sometimes, the paper appeared even before a group or party framework had been established. Activists clustered around the printing press, and the appearance of an 'official' organ would stimulate development elsewhere. Certainly, a particular paper or journal could represent a faction within the revolutionary movement; indeed, the factional development of left-wing revolutionaries like the Social Democrats can be charted through the existence of various newspapers, to such an extent. National identities were forged through an active press; for example, in October 1905 restrictions on Ukrainian publications were dropped, and what was at first a trickle of Ukrainian-language publications became a cascade. A transformative process occurred as many people began to read about politics, culture and the arts in their own languages.

Censorship greatly affected what could and could not be published in the late Imperial period. Censorship was a complex matter which evolved over time and was impacted upon by regional, political and administrative considerations. In Russia there were two types of general press censorship: preliminary and punitive censorship, the former of which included the greatest proportion of all privately printed publications and which was abolished in the cities from 1905 to 1906. In preliminary censorship the manuscript (and sometimes proof sheets) were submitted to the censor's office, whilst for the latter type only the finished product was submitted. The former meant two versions of a manuscript, including an original and a revised version, could be submitted to the censor's office, with red marker highlighting the extracts of an original manuscript that the censor's office desired changing. In practice this meant content was heavily restricted: many publications were hit by costly delays and extensive revision. The press law of 1905–6 abolished preliminary censorship in the cities, and Article 79 of the new Fundamental Laws of April 1906 established the basic right of free expression. Together these allowed greater press freedoms, but after 1905–6 the government still had controls at its disposal that restricted what could be printed. On publication a newspaper or magazine was required to submit a specified number of issues to a committee or official for 'press affairs', which could allow for confiscation of individual issues or the suspension of a particular publication. Additionally, new emergency regulations were developed whereby violations of the new press law could be punished with fines and imprisonment. In fact, the scale of government repression of the press reached its zenith in 1907; throughout this period, the previous laws remained in place for the provincial press, and new publications could only be started here with the express permission of the Minister of the Interior.[20]

But, there were ways round the censors. One was to avoid them entirely: some radical newspapers and journals read in Russia were published abroad and then smuggled into the country. One example was the anarchist journal *Burevestnik* (*The Stormy Petrel*), founded in Paris in 1906 with a small but committed readership; other exile publications included *Golos truda* (*The Voice of Labour*) published in New York City from 1911.[21] Within Russia, astute editors worked out ways to avoid repression, which could include self-censorship; certain themes could be discussed in Aesopian language, or, in some cases, the title of a paper was changed to evade further restrictions. In *Pravda*, one would read not about the 'Russian Social Democratic Workers' Party' (the name was not allowed), but instead about 'consistent Marxists' or 'consistent democrats'. Sensitive news such as reports on strikes or disorders in Russia could appear in a different guise, for instance disguised as a report from abroad. Another way of dodging the censors was to change the newspaper's name whilst preserving a completely unchanged editorial line. These various techniques of evasion are sometimes known as 'camouflage' in the literature. In practical terms, the rapid expansion of the press after 1905 meant the administration increasingly struggled to control it, as the quantity of publications made enforcing the existing controls difficult.

A word must be said about literacy. Though rates were on the rise, a great many Russians were still illiterate during the entire late Imperial period, which necessarily affects any discussion of whether newspapers can be said to reflect that nebulous concept of 'public opinion'. Literacy in rural Russia was much lower than in the cities, perhaps no more than 6 per cent in the 1860s, though this began to climb slowly towards the end of the nineteenth century.[22] According to the 1897 census, 21 per cent of the Russian empire was literate, a figure that rose to around 40 per cent on the eve of the First World War, with rates rising much more quickly in urban Russia.[23] Press freedoms were much greater in urban areas, where the audience for the press was more concentrated. Though in a minority, geographical concentration meant that literate people were increasingly close to one another and able to discuss key issues. In both urban and rural areas, newspapers could have particular uses in a climate of increasing literacy, not only by teaching people to read but instructing them, through the selection of preferred content, how to interpret key themes, events and debates of the day. Finally, the financial backing of major newspapers influenced the quality, remit and reach of their journalism. Good salaries and esteem attracted high quality journalists, who played important roles in articulating major discourses of the day. Wealthy newspaper owners had social power and influence, increasingly so as the newspaper became firmly established as a public institution, which in turn reflected the issues discussed and debated in the press. The following analysis is largely focused on the consumption, rather than production end of newspapers, but remarks about the social context need bearing in mind as sources inevitably reflect wider society.

Historiography

In practical terms, the use of newspapers as a source in Russian history was encouraged by the gradual accrual of collections of major Russian newspapers in large libraries in Europe and America. For a long time now, rich and varied historical studies of a wide variety of themes in late Imperial history have drawn on press comment. But, in contrast to studies that use the press as a source, assessments about newspapers and the institutions of the press are few and far between. However, over time a rich and complex picture of the world of the late Imperial press has emerged through diverse historical writing on the topic.

Serious attention was first given to the pre-revolutionary press in the Soviet Union, and this focused on the interaction between the press and the workers' movement in the late Imperial period. Studies touched on the role of the press during the 1905–7 revolution, particularly on its contribution towards the creation of distinctly working-class identities. Newspapers such as *Rabochaia gazeta* (*Workers' Gazette*) and *Rabochii zhizn'* (*Workers' Life*) identified issues such as workers' rights, the right to strike, the issues and interests of unemployed workers, the struggle with the extreme right in Russia's towns and cities and conflict with the government. In doing so, these newspapers articulated a set of distinctly working-class concerns through the creation of a distinct language and set of banners and symbols associated with these movements.[24] After the revolutions of 1917, work on the 'bourgeois' press began to be undertaken within the Soviet Union, which contained detailed information about circulation figures and also the range of newspapers available. In the West, early studies focused on newspapers such as *Pravda* (*Truth*) and *Izvestiia* (*News*) as well as figures in the radical press, including assessment of important issues such as the relationship between the pre-revolutionary radical press and tsarist censors.[25]

Once the revolutionary actors had been identified, the diversity of the late Imperial press came under greater scrutiny. Studies in English of major liberal newspapers – known as the 'bourgeois' press in Soviet scholarship – emerged in the 1960s. Thomas Riha traced the development of *Rech'*, one of the most important liberal publications from 1906 to 1917.[26] Case studies extended to the conservative press, and the influence, world views and contributions to Russian journalism of significant figures like Prince Vladimir Meshcherskii, who at one stage had the ear of Alexander III, and the press baron Aleksandr Suvorin, who managed to establish his own publishing empire, including the major daily newspaper *Novoe vremia*.[27] Studies show that far from being ideological monoliths, these newspapers were complex institutions in their own right. In the Soviet Union too, scholarly interest expanded to include a wider variety of pre-revolutionary newspapers as seen in B. I. Esin's works.[28] Together such studies provided a more complete image of the pre-revolutionary press by identifying the breadth of political interests, diversity of major newspapers, their financial backing and information on selected content.

Meanwhile the processes that governed the mediated reality of the Russian press began to be studied more deeply. The relationship of the press with the tsarist establishment and censorship after 1865 began to be scrutinized.[29] As discussed above, press censorship placed restrictions on the national and provincial press, but editors exploited legal loopholes and new press freedoms after 1905–6 in bringing commercial publications to a mass audience.[30] Attention began to be given to the press as a complex institution in its own right, notably in the work of Louise McReynolds, which revealed more about the development of the commercial press, and, in examining the emergence of careers such as the newspaper reporter and war correspondent, contributed hugely to our knowledge of journalism in the period.[31]

Subsequent interest shifted away from the relationship between the state and newspapers towards the readers of the late Imperial press. Historians began to interpret the impact of the press on audiences, and its contribution towards what one might hesitantly call 'popular culture'.[32] Jeffrey Brooks examined the emergence of different secular, rational and cosmopolitan values in sources including newspaper serials and the mass circulation press after 1861. Unlike broadsheets such as *Novoe vremia*, newspapers such as *Moskovskii listok* (*The Moscow News Sheet*) and its editor Nikolai Pastukhov first and foremost targeted a mass audience, and, in so doing, played an important role in the development of popular fiction in the late nineteenth century. Driven by commercial interests, Pastukhov's journalism broke with press standards by displaying a rough, even plebeian quality, and (in spite of his own conservatism) Pastukhov clashed with authorities and those who saw themselves as the moral arbiters of Russian print culture. Innovations of his journalism such as an 'advice and answer' column opened up a new space for readers to communicate with the press, and thus contributed towards an important shift in power between reader and text, influencing discursive possibilities. Increasingly the readers of the press were portrayed as active and dynamic subjects who responded to press agendas in diverse and sometimes surprising ways: for instance, readers could be class conscious, or take a more individualistic approach.[33]

In assessing the creation of social identities in the space between reader and text, work focused closely on conceptions of subjectivity amongst the press's diverse readership, including those who sat at the interstices of class experience. In his work on the printing industry, Mark D. Steinberg illustrated how reception of press comment contributed to perceptions of 'the self' amongst working-class Russians. This went far beyond earlier studies by not merely identifying the demands articulated by workers but placing them within part of a wider moral vision of naturalistic dignity and workers' rights. Significant too were worker contributions to newspapers such as stories, poems and letters, and hence their influence on the content of the commercial press.[34] Further work emerged on the types of press in late Imperial Russia, including the so-called 'boulevard' or 'penny press' aimed at mass audiences, which focused on the cultural role of these new press forms and the development of reader selfhoods. Joan Neuberger's study of hooliganism included close scrutiny of the boulevard press, and concluded that the image of the 'hooligan' was defined, articulated and contested in the pages of this type of newspaper.[35] Furthermore, her work uncovered the important point that fears of hooliganism reflected upon readers' own real and perceived social identities. As Neuberger writes, '*Peterburgskii listok* constructed a Russian variant of the culture of respectability that predominated in the "civilized" west'.[36] Writing on the press encompassed the realities clarified and articulated by the press and the reciprocal arrangements between text and reader, and how one influenced the other as proximity between the two diminished. As Daniel R. Brower put it, 'the boundary separating the journalists and readers of the penny press was thus very porous ... this press sought to give the reader the impression of being on an equal footing with the authors of its articles'.[37]

As more attention has been given to textual patterns and the articulation of key concepts in the late Imperial press, the mediated cultural space between readers and text has become more clearly defined. Examination has, once again, turned to the content of newspapers, but now informed by debates about subjectivity and selfhood amongst the readership. Newspapers have been used to chart popular interests in crime, scandal, sport, art, culture and entertainment as well as high politics.[38] For instance, Katia Dianina has focused on the newspaper as 'the principal forum for this dialogue between art and society', and the contribution of artistic culture as presented in the news towards the concept of a national community.[39] Mark D. Steinberg used urban journalism in his study of moral ambivalences in turn of the century St Petersburg to assess how residents contemplated a bleak future of crime, moral decay, decadence, suicide and death.[40] What is remarkable from reading studies that use the commercial press is the range of publications now available and how diverse voices from the past resonate so clearly within them. Work on the press has developed to include a vast array of discourses, including (but not limited to) concepts of power, nation, empire, class and identities.

Newspapers formed part of what Laura Engelstein has called the 'theatre of public life' in the late Imperial period, and sophisticated work has located how press interests shaped debates about culture, society and politics.[41] As our knowledge of the thematic range of the press has developed, recent studies have expanded understanding of the Russian provincial press and newspapers in an earlier period.[42] We have seen how newspapers could specialize in providing for largely or wholly non-Russian audiences within the empire. Our image of the institutional frameworks that allowed for such articulation is clearer, but it is still often difficult to speak confidently about audience reception to newspapers in many cases.

Interpretation

By now it should be apparent that reading a newspaper is not likely to be as straightforward a process as it might initially appear. Historians must look for clues to unlock deeper meanings as well as show awareness of superficial issues apparent from the text. As outlined by Stephen Vella, investigation can be divided into three broad areas of institutional structure (social context), format (textual content) and content (the text), with readers taking an active approach towards all three areas, asking a series of important, related questions.[43]

The institutional setting of the newspaper is important to consider if the reader wishes to know more about how a newspaper reflected the distribution of power in society. Questions that can be applied to reading newspapers in different social contexts can be asked of the Russian press, with the problem that sometimes further information about the institution of the newspaper is lacking. This can include technical information like print runs, but also the internal politics of the newspaper, including power struggles within hierarchies. The Russian empire was remarkably diverse, which naturally affects the type of questions we should ask about its newspapers. These can include: do we know anything about the owners and editors of the newspaper? Does the newspaper have any particular social, political, national, religious or cultural affiliations? What was the reach of the newspaper? Was it local, regional or national in coverage? Did it have a large print run? How did the newspaper make money? Did it rely primarily on subscribers or on street sales? Did advertisements appear in the newspaper – if so, who were they aimed at? Such questions can shed light on the readership of the paper, and issues such as the social class, gender and age of readers.

In late Imperial Russia newspapers catered for a range of tastes and content reflected a variety of government and commercial interests. A press reliant on street sales and advertising would operate in a different way to one reliant on government funds, responding more keenly to the tastes – real and perceived – of a mass readership. For instance, the widely circulating *Gazeta kopeika* (*Kopeck Gazette*) displayed liberal sensibilities which reflected the views of its owner, M. B. Gorodetskii. Gorodetskii showed sympathy with his readership and his paper was a remarkably successful commercial enterprise which included a broad range of content. According to Louise McReynolds, this prominent example of the kopeck press provided 'integration and escapism' for its readers.[44] The newspaper provided for the political views of a liberal readership, but covered non-political subjects, as demonstrated by its inclusion of the feuilleton – a type of non-political supplement attached to the main pages of the newspaper, consisting of topics such as gossip, literature, art criticism and fashion. In contrast, a newspaper such as *Pravitel'stvennyi vestnik* (*The Government Herald*) had the function of providing a direct line to major issues as perceived by the government. As a state organ and not dictated to by commercial pressures, it was much less responsive to readers' tastes than a paper like *Gazeta kopeika* and its coverage tended to be more narrowly focused on the activities of the Imperial family, foreign conflict and national and international news.

Looking at individual newspapers, we can ask questions about format. Newspapers do not simply report what happened, but present a certain vision in creating a style and mood within their pages. We need to consider *how* the facts are presented, as the appearance and visual styles of newspapers are deliberately chosen and designed to alter readers' perceptions. As technology improved during the late Imperial period, the visual possibilities of the newspaper increased. Firstly, can the entire newspaper be seen? If observing a clipping or a single article in translation, this will affect how the newspaper is read. If the entire paper (or a series of pages) can be seen, then observe whether the article in question is displayed prominently or hidden away towards the end of the paper. Has it been afforded much space? Does it have any relationship with other articles in the newspaper? Consider what does the masthead looks like – is the font used here and throughout the paper evocative of a certain tone? Are there any illustrations? If so, are these large and high quality? What do they represent? Look at the advertisements, if there are any. Where are these placed? Are they large? Do they complement in any way the content of articles in the paper? Do they represent or conflict with other content in the newspaper?

Attention can then be turned to the text itself. Newspaper viewpoints were based around selected issues, with the editorial line providing a 'reality' with an intended effect on the reader. Considering firstly the writer of a contribution, questions might include whether we know who the author is. If so, how much is known about them? When and where was the article written? Does it reflect upon contemporary themes or interests? What major viewpoints are articulated? Does the article position itself for or against a particular point of view? What events are covered or referred to? Attention might shift to the imagined readership. Look closely at the language used – is there any interesting use of metaphor, tone, or is it phrased as an appeal of any sort? Is it addressed to anyone in particular? If so, how is this reader addressed? Are there any clues as to what the identity of this reader is perceived to be? Is it addressed to a local, national or international audience? The reader should consider the veracity of the source. Is anything known about the author's sources? Can the accuracy of these be questioned? Is there any important information that is left out? Thinking about historical change, is there a sense of historical development in any way? What past events (if any) are referred to? Thinking about the impact of the source, does the article confirm expectations, or modify them in any way?

We can then place the source in wider context, considering it alongside other sources that cover the same topic or theme. Does the article or extract demonstrate inter-textuality – that is, does it refer to other texts or newspaper? If so, how are these reported? Often events and stories unfolded across different newspapers as well as different types of sources, so when examining a particular story or issue the reader should consider how widely the event or theme was covered in both the contemporary press and in other sources.

Case study: *Novoe vremia* and the murder of Grand Duke Sergei Aleksandrovich

The example below focuses on responses in the newspaper *Novoe vremia* to the death of Nicholas II's uncle Grand Duke Sergei Aleksandrovich from a terrorist attack in February 1905. This example offers a test for ways in which newspapers can be read, as the event intersected with a number of concerns of the day.

Published in St Petersburg, *Novoe vremia* was set up in 1868 and ran until 1917, when it was closed by the Bolsheviks. Initially it was not wildly successful, but it rose to prominence after being taken over in 1876 by Aleksei Suvorin, becoming one of the most influential of all Russia's daily newspapers. A major figure within Russian publishing, Suvorin also established the thick journal *The Historical Herald* in 1880. Suvorin was the sole owner of the newspaper until 1911, when he relinquished full control but continued to sit on the board. He had strong influence over the content of the newspaper and contributed to its editorial frequently. In the later nineteenth and early twentieth centuries, *Novoe vremia* was one of the most widely circulating national dailies, with circulation figures of 30,000 in 1895, 60,000 in 1900, 71,500 in 1905 and 80,000 in 1915.[45] Moreover, it had many influential readers, being widely read by urban professionals including government ministers. The paper's advertisements, including those from the state, brought in plenty of money. Its editorial line was conservative and broadly pro-government (something that led to the paper being disparaged in liberal circles), but it had quite a wide variety of contributors. Suvorin himself held moderately conservative views as an adult on most political matters, but contributors included the ultra-nationalist Mikhail Men'shikov, and in the 1870s and 1880s a few former radicals too. The paper contained a broad range of content including national politics, with significant sections given over to national news, local and government news, international affairs, economics and transportation as well as stories of general interest. Key stories could include tales of war, rebellion and defence, crime, public welfare, education, accidents and disasters. Though it was serious-minded, the newspaper included content about entertainment, such as literature and theatre reviews as well as reports on science and inventions.

The murder of Grand Duke Sergei Aleksandrovich on 4 February 1905 was a major shock for the autocracy.[46] He had been governor-general of Moscow, a member of the State Council, and patron of a range of learned societies. He was a significant figure within the political and cultural life of Imperial Russia, a member of the Imperial court, but hated by many for his aloof manner and cold relations with other people. He was assassinated by I. P. Kaliaev of the combat organization of the Socialist Revolutionary Party, a group that used political terror to shake the confidence of the government and incite insurrection. Kaliaev had killed the duke in the grounds of the Kremlin in Moscow by throwing a bomb into his carriage as it passed through the city's streets. Such was the force of the explosion it was said that the duke's body parts were found in the surrounding area for several days afterwards. Such a dramatic attack on the autocracy was obviously a lightning rod for conservative discontents, and as a newspaper with such an editorial, *Novoe vremia* was among the press organs expressing concern. Sergei was one in a series of assassinations of political and Imperial figures, including Alexander II in 1881, the Minister of the Interior Viacheslav von Pleve in July 1904, and the governor-general of the Grand Duchy of Finland, Nikolai Bobrikov, who had been assassinated only one month before Pleve. The timing of the event was crucial, occurring during an upsurge in strikes and unrest, an uncertain military conflict against Japan, and the wider mobilization of political opposition to autocracy. News of the violent end of the Duke and reaction to this continued for weeks afterwards in the newspaper. Here are a series of extracts from *Novoe vremia's* coverage of the events, on 5, 6, 7 and 17 February:[47]

[Editorial]

In Moscow today, at 3 o'clock in the afternoon, on Senate Square in the Kremlin, Grand Duke Sergei Aleksandrovich, his Imperial Highness, was viciously killed by a bomb thrown at him. News of this terrible incident spread like lightning across all of Moscow. By 4 o'clock in the afternoon crowds of thousands of people surrounded the Kremlin on the side of the Spaska and Nikol'skii Gates.

...

The terrible murder of Grand Duke Sergei Aleksandrovich will cause deep shock to the whole of Russia. We will repeat what has been said about each of these attempts, which have, alas, become so frequent in recent years! To spill blood is always a crime; some of these murderers have a robber's motivation, others those of the executioner, but all are equally intolerable to peaceful civilians. How do we stop these murders becoming more frequent?

...

Who are these murderers? The answer to this question is important, if only for justice. But much more important is another question: why was there no warning of this crime? For several decades, the revolutionary parties have committed terrorist acts. They have organized, they have openly published proclamations, they have published 'sentences' in their leaflets and their 'executioner' will know everything that is being done by the government; but, our police do not know what murders they have been involved in over the past dozen years.

...

May God help the Emperor to save all of the kindness of his heart in this terrible year of misery and trials. May God help him strengthen his courage amidst the blows of fate and his faith in the Russian people, who understand his sorrows and grief, and shares them with their habitual and profound feeling.

(*Novoe vremia*, 5 February 1905, p. 3)

[News article from a special correspondent]

The murder of Grand Duke Sergei. Moscow, 4 February. 4 o'clock.

Today, at about 3 o'clock, a deafening explosion was heard in the Kremlin, from which the buildings of the city barracks, the walls of the Historical Museum and other nearby buildings were shaken. The glass in the surrounding windows was broken by this.

...

I went to the Town Hall, where the assembled administration and the judicial authorities interrogated the criminal. I was informed there (at 5 o'clock) that the detainee was either stubbornly silent, or uttering phrases irrelevant to the case. He was extremely excited on the way from Red Square to the city port, shouting freedom, freedom!

Passers-by, seeing this scene, thought that they were leading a drunk who had accidentally fallen and smashed his face.

(*Novoe vremia*, 6 February 1905, p. 4)

[News article]

Moscow, 6 February. In the Kremlin, the place where Grand Duke Sergei Aleksandrovich was killed, a metal cross with a suspended lamp was erected on a stone foundation. The cross was built at the expense of the Kiev regiment; the lamp, at the expense of the Preobrazhenskii regiment. The coffin of the Grand Duke is covered with a mass of wreaths, most of which are silver. Wreaths were sent by all of the Grand Duke's regiments, in addition to those from the Preobrazhenskii regiment and the Strelkov battalion of the imperial family. Memorial services were held all day at the Grand Duke's grave.

(*Novoe vremia*, 7 February 1905, p. 2)

A telegram from his excellency was reported in the newspaper *Moskovskie vedomosti*, compiled in the following terms.

[News article]

Having gathered on the 9th day of the untimely martyr's death of Grand Duke Sergei Aleksandrovich, the unforgettable honorary member and chairman of the All-Russian Archaeological Society, having prayed for his soul's repose and mourned his irreplaceable loss, the Imperial Moscow Archaeological Society provides feelings of boundless devotion at the sacred feet of your imperial majesty and prays to the Almighty: may he give the Leaders of the Russian land invincible strength and complete victory over all of our enemies, both foreign and domestic; regarding our dear motherland, may he grant peace of mind to the Royal Family and to your majesty.

Chairman Count Uvarov, Secretary Trutovskii.

(*Novoe vremia*, 17 February 1905, p. 1)

These extracts illustrate how the death was presented, though questions can be asked too about how the facts of the matter were established. The first editorial which ran a day after the events themselves presented a snap response to the murder. It establishes basic context, informing a fact-minded public when and where Sergei was killed. Throughout these extracts we learn a little about Sergei himself, including the emotion his death allegedly caused in the wider public, a little about his military connections, and information about his social status, which identified his contribution to wider society. The official response to his death is reflected upon on 6 February, which concentrates on the day he was killed. Later, we read more about the social responses and grief that his death unleashed. Though the newspaper concentrates on establishing facts and is quite particular in its descriptions of Sergei's repose, we certainly do not learn everything about the case from these extracts, with more comment on the official response than that of the general public.

The drama is clear from the initial editorial. Sergei was 'viciously killed' in a 'terrible' event that will cause 'deep shock' to the 'whole of Russia'. Not much distance is implied between the writer of the editorial and the reader: moreover, it is assumed that everyone in the country will share in the grief caused. The connections between the imperial family and the people are minimal: 'everything bends before this grief'. This line does not change much over time, and the language used was dramatic: for example, a telegram from the Archaeological Society (mentioned 17 February above) informs us Sergei is an 'irreplaceable loss' to Russia and only 'complete victory' in the wake of his death over the 'enemies' of the land can avenge his passing. The extracts include a range of contributors, including editors, news correspondents and telegrams from the organizations that Sergei patronized. Including diverse respondents as well as repeating key details and commenting on 'the crowds' observing his grave are suggestive of the popular impact of Sergei's death. Dwelling on the emotion the murder caused confirms the importance of the deceased in the mind of the reader.

The story is also a window on the wider context of life in late Imperial Russia, and what conservative publications described as a 'time of troubles'. It claimed that the death is part of a 'terrible year of misery and trials'. Though not explicitly described, crises such as the strikes, riots and disorders seen during 1905 and uncertain progress during the Russo-Japanese War of 1904–5 are part of the mental world created by these articles: the war in particular was discussed in articles surrounding these extracts on the same pages. Alexander II's death is not mentioned and neither are those of various government ministers from 1901 to 1904, but we are told that 'murders ... have become so frequent in recent years', a clear reference to cases of anti-state violence. Reading the press closely involves considering what messages are communicated explicitly, and what is implied.

Some elements of the case are not discussed in much or in any detail. The unnamed assassin remains a distant figure throughout; though we hear his cries for 'freedom', he appears taciturn though somewhat clownish: 'passers-by, seeing this scene, thought that they were leading a drunk who had accidentally fallen and smashed his face'. In this way, the terrorist himself is dehumanized, with little said about the cause he represented beyond a vague and contestable notion of freedom. We are told that the 'revolutionary parties' have caused a great deal of suffering in Russia, but they are not described in depth and their causes are not sketched out in any detail. In contrast the case for Sergei's death being a significant blow is repeatedly and continually stressed: all of the focus is on the causes that the ex-member of the imperial family had stood for and how these were related to contemporary Russian governance.

Such reports are revealing in how they present the leading figures to the audience, addressing a readership of politically and socially aware people keyed into the major debates of the day. It is suggested that the Russian people as well as the readers of this particular newspaper were invested in the struggles of Russia's rulers and cared about their fates. The newspaper assumed an engaged reader for these stories but took a relatively loyal position on the assassination as a broadly pro-state organ that shared the concerns of high officialdom at a wave of attacks on Russia's rulers.

Conclusion

Newspapers are in the business of establishing 'the facts', but taking a purely literal approach towards the press in the late Imperial period will produce a limited, narrow reading of this invaluable and rich resource. In Russia, as elsewhere, newspapers do more than provide 'snap opinion': they function as repositories of cultural meaning, reflecting dominant discourses and practices of an age. In presenting a record of daily, monthly and annual change, newspapers build a record of the world around us, engaging with selected themes of the day in creating an impression of wider society. Thinking particularly about the Russian case, as well as identifying the content newspapers carry, we need to consider processes of censorship, administrative control, literacy patterns and changing social identities. By doing this, we can come to a more complex, nuanced picture of how the newspaper operated; focusing on the social interactions that reading and consuming newspapers foster can tell us much about the press as an institution, but also the world around them and the past we seek to understand. More work needs to be carried out on the institutions of the late Imperial press, and properly interdisciplinary approaches to the problems of the period using newspapers as one in a series of texts should be adopted. Some of the path-breaking ways in which scholars have assessed and utilized the Russian newspaper can signal the uses of these texts as a formidable part of the historian's toolkit.

Notes

1 I would like to thank Peter Waldron and Joan Neuberger for their comments on an earlier draft of this chapter.
2 The chapter uses 'press' to reference print media, including newspapers and journals. A key difference between the two was that most newspapers were published much more frequently than journals, and so were more concerned with creating an effect of immediacy.

3 Quoted in Mark D. Steinberg, *The Russian Revolution, 1905–1921* (Oxford: Oxford University Press, 2017), p. 125.

4 Stephen Vella, 'Newspapers', in Miriam Dobson and Benjamin Ziemann (eds.), *Reading Primary Sources: The Interpretation of Texts from Nineteenth- and Twentieth-Century History* (London: Routledge, 2009), pp. 192–208.

5 Anthony Smith, 'The Long Road to Objectivity and Back Again: The Kinds of Truth We Get in Journalism', in George Boyce, James Curran and Pauline Wingate (eds.), *Newspaper History from the Seventeenth Century to the Present Day* (London: Constable, 1978), p. 168.

6 Steinberg, *The Russian Revolution*, p. 4.

7 Ibid., pp. 158–9.

8 A single microfilm reel in the Library of Congress European Reading Room on 'revolutionary newspapers' aggregates a variety of newspapers from the end of 1917 until the start of 1918, including major publications like *Pravda* (*Truth*) and *Izvestiia* (*News*).

9 '*Novaia zhizn'*, 5 May 1917', and '*Rabotnitsa*, 20 May 1917', in Mark D. Steinberg (ed.), *Voices of Revolution, 1917*, documents translated by Marian Schwartz (London: Yale University Press, 2001), pp. 98–9.

10 Louise McReynolds, *The News Under Russia's Old Regime: The Development of a Mass-Circulation Press* (Princeton, NJ: Princeton University Press, 1990), p. 19.

11 Ibid., pp. 20–1. The *Northern Post* was renamed *Pravitel'stvennyi vestnik* (*The Government Herald*) in 1869.

12 Figures in McReynolds, *The News Under Russia's Old Regime*, Appendix A, Tables 1 and 3.

13 Ibid., Appendix A, Tables 4 and 5.

14 Ibid.

15 Figures in Jeffrey Brooks, *When Russia Learned to Read: Literacy and Popular Culture, 1861–1917* (Princeton, NJ: Princeton University Press, 1985), p. 118.

16 McReynolds, *The News Under Russia's Old Regime*, Appendix A, Table 3.

17 'Proekt osnovnykh gosudarstvennykh zakonov' (Project of the Fundamental Laws of the State), *Rech'*, 11 April 1906, 45, pp. 2–3.

18 On *The Herald*, see Anton A. Fedyashin, *Liberals under Autocracy: Modernization and Civil Society in Russia, 1866–1904* (Madison, WI: University of Wisconsin Press, 2012).

19 Katia Dianina, *When Art Makes News: Writing Culture and Identity in Late Imperial Russia, 1851–1900* (Dekalb, IL: Northern Illinois University Press, 2013).

20 Benjamin Rigberg, 'The Efficacy of Tsarist Censorship Operations, 1894-1917', *Jahrbücher für Geschichte Osteuropas*, 14 (1966), pp. 327–46; Caspar Ferenczi, 'Freedom of the Press Under the Old Regime, 1905–1914', in Olga Crisp and Linda Edmondson (eds.), *Civil Rights in Imperial Russia* (Oxford: Clarendon Press, 1989), pp. 191–214 (pp. 195–9).

21 Paul Avrich, *The Russian Anarchists* (Edinburgh, WV: AK Press, 2005), pp. 114–15.

22 Figures in Brooks, *When Russia Learned to Read*, p. 4.

23 On rural literacy, see Brooks, *When Russia Learned to Read*, pp. 241–5; on urban literacy, see Gregory Guroff and S. Frederick Starr, 'A Note on Urban Literacy in Russia, 1890–1914', *Jahrbücher für Geschichte Osteuropas*, 19 (1971), pp. 520–31.

24 D. I. Kol'tsov, 'Rabochie v 1905–1907 gg.', in L. Martov, P. Maslov and A. Potresov (eds.), *Obshchestvennoe dvizhenie v Rossii v nachale XX-go veka*, vol. 2, part 1 (St Petersburg: Obshchestvennaia pol'za, 1910), pp. 288–92.

25 W. Bassow, 'The Pre-Revolutionary Pravda and Tsarist Censorship', *American Slavic and East European Review*, 13 (1954), pp. 47–65.

26 Thomas Riha, "*Riech*': A Portrait of a Russian Newspaper', *Slavic Review*, 22 (1963), pp. 663–82.

27 W. E. Mosse, 'Imperial Favourite: V. P. Meshchersky and the Grazhdanin', *Slavonic and East European Review*, 59 (1981), pp. 529–47; David R. Costello, 'Novoe Vremia and the Conservative Dilemma, 1911–1914', *Russian Review*, 37 (1978), pp. 30–50.

28 B. I. Esin, *Russkaia dorevoliutsionnaia gazeta. 1702–1917* (Moscow: MGU, 1971); idem., *'Russkaia gazeta' i gazetnoe delo Rossii* (Moscow: MGU, 1981); idem., *Puteshestvie v proshloe* (Moscow: MGU, 1983).

29 Rigberg, 'Efficacy', pp. 337–8; Charles Ruud, *Fighting Words: Imperial Censorship and the Russian Press, 1804–1906* (Toronto: University of Toronto Press, 1982), chs. 9–12.

30 Ferenczi, 'Freedom of the Press', pp. 191–214.

31 McReynolds, *The News Under Russia's Old Regime*, pp. 146–67.

32 For further comment, see Robert Chartrier, *The Cultural Uses of Print in Early Modern France*, trans. Lydia Cochrane (Princeton, NJ: Princeton University Press, 1987), pp. 3–6.

33 Brooks, *When Russia Learned to Read*, pp. 117–23.

34 Mark D. Steinberg, *Moral Communities: The Culture of Class Relations in the Russian Printing Industry* (Berkeley, CA: University of California Press, 1992), pp. 235–6, 242–5.

35 Joan Neuberger, *Hooliganism. Crime, Culture and Power in St. Petersburg, 1900–1914* (London: University of California Press, 1993), p. 15.

36 Ibid., p. 17.

37 Daniel R. Brower, 'The Penny Press and Its Readers', in Stephen P. Frank and Mark D. Steinberg (eds.), *Cultures in Flux: Lower-Class Values, Practices, and Resistance in Late Imperial Russia* (Princeton, NJ: Princeton University Press, 1994), p. 153.

38 See for instance Louise McReynolds, *Russia at Play: Leisure Activities at the End of the Tsarist Era* (Ithaca, NY: Cornell University Press, 2003); idem., *Murder Most Russian: True Crime and Punishment in Late Imperial Russia* (Ithaca, NY: Cornell University Press, 2012).

39 Dianina, *When Art Makes News*, p. 7.

40 Mark D. Steinberg, *Petersburg Fin de Siècle* (New Haven, CT: Yale University Press, 2011), pp. 34–46.

41 Laura Engelstein, 'Revolution and the Theater of Public Life in Imperial Russia', in Isser Woloch (ed.), *Revolution and the Meanings of Freedom in the Nineteenth Century* (Stanford, CA: Stanford University Press, 1996), pp. 314–47.

42 Russian-language literature on regional papers is summarized in V. V. Shevtsov, *Tomskie gubernskie vedomosti' (1857–1917 gg.) v sotsiolkul'turnom i informatsionnom prostranstve sibiri* (Tomsk: Tomskii gosudarstvennyi universitet, 2012), pp. 13–16; this source is cited in a recent article which is also useful for the history of the press from 1700–1850: Alison K. Smith, 'Information and Efficiency: Russian Newspapers, ca. 1700-1850', in Simon Franklin and Katia Bowers (eds.), *Information and Empire. Mechanisms of Communication in Russia, 1600–1854* (Cambridge: Open Book Publishers, 2017), pp. 185–211.

43 Vella, *'Newspapers'*, p. 196. Adopting Vella's terminology, this section uses a 'questioning' approach in interpreting newspapers.

44 McReynolds, *The News Under Russia's Old Regime*, p. 230.

45 Figures in McReynolds, *The News Under Russia's Old Regime*, Appendices A, Table 6.

46 Russia used the Julian calendar until February 1918; in the nineteenth century the Russian calendar was twelve days behind the West. Between 1900 and 1918 the difference was thirteen days. I have kept to the so-called old style for all dates before 1918.

47 *Novoe vremia*, issues of 5, 6, 7 and 17 February 1905. All of the translations offered in this section are my own.

Further reading

Brooks, Jeffrey, *When Russia Learned to Read: Literacy and Popular Culture, 1861–1917* (Princeton, NJ: Princeton University Press, 1985).

Dianina, Katia, *When Art Makes News: Writing Culture and Identity in Late Imperial Russia, 1851–1900* (Dekalb, IL: Northern Illinois University Press, 2013).

Ferenczi, Caspar, 'Freedom of the Press under the Old Regime, 1905–1914', in Olga Crisp and Linda Edmondson (eds.), *Civil Rights in Imperial Russia* (Oxford: Clarendon Press, 1989), pp. 191–214.

Frank, Stephen P., and Mark D. Steinberg (eds.), *Cultures in Flux: Lower-Class Values, Practices, and Resistance in Late Imperial Russia* (Princeton, NJ: Princeton University Press, 1994).

Hickey, Michael C. (ed.), *Competing Voices from the Russian Revolution* (Oxford: Greenwood, 2011).

McReynolds, Louise, *The News Under Russia's Old Regime: The Development of a Mass-Circulation Press* (Princeton, NJ: Princeton University Press, 1990).

_____, *Murder Most Russian: True Crime and Punishment in Late Imperial Russia* (Ithaca, NY: Cornell University Press, 2012).

Neuberger, Joan, *Hooliganism: Crime, Culture and Power in St. Petersburg, 1900–1914* (London: University of California Press, 1993).

Rigberg, Benjamin, 'The Efficacy of Tsarist Censorship Operations, 1894–1917', *Jahrbücher für Geschichte Osteuropas*, 14 (1966), pp. 327–46.

Ruud, Charles, *Fighting Words: Imperial Censorship and the Russian Press, 1804–1906* (Toronto: University of Toronto Press, 1982).

Smith, Alison K., 'Information and Efficiency: Russian Newspapers, ca. 1700-1850', in S. Franklin and Katia Bowers (eds.), *Information and Empire: Mechanisms of Communication in Russia, 1600–1854* (Cambridge: Open Book Publishers, 2017), pp. 185–211.

Steinberg, Mark D., *Proletarian Imagination: Self, Modernity and the Sacred in Russia, 1910–1925* (Ithaca, NY: Cornell University Press, 2002).

_____, *The Russian Revolution, 1905–1921* (Oxford: Oxford University Press, 2017).

Online sources

Gosudarstvennaia publichnaia istoricheskaia biblioteka Rossii (*State Public Historical Library of Russia*) <http://elib.shpl.ru/ru/nodes/9347-elektronnaya-biblioteka-gpib>

Digital Collections University of Wisconsin-Madison Libraries. Russian Satirical Journals <http://digital.library.wisc.edu/1711.dl/EastEurope.RussianSatirical>

7   Surveillance reports[1]

Dakota Irvin

Introduction

'Among Soldiers: Dissatisfaction is openly expressed with the existing authorities, whom the soldiers do not want to fight for. The situation is serious and at the first sign of reversals at the front, it could become threatening'.[2] This surveillance report, from an anti-Bolshevik (White) counter-intelligence officer in the Urals city of Ekaterinburg in 1919, identified an alarming disposition among soldiers at the front lines of the Russian Civil War. Documents such as this, known as surveillance reports on the mood of the population (*svodki o nastroenii naseleniia*, or *svodki*), sought to collect and interpret the attitudes, opinions and behaviors of ordinary citizens. Covering a distinct period ranging from one week to one month, *svodki* attempted to document the predominant attitudes of different segments and classes of the population toward the major issues of the day, from food shortages and the cost of living, to political opposition and armed resistance. With their origins in the First World War, surveillance reports emerged as an invaluable instrument not only to assess the mood of the public, but also to transform it. By reducing society to essentialist categories such as 'workers', 'soldiers' and 'white-collar workers', mass surveillance reflected twentieth-century states' increased understanding of populations as raw, malleable materials that could be sculpted into an ideal ideological form. Surveillance and information gathering, carried out by the regular police, military authorities, and the Communist Party, expanded the state's reach into villages, workplaces and individual homes.

For historians, *svodki* present a rare opportunity to examine how the Soviet system functioned from the inside; to see and hear with the 'eyes and ears of the regime'.[3] The reports expose the methods of rule, political priorities, ideological frameworks and revolutionary aspirations of the regimes that created them. The evolution of Russian and Soviet surveillance practices, from the First World War to the heights of Stalinist Terror, raises broader questions about social engineering and the use of political violence in twentieth-century history. Furthermore, with the absence of reliable sources on public opinion, *svodki* can paint a revealing picture of social and individual experiences outside of the regime's official narrative. While focused primarily on dissent and opposition, *svodki* candidly document the immense challenges of everyday life and individual survival strategies during this period.

Surveillance reports have had a significant impact on secondary literature and major historiographical debates. *Svodki* played an important role in the emergence of the 'totalitarian' framework in Soviet history by documenting the expansive surveillance apparatus in the Soviet Union. The opening of the Soviet archives in the 1990s spurred a wave of new studies and discussions about state surveillance practices that challenged earlier narratives and influenced decades of future work. According to Peter Holquist, *svodki* 'have become nearly *de rigueur* for any study of the Soviet period'.[4] When contextualized and compared with other sources, surveillance reports have much to tell us about previously obscured topics in Russian and Soviet history.

This chapter presents a case study of Bolshevik and White *svodki* from the Russian Civil War. Although much of the historical scholarship has focused on surveillance under the rule of Joseph Stalin, I instead examine the years 1918–19 during the Civil War period, when the Reds and Whites struggled to determine the future of the country, and wartime policies of information gathering and monitoring became institutionalized. The formative experience of the Civil War deeply influenced Soviet state practices, and the surveillance system developed during this time contributed to the atmosphere of fear and paranoia that drove political terror in the 1930s. Rather than treating the higher echelons of the secret police apparatus in Moscow, I shift the focus to the provinces, and to the city of Ekaterinburg, in order to capture the local dynamics of state surveillance. A local perspective nuances national studies by raising fresh questions about the limits of state power and highlighting diverse and often contradictory processes of events outside of the capital. For the time being, Russian provincial archives also offer access to *svodki*, although the majority of surveillance documents remain closed to researchers in the archives of the security services.

The use of *svodki* in historical scholarship

Given the closed and secretive nature of the Soviet system, *svodki* have provided scholars the rare opportunity to assess popular sentiments outside of the regime's official documents. The distinguished scholar of Stalinism, Sheila Fitzpatrick, has called *svodki* 'the nearest approximation of public opinion surveys', although they are not without methodological challenges, as will be discussed later.[5] One of the major obstacles facing a researcher interested in *svodki* was, and remains, access and availability. Before the fall of the Soviet Union in 1991, Western scholars drew on archival collections available in the United States, in particular the records of the Smolensk Archive. During the Second World War, advancing German armies captured the records of the Smolensk Oblast Communist Party Committee, which eventually fell into US hands after the conclusion of the war. In 1956, Merle Fainsod concluded after analysing this collection, which included *svodki*, that the Soviet Union had been governed by a vast and intrusive 'totalitarian' state, which utilized surveillance and repression to control its citizens and hold onto power. In Smolensk, the powerful secret police relied on informers, denunciations and arrests to cast a dragnet over Soviet society, with the state monitoring and recording all aspects of everyday life.[6] For much of the Cold War period, this 'totalitarian' paradigm in Soviet history prevailed as a widespread academic and popular understanding. However, after gathering dust for decades after Fainsod's study, a new generation of historians tapped the archive's contents to produce groundbreaking studies on subjects such as the nature of Soviet governance, Stalinism in the provinces, and the Great Terror.[7] These so-called 'revisionists', which included among their ranks Sheila Fitzpatrick, challenged the totalitarian narrative, complicating our understanding of how the Soviet regime governed.[8]

The opening of the former Soviet archives in the early 1990s provided Western and Russian scholars unprecedented, although not unlimited, access to central and local records. The arrival of published collections of surveillance reports from the 1920s and 1930s further offered researchers the ability to work with *svodki* without stepping foot in a Russian archive.[9] In the 1990s and early 2000s, *svodki* as a source played a leading role in many important historical discussions. Sarah Davies worked extensively with *svodki* in her study of popular opinions under Stalinism, concluding that surveillance reports demonstrated that the regime's attempts to establish cultural hegemony had come up short: 'the Stalinist propaganda machine failed to extinguish an autonomous current of public opinion'.[10] A special 1997 issue of the journal *Cahiers du Monde russe* on newly available Soviet sources included several contributions on surveillance reports, including Lesley A. Rimmel's study of popular opinion in 1930s Leningrad. Using *svodki* to illuminate tensions between Soviet authorities and society and within society itself, Rimmel showed how surveillance reports can 'help to humanize an inhuman era' by giving voice to individual experiences and creating a complex mosaic of daily life under Stalinism.[11] Drawing on surveillance reports of the secret police in the 1920s, the Joint State Political Directorate (OGPU), D'Ann R. Penner fleshed out popular opinions among Cossacks in the Don region, underlining sundry political attitudes toward the Soviet regime, driven by both ideological and quotidian concerns.[12] These contributions convincingly demonstrate how *svodki* can provide a window into popular opinions and experiences traditionally absent from bureaucratic documents, as well as what James C. Scott termed 'hidden transcripts' – subaltern strategies of critique and resistance.[13] Moreover, Donald J. Raleigh positions *svodki* as an example *par excellence* of the Bolsheviks own 'hidden transcripts' – an 'internal' language of those in power that diverged and complimented 'external' pronouncements in propaganda and the press.[14]

In addition to opening new doors in the study of social history, *svodki* have also broadened our understanding of political transformations in the Soviet Union and beyond. In the 1990s and 2000s, a new generation of scholars drew on methodological approaches from the study of Nazi Germany and the Holocaust to reinterpret the concept of 'totalitarianism' in Soviet history. Zygmunt Bauman's investigation of the state's 'methods of social engineering' to remake, master, and mould society as a 'garden' inspired studies of Soviet practices of surveillance, propaganda and mass mobilization that challenged existing narratives.[15] In uncovering contemporaneous anti-Bolshevik *svodki* from the Russian Civil War, which shared a similar structure and ethos to their Soviet counterparts, Peter Holquist argued that mass surveillance and 'enlightenment' (rather than propaganda) were not unique to Bol-shevism, but rather representative of twentieth-century 'modern' state practices. These policies and their implementation arose from a shared Russian and European political culture of 'modernity' that was transformed by the outbreak of total war after 1914. Holquist and others point to deep continuities among pre-revolutionary, First World War, and Soviet use of information to control and shape society.[16] David L. Hoffman asserts that Stalinist leaders deployed surveillance and infor-mation collecting in the service of creating the 'New Soviet Person' by transform-ing individual subjectivities into expressions of the regime's ideological project. Surveillance practices introduced during the First World War expanded rapidly during the 1920s and 1930s, creating a complex system of agents and informers that strove to eradicate behaviours and mentalities deemed incompatible with the Stalinist order.[17]

The evolution of Soviet surveillance has also influenced narratives about the dynamics of mass violence and terror under Stalinism. The *svodki* from the Civil War, which included colourful language and glaring contradictions, transformed by the 1920s and 1930s into standardized reports structured around templates com-prised of contemporary slogans and political categories.[18] As Fitzpatrick notes in her work on peasants during collectivization, surveillance reports contained 'their own built-in bias: these channels existed specifically for the purpose of transmit-ting bad news'.[19] Tracy McDonald, in her study of the Riazan countryside, docu-mented a process where local and regional offices of the OGPU forwarded only the most sensational and troubling reports to the centre, presenting 'an unrelenting picture of rape, murder, banditry, arson, mayhem, and corruption' in the provinces. These chaotic scenes served to reinforce the regime's use of violence during collec-tivization.[20] By the early 1930s new practices such as internal passports bolstered the surveillance apparatus, and the secret police and Communist Party continued to circulate only the most threatening reports on the mood of the population.[21] As a result, the leadership became increasingly alarmed at the unrest brewing in the cities and the countryside, and 'thus ended up feeding on its own propaganda'. This paranoia, aided by the transmission of alarming *svodki*, emerged as a key con-tributor to the use of political violence in the Great Terror.[22] Surveillance reports have complicated our understanding of Soviet social and political history, offering glimpses into popular attitudes toward the regime as well as underlining the entan-glements between information collection and political violence.[23]

The researcher must take care, however, when analyzing *svodki*, as they pres-ent a variety of methodological challenges. As Rimmel cautions, 'ascertaining the veracity of government *svodki* will always be an art, not a science, that must be informed by one's knowledge of the era and supplemented by other kinds of sources'.[24] Nicolas Werth, a historian with extensive experience analyzing *svodki* from the Civil War until the 1930s, suggests that the reports themselves cannot pro-vide 'definitive answers'; rather, they offer the opportunity to ask questions, tests hypotheses, and open new lines of inquiry.[25] Similarly, Viktor Danilov and Alexis Berelowitch warn that *svodki* readers must always keep in mind that security agen-cies generated the reports with specific goals in mind, and while they can provide valuable insights into the experience of victims of political terror, this perspective is indelibly refracted through the eyes of the state.[26] Penner calls our attention to the anonymous creators of the *svodki*, who were in many cases unqualified, lower-level operatives tasked with drawing analytical conclusions about the mood of the population while fitting them into an established ideological framework. Penner does observe, however, that local surveillance reports carried more reliable information than those heavily edited versions that reached the top echelons of power.[27]

For these reasons, and other methodological concerns, some scholars have been keen to stress the limits of Soviet *svodki* as a source. Terry Martin argued that the imposition of ideological and social categories when compiling surveillance reports, particularly regarding the peasantry, led to the creation of 'artificial class divisions' that ultimately 'distort[ed] social reality'.[28] Ehren Park and David Brandenberger reject *svodki* as 'objective indices of public opinion or social unrest', asserting that they 'were essentially written by policemen for policemen'. Such anecdotal or often fabricated or exaggerated reports lack essential context, and without a clear understanding of the process of compilation, they hold limited value for analyzing Soviet society.[29] Jeremy Smith furthermore calls into question the reliability of statistics provided in surveillance reports, pointing to discrepancies in standards, collection practices and measurements, as well as the personal and political motivations of individual preparers. Smith concludes, 'it is hard to tell whether the reports represent an illustrative selection or a comprehensive listing'.[30] Nevertheless, while acknowledging the potential drawbacks and methodological questions raised by analyzing *svodki*, most scholars concur that they remain a valuable and promising avenue for further research, despite worsening archival access in the countries of the former Soviet Union.

Unfortunately for researchers interested in Soviet *svodki*, the opening of the archives yielded only ephemeral access to the files of the security services, which include the All-Russian Extraordinary Commission for Combatting Counter-Revolution and Sabotage (*Cheka*), the OGPU, the NKVD (People's Commissariat of Internal Affairs), and the KGB (Committee for State Security). The archives of the successor to these institutions, the FSB (Federal Security Service), have never been fully opened, and in today's political climate, remain difficult, if not impossible, for foreign or even Russian historians to access. Provincial archives, particularly the former archives of the Communist Party, have preserved many *svodki* from the Revolutionary and Civil War era, although accessibility is varied and increasingly limited. In Ekaterinburg, the Centre for the Documentation of Social Organizations of Sverdlovsk Oblast (TsDOOSO), the former party archive, provided the Soviet *svodki* discussed in this chapter. Since the provincial *Cheka* (*Gubcheka*) was nominally subordinated to the provincial Communist Party Committee (*Gubkom*), its collections often contain *svodki* and other documents from the security services. Many historians have thus turned to provincial archives as a way to find sources unavailable in the centre.

Anti-Bolshevik *svodki* are widely available to researchers in Russian state and regional archives. The State Archive of the Russian Federation (GARF) in Moscow holds extensive collections of the White movement across Russian and foreign territories, which are available online and allow limited searching functions. Both civilian and military institutions generated surveillance reports, and for the Whites in the East and Siberia, *fondy* (collections) for the Omsk Ministry of Internal Affairs (f. R1700), the Militia Department (f. R147), and the Ministry of Justice (f. R4369) all contain various civilian *svodki*. Military surveillance, one of the most powerful and feared forces in the anti-Bolshevik movement, can be found at the Russian State Military Archive (RGVA), although researchers should take care to obtain the proper permission and letters to receive access to the archival collections. The White military *svodki* presented in this chapter are from the Administration of the Siberian Army (f. 39736) records at RGVA. Finally, the Wrangel Military Archive at the Hoover Institution at Stanford University holds extensive records of military authorities from the Civil War in Southern Russia.

Historical context: surveillance and *svodki* in the Russian Revolution and Civil War

State surveillance and information gathering existed long before the 'totalitarian' regimes in the Soviet Union and Nazi Germany. In Russia, Tsar Nicholas I established the 'Third Department of His Imperial Majesty's Own Chancellery', a secret political police force, as a response to the Decembrist Uprising of 1825.[31] With a relatively small staff and a limited mandate to exercise oversight, the Third Department proved less effective than Western and Soviet historians often suggest, and after a series of high profile assassinations, it was dissolved in 1880 and replaced with the Police Department of the Ministry of Internal Affairs and the Department for Protecting Public Security and Order, known popularly as the *Okhranka*. The *Okhranka* waged a sustained yet unsuccessful campaign against the burgeoning revolutionary movement throughout the final decades of the Russian Empire, infiltrating socialist and terrorist organizations and keeping tabs on individual threats to the imperial order.[32] However, as Peter Holquist observes, the *Okhranka*'s work was consciously defined as 'oversight' (*nadzor*), rather than the Russian word for surveillance (*osvedomlenie*), 'a term invariably implying a two-way circuit of information'.[33] The tsarist state was concerned above all in maintaining security and order, rather than cataloguing information about the subjects it ruled over, and 'it certainly did not conceive of these sentiments as "political" in any modern sense'.[34]

The emergence of a modern surveillance programme occurred in Russia and across Europe during the First World War, a time marked by total mobilization of resources and subjects. Warring European states embarked on ambitious projects to 'manage' their populations as if they were material resources. Their efforts included perlustration (the intercepting and reading) of soldiers' and civilians' mail and generating detailed reports about attitudes toward the war effort and the government. However, the central state did not act alone in in these endeavours. Army commanders commissioned extensive reports on the mood among the soldiers and their attitudes toward the war, while local authorities in Russia's vast provinces sought to gauge the contours of public opinion on the ground. After a year of war and the spread of antisemitic accusations that Jews shirked military duty and created shortages by hoarding goods, central and local officials began regularly recording the mood of the Jewish population.[35] Surveillance reports also helped justify the mass deportations of 'unreliable' groups from frontline territories, often the Empire's non-Orthodox populations, who fell under suspicion of sympathizing with the Germans.[36] The First World War contributed to the expansion and institutionalization of practices with the aim of recording, explaining and shaping the opinions of civilian and military populations in the service of consolidating power.

The February Revolution of 1917 ushered in a wave of new freedoms and civil liberties and swept away despised institutions such as the *Okhrana* and the tsarist police. But rather than curbing surveillance and monitoring practices, the Provisional Government, the successor of the tsarist autocracy, expanded their reach. Well aware of the simmering social and political tensions that had brought down Nicholas II, the country's new leaders paid close attention to public opinion and surveillance. Widespread perlustration of civilian and military post continued unabated, commissars monitored attitudes among soldiers, and the highest echelons of the Provisional Government collected information about the mood of the population. It went as far as creating colour-coded maps measuring loyalty in the provinces.[37] The Provisional Government had good reasons to fear social unrest and popular discontent, especially outside of the capitals, as the establishment of a new political order proceeded chaotically and unevenly. A surveillance report sent to the Ministry of Internal Affairs from a rural commissar in Perm province in March 1917 offers a glimpse at these challenges: 'the population is left on its own, as rural governments do not enjoy any authority to preserve order and calm ... It is advisable to send lecturers as soon as possible to explain to the population the necessity of preserving order'.[38] Ultimately, as Hoffman observes, 'under the Provisional Government, then, surveillance became more developed, more routinized, and more political'.[39]

The October Revolution of 1917 propelled Russia toward fratricidal civil war. As opponents gathered on the peripheries of European Russia to organize armed resistance, determined political opposition and popular unrest presented grave challenges to the establishment of Soviet power. Yet even after taking power, Soviet leaders did not envision creating an all-encompassing surveillance apparatus to shape the minds and attitudes of the population over whom they now ruled. Instead, the regime exploited and expanded existing institutions that had emerged during the First World War, and which proved well-suited to the conditions of the Civil War. Perlustration of mail continued but its scope widened, as censors collected and recorded information not just from soldiers and those officially under suspicion, but all post circulating in the country. *Svodki* compilers relied on a variety of sources, including intercepted correspondence, intelligence and informer networks, news bulletins, letters to newspapers, and reports from local party activists.[40] Multiple institutions, including the Communist Party, civilian government, and military structures, generated their own surveys of the population's moods.[41] Founded in December 1917, the *Cheka* emerged as one of the regime's most feared instruments. Its agents undertook a relentless campaign against perceived enemies of the Soviet regime, culminating in mass arrests and violence during the Red Terror of 1918. The *Cheka* also assumed oversight over the surveillance apparatus, gathering *svodki* while evaluating reports created by other local and national organizations. Crucially, the secret police demanded not only the collection of information about the population's attitudes, but also its interpretation. It was not enough to record and document: this new form of surveillance required evaluation, explanation, and action.[42]

As the Civil War intensified and White armies threatened the existence of the Soviet regime, information became a valuable resource to be hoarded, similar to fuel, ammunition and food. These materials about the attitudes of people living across the country were then employed to realize social and political transformation. As Hoffman notes, 'Soviet leaders did not seek to discern popular sentiment in order to accommodate it'; rather, this information provided a mechanism to overcome Russia's 'bourgeois' traditions and psychologies and to realize socialist transformation. Popular attitudes toward the Soviet project, along with questions about food supply, wages, living conditions, education, and other concerns, assumed a new political significance. The regime came to view opposition or lack of enthusiasm for its policies as hostile leftovers from Russia's pre-revolutionary past, a challenge to be overcome by shaping hearts and minds. As a result, Soviet leaders cast their suspicions and dragnets not on individuals but on entire social classes, whose collective members carried the germs of counter-revolution.[43] Surveillance worked hand in hand with 'enlightenment', a euphemism for propaganda employed by both sides during the Civil War. Enlightenment measures included the circulation of printed materials, the work of local 'agitators' who spread regime messages on the ground, and 'reading huts' where peasants could gather to receive the latest news.[44] Information gathered through surveillance thus became a vital tool for moulding attitudes and behaviours in the service of a revolutionary, socialist transformation.

The Bolsheviks' victory in the Civil War has long been attributed to the use of surveillance, information gathering and propaganda. A leading scholar of the Russian Civil War, Peter Kenez, argued that the Bolsheviks 'were better in getting their message across to the people', not least because 'no previous state had similar ambitions, and no leaders had paid comparable attention to the issue of persuasion'.[45] According to Kenez, the Whites lacked a coherent ideology, and therefore their limited use of propaganda and surveillance failed to convey their message to the masses.[46] However, the Bolsheviks did not have a monopoly on these practices. While the anti-Bolshevik movements lacked aspects of the Bolsheviks' transformational agenda and expanded definition of the 'political', they engaged in widespread surveillance and 'enlightenment' practices.[47] In Southern Russia, White armies drew on networks of informants, agitators, and undercover agents to compile reports on attitudes among locals.[48] Intelligence and counterintelligence agencies clandestinely coordinated between anti-Bolshevik organizations in Soviet Russia and provided information on social and political conditions.[49] In the Don region, Cossack leaders founded the Don Information

Bureau, an organization that collected information gathered through surveillance and transmitted the regime's propaganda. For Holquist, the bureau's efforts represented 'the attempt to construct a political circuit between citizens and authority, with information as the necessary conduit'. Thus, gathering surveillance and using information to transfigure a pliable population was not a distinct feature of the Bolshevik revolution; rather, it reflected long-simmering trends in Russian political culture and the emergence of modern strategies of governance during the First World War.[50] The institutionalization of these methods, forged in the Civil War, shaped the course of Soviet history and played a central role in cultivating the Stalinist terror of the 1930s.[51]

Case study: *svodki* from the Civil War in Ekaterinburg, 1919–20

The following case study examines *svodki* created in the provincial city of Ekaterinburg during the Russian Civil War. Founded by Peter the Great in 1723 and known as the 'capital of the Urals', Ekaterinburg in 1917 was an important industrial city of more than 70,000 that lay at the intersection of several major railroad lines. After the October Revolution, the Bolsheviks held power until July 1918, when anti-Bolshevik forces led by soldiers of the Czechoslovak Legion captured the city and drove Soviet power out of the Urals. For the following year, residents lived under several White governments, including the dictatorship of Admiral Aleksandr Kolchak, before the Red Army's successful offensive recaptured Ekaterinburg in July 1919. Even though the front had moved far beyond the Urals, in the first years after the Civil War the local branch of the secret police, the *Gubcheka*, ruthlessly repressed real and imagined enemies, such as White 'bands', Red Army deserters and peasant uprisings. The quick succession of Whites and Reds regimes offers the ideal conditions for examining surveillance practices and *svodki*, not least because Ekaterinburg emerged as an operational centre and the headquarters of both regimes' secret police. Furthermore, analyzing documents from a provincial region outside of European Russia allows for a more nuanced understanding of both the Civil War and state surveillance practices.

Red and White *svodki* from the Civil War shared many common features. With titles usually consisting of 'Report on the Political Situation' or simply 'Report on the Situation', these documents covered a distinct time, ranging generally from one week to one month. Each *svodka* was broken down into several essentialist categories, with the aim of capturing a range of opinions of society, classes, and social organizations. Headings included 'among workers', 'among soldiers', 'among white-collar workers' (*sluzhashchie*), 'public opinion' (which connoted the *intelligentsia*), and others. These summaries attempted, in several paragraphs, to describe and record the mood and general disposition of these groups toward the major political questions of the day, such as the war, the current government, the food supply situation, working conditions and a host of others. The sources for the *svodki* included police reports, local party activists, telegraph news, newspaper articles, informant networks, denunciations, and widespread perlustration of private correspondence.[52]

Let us start by analysing two *svodki* compiled seven months apart in Ekaterinburg during the height of the Civil War, concerning the mood of workers. The first, from the anti-Bolshevik Counter-Intelligence Department of the Siberian Army garrisoned in Ekaterinburg, details the week of 23–30 May 1919. This was a time of heightened anxiety for the Whites, as a failed offensive in April had been followed by a swift counterattack from the Red Army that directly threatened the Urals. Reversals on the battlefield contributed to growing social unrest and dissatisfaction with the Kolchak regime, as well as increased surveillance by concerned White authorities.

> Constant secret meetings of workers' representatives of all factories in urban settlements [have been observed]. Their mood is agitated, with accusations against the authorities of inaction and failing to protect the interests of the working class. There is general indignation toward the failure to curb the increasing cost of living. Salaries are too low. Recently, a defiant attitude of workers to the administration of factories has been noticed, manifesting itself in the failure to fulfill urgent government orders. There are also cases of workers' refusals to carry out the work assigned to them.[53]

In the first half of the report, the counterintelligence officer responsible for the *svodka* identifies agitated moods and nascent political organization among workers in Ekaterinburg as challenges to the regime. Well aware of the Whites' unpopularity among the working classes – a result of political repression and draconian labour policies – many anti-Bolshevik military *svodki* treated 'workers' as an innately hostile social category.[54] Comparing the report with contemporaneous documents from critics of the regime shows that military intelligence accurately summarized many popular complaints. Interestingly, the causes of unrest are presented primarily in economic terms, with issues such as salaries, cost of living and labour rights blamed for the agitation. But when these restive workers translated attitudes into deeds, their actions assumed a political nature, such as the 'failure' to deliver government production orders – a serious crime in the eyes of the state. This could also have been a tactic to assign blame for falling production on workers' attitudes rather than the owners' or the government's mismanagement. This *svodka* encapsulates the Whites' suspicion of workers as a class, similar to the Bolshevik attacks against the 'bourgeoisie', while also entangling political and economic concerns that contributed to resistance.

The hostile approach toward the working classes in the first *svodka* might help readers recognize that this document came from the anti-Bolshevik movement. However, a second illuminating example comes by way of the Ekaterinburg *Gubcheka*, from December 1919, months after Ekaterinburg had been captured from the Whites. With the Civil War continuing to rage in Siberia, the situation in the city remained tense as the secret police rooted out suspected collaborators and enemies of the regime. Thousands of residents fled Ekaterinburg with the White armies, and those who remained, including traditional supporters of the Bolsheviks, fell under suspicion and increased surveillance. Additionally, many workers in Ekaterinburg's major factories met the new authorities with indifference and even resistance, despite the Communist Party's claim to represent and personify their collective interests.

> The shortage of food has been taken advantage of by the counter-revolutionary elements and Kolchak's agents, who have campaigned and urged the workers to go on strike. This intensified agitation was conducted among the workers of the mint of the city of Ekaterinburg …. It was led by the old workers of the mint, who have been working here for several years and enjoy some popularity among the less conscious workers. As a result of this, on 12 December, the mint workers walked out of work and demanded food rations …. The *Gubcheka* has registered [the instigators] with the Secret Operations Department, installed surveillance [at the factory], and begun an investigation.[55]

As with the White *svodka*, the *Gubcheka* agents compiling this December 1919 report identified the causes of unrest as economic: the striking workers wanted food, not political change. Yet the Bolshevik secret police ascribed an overtly political nature to these demands, labelling the organizers as 'counter-revolutionary elements and Kolchak's agents' taking advantage of shortages. It was damaging for the revolutionary project to have senior workers, natural Bolshevik constituents, organizing labour resistance against the 'owners' of the factory, the Soviet state. Walking out or striking was thus a political crime against the regime; accordingly, the same report blamed 'Mensheviks' and 'White-Guard organizations' for labour unrest observed at other city factories and among workers at the railway station.[56] The designation of 'less conscious' workers reflected the Bolsheviks' ideological construction of the 'worker' as a revolutionary subject: opposition to Soviet labour policies reflected the 'immaturity' of elements of the Russian working class, which made them susceptible to 'Menshevik' propaganda.[57] In this way, Soviet authorities 'ascribed' class identities onto its subjects in order to simplify social organization and to define allies and enemies of the regime.[58] Bolshevik ideology thus provided an iron framework to interpret attitudes and actions, contributing to a broadening definition of what constituted 'political'.[59] *Svodki* such as this transmitted a Manichean picture of counter-revolutionary agitation and political resistance through the hierarchies of the Soviet state, which responded with increased efforts to eliminate resistance and reshape society in its own image.

Soviet security services did not blame all shortcomings and public unrest on 'saboteurs', 'counter-revolutionary agents' or Mensheviks, however. *Gubcheka svodki* from 1919 to 1920 in Ekaterinburg reflect a desperate awareness of the weak foundations of Soviet power. The introduction of War Communism in 1918, the abolition of private trade, and forced grain requisitions led to violent clashes with the peasantry, including large-scale armed rebellions. Deserters, former White soldiers, and 'bandits' still roamed the remote forested regions of the Urals, raiding rural settlements and killing Soviet representatives. Despite emerging victorious against the Whites, Soviet rule remained weak and unable to impose its authority through poorly staffed and underfunded local institutions. Surveillance reports from this time period often included categories such as 'shortcomings of soviet work', which outlined the failures of local administrations. One particularly damning report came on the militia (police) and the fledgling Soviet judicial system:

> Local administrative departments are weak. There is almost no recording of those who fled with the Whites returning. There is also no registration of the population, which contributes to the concealment of deserters and counter-revolutionary elements. The local militias are organized poorly. There is no discipline, and militiamen often get drunk and neglect their duties. The detainees held by the militia are poorly guarded and there are frequent escapes .... The local people's courts[60] are also not functioning well. They are filled with a majority of non-party members from the old system and not yet trained in the new law.[61]

Turning their gaze inwards, these *Gubcheka* agents evinced concern about the troubled functioning of the early Soviet government, in particular local soviets' management of discipline and security. After the defeat of the Whites and execution of Admiral Kolchak in February 1920, many of those who had fled returned to Ekaterinburg, causing local officials to worry about the incomers' political 'reliability'. The failure to register White refugees, and even all segments of the population, presented a threat to security and the ability of the secret police to conduct proper surveillance. This *svodka* also establishes a direct connection between the labour unrest that 'counter-revolutionary elements' in the previous document stirred up and the failure of the local administration to secure the city. Lack of discipline and drunkenness among militiamen had led to escapes and the breakdown of policing, an essential tool of the *Gubcheka*'s surveillance apparatus. Finally, the political reliability and past education of court employees undermined the revolutionary mission of the Soviet justice system, although it must be noted that by this time very few people across the entire country had been trained in the 'new law'. Moreover, the lack of Communist Party members in any civilian institution drew suspicion from the security services and the party itself, although the latter lacked the manpower to staff these organizations. Soviet *svodki* presented a chaotic, disorderly, and violent picture of Soviet power in the localities, one that frequently explained shortcomings and undesirable circumstances as the result of political opposition, thereby justifying the use of force.

While *svodki* reflect the assumptions of the intelligence officers and secret policeman who created them, they present candid understandings of the political situation on the ground. Diverging from other public proclamations and internal reports, some even offer criticism of the regime. Consider this prescient analysis of workers' unrest by a White counter-intelligence officer in June 1919 on the eve of the Ekaterinburg's fall to the Red Army:

> Calmness among the workers can come only when the government follows its declarations. That is, a democratic state which, through its social policy, will provide the people and the working masses access to the material and cultural

progress of the country, to give them a vital interest in it and the opportunity to realize their share in the overall productivity through increased wages, reduced working hours and improved living conditions.[62]

This fragment appears in an otherwise standard *svodka* compiled during the final days of anti-Bolshevik rule in Ekaterinburg. The officer does not indicate that these lines were quoted from material gathered by surveillance, and the report, written as a narrative, frequently refers to 'reactionary elements' gaining power in the military and the government. With forthright clarity, the report criticizes the government's failure to deliver its promises and concisely articulates popular political and economic criticisms of the White regime. The counter-intelligence officer did not necessarily evince support for the opposition, acknowledging only that the 'left-wing movement has been given special impetus by the unprecedented rise in cost of living and the total absence of daily necessities'.[63] But this sober reporting must be read as an explicit criticism of the government and its actions, effectively blaming the Whites for causing agitated moods rather than categorizing the population's complaints as political dissent. It also raises the broader question of how 'societal calm' could be achieved when secret policemen had little faith in the regime. The *svodka* succinctly outlines the roots of the political crisis that the Whites' critics also articulated: failed government leadership, hostility to workers and economic collapse. When analysed alongside other sources, this *svodka* provides illuminating insights into the history of the anti-Bolshevik movement and the political dynamics of the time.

Conclusion

Surveillance reports on the mood of the population offer unique perspectives and insights not otherwise found in Russian and Soviet archival documents. They express the priorities and anxieties of the state institutions that created them, providing a window into the internal functioning of Soviet and anti-Bolshevik governments, and uncovering the logic of what behaviours constituted 'political' action. Surveillance not only compiled information, but also interpreted and acted upon it. *Svodki* emerged as a vital instrument in the Soviet transformation of society and individual subjectivities, providing the justification and targeting for the regime's 'enlightenment' campaigns, as well as repression and violence. The process of creating the *svodki*, compiling surveillance information and tapping informant networks and denunciations, speaks to the bureaucratic ethos of the Soviet regime and the influence of wartime practices. An understanding of Soviet surveillance reports and practices is necessary for any analysis of the mass violence and political terror that marked the Stalinist 1930s and postwar years. *Svodki* help to uncover 'hidden transcripts' and subaltern strategies of resistance and survival. In their frequent cataloguing of opinions, agitated moods, rumors, anti-government jokes, labour organization, and societal demands, *svodki* shine a light on how ordinary citizens understood, responded to and resisted the state's attempts to radically transform society. These reports should not be accepted uncritically, or without contextualization, and cannot tell the entire story on their own. But as a colourful tile of a larger mosaic, *svodki* are a vitally important source in the study of Russian and Soviet history.

Notes

1 Thanks to Donald J. Raleigh for comments on an earlier draft of this chapter.
2 Russian State Military Archive (RGVA), f. 39736, op. 1, d. 121, l. 11.
3 V. S. Izmozik, *Glaza i ushi rezhima: Gosudarstvennyi politicheskii kontrol'za naseleniem sovetskoi Rossii v 1918–1928 gg.* (Saint Petersburg: Izd-vo Sankt-Peterburg. Un-ta ekonomiki i finansov, 1995).
4 Peter Holquist, 'Anti-Soviet *Svodki* from the Civil War: Surveillance as a Shared Feature of Russian Political Culture', *Russian Review*, 56 (1997), pp. 445–50 (p. 445).
5 Sheila Fitzpatrick, 'Impact of the Opening of Soviet Archives on Western Scholarship on Soviet Social History', *Russian Review*, 74 (2015), pp. 377–400 (p. 387).
6 Merle Fainsod, *How Russia Is Ruled* (Cambridge, MA: Harvard University Press, 1967), pp. 390–1, 456–7.
7 For example, see Merle Fainsod, *Smolensk under Soviet Rule* (Cambridge, MA: Harvard University Press, 1958); J. Arch Getty, *Origins of the Great Purges: The Soviet Communist Party Reconsidered, 1933–1938* (Cambridge: Cambridge University Press, 1985); Roberta T. Manning, 'Government in the Soviet Countryside in the Stalinist Thirties: The Case of Belyi Raion in 1937', *The Carl Beck Papers in Russian and East European Studies*, 301 (1984).
8 For example, see Sheila Fitzpatrick, *Education and Social Mobility in the Soviet Union, 1921–1932* (Cambridge: Cambridge University Press, 1979); Lynne Viola, *The Best Sons of the Fatherland: Workers in the Vanguard of Soviet Collectivization* (New York, NY: Oxford University Press, 1987); Alexander Rabinowitch, *The Bolsheviks Come to Power: The Revolution of 1917 in Petrograd* (New York, NY: Norton, 1976); Getty, *Origins of the Great Purges*; Manning, 'Government in the Soviet Countryside in the Stalinist Thirties'.
9 For example, see Nicolas Werth and Gaël Moullec (eds.), *Rapports secrets soviétiques: La société russe dans les documents confidentiels (1921–1991)* (Paris: Gallimard, 1995); G. F. Dobronozhenko (ed.), *VChK-OGPU o politicheskikh nastroeniiakh severnogo krest'ianstva, 1921–1927 gody. Po materialam informatsionnykh svodok VChK-OGPU* (Syktyvkar: Syktyvkarskii gos. universitet, 1995); A. Berelowitch and V. Danilov (eds.), *Sovetskaia derevnia glazami VChk-OGPU-NKVD, 1918–1939*, vol. 1 (Moscow: ROSSPEN, 2000); R. Podkur and V. Chentsov, *Dokumenty organov gosudarstvennoi bezopasnosti USSR 1920–1930-x godov: istochnikovedcheskii analiz* (Ternopol: Zbruch, 2010).
10 Sarah Davies, *Popular Opinion in Stalin's Russia: Terror, Propaganda, and Dissent, 1934–1941* (Cambridge: Cambridge University Press, 1997), pp. 183–4.
11 Lesley A. Rimmel, '*Svodki* and Popular Opinion in Stalinist Leningrad', *Cahiers du Monde russe*, 40 (1999), pp. 217–34 (p. 233).
12 D'Ann R. Penner, 'Ports of Access into the Mental and Social Worlds of Don Villagers in the 1920s and 1930s', *Cahiers du Monde russe*, 40 (1999), pp. 171–97 (pp. 174–8).
13 James C. Scott, *Domination and the Arts of Resistance: Hidden Transcripts* (New Haven, CT: Yale University Press, 1990), p. xii.
14 Donald J. Raleigh, 'Languages of Power: How the Saratov Bolsheviks Imagined Their Enemies', *Slavic Review*, 57 (1998), pp. 320–49.
15 Zygmunt Bauman, *The Holocaust and Modernity* (Ithaca, NY: Cornell University Press, 2000), p. 18.

16 Holquist, 'Anti-Soviet *Svodki* from the Civil War,' pp. 445–50; idem., *Making War, Forging Revolution: Russia's Continuum of Crisis, 1914–1921* (Cambridge, MA: Harvard University Press, 2002).

17 David L. Hoffman, *Cultivating the Masses: Modern State Practices and Soviet Socialism, 1914–1939* (Ithaca, NY: Cornell University Press, 2011), pp. 200–11, 235–7.

18 Andrea Graziosi, 'The New Soviet Archival Sources: Hypotheses for a Critical Assessment', *Cahiers du Monde russe*, 40 (1999), pp. 13–63 (p. 36).

19 Sheila Fitzpatrick, *Stalin's Peasants: Resistance and Survival in the Russian Village after Collectivization* (New York, NY, and Oxford: Oxford University Press, 1994), p. 327.

20 Tracy McDonald, *Face to the Village: The Riazan Countryside under Soviet Rule, 1921–1930* (Toronto: University of Toronto Press, 2011), pp. 24–6.

21 David R. Shearer, *Policing Stalin's Socialism: Repression and Social Order in the Soviet Union, 1924–1953* (New Haven, CT: Yale University Press, 2009), pp. 179, 249.

22 Graziosi, 'The New Soviet Archival Sources', p. 38.

23 Recent works that utilize *svodki* include Jeffrey W. Jones, *Everyday Life and the Reconstruction of Soviet Russia During and After the Great Patriotic War, 1943–1948* (Bloomington, IN: Slavica Publishers, 2008) and Rósa Magnúsdóttir, *Enemy Number One: The United States of America in Soviet Ideology and Propaganda, 1945–1959* (New York, NY: Oxford University Press, 2018).

24 Rimmel, '*Svodki* and Popular Opinion in Stalinist Leningrad', p. 233.

25 Nicolas Werth, 'Une source inédite: les svodki de la Tchéka-OGPU', *Revue des Études Slaves*, 66 (1994), pp. 17–27 (p. 27).

26 Viktor Danilov and Alexis Berelowitch, 'Les documents de la VČK-OGPU-NKVD sur la campagne soviétique, 1918–1937', *Cahiers du Monde russe*, 35 (1994), pp. 633–40 (p. 639).

27 Penner, 'Ports of Access into the Mental and Social Worlds of Don Villagers', pp. 174–5.

28 Terry Martin, 'Obzory OGPU i sovetskie istoriki', in Iu. L. D'iakov (ed.), *"Sovershenno sekretno:" Liubianka-Stalinu o polozhenii v strane (1922–1934 gg.)*, Vol. 1, Part 1 (Moscow: IRI RAN, 2001), p. 24.

29 Ehren Park and David Brandenberger, 'Imagined Community? Rethinking the Nationalist Origins of the Contemporary Chechen Crisis', *Kritika: Explorations in Russian and Eurasian History*, 5 (2004), pp. 543–60 (p. 554).

30 Jeremy Smith, 'Nation Building and National Conflict in the USSR in the 1920s', *Ab Imperio*, 3 (2001), pp. 221–65 (pp. 248–9).

31 For more on the Third Department, see Sidney Monas, *The Third Section: Police and Society in Russia under Nicholas I* (Cambridge, MA: Harvard University Press, 1961).

32 For more on the *Okhrana*, see Jonathan W. Daly, *The Watchful State: Security Police and Opposition in Russia, 1906–1917* (Dekalb, IL: Northern Illinois University Press, 2004), Z. I. Peregudova, *Politicheskii sysk v Rossii (1880–1917)* (Moscow: Rossiiskaia politicheskaia entsiklopedia, 2000).

33 Peter Holquist, '"Information is the Alpha and Omega of Our Work": Bolshevik Surveillance in its Pan-European Context', *Journal of Modern History*, 69 (1997), pp. 415–50 (p. 420, note 15).

34 Holquist, 'Anti-Soviet *Svodki*', p. 448.

35 Peter Gattrell, *Russia's First World War: A Social and Economic History* (London: Routledge, 2005), pp. 88–90; Oleg Budnitskii, *Russian Jews Between the Reds and the Whites, 1917–1920*, trans. Timothy J. Portice (Philadelphia, PA: University of Pennsylvania Press, 2012), p. 186.

36 Eric Lohr, *Nationalizing the Russian Empire: The Campaign Against Enemy Aliens during World War I* (Cambridge, MA: Harvard University Press, 2003), pp. 152–3.

37 Hoffman, *Cultivating the Masses*, p. 186.

38 Center for the Documentation of Social Organizations of Sverdlovsk Oblast (TsDOOSO), f. 41, op. 2, d. 348, l. 10.

39 Hoffman, *Cultivating the Masses*, pp. 186–7.
40 Matthew E. Lenoe, 'Letter-Writing and the State. Reader Correspondence with Newspapers as a Source for Early Soviet History', *Cahiers du Monde russe*, 40 (1999), pp. 139–69 (p. 143).
41 Hoffman, *Cultivating the Masses*, pp. 195–7.
42 Holquist, '"Information is the Alpha and Omega of Our Work"', pp. 430–2.
43 Hoffman, *Cultivating the Masses*, pp. 197–200.
44 Holquist, '"Information is the Alpha and Omega of Our Work"', p. 435.
45 Peter Kenez, *The Birth of the Propaganda State: Soviet Methods of Mass Mobilization, 1917–1929* (Cambridge: Cambridge University Press, 1985), p. 4.
46 Ibid., pp. 63–4.
47 Christopher Lazarski, 'White Propaganda Efforts in the South during the Russian Civil War, 1918–19 (The Alekseev-Denikin Period)', *Slavonic and East European Review*, 70 (1992), pp. 688–707.
48 Hoffman, *Cultivating the Masses*, pp. 197–8.
49 Viktor Bortnevski, 'White Intelligence and Counter-Intelligence during the Russian Civil War', *Carl Beck Papers*, 1108 (1995), pp. 1–36.
50 Holquist, 'Anti-Soviet *Svodki*', pp. 446–8.
51 See Sheila Fitzpatrick's influential chapter, 'The Civil War as a Formative Experience', in Abbot Gleason, Peter Kenez and Richard Stites (eds.), *Bolshevik Culture* (Bloomington, IN: Indiana University Press, 1985), pp. 47–76.
52 As Donald J. Raleigh notes, by 1920 the *Cheka* had assumed total control over perlustration and surveillance of mail; Donald J. Raleigh, *Experiencing Russia's Civil War: Politics, Society, and Revolutionary Culture in Saratov, 1917–1922* (Princeton, NJ: Princeton University Press, 2002), p. 391.
53 RGVA, f. 39736, op. 1, d. 121, l. 10.
54 For more on the Whites' hostility toward workers, see Smele, *Civil War in Siberia*, pp. 340–61.
55 TsDOOSO, f. 76, op. 1, d. 780, l. 29.
56 Ibid.
57 Raleigh, *Experiencing Russia's Civil War*, pp. 365–7.
58 Sheila Fitzpatrick, 'Ascribing Class: The Construction of Social Identity in Soviet Russia', *Journal of Modern History*, 65 (1993), pp. 745–70 (pp. 745–6).
59 Holquist, '"Information is the Alpha and Omega of Our Work"', p. 437.
60 People's courts were established in November 1917 after the October Revolution, with the intent of constructing an entirely new 'revolutionary' legal system on the shattered foundations of the 'bourgeois' courts. The practices and rulings of these locally-elected courts varied widely across Soviet territories, and came to be used as an instrument to maintain social stability and curb the spread of vigilante justice (*samosud*); Aaron B. Retish, 'Controlling Revolution: Understandings of Violence through the Rural Soviet Courts, 1917–1923', *Europe-Asia Studies*, 65 (2013), pp. 1789–806 (pp. 1793–4).
61 TsDOOSO, f. 76, op. 1, d. 780, l. 17.
62 RGVA, f. 39736, op. 1, d. 121, l. 12.
63 Ibid.

Further reading

Daly, Jonathan W., *The Watchful State: Security Police and Opposition in Russia, 1906–1917* (Dekalb, IL: Northern Illinois University Press, 2004).
Fainsod, Merle, *How Russia Is Ruled* (Cambridge, MA: Harvard University Press, 1967).
Fitzpatrick, Sheila, 'Impact of the Opening of Soviet Archives on Western Scholarship on Soviet Social History', *Russian Review*, 74 (2015), pp. 377–400.

Graziosi, Andrea, 'The New Soviet Archival Sources: Hypotheses for a Critical Assessment', *Cahiers du Monde russe*, 40 (1999), pp. 13–63.

Hoffman, David L., *Cultivating the Masses: Modern State Practices and Soviet Socialism, 1914–1939* (Ithaca, NY: Cornell University Press, 2011).

Holquist, Peter, 'Anti-Soviet Svodki from the Civil War: Surveillance as a Shared Feature of Russian Political Culture', *Russian Review*, 56 (1997), pp. 445–50.

———, '"Information is the Alpha and Omega of Our Work": Bolshevik Surveillance in its Pan-European Context', *Journal of Modern History*, 69 (1997), pp. 415–50.

———, *Making War, Forging Revolution: Russia's Continuum of Crisis, 1914–1921* (Cambridge, MA: Harvard University Press, 2002).

Kenez, Peter, *The Birth of the Propaganda State: Soviet Methods of Mass Mobilization, 1917–1929* (Cambridge: Cambridge University Press, 1985).

McDonald, Tracy, *Face to the Village: The Riazan Countryside under Soviet Rule, 1921–1930* (Toronto: University of Toronto Press, 2011).

Penner, D'Ann R., 'Ports of Access into the Mental and Social Worlds of Don Villagers in the 1920s and 1930s', *Cahiers du Monde russe*, 40 (1999), pp. 171–97.

Rimmel, Lesley A., '*Svodki* and Popular Opinion in Stalinist Leningrad', *Cahiers du Monde russe*, 40 (1999), pp. 217–34.

Shearer, David R., *Policing Stalin's Socialism: Repression and Social Order in the Soviet Union, 1924–1953* (New Haven, CT: Yale University Press, 2009).

Smele, Jonathan D., *Civil War in Siberia: The Anti-Bolshevik Government of Admiral Kolchak, 1918–1920* (New York, NY: Cambridge University Press, 1996).

8 Soviet autobiographies

Katy Turton

Introduction

Shortly after the seizure of power by the Bolsheviks in October 1917, the American journalist John Reed decided to travel out of Petrograd with a group of Red Guards in order to further his understanding of the unfolding revolution. Stopped by soldiers en route to Romanov, Reed was almost shot because his pass, which did carry the seal of the Military Revolutionary Committee, did not match those of his companions and, on top of this, the soldiers could not read. It was only after a local woman read the pass out to the soldiers that Reed's life was spared and only after a literate member of the local Regimental Committee re-read the pass and explained who Reed was that he was properly welcomed by the local troops.[1] Identity, or rather being able to prove one's identity, was all in the Soviet regime. A written, verified and acceptable autobiography was the most important document a Soviet citizen could produce. It defined a citizen's status, guaranteed his or her access to education, employment, housing, food, health care, and established his/her legal and political rights. Conversely, a less than satisfactory autobiography could expose an individual as a class or state enemy and doom that person to a variety of deprivations and punishments. During the worst times of the Terror, the life stories of citizens were distorted and falsified to justify their arrest, imprisonment, exile or execution.

Western scholars are used to exploring autobiographies as documents written at the whim of the individual, for private or personal reasons (including to make money), and shared voluntarily with the reading public. They are distinct from memoirs because rather than deal with a particular part of an individual's life, often their public achievements, they focus on the total life of the individual up to the point of writing, including in particular his or her internal experience.[2]

When faced with Soviet autobiographies, it is important to remember that these documents tend not to meet any of these criteria. In the Soviet Union, autobiographical documents were written at the behest of, and submitted to, societies, organizations, committees, the Party and the state, for official reasons and were permanently available to the political police.[3] Other autobiographies were commissioned by the state to be published for educational and ideological reasons.[4] A collective, rather than an individual, identity was central to these works and, some have argued, such autobiographies were written as much to conceal the authentic self as to reveal it. In fact, it is generally agreed that Russian autobiographies written in the late Imperial and the post-Soviet period do not follow the classic Western model, embodied in the works of Rousseau.

On the other hand, autobiographies around the world are recognized as highly unstable sources which regularly stretch or defy the parameters of the genre and scholars of a variety of disciplines must grapple with their contradictory nature. Autobiographies seem to offer both the greatest opportunity for insight into the personal feelings, thoughts and motivations of an individual and the greatest challenges in disentangling the unpredictable and unreliable influences of such factors as memory and hindsight, political context and self-censorship, personal motivations and literary traditions on the texts. Thus, scholars in a range of fields have developed methodologies to deal with the multiple challenges such sources pose and have successfully based diverse studies on them, from in-depth analyses of individual autobiographies and micro-histories to prosopographical studies of multiple autobiographies by a particular group.[5]

In broad terms, there are two approaches to autobiographies. The first, literary approach, considers autobiographies both as individual texts and as examples of the genre and explores their contents to gain an understanding of autobiography itself.[6] The autobiographical narrative as a performance is central here, with attention paid in particular to language and linguistic choices. The second, more historical approach, uses autobiographies as sources to gain an understanding of the subject of a particular autobiography or to further knowledge of the society to which the autobiographer belonged. While the former is concerned above all with the structure and performance of the autobiography, the latter is more interested in the contents and their authenticity.[7]

Historians continue to debate whether autobiographies can be understood as an authentic retelling of an individual's life based on verifiable details or whether the amorphous nature of the genre, the instability of the narrative 'I' and the difficulties posed by the unreliability of memory and hindsight prevent autobiographies being used as historical documents at all.[8] In the earliest stages of historical enquiry, eye-witness testimony was seen as the most reliable form of source material, but with the professionalization of the discipline and the increased emphasis on scientific and empirical enquiry, autobiography became discredited as evidence.[9] Later, the advent of gender and post-colonial studies, as well as the development of the theories of structuralism, post-structuralism and post-modernism, restored interest once more in autobiographical materials precisely because they disrupted the dominant narrative of white, imperialist patriarchy and seemed to offer avenues of historical study that allowed for disenfranchised voices to be heard.[10] While the value of autobiographical sources remains contested, few historians can avoid the use of such materials at some point in their career so it is important to understand how to approach them. There are numerous excellent guides to studying autobiographies, including Carlson's introduction to autobiographies in Dobson and Ziemann's *Reading Primary Sources: The Interpretation of Texts from Nineteenth- and Twentieth-Century History* and the in-depth study of Smith and Watson's *Reading*

Autobiography: A Guide for Interpreting Life Narratives.[11] Most researchers combine in some way strategies from the literary and historical approach. This chapter will explore some of the specific approaches which can be taken to understand Soviet autobiographies, particularly in their wider historical context.

The subject

It is well established that the 'I' of an autobiography is a fractured one with scholars agreeing that there are often at least three 'I's' to read for.[12] There is the authorial 'I', the narrating 'I' and the 'I' of the narrator's past. All three 'I's can tell the historian a great deal, though none are necessarily reliable narrators of the autobiographer's life. It is a common feature of autobiographies that the author attempts to embody his/herself of the past, describing their feelings or actions as a child or younger self inside the moment of the experience being recalled. Inevitably, these descriptions are filtered through memory, hindsight and later meanings assigned to the past. The narrating 'I' is the self the author presents to the reader, but (intentionally or not) it is not necessarily the same as the authorial 'I', the individual whom historians have researched using other documents. Analysis of autobiographies invariably involves efforts to establish the contours of the three 'I's and assessing what the differences between them tell the reader about the author's intentions as autobiographer.

In the dominant or classic Western model, the autobiographer offers a chronological account of his (*sic*) life, framing it as his individual struggle to become the self he is now, through trials and struggles of various kinds.[13] Historians of women, of other ethnic groups, or of the non-elite have highlighted the inadequacy of this 'universal' autobiographical model. Studies of women's autobiographies, for example, have shown that the female self often portrays such struggles in far more relational terms, stressing collective effort and relationships with others: mothers with daughters and vice versa, wives with husbands. Tied to this, women often discuss their identity in relation to the ideal female promoted by the particular society to which they belong, highlighting how they failed or refused to live up to it.[14] Of course, subscribing to the notion of clearly defined gender differences in autobiographical writing is not without its dangers. In a comparison of male and female Russian Populist autobiographies, for example, Hoogenboom noted that while all fourteen of the female autobiographers referred to their childhood, only nine out of the thirty male writers did.[15] This statistic shows a gendered divergence, but also a significant overlap in approaches between the genders too. Hoogenboom argued it was also important to note that working-class male authors shared similar concerns to the women autobiographers.[16] Similarly, gender is not an automatic indicator of whether emotional issues will be included in or omitted from an autobiography.[17]

Russians began to write autobiographies partly in response to the emergence of this new genre in the West, but partly as a result of internal developments. As Greenleaf points out, Catherine the Great's first autobiographical writings were composed before any of the 'great' autobiographies like those by Rousseau,

Franklin or Hume had been written.[18] It is also well established that most Russian and Soviet autobiographies diverge from classic Western models.[19] Late Imperial Russian autobiographers described a more collective self than the Western individual, offering, for instance, long family histories to explain the self's context, rather than beginning only with their own childhood.[20] Indeed, not all Russian researchers would even use the term autobiography because of the lack of 'emphasis on individuality' in Russian autobiographical writing.[21] Another feature of pre-revolutionary autobiographies is that they are often presented as fictionalized accounts.[22] Tolstoy's *Childhood* (1852) is the classic example of this genre; others include Sofia Kovalevskaia's *A Russian Childhood* (1889) and Maxim Gorky's autobiographical work, *Childhood* (1913).[23]

As might be expected, most Soviet autobiographies very deliberately stressed collective identity or collective endeavour where possible given the importance of communality in their society. In this context, autobiographers wrote about their lives not because they were exceptional in some way, but rather because they were representative of experiences shared by a whole group of people.[24] Nadezhda Konstantinovna Krupskaia is credited for coining the term collective biographies to describe such texts, though it should be highlighted that collective biographies can be found in other cultures.[25] Krupskaia was thinking specifically of works written by veterans of the revolutionary struggle, for example women who had participated in the October Revolution, but other groups, like collective farmers and Stakhanovites, produced similar autobiographies.[26] The state regularly commissioned collective biographies which were seen as performing the social function of being educational tools to demonstrate the qualities of model citizens and to set out how group endeavour had brought about great achievements in the Soviet project.[27]

Collective writing was also an approach informally adopted by other communities to help them produce autobiographies which captured their shared experience, including, for example, members of non-Bolshevik parties who for a time were allowed to share their own version of the pre-revolutionary period. Amongst these autobiographers, it was not unusual for individuals to turn to their comrades to verify their recollection of an event or even to draw on their comrades' own portrayal of it, using everything from similar phrases to direct quotation.[28] They also asked the same questions of themselves as autobiographical subjects, for example, what in their lives had sparked their turn to revolutionary beliefs and activities.[29] Childhood was often discussed not in the context of the formation of the self, but as the site of the formation of the revolutionary.[30]

There is a certain instability in collective biographies, however, for in the end, each individual wrote his/her own version of their life and this could involve experiences or perspectives that deviated from the norm or model established by the collective. Thus, the Populist Nikolai Apollonovich Charushin did not find in his childhood the types of experiences and crises his comrades underwent which drove them to embrace socialism.[31] Alternatively, autobiographers might find themselves rejecting one form of collective identity for another. The women who wrote about their participation in the October Revolution had to distance themselves from those women who did not participate and instead highlight their comradeship with male Party members who acted as their mentors.[32] For some scholars, it is in these divergences between the collective biography and the individual autobiography that the most authentic 'I' is to be found.

Authenticity

One of the important tasks the narrating 'I' fulfils is to assert the authenticity of the autobiography, whether by addressing the reader directly, reflecting on the mechanics of writing an autobiography, or simply by seeming to be the actual interior voice of the author. Debate over the authenticity of Soviet autobiographies is particularly fraught and discussion continues over whether the self presented in Soviet autobiography can ever be understood as authentic. One school of thought assumes that the Soviet self presented in official autobiography was inherently different to the private Soviet self. Soviet autobiographies were written entirely to make the subject's life adhere to the ideal self promoted, if not required, by an oppressive state.[33] Certainly, many citizens were given specific guidance on what topics to address by the body for which the autobiography was being written, including medical centres, educational institutions, work places and of course the Party. A typical autobiographical questionnaire in the New Economic Policy (NEP) period (1921–28) would include questions about the citizen's family background, childhood, education, employment, outlook, disagreements with family members over outlook, peers, and activities in the Revolution and the Civil War.[34] The autobiographer, this school argues, would unite these themes in a predictable narrative of discovery of Bolshevism, conversion to this ideology and personal development towards becoming an ideal Soviet citizen, eschewing all other paths.[35] Halfin is categorical:

> Biographical details not directly relevant to this scheme were omitted. Only events that contributed to the revelation of Communist truth were worthy of inclusion in the life story of the protagonist. Thus we should not confuse this particular mode of autobiography with a chronicle of the applicants' life.'[36]

In such autobiographies, the personal was omitted in favour of the public self, sometimes to the point where the autobiography was written in the third rather than first person. In a break from earlier traditions, Soviet autobiographers often hid their longer family history, sometimes going as far as changing their names to disassociate themselves from a past that did not fit with the Soviet Union's expectations of what made a good citizen.[37] For this school of thought, the real self was only revealed to a trusted few, in the privacy of one's own home and not committed to paper.[38]

Other historians, however, prefer to return some authenticity and agency to the Soviet autobiographer, arguing that to dismiss their accounts as false or 'insufficient' is to impose the scholar's assumptions and priorities on the subjects.[39] Kelly warns that if historians constantly doubt what autobiographers write it 'distracts attention from the actual ways of telling in Soviet official autobiographies'.[40] Indeed, this approach argues that Soviet autobiographers wrote in a way that reflected their belief system and which felt authentic to them. Hellbeck's work on diaries in the 1930s supports this view. He argues that the early Soviet era marked a period of productive autobiographical work. As literacy increased and state interest in autobiographies intensified, Soviet citizens became more conscious of the need to record the development of their selfhood. Diarists often expressed genuine belief in the Soviet project and a desire to shape their selves according to the ideal Soviet model, without the prompting of official questionnaires.[41] Thus, Hellbeck's study suggests, we should see more authenticity in official autobiographies as well.

Scholars who take this perspective argue that the repetition of Soviet terms and phrases, which can make autobiographies sound rehearsed, formulaic and insincere, is not mindless parroting of unconsciously absorbed propaganda, a demonstration of wholesale acceptance of ideology nor the deliberate manipulation of language to conceal another self. Rather, 'speaking Bolshevik', as Kotkin terms it, was a way for Soviet citizens to site themselves in their society, express their views in language that all would understand, and establish a context in which they could then voice their own individual thoughts, hopes, fears and even criticisms.[42]

Narratives

Scholars seeing authenticity in Soviet autobiographies would also point out that to assume such works are not genuine because of their formulaic nature is to ignore the fact that recognizable narrative structures can be found in autobiographies across the globe. In making sense of their life, autobiographers of all types tend to draw on narrative structures embedded in their particular culture, in fictional works, myths, religious texts and political systems.[43] A great deal of autobiographical study explores the way in which subjects appropriate such narratives to express their experiences or to demonstrate how they found themselves in conflict with them, particularly women, non-white or non-elite writers.

In trying to identify the narrative structures being used, it is vital to remember that the Soviet period was not monolithic. In different periods, different narratives emerged, depending on the political climate, the economic programmes of the day and varying societal concerns. The enemies of the 1920s were not the same as the enemies of the 1930s, the war or the post-war period. The economic priorities of the state shifted over time and societal ideals, for example, those concerning what an ideal family looked like, changed. Lastly, the intensity of censorship in place strengthened and weakened in cycles, according to the level of state anxiety about enemies, and censorship was applied unevenly depending on the topics discussed.[44] As with most autobiographies, it is critical that the time and context in which Soviet autobiographies were written are understood.

Scholars have identified numerous narrative structures in Soviet autobiography. Above all and almost inevitably given the seismic events of the Revolution and

Civil War, before and after tales are to be found in many autobiographies, whether written by those who fled Russia to escape Bolshevik persecution or by others who stayed and participated willingly in the socialist state.[45] While the former portrays an idyllic pre-revolutionary period which the Revolution brings to an abrupt end and replaces with a period of loss of property and rights, of personal insecurity and of the creation of an alien culture, the latter depicts the barbaric, unequal and oppressive nature of Tsarist Russia which is replaced with a better society grounded in new opportunities and revolutionary ideals.[46] Another recognizable narrative is the so-called 'darkness to light' tale which describes the process of becoming a Bolshevik, as discussed previously. Later in the Soviet regime, a common story was that of the 'struggle for socialism'. As the state undertook huge economic projects such as collectivization and industrialization, autobiographers began to describe their lives in terms of the sacrifices they were required to make now in order to build a better future.[47]

Recognizing the existence of these narratives is not to argue that such common structures distort autobiographies. In fact, they tell us a great deal about the social, political and cultural moment in which the autobiographer is writing. It must also be remembered, for example, that these narratives did genuinely reflect the experiences of some Soviet citizens. Many working-class women, for example, did see an improvement in their lives during the Soviet period in the form of new legal, educational and political rights.[48] Others were genuinely untouched by the Purges and supported the removal of corrupt Communists from their positions of power.[49]

Of course, just as the narratives themselves are of interest, so too are divergences from them. It is always interesting to note places where the narrative makes anachronistic claims that are clearly included because of the current political climate. References to Trotsky or other leaders who fell foul of the regime, as a pernicious enemy whom the narrator had always suspected or their conspicuous omission from a narrative are important. More broadly, comparing the changing portrayal of a particular group can also be illuminating. Thus, while the state celebrated women's contribution to the war effort during the Second World War, it rapidly returned to a more traditional portrayal of women's role in the post-war period. Those women who wrote their autobiographies about their involvement in the war found that they were out of step with the new domesticity being promoted.[50]

If autobiographies are dependent, to a lesser or greater degree, on the culture and society in which they are produced for narrative structure, then it is understandable that in the post-Soviet period, autobiographies underwent a crisis. As Elena Zdravomyslova puts it, all the former foundations of Russian autobiography had changed, including 'the borders of states, the political configurations, the stratification design of society', as well as gender norms.[51] There were two consequences. Autobiographers took a far greater interest in their interior selves and the construction of self, and were 'eager to share their self-understandings'.[52] On the other hand, those wishing to share their sense of self were hostile to the many researchers keen to use the new openness of Russian society to speak to those who had lived in the Soviet period. The autobiographers did not want experts to interfere with or interpret their narrative.[53]

In the 1990s, different narratives emerged in the relative freedoms of post-Soviet Russia, though these too were shaped by the new capitalist society being built. Publishers and their audiences wished to read about victims of the Soviet regime, those who had suffered in collectivization or during the Purges.[54] Just as dissenters in the Soviet regime had limited if any opportunities to express their views, after the fall of Communism, those who continued to believe in the Soviet project wholeheartedly or those who revered Stalin's role in bringing victory to the Soviet Union in the Second World War found it harder to make their views public.[55]

Audience

As the above makes clear, in the Russian and Soviet context, audience is also an important element of autobiographical writing. According to the Western model, autobiographies are published voluntarily and they are bought by individuals, unknown to the author, who choose one over another, according to their personal taste and circumstances. As Popkin puts it, autobiographers 'have made a deliberate decision to share their stories with readers they do not know'.[56]

In contrast, autobiographers writing for publication in the late Imperial, Soviet and post-Soviet period were writing for a specific audience and all were aware that their first reader would likely be a censor. Imperial Russian autobiographies, for example, were sometimes used as a way of reaching out to fellow reform-minded subjects. Political and historical texts were censored heavily, so writers produced autobiographical works instead so that social problems such as the condition of the peasantry could be highlighted by presenting it in the innocent context of an individual's travels around the countryside.[57]

In the Soviet Union, autobiographical documents were most often commissioned by their intended audience: Party committees, societies, places of employment or educational institutions. Authors sometimes presented their autobiographies orally in front of a group of people known to them, for example, at a meeting of their fellow Stakhanovites or to a local Party cell. In the latter situation, autobiographers would often undergo 'grueling scrutiny' by those present.[58] In the pre-war period, there was such 'suspicion of falsified autobiographies' in Party membership applications that autobiographers could expect that their comrades and colleagues had been approached or encouraged to 'advance denunciatory material' against those not worthy of becoming Communists.[59] Such writers also knew that their autobiographies would be made available to the political police in whatever guise it was known at that time. Unsurprisingly, these autobiographies regularly included the names of prominent Communists whom the individual knew so that they might be approached for affirming references.

Autobiographies commissioned for publication tended to be written with the Soviet, as opposed to an international, population in mind, especially youngsters. They were to be designed to act as educational materials to help individuals shape themselves into ideal Soviet citizens. Autobiographies written for a more private audience can be found. Caches of autobiographies are held in the archives of philanthropic and non-partisan bodies such as the Society of Former Political Prisoners and Exiles. Those applying for membership were asked to provide short autobiographies.[60] Of course, in this context, less was at stake than when applying for Party membership and this type of organization could not mete out consequences more punitive than a rejection of the individual as a member for an unsuitable autobiography. Citizens often voluntarily included autobiographical statements in letters to Communist leaders.[61] What is striking about this private correspondence, as Fürst has discussed, is that while the autobiographies were used to show deep belief in the Soviet ideal and a passionate wish for life to match up to it, the letters often concluded with expressions of confusion and concern that it does not.[62]

Writing for the post-Soviet audience is no less complicated. The constitution of the Russian Federation adopted in 1993 states in Article 29 that 'the freedom of mass communication shall be guaranteed. Censorship shall be banned'.[63] After a brief spell of relative freedom, however, state interest and control over publications has increased again.[64] Of late, Russia has consistently received a low rating in the Press Freedom Index (148 out of 180 as of 2018)[65] and a combination of unclear laws against vaguely defined harmful content which are arbitrarily applied disrupts the provisions of the constitution.[66] Writers have increasingly resorted to self-censorship to avoid falling foul of the government.[67]

The Autobiography of a Sexually Emancipated Communist Woman

Alexandra Mikhailovna Kollontai's *Autobiography of a Sexually Emancipated Communist Woman* is a particularly interesting case study for exploring all these questions. A Menshevik turned Bolshevik in the Imperial period, then Commissar of Social Welfare in the first Bolshevik government, leader of the Zhenotdel (the women's department of the Secretariat of the Bolshevik Central Committee) and latterly a Soviet diplomat, Kollontai wrote autobiographical texts in the late Imperial period and the Soviet period and so was familiar with the ways in which the contours of the genre itself were changed by the times.[68] Her most famous autobiography is her *Autobiography of a Sexually Emancipated Communist Woman*, which was written in 1926 and published in Germany in 1927 as part of a series on Leading European women. The version quoted below, which was published in 1971 in the United States of America and can be read in full at the Marxists Internet Archive, is particularly interesting for it combines the published text with the sections removed by Kollontai herself during the editing process, these being highlighted in italics.[69]

Kollontai begins as many autobiographers do with a discussion of the act of writing an autobiography:

> Nothing is more difficult than writing an autobiography. What should be emphasized? Just what is of general interest? It is advisable, above all, to write honestly and dispense with any of the conventional introductory protestations

of modesty. For if one is called upon to tell about one's life so as to make the events that made it what it became useful to the general public, it can mean only that one must have already wrought something positive in life, *accomplished a task that people recognize.* Accordingly it is a matter of forgetting that one is writing about oneself, of making an effort to abjure one's ego so as to give an account, as objectively as possible, of one's life in the making and of one's accomplishments. I intend to make this effort but whether it will turn out successfully is something else again. At the same time I must confess that, in a certain sense, this autobiography poses a problem for me. For by looking back while prying, simultaneously, into the future, I will also be presenting to myself the most crucial turning points of my being and accomplishments. *In this way I may succeed in setting into bold relief that which concerns the women's liberation struggle and, further, the social significance which it has.*[70]

Several points of interest should be noted in these opening sentences. First is Kollontai's rejection of the 'conventional introductory protestations of modesty' which is in part a reference to the tradition whereby women writers in the nineteenth century apologized for writing or expressed their inadequacy as authors, even as they wrote.[71] Writing was still very much a male domain at that point and female authors often felt the need to justify their encroachment into this realm.[72] The second is Kollontai's argument that autobiographies should be 'useful to the general public'. Even though Kollontai was not writing for a Soviet audience, she still, here, expressed the Soviet belief that autobiographies should be educational. Lastly, note her efforts to make her words sound authentic. She stresses the need to 'write honestly' and to 'give an account, as objectively as possible'.[73]

Kollontai also refers to the tussle which many revolutionary writers experienced. They were singled out to write their autobiography because of their 'accomplishments' but felt they must at the same time 'abjure' their 'ego' in order to remain part of the collective society to which they belonged. In fact, Kollontai consistently defies the Soviet 'collective' identity as well as the allegedly female habit of acknowledging help and support in her achievements and describes her policy work, publications and diplomatic victories as very much the result of her own efforts. She states emphatically at one point: 'Not a single one of the men who were close to me has ever had a direction-giving influence on my inclinations, strivings, or my world-view. On the contrary, most of the time I was the guiding spirit.'[74] She also confidently describes her expertise, based on her own scholarship and research, on such matters as maternity policy and throughout her autobiography points to the numerous times she was the first (if not only) woman to achieve something. She portrays herself as initially being the sole campaigner in the RSDRP for work to be conducted amongst women and highlights that she was the first woman ever to hold a full ministerial post in a government,[75] as well as the first woman ever to be appointed as an ambassador.

Kollontai's sense of individuality, if not isolation, comes across strongly too when she refers to several periods in which she endured direct attacks on her personally by a hostile press: in 1917 when 'bourgeois newspapers' labelled her as a 'mad female Bolshevik', in the early Soviet period when the conservative press published criticisms of her conversion of the Alexander Nevsky monastery into 'a home for war invalids', and when the 'White' press 'tried to make a real monster of immorality' of her when she was first appointed as an ambassador.[76]

Occasionally, Kollontai makes comments more geared towards the notion of collective identity and achievement. For example, her introductory description of the October Revolution asks 'was there altogether an individual will at that time? Was it not only the omnipotent storm of the Revolution, the command of the active, awakened masses that determined our will and action?' Kollontai also highlights in several places the way in which her own individual achievements served the greater good, in her case 'the women's liberation struggle'. Indeed, in the concluding paragraph, Kollontai asserts again that her 'achievements are only a symbol' of the 'millions of women' who have been 'drawn into productive work' by the Revolution.[77]

As mentioned above, two key narratives to be found in Soviet autobiographies are the 'darkness to light' tale of conversion to Bolshevism and the before and after comparison of pre- and post-revolutionary society. Kollontai includes both in her autobiography. Of her socialist awakening, she writes:

> That I ought not to shape my life according to the given model, that I would have to grow beyond myself in order to be able to discern my life's true line of vision was an awareness that was mine already in my youngest years. [...] I was particularly and painfully shocked by the little peasant children who were my playmates. [...] Already early in life I had eyes for the social injustices prevailing in Russia.[78]

Like many Socialist autobiographers, Kollontai looked to her childhood to explain her conversion to revolutionary politics. Here we note the split between the narrating 'I' and the 'I' of the author's past, though it is not very pronounced. Kollontai does not attempt to immerse herself in her childhood and she recreates her impressions, thoughts and feelings from that time in only the most cursory fashion. More important here is her reference to her early understanding of the need to break free from 'the given model'. This has layers of meaning. It is a common trope in women's autobiographies that there was a constant tension between the gendered path set out for women by their society and the path they chose. For revolutionary women like Kollontai, divorcing a husband and leaving a child in the care of others in order to embark on a political career was a demonstration of their rebellion not only against the confines of their own lives, but also against the patriarchal expectations of Tsarist society itself.[79] The second meaning of the 'given model' phrase is that it explains how an aristocratic woman became a socialist. This was something which many Bolsheviks, male and female, had to do, for the majority of leading figures of the Party in the 1920s came from wealthy if not aristocratic backgrounds and this was at odds with Marx's theory that the revolution would be achieved by the working class. Thus, it was critical that Kollontai could trace her development from class enemy to committed socialist.

It is in Kollontai's discussion of life before and after the revolution that she makes her most candid and confessional comments.

> To avoid any misunderstanding, however, it should be said here that I am still far from being the type of the positively new women who take their experience as females with a relative lightness and, one could say, with an enviable superficiality, whose feelings and mental energies are directed upon all *other things* in life but *sentimental love feelings.* After all I still belong to the generation of women who grew up at a turning point in history. Love with its many disappointments, with its tragedies and eternal demands for perfect happiness still played a very great role in my life. An all-too-great role! It was an expenditure of precious time and energy, fruitless and, in the final analysis, utterly worthless. We, the women of the past generation, did not yet understand how to be free. The whole thing was an absolutely incredible squandering of our mental energy, a diminution of our labour power which was dissipated in barren emotional experiences. It is certainly true that we, myself as well as many other activists, militants and working women contemporaries, were able to understand that love was not the main goal of our life and that we knew how to place work at its centre. Nevertheless we would have been able to create and achieve much more had our energies not been fragmentized in the eternal struggle with *our egos and with* our feelings for another. It was, in fact, an eternal defensive war against the intervention of the male into our ego, a struggle revolving around the problem-complex: work or marriage and love? We, the older generation, did not yet understand, as most men do and as young women are learning today, that work and the longing for love can be harmoniously combined *so that work remains as the main goal of existence.* Our mistake was that each time we succumbed to the belief that we had finally found the one and only in the man we loved, the person with whom we believed we could blend our soul, one who was ready fully to recognize us as a spiritual-physical force.[80]

The above extract is one of several places in her autobiography where Kollontai combines discussion of her struggle to free herself from emotional dependency on men with descriptions of the way in which the new Soviet regime has emancipated women from the old-style unhealthy romantic relationships between men and women and enabled them to fulfil their own needs, as well as enter into relationships with the opposite sex as equals. Like many autobiographers whose lives straddled the Revolution and Civil War, Kollontai is deeply aware of generational divides and the fact that she lived through a historical 'turning point'.

It is noticeable, however, that despite being open about the nature of her first marriage, she does not refer explicitly to any of her other relationships and mentions her son only briefly. She comments at one point that in 1922 'personal and family cares' helped ensure that 'months' 'went by without fruitful work'.[81] Many, especially female, Soviet autobiographers similarly describe family matters tangentially and often in the context of the way in which domestic concerns prevented them from conducting useful activities. While some scholars would view this as a sign of the artificial nature of Soviet autobiographies which prevented individuals from being emotionally candid, others would argue that this demonstrates the importance which Soviet citizens assigned to serving the cause and the state and their genuinely held belief that personal matters were less important than the great tasks which faced the country.[82]

Kollontai's autobiography, with its reinserted deletions, seems to offer a unique opportunity to assess the extent to which the published text was authentic. Do the deletions offer the reader greater insight into Kollontai's thoughts and feelings? Certainly, there are aspects of her autobiography which, when contextualized, seem to point to a degree of self-censorship at work. In fact, one reviewer argues that even 'the deleted material does not appreciably alter the tone of reserve and caution that pervades the self-censored manuscript'.[83] However, certain deletions are worthy of attention.

Kollontai's comment that at the time of writing she had been a Communist for thirty years is a particularly striking one. It is always important to identify anachronistic terms in an autobiography for they often signpost the influence of hindsight. The term Communist is out of place here as it was a term that only came into use when the Party renamed itself in 1918, that is, long after Kollontai joined the Party. Calling herself a long-standing Communist in her autobiography, however, was a means for Kollontai to assert her loyalty to the cause and gloss over her various disagreements with the Party line. In the 1920s, it was still the ultimate badge of honour to have been a member of the RSDRP (Russian Social Democratic Workers' Party) from the Party's inception and even better to have been a consistent Bolshevik since the Party's split in 1903. The so-called Old Bolsheviks were seen as more reliable and experienced than those who had joined in 1917, for there was always a danger that recent recruits had become members for personal reasons of ambition or self-preservation. After Lenin's death in January 1924, it was also increasingly important to be able to demonstrate persistent loyalty to Lenin throughout the underground period, especially as the Party began to tear itself apart over economic and political questions.

Kollontai had been a social-democrat for thirty years, but had in fact become a Menshevik when the Party split and only became a Bolshevik when Lenin's faction was the only socialist group to oppose the world war. She deleted a long, nuanced section on her membership of the RSDRP during the pre-revolutionary period which described her disagreements with her fellow Mensheviks and removed a comment that in 1907–8 she had 'no desire to pass over to the Bolsheviks'. She left in her statement that she 'officially joined' the Bolsheviks in 1915, but strangely left out her reference to her 'lively correspondence with Lenin' at that time which had in fact been published in Russia, as well as her comment that she was 'the only one of his Party comrades' who supported Lenin's April Theses.[84]

Perhaps she thought it better not to dwell on her relationship with Lenin, for she had not remained loyal to him. Instead, for example, she had resigned from her post of Commissar of Social Welfare over the Brest–Litovsk treaty. She deleted the line in her autobiography where she explained her resignation 'on the grounds of total disagreement with the current policy'.[85] Kollontai was then removed from the Zhenotdel leadership for her outspoken criticism of the government's policies on women and narrowly avoided expulsion from the Party over her involvement in the Workers' Opposition in 1922. As we saw above, she referred to 1922 as a year without fruitful work. She made no reference to her membership of the Workers' Opposition, but did, stridently, reassert her view that the Bolsheviks' policies on marriage and illegitimacy were not as progressive as the government claimed. She mentioned Western and White press attacks on her, but did not refer to the criticism she received in the Soviet press.

One last important detail to bear in mind is the year Kollontai was writing. A tense year for the Party, 1926 saw the United Opposition of Zinoviev, Kamenev and Trotsky under sustained attack by Stalin and his supporters. Kollontai faced criticism again for her views on women's emancipation and she was given a new diplomatic posting in Mexico, which her biographer interpreted as a type of political exile.[86] She did not join the Opposition although she was asked to do so, but she also did not reject her comrades. Of four, mostly positive, references to Trotsky in her autobiography, she left in three, including a direct reference to the fact that Trotsky and Lenin were in different Party factions before the war. She also left in her description of her former partner and former Workers' Opposition member Alexander Shliapnikov, who had only recently been investigated and rebuked by the Central Control Commission, as 'a good friend and Party comrade'.[87]

Scholars of Kollontai have differing opinions of this work. Cathy Porter, one of Kollontai's first Western biographers, contrasted this autobiography negatively with the 'engagingly honest insights into her personal and political thoughts' which can be found in her other earlier writings, some published in the 1920s. This 1926 work, however, in her view, had a 'certain dismal leadenness'.[88] In contrast, another biographer, Barbara Clements argues that the 1926 autobiography is 'a more revealing piece' than the autobiographical article Kollontai produced in 1921 for the Soviet Granat encyclopaedia, the latter offering 'only delicate clues to the more controversial aspects of her life'.[89] She also stresses that the deletions made to the 1926 work were made by Kollontai herself.[90] While this latter comment highlights the importance of self-censorship, it also reminds us that in the end, autobiographies do not necessarily tell us about the author's past, but rather they tell us what the author wishes to tell us about their past in the particular moment of writing.[91]

As a postscript, it is worth mentioning the issue of reading autobiographies (and any Russian source) in translation. A full discussion is beyond the scope of this chapter, but simply considering how Kollontai's autobiography title has been translated highlights an example of the problems that can arise. When Kollontai wrote this for a German series about women of Europe, she entitled it *The Aims and Worth of My Life*.[92] In 1970, it was published again in Germany under the title *Autobiographie einer sexuell emanzipierten Kommunistin*.[93] It is interesting that the American translator of the work into English, Salvator Attanasio, chose to use the latter, rather than the former title. Certainly, Kollontai was a champion of the sexual emancipation of women throughout her life and quite open about her relationships, but the choice to forefront this in the title of her autobiography mirrors a trend in the historical treatment of Kollontai whereby a significant number of scholars have focused on Kollontai's personal life at the expense of the other aspects of her career, sometimes using dismissive if not sexist language.[94] Translation is an art not a science and those using translated sources must always be aware that the prejudices and perspectives of the time and the translator affect the language choices made.

Autobiography remains one of the most challenging source genres to use as a historian, but no doubt this is where half of its attraction lies. Unravelling an autobiography's complex structure, identifying the different voices of the narrating 'I's and considering the nuances of meaning which are generated by the interplay between the individual text and recognizable narrative structures produce a wealth of information and material for the historian. An autobiography can provide insights into an individual life, as well as into the society in which the subject lived, its social and political mores, as well as its artistic culture. It can highlight class, gender and ethnic norms and the avenues by which individuals could embrace or defy them. In the Russian and Soviet context, they provide an important reminder that Western autobiography is by no means the 'universal' model and that geographical, historical, social, political, cultural and ideological context are fundamental in shaping how individuals see and write about themselves.

Notes

1 John Reed, *Ten Days that Shook the World* (London: The Folio Society, 2006), pp. 203–4.
2 Margaret Ziolkowski, 'Diaries of Disaffection: Some Recent Russian Memoirs', *World Literature Today*, 61 (1987), pp. 199–202 (p. 201).
3 Marianne Liljeström, Arja Rosenholm and Irina Savkina, 'Introduction', in Marianne Liljeström, Arja Rosenholm and Irina Savkina (eds.), *Models of Self: Russian Women's Autobiographical Texts* (Helsinki: Kikimora Publications, 2000), p. 7.
4 Catriona Kelly, 'The Authorised Version: The Auto/Biographies of Vera Panova', in M. Liljeström et al., *Models of Self*, p. 65.
5 Jeremy D. Popkin, 'Historians on the Autobiographical Frontier', *American Historical Review*, 104 (1999), pp. 725–48 (p. 729).
6 Marianne Liljeström, Arja Rosenholm and Irina Savkina, 'Introduction', in M. Liljeström ed., et al., *Models of Self*, p. 5.
7 Choi Chatterjee and Karen Petrone, 'Models of Selfhood and Subjectivity: The Soviet Case in Historical Perspective', *Slavic Review*, 67 (2008), pp. 967–86 (p. 968).
8 Marcus C. Levitt, 'Siniavskii's Alternate Autobiography "A Voice from the Chorus"', *Canadian Slavonic Papers*, 33 (1991), pp. 46–61 (p. 47).
9 Paul Thompson (ed.), *Voice of the Past* (Oxford: Oxford University Press, 2000), http://ebookcentral.proquest.com/lib/qub/detail.action?docID=684602 (accessed 22 March 2017).

10 Marcus Moseley, 'Jewish Autobiography: The Elusive Subject', *Jewish Quarterly Review*, 95 (2005), pp. 16–59 (p. 17); Monika Greenleaf, 'Performing Autobiography: The Multiple Memoirs of Catherine the Great (1755–96)', *Russian Review*, 63 (2004), pp. 407–26 (p. 410); Gershon Bacon, 'Introduction', *Nashim: A Journal of Jewish Women's Studies and Gender Issues*, 7, Autobiography and Memoir (5764/2004), pp. 7–10 (p. 7).
11 David Carlson, 'Autobiography', in Miriam Dobson and Benjamin Ziemann (eds.), *Reading Primary Sources: The Interpretation of Texts from Nineteenth- and Twentieth-Century History* (London: Routledge, 2008), pp. 174–91; Sidonie Smith and Julia Watson, *Reading Autobiography: A Guide for Interpreting Life Narratives* (Minneapolis, MN: University of Minneapolis Press, 2001). Smith and Watson include an excellent 'tool-kit' for analysing autobiographies in their work.
12 Smith and Watson, *Reading Autobiography*, pp. 167–8.
13 Moseley, 'Jewish Autobiography', p. 27; Rockwell Gray, 'Autobiography Now', *Kenyon Review*, New Series, 4 (1982), pp. 31–55 (p. 41).
14 Sian Chalke, 'Autobiography: Liubov Mendeleeva-Blok', *New Zealand Slavonic Journal* (1996), pp. 199–207 (pp. 200, 201); Hilde Hoogenboom, 'Vera Figner and Revolutionary Autobiographies: The Influence of Gender on Genre' in Rosalind Marsh (ed.), *Women in Russia and Ukraine* (Cambridge: Cambridge University Press, 1996), p. 79.
15 Hoogenboom, 'Vera Figner', p. 81.
16 Ibid., p. 81.
17 Katy Turton, *Family Networks and the Russian Revolutionary Movement, 1870–1940* (Basingstoke: Palgrave Macmillan, 2018), p. xvii.
18 Greenleaf, 'Performing Autobiography', p. 410.
19 Nancy L. Cooper, 'A Chapter in the History of Russian Autobiography: Childhood, Youth, and Maturity in Fonvizin's "Chistoserdechnoe Priznanie v Delakh Moikh i Pomyshleniiakh" (A Sincere Avowal of My Deeds and Thoughts)', *Slavic and East European Journal*, 40 (1996), pp. 609–22 (p. 609).
20 Moseley, 'Jewish Autobiography', pp. 35, 37.
21 Liljeström et al., 'Introduction', in Liljeström et al., *Models of Self*, pp. 6–7.
22 Ibid., pp. 6–7.
23 Barry Scherr, 'Gor'kij's Childhood: The Autobiography as Fiction', *Slavic and East European Journal*, 23 (1979), pp. 333–45 (p. 334).
24 Sheila Fitzpatrick, 'Lives and Times', in Sheila Fitzpatrick and Yuri Slezkine (eds.), *In the Shadow of Revolution: Life Stories of Russian Women: From 1917 to the Second World War* (Princeton, NJ: Princeton University Press, 2000), p. 15.
25 Popkin, 'Historians on the Autobiographical Frontier', p. 732.
26 Liljeström, 'The Remarkable Women: Rituality and Performativity in Soviet Women's Autobiographical Texts from the 1970s', in Liljeström, et al., *Models of Self*, p. 81.
27 Ibid., p. 81.
28 Ben Eklof and Tatiana Saburova, *A Generation of Revolutionaries: Nikolai Charushin and Russian Populism from the Great Reforms to Perestroika* (Bloomington, IN: Indiana University Press, 2017), p. 325.
29 Ibid., p. 13.
30 Ibid., p. 13; Hoogenboom, 'Vera Figner', p. 79.
31 Eklof and Saburova, *A Generation of Revolutionaries*, p. 15.
32 Liljeström, 'The Remarkable Women', pp. 82, 95, 97.
33 Chatterjee and Petrone, 'Models of Selfhood', pp. 974–6.
34 Igal Halfin, 'From Darkness to Light: Student Communist Autobiography During NEP', *Jahrbücher für Geschichte Osteuropas*, 45 (1997), pp. 210–36 (p. 212).
35 Liljeström et al., 'Introduction', p. 7; Elena Zdravomyslova, 'A Cultural Paradigm of Sexual Violence Reconstructed from a Woman's Biographical Interview', in Liljeström et al., *Models of Self*, p. 212.

36 Halfin, 'From Darkness to Light', p. 212.
37 Zdravomyslova, 'A Cultural Paradigm', pp. 211–12.
38 Ibid., p. 212; Chatterjee and Petrone, 'Models of Selfhood', p. 986.
39 Kelly, 'The Authorised Version', p. 68.
40 Ibid., pp. 67–9.
41 Jochen Hellbeck, 'Working, Struggling, Becoming: Stalin-Era Autobiographical Texts', *Russian Review*, 60 (2001), pp. 340–59, especially, pp. 341, 347–9.
42 Juliane Fürst, 'In Search of Soviet Salvation: Young People Write to the Stalinist Authorities', *Contemporary European History*, 15 (2006), pp. 327–45 (p. 333).
43 Kelly, 'The Authorised Version', p. 68; Moseley, 'Jewish Autobiography', p. 50; Liljeström et al., 'Introduction', p. 8.
44 Fitzpatrick, 'Lives and Times', p. 4.
45 Ibid., p. 16.
46 Yuri Slezkine, 'Lives as Tales', in Fitzpatrick and Slezkine, (ed.), *In the Shadow*, pp. 20–1.
47 Halfin, 'From Darkness to Light', p. 212; Yuri Slezkine, 'Lives as Tales', in Fitzpatrick and Slezkine, (ed.), *In the Shadow*, p. 25.
48 Fitzpatrick, 'Lives and Times', in Fitzpatrick and Slezkine, *In the Shadow*, p. 12.
49 Ibid., p. 8.
50 Irina Novikova, 'A War in Her Own Translation: Elena Rzhevskaya's *Distant Rumble*', in Liljeström et al., *Models of Self*, p. 158.
51 Zdravomyslova, 'A Cultural Paradigm', p. 210.
52 Ibid., p. 210.
53 Ibid., p. 210.
54 Fitzpatrick, 'Lives and Times', in Fitzpatrick and Slezkine, *In the Shadow*, p. 5.
55 Hellbeck, 'Working, Struggling, Becoming', p. 359; see also Marianne Liljeström, *Useful Selves* (Saarijärvi: Kikimora Publications, 2004), p. 9.
56 Popkin, 'Historians on the Autobiographical Frontier', p. 726.
57 Levitt, 'Siniavskii's Alternate Autobiography', p. 48.
58 Halfin, 'From Darkness to Light', p. 224.
59 Ibid., p. 221.
60 Hoogenboom, 'Vera Figner', p. 79.
61 Fitzpatrick, 'Lives and Times', p. 6.
62 Fürst, 'In Search of Soviet Salvation', pp. 339–40.
63 'The Constitution of the Russian Federation'. <www.constitution.ru/en/10003000-01.htm> (accessed 30 May 2018); A. M. Chenoy and R. Kumar, *Re-emerging Russia: Structures, Institutions and Processes* (Basingstoke: Palgrave Macmillan, 2017), p. 35.
64 Neil Robinson, *Institutions and Political Change in Russia* (Houndmills: Macmillan Press, 2000), pp. 190–1; Richard Sakwa, *Putin. Russia's Choice* (London: Routledge, 2008), p. 115.
65 '2018 World Press Freedom Index'. https://rsf.org/en/ranking (accessed 30 May 2018).
66 Alyssa Rosenberg, 'How censorship works in Vladimir Putin's Russia', 9 February 2016. https://washingtonpost.com/news/act-four/wp/2016/02/09/how-censorship-works-in-vladimir-putins-russia/?noredirect=on&utm_term=.0de2a9f1bf55 (accessed 30 May 2018).
67 Sakwa, *Putin. Russia's Choice*, p. 153.
68 Kollontai's autobiographical works are: Po rabochei Evrope [Around Workers' Europe] (1912); Otryvki iz dnevnika 1914 g. [Fragments from a Diary] (1920s); V tiur'me Kerenskogo [In Kerensky's Prison] (1920s); Avtobiograficheskii ocherk [An Autobiographical Sketch] (1921); Autobiographical article in the Soviet Granat encyclopedia (1925–1927); Ziel und Wert meines Lebens [The Goal and Worth of my Life] (1927) later published as Alexandra Kollontai, *The Autobiography of a Sexually Emancipated Communist Woman* trans. by Salvator Attansio (New York, NY: Herder and Herder, 1971) https://marxists.org/archive/kollonta/1926/autobiography.htm

(accessed 31 May 2018); Den första etappen [The First Steps], (1945); Barbara Evans
Clements, *Bolshevik Feminist: The Life of Aleksandra Kollontai* (Bloomington, IN:
Indiana University Press, 1979), pp. 315–16.
69 Kollontai, *Autobiography.*
70 Ibid.
71 Chalke, 'Autobiography', p. 201.
72 Liljeström et al., 'Introduction', p. 5.
73 Kollontai, *Autobiography.*
74 Ibid.
75 This is correct in fact, if not in spirit, as Sofia Vladimirovna Panina was both deputy
Minister of State Welfare and Deputy Minister of Education in the Provisional
Government before October 1917.
76 Kollontai, *Autobiography.*
77 Ibid.
78 Ibid.
79 Turton, *Family Networks*, pp. 15–16.
80 Kollontai, *Autobiography.*
81 Ibid.
82 Gary Kern, 'Trotsky's Autobiography', *Russian Review*, 36 (1977), pp. 297–319
(p. 297).
83 Jeri Laber, 'Review of *The Autobiography of a Sexually Emancipated Communist
Woman*', *Slavic Review*, 31 (1972), pp. 678–9 (p. 679).
84 Kollontai, *Autobiography.*
85 Ibid.
86 Cathy Porter, *Alexandra Kollontai* (London: Virago, 1980), p. 435.
87 Kollontai, *Autobiography*; Barbara C. Allen, *Alexander Shliapnikov: 1885–1937: Life of
an Old Bolshevik* (Leiden: Brill Academic Publishers, 2015), p. 277.
88 Cathy Porter, 'Introduction', in Porter, *Alexandra Kollontai*, no page numbers.
89 Clements, *Bolshevik Feminist*, p. 315.
90 Ibid., p. 315.
91 Carlson, 'Autobiography', p. 183.
92 Porter, 'Introduction', no page numbers.
93 Clements, *Bolshevik Feminist*, p. 329.
94 This is discussed at length in Moira Donald, '"What Did *You* Do in the Revolution,
Mother?": Image, Myth and Prejudice in the Russian Revolution', *Gender and History*,
7 (1995), pp. 85–99.

Further reading

Primary source collections

Bisha, Robin, Jehanne M. Gheith, Christine Holden and William G. Wagner (eds.), *Russian
Women, 1698–1917: Experience and Expression* (Bloomington, IN: Indiana University
Press, 2002).
Fitzpatrick, Sheila, and Yuri Slezkine (eds.), *In the Shadow of Revolution: Life Stories
of Russian Women: From 1917 to the Second World War* (Princeton, NJ: Princeton
University Press, 2000).

Secondary materials

Chatterjee, Choi, and Karen Petrone, 'Models of Selfhood and Subjectivity: The Soviet Case
in Historical Perspective', *Slavic Review*, 67 (2008), pp. 967–86.
Dobson, Miriam, and Benjamin Ziemann (eds.), *Reading Primary Sources: The Interpretation
of Texts from Nineteenth- and Twentieth-Century History* (London: Routledge, 2008).

Halfin, Igal, 'From Darkness to Light: Student Communist Autobiography During NEP', *Jahrbücher für Geschichte Osteuropas*, 45 (1997), pp. 210–36.

Hellbeck, Jochen, 'Working, Struggling, Becoming: Stalin-Era Autobiographical Texts', *Russian Review*, 60 (2001), pp. 340–59.

Liljeström, Marianne, Arja Rosenholm and Irina Savkina (eds.), *Models of Self: Russian Women's Autobiographical Texts* (Helsinki: Kikimora Publications, 2000).

Liljeström, Marianne, *Useful Selves* (Saarijärvi: Kikimora Publications, 2004).

Marsh, Rosalind (ed.), *Women in Russia and Ukraine* (Cambridge: Cambridge University Press, 1996).

Popkin, Jeremy D., 'Historians on the Autobiographical Frontier', *American Historical Review*, 40 (1999), pp. 725–48.

Smith, Sidonie, and Julia Watson, *Reading Autobiography: A Guide for Interpreting Life Narratives* (Minneapolis, MN: University of Minneapolis Press, 2000).

Thompson, Paul (ed.), *Voice of the Past* (Oxford: Oxford University Press, 2000).

9 'Read all about it!'

Soviet press and periodicals

Andy Willimott

In October 1917 the Bolsheviks promised to remake Russia, global politics, and mankind itself. 'A new culture with a new vocabulary and new moral tone was disseminated widely', notes Laura Engelstein.[1] The newspaper, the periodical, alongside the tribune and the public meeting hall, were at the heart of this new world of words. Street kiosks became the hubs of revolutionary hubbub. Factory noticeboards overflowed with radical overtures. New words promised new horizons. 'The Bolshevik idiom', Engelstein explains, 'was part of a more pervasive socialist culture which had begun, under the impact of 1905, to expand beyond the radical fringe'.[2] It extended a language of 'dignity', 'freedom', 'democracy', 'justice', and 'equality'. On the eve of the October Revolution, the daily newspaper *Russkie vedomosti* (*Russian News*) reported: 'There is no authority, no legality, and no effective political action in Russia, but there is an abundance of political words'.[3] As the Bolsheviks seized power, they advanced on a wave of political words and sought to unleash the full, uncompromised potential of Russia's socialist discourse.

At the same time, as the Bolsheviks moved to consolidate Soviet power, they placed severe restrictions on press freedom and political opposition. A party-state system of governance emerged that dictated the boundaries of socialist discourse. And so, focusing on the restrictions of the Soviet state, many scholars went on to underestimate the value of Soviet newspapers and periodicals as a source base. The Soviet press was often blanketly written-off as unreliable propaganda – a suspicious and devious appendage of a suspicious and devious system. In the wake of the Grand Alliance, as Cold War battle-lines hardened, some Western scholars perpetuated a view of the Soviet Union as a monolithic 'propaganda state'. An old Soviet anecdote offered a neat refrain for adherents of the totalitarian explanation of the Soviet system: 'There is no news in *Pravda* [*Truth*] and no truth in *Izvestiia* [*News*]'. The Soviet press was presented as little more than a façade, part of an ideological 'fraud' intent on peddling 'counterfeit' portrayals of reality.[4] Kremlinologists – as they were labelled – scanned over Soviet newspapers, just as they looked to the positioning of Soviet leaders atop Lenin's mausoleum on parade days, searching for clues as to which party person was on the ascendancy. But, concerned only with the inner circles of power, they read 'between the lines', largely overlooking content.

What the totalitarian model and Kremlinology fundamentally overlooked was the range, meaning, and nuance to be found in Soviet newspapers and periodicals. The Soviet newspaper typically contained reports, resolutions, appeals, and letters from citizens, as well as a topical chronicle of events. Key political developments can be charted alongside contemporaneous responses. The press organs of the party (*Pravda*), the Communist Youth League (*Komsomol'skaia pravda*), and those that emerged from different workers', soldiers', and political organisations (such as *Soldatskaia pravda* [*Soldiers' Truth*] and *Izvestiia*) reflected different editorial priorities, especially in the early years of the Soviet state. Within the parameters of ideological acceptability, divergence of opinion, preoccupation, and understanding can be discerned. Human-interest stories and citizens' voices also capture some of the lived experience of the Soviet Union.

The Soviet periodical contained extended thought-pieces, fictional and non-fictional stories, and advice literature. Like all periodicals, they were often specialised, or focused on a certain theme, and published at regular intervals. For instance, *Iunyi communist* (*Young Communist*), published by the Communist Youth League, was a biweekly targeted at young people; *Narpit* (*People's Nutrition*), established by the body in charge of improving the public diet, was a bimonthly that reported on communal dining and municipal canteen projects; and *Bol'shevik* (*Bolshevik*) was a biweekly politico-economic publication of the central committee. Some publications were more specialised than others, but a great variety of themes and concerns acquired a print outlet. What is more, as recent research has shown, the words printed in these publications could fire as well as frame the imagination – these words could appeal and obscure, they were full of meaning and vacuous for different readers at different points in time.

In recent years, digitisation projects have made working with print sources much simpler, bringing together full or partial runs of large swathes of titles published over many years, and making them searchable. The online library subscription database *EastView*, for instance, contains digitised copies of numerous print sources, including *Pravda*, *Izvestiia*, *Moscow News*, and *Literaturnaia gazeta* (*The Literary Gazette*). Most recently, the National Library of Russia developed a catalogue system that allows researchers to search for available scanned copies of historical newspapers on any given calendar-day from 1703 to 2017. This provides the researcher with a tool that could hasten the piecing together of historical and discursive sequences. Although, it has to be said, at this moment in time digitisation projects remain imperfect and incomplete. The search facilities on these systems are not always reliable indicators of the full range of content. Researchers still need to have their wits about them and develop a good working knowledge of the materials they search. For in-depth, qualitative work, in particular, nothing can yet give a sense of 'the times' like the ephemeral object itself. Although, as Boris Kolonitskii has warned, 'hurry!' for it is thought that the poor quality paper upon which some of the earliest revolutionary and Soviet publications were printed could only have a lifespan of about one hundred years.[5]

For those with Russian, numerous university and national libraries maintain well-catalogued collections of Soviet newspapers and periodicals either in hard copy or on microfilm, although these collections can be sporadic or broken, with materials from the early years of the Soviet state in much shorter supply. Publications such as *Komsomolskaia pravda* are partially accessible in the UK via the British Library or the UCL School of Slavonic and East European Studies Library. Likewise, the Library of Congress, in Washington, DC, hosts a number of Russian and Soviet daily publications on microfilm. Generally speaking, however, substantial collections of Soviet periodicals are harder to come by outside of Russia. Indeed, to gain access to large swathes of different Soviet newspapers and periodicals, and the ability to read across a range of publications, researchers must visit institutions such as the State Public Historical Library of Russia, in Moscow. Here research is dictated less by the nature of the collection than by the approach of the scholar or the quantity of reading one can undertake.[6]

There are also many interesting collections of translated materials available for students without Russian. Even for the seasoned researcher, reading through these collections and observing the juxtaposition of different articles can be a valuable exercise. Mark D. Steinberg's *Voices of Revolution, 1917* (2001), for instance, contains a wide selection of contemporary newspaper reports, readers' letters, and published resolutions. While William G. Rosenberg's *Bolshevik Visions* (1984) includes a dazzling array of newspaper and periodical articles in translation.

'No news in *Pravda* ...'

The way Soviet newspapers and periodicals have been approached by scholars closely reflects changing historiographical and theoretical developments in the field. While the scholarship on the Soviet Union was dominated by the 'T-model' (totalitarian), throughout the 1950s and 1960s, a reductive view of Soviet print media persisted. Works such as George Counts and Nucia Lodge's *The Country of the Blind: The Soviet System of Mind Control* (1949) and Merle Fainsod's *How Russia Is Ruled* (1953) set the tone, stressing the omnipotence of the Soviet leadership, rendering Bolshevik/Soviet ideology as a fixed concept of control, and reducing the press to a means of maintaining that control or extending the whim of the leader. Short shrift was given to the social dynamics, improvisations, and indeterminacies of Soviet policy.[7]

From the mid-1960s, a new generation of historians, many inspired by the possibilities of 'social history', started to challenge the reductive and determinate narrative espoused under the influence of the T-model.[8] Taking advantage of expanded cultural-exchange programmes and acquiring some access to state archive materials in the process, this generation were more inclined to consult Soviet newspapers and periodicals to corroborate and texture their findings. They looked beyond high politics and 'great men', revealing the social and structuralist forces at play in Russian/Soviet history. They revealed the role of popular support for socialism in 1917, as well as worker enthusiasm for rapid industrialisation from the end of 1920s.[9] Historians such as Sheila Fitzpatrick and Lynne Viola, amassing materials from the archives and triangulating this with print media, showed how genuine enthusiasm among young activists helped shape the mobilisation drives that launched the First Five-Year Plan.[10] Lewis Siegelbaum and Donald Filtzer mined industrial-sector periodicals for qualitative and quantitative evidence that would help reconstruct the social realities of working life under early Stalinism. They produced shop-floor studies and micro-histories illuminating cases of worker autonomy and bargaining that undermined the overly simple totalitarian image of ubiquitous and ridged conformity.[11]

Similarly, Alexander Rabinowitch used newspapers, in conjunction with other sources, to chart the unfolding political drama of 1917. Not a social historian, Rabinowitch was interested in the development of Bolshevik politics across 1917. But like those that extended social history to the study of the Soviet Union, Rabinowitch challenged determinative accounts. Undertaking a close reading of the various press organs attached to the Bolsheviks and different Bolshevik divisions, Rabinowitch overturned the orthodox view of the party as a disciplined, monolithic organisation subservient to Lenin. He revealed the chaos and improvisation of Bolshevik politics in 1917. He showed that Lenin had to respond to events and popular forces, and that the party was often split when it came to determining the best course of action.[12] Shifting editorial prerogatives, heated op-eds and counter op-eds, as well as inter-newspaper references or rebukes were a staple of the press in 1917 – all of which can be used to draw out the ideological and strategic fissures within the Bolsheviks and the wider socialist movement.

The most significant shift in the way scholars approached the Soviet press and periodical was bought about by the 'cultural' and 'linguistic turn' – the principle influences of which included French social and cultural theorists, Michel Foucault and Pierre Bourdieu; German political theorist, Jürgen Habermas; American cultural anthropologist, Clifford Geertz; and Russian literary theorist, Mikhail Bakhtin.[13] This shift precipitated a move away from historical materialist and structuralist influences which had proposed that the 'social environment' dictated the formation of accepted (even rational) social categories, such as 'class', 'gender' and 'nation'. Across many disciplines and areas of research, scholars began to contest the assumed naturalness of these categories. No longer taken at face value, Ronald G. Suny explains, categories were increasingly viewed as 'historical constructions made by human actors who in turn are reconstituted by the very products of their making'.[14] From this perspective, structure was no longer seen to determine culture; culture was seen to play a constructive role in the formation of human organisation. Attention moved to how and why human actors invested and participated in certain 'constructions'. Culture was seen as contested, not an addendum or reflexion. And nothing – not science, nor rationality – was seen to be above the 'linguistic process'. Language and texts, it was stressed, reflect the artificial or constructed nature of cultural accounts and the wider human experience.

In general, there was a move toward a greater focus on discourse, language, and culture. The old analytical lenses of politics, society, and economics were no longer deemed sufficient on their own. Researchers started to study cultural phenomena, such as rituals and festivals, popular and ethnic culture, and the daily life of ordinary people. Politics was now understood to be embedded in everyday life.

Historians became interested in mentalities, attitudes, identity, images, symbols, rituals, and mythology – the things hidden beneath the surface of events, structures, and ideologies, as well as society, politics, and economics.[15] The result was a new-found appreciation for that which was once disregarded as 'counterfeit' or 'fraudulent' – the world of words that helped make and shape the Soviet experiment.

Stephen Kotkin's influential study, *Magnetic Mountain* (1995), which borrowed insights from Foucault, argued that Stalin's subjects learned to 'speak Bolshevik'. He highlighted the interaction between discourse and identity-formation at the heart of the Stalinist project. Kotkin took Soviet discourse seriously. He viewed Stalinism as a welfare-state project – an amalgam of transnational modern visions – with a constructed 'attendant consciousness'. In his own words, Kotkin looked upon Stalinism 'not just as a political system', but as a 'set of values, a social identity, a way of life'. Kotkin set out to show 'how certain ways of thinking and accompanying social practices fit into the grand strategies of Soviet state building'. He presented Stalinism as 'a new civilisation' with which individuals could self-identify or at least recognise the terms of reference.[16] The world of words – and the human interaction with these words – was a central preoccupation for Kotkin.

Within the field more broadly, the composition of texts and the voice of the subject gained in importance around this time. Scholars of the Soviet past approached published records, diaries, and discursive trails with fresh impetus. Jochen Hellbeck and Igal Halfin extended on Kotkin, using diaries and 'red biographies' to demonstrate how subjects identified with 'official discourse', going so far as to suggest that discourse 'creates a world for its users'.[17] Boris Kolonitskii looked at how rumour desacralised the Russian monarchy and how radical language and symbols gave people something around which to unify in 1917.[18] Katerina Clark probed Soviet literature and other discursive mediums in search of what she called the 'cultural ecosystem' from which revolution was constructed and understood.[19] Catriona Kelly traced the construction of Russian culture in numerous ways, including a study into the evolution of advice literature through etiquette manuals, guides to hygiene and house management, and treatises on upbringing.[20]

Drawing heavily on newspapers, periodicals, and printed sources, the historian Mark D. Steinberg has long seen the world of words as a means of illuminating Russian's encounter with modernity (and the discourses that helped make it). In his book *Moral Communities* (1992), Steinberg used printed sources to put 'culture ... back into social history', showing how working-class communities were galvanised by a sense of solidarity and morality that drew on values, norms, and perceptions formed and perpetuated through the myriad stories and voices that made the modern discourse of *fin de siècle* Russia. Steinberg has challenged cases of theoretical overreach – when discourse is used to deny human agency – extending the 'cultural turn' further than it usefully goes. But he maintains that discourse gave language to grievances and experiences felt in society. And, in turn, he has shown how letters to the press and workers' writings offer a means of accessing how this language was appropriated. This presents the newspaper and periodical not as an uncomplicated reflection of a time, nor as the perpetrators of a purely constructed matrix – a language that 'creates a world for its users' – but as a means of getting to grips with the circulation of ideas and values and varying appropriations that gave meaning to contemporary situations.

'Read all about it': history as experience

Although aware of the limitations of printed sources, Steinberg has stressed their value with regard to capturing the lived experience of history. With these materials, he insists, the historian can seek to 'tell the story of the Russian Revolution as *experience*, as people thinking and feeling about history as it unfolded in their own lives and as they took part in making history.'[21] The Russian Revolution has been viewed from many different angles. 'Traditional approaches', Steinberg explains, have focused on causes: 'why, for example, did the tsarist autocracy collapse in February 1917 and then the liberal government that replaced it fall to the Bolsheviks[?]' 'The usual answers', he continues, 'emphasize the role of institutions, leaders, and ideologies, and the unfolding story itself as a causative structure: events shaped the events that followed.'[22] 'Revisionist' social history put the spotlight on societal structures, leading historians of the Russian Revolution and the Soviet Union to emphasise the role of social polarisation and social stratification. But, as 'social history evolved into a new cultural history', Steinberg continues,

> historians have looked more to the complex and elusive world of mentalities and attitudes beneath the surfaces of events, structures, and ideologies towards 'discourse' – words, images, symbols, rituals, and myths – as not only revealing attitudes but shaping how people are able to understand their world and act in it.

'Experience', Steinberg advances, 'intersects with … these traditions and innovations as we ask what the past meant to people then, as lived history.'[23]

The value of printed sources is their ability to give the historian an insight into the past's own 'knowledge and interpretations of itself'. Historians have long struggled to recreate a sense of the past as it was then. Most understand that this is an impossible task, but that an imperfect attempt is better than no attempt at all. 'Every student', notes Steinberg, 'is taught that "primary sources" (documents created during the time under study) are better than secondary sources as more direct reflections of the past itself.' 'Of course', Steinberg adds, 'there is as much desire as science in this.'[24] Like a bee seeking nectar, the historian finds that primary documents offer a higher *experience*-reward return. But, it is worth stressing, such documentation offers only fleeting traces and interpretations, not complete views. Historians must also be extremely attentive and knowledgeable of historical contexts when reading these texts. Chronological proximity does not equate to accuracy or purity. We must be wary of the influences that came to bear on those that created primary evidence, as well as the parameters in which they were working – the things that might have affected what our subjects could or could not say, and how they said it.

Newspapers and periodicals are no different to other primary sources in this respect. But, as Steinberg puts it, 'For the historian of experience, the newspaper would seem to give us the past's own present, lived historical experience before it was rewritten to fit a story'. Steinberg acknowledges the essayist Walter Benjamin's call for a new history of modernity in the 1930s – a call that cited a preference for the newspaper and 'lived experience' (*erlebnis*) over detached and desalinised historicism.[25] 'I admit to the seductiveness of this ideal', explains Steinberg.

> I have long been drawn to newspapers as a source ... But I try not to be naïve, for newspaper writers certainly were not. Journalists knew that the stories they reported were filtered by incomplete evidence, unreliable or false witnesses, and their own choices and purposes. They had stories to tell and motives in telling them, ranging from selling papers to advancing a political cause – and Russian journalists had the added pressure of government censorship.[26]

From this perspective, the daily newspaper, handled with due consideration, is presented as a particularly good means of getting closer to everyday life. These fast-paced, immediate, and ever-updating reflections on contemporary events do not present a solitary vision of the 'truth' (in the manner understood by Leopold von Ranke). Rather they provide snapshots of what was considered relevant to, and by, contemporaries at the time of publication. They can also capture the mood, as seen in this example from *Ezhednevnaia gazeta-kopeika* (*The Daily Kopeck Gazette*), 11 March 1917:

> The nightmare yoke fell. Freedom and happiness – forward.
>
> 'Hurrah! Hurrah! Hurrah!'
>
> With thunderous roar, the thousand-voiced cry of the elate people cheer ...[27]

In turn, discovered Steinberg, one navy seaman absorbed and expressed this mood, conveying his experience of 'this time' in a poem he sent to *Izvestiia*:

> Dawn has broken, Arise, tribe oppressed,
> Arise, oh people bound in chains.
> Seed Once under the brutal yoke,
> Has now brought forth bountiful fruit.
> Unbend your mighty shoulders,
> Who would dare block your path bought with blood?
> No henchmen of monarch's thrones,
> Will take away your progress, your freedom flag!
> Who would trespass on your temple holy,
> Or dare defile that sacred site?
> No one, for you are a hero, a mighty titan,
> All men fall silent in your sight.[28]

In the Soviet context, we must be aware that press freedom and press diversity became more restricted and formulated as the years went by. This is a critical observation often levelled at *Pravda* and *Izvestiia*. With the seizure of power in October 1917, organs of the Soviet, most notably *Izvestiia*, came under Bolshevik control. The Decree on the Press, issued by the Bolsheviks in late October 1917, then targeted 'counter-revolution' and those that called for 'open resistance or disobedience'. It resulted in the closure of many liberal and rival socialist presses.[29] As the Civil War set in, non-socialist parties, such as the Constitutional Democrats (Kadets), were outlawed as 'enemies of the people'. By December, the 'All-Russian Extraordinary Commission for the Struggle Against Counter-revolution and Sabotage', better known as the *Cheka*, was established to root out and suppress opposition to the revolution. The Soviet system emerged amid a state of civil war and entrenched political suspicion. The Civil War was a brutal and vicious affair, with unspeakable violence perpetrated by all involved. For those that emerged as victors, it justified continued political restriction.

These restrictions place obvious limitations on the historian's pursuit of the lived experience. But a nuanced understanding of Soviet history still enables the researcher to discern shifts in discursive patterns over the years, as well as themes of genuine concern within published readers' letters, for example. Careful reading of later publications can still add texture to our renderings of Soviet life past.

Indeed, it should be noted, as the editor of *Pravda* in the 1920s, Nikolai Bukharin was convinced that amateur letter-writing was a means of developing an authentic proletarian consciousness. He initiated a 'Workers' Life' column in *Pravda*, publishing correspondence from ordinary people. He saw this as a way of developing the 'small grass root cells' that would form 'Soviet public opinion' (*Sovetskoe obshchestvennoe mnenie*), as well as the greatly anticipated social initiative that Marx and Engels insisted was destined to advance revolution.[30] Bukharin even became a self-appointed advocate for the *rabsel'kor* (worker-village correspondent) movement, encouraging readers to write in to Soviet newspapers and periodicals on matters close to home. Obviously, published letters were subject to editorial selection. But they still provide an insight into sections of Soviet society. As the historian Zenji Asaoka observes, Bukharin did not see this as a means of fostering political pluralism along the lines of liberal democracy, but he did expend a great deal of energy protecting *rabsel'kor*.[31]

Bukharin viewed all of this as part of an emerging discourse on Soviet *obshchestvennost'* – a term that defies easy translation, but which, it has been suggested, denotes Soviet 'civic-mindedness'. That is, a variation of civil society as understood in the West, a public sphere, a form of professional association, a public identity or an imagined civic community engaged in constructing a collective vision of socialist society. This was a vision of civic or public agency quite specific to Soviet socialism – something permitted up to the point it was deemed 'opposition', or to the point at which it challenged the Bolshevik party's right to govern and arbitrate. It was for those with an interest in the development of socialist ideology and Soviet revolutionary imperatives. In *Historical*

Materialism, Nikolai Bukharin argued that having spent their early years fighting to establish a new state, it was now time to refocus their efforts on Soviet *obshchestvennost'*.[32]

This idea of *obshchestvennost'*, some form of Soviet public dialogue, albeit restricted, can be seen in the 'Workers' Life' columns of later years. Some sections of Soviet society still felt encouraged to perform the role of good socialist citizen or opinion leader; others engaged in what Oleg Kharkhordin has called 'loyal critique of the regime's dysfunctions.'[33] Careful and considered researchers can gain considerable insight from both the 'loyalty' and 'criticism' of published correspondence and other contemporary writings. As Karl Loewenstein has shown, *obshchestvennost'* was resurgent under Nikita Khrushchev, particularly among literary figures keen to associate with, and advance reform.[34] If we accept, as Michael David-Fox has proffered, that some form of 'civil participation may have to be considered a feature of totalitarian dictatorship as well as a backbone of middle-class democracy', then such voices must be considered *telling* – even if they do not tell the 'whole truth'.[35] And, as ever, silences can be as revealing as anything else. Editorial choices are telling, too. Far from being 'fraudulent' – something to avoid because it will mislead the researcher – Soviet newspapers can be seen as a constructive source base when approached with due consideration.

New words, new worlds

Periodicals, it should be understood, were also an intrinsic part of the Soviet experience. As the German traveller Klaus Mehnert observed at the beginning of the 1930s, 'Periodicals are taken in everywhere'.

> The periodical plays a more important part in the Soviet Union than in any other country in the world. Four hundred different journals, not including newspapers, which are read by the great mass of the people are included alone in the German edition of the catalogue of Soviet Russian periodicals for the year 1932. The number of those journals intended specifically for youth is growing particularly fast, and their circulation runs well into millions already.

Mehnert noticed that 'Every level space in the Moscow bookshops' is taken up with periodicals and pamphlets 'dealing with burning questions'.

> There are little booklets consisting of eight printed pages and costing from two kopeks [...] I came across a hundred pamphlets concerning the Komsomol alone; fresh from the press they flooded the whole Union.[36]

'I have found that particularly important articles are much more thoroughly discussed [here]', Mehnert continues.

> [T]hey always provide a definite attitude to topical questions. The fact that views on the most important questions of the day, which seem to us to be

settled once and for all, do not follow the beaten track places Russian youth in a difficult position. These tracks are being laid bit by bit ... New solutions are always being tried. One must be well posted if one wishes to keep up.

The Soviet periodical is shown to be modern in form and content. This 'scientific' format, published in regular instalments and targeting specific areas of life, confidently showed the way forward on a number of 'topical questions'. 'A young Communist', Mehnert explains, 'looks in the periodical for the answer.' Soviet periodicals displayed all the arrogance of (socialist) modernity, imbued with the belief that the world can be made anew along rational lines. They were ever-updating for the ever-improving citizen of socialism. They were part of a fast-moving and ambitious vision. Books were unchanging, the periodical continued to progress. And, as Mehnert witnessed, the periodical became a particularly important part of youth life at this time.

Periodicals such as *Molodaia gvardiia* (*Young Guard*) formed part of the youth activist dialogue with Soviet ideology. According to the journal's own editorial brief, it was devoted to 'literature and art, general politics, and popular science'. Youth periodicals like this spoke to a 'new way of life' (*novyi byt*) and cultural transformation. What is more, they were direct and they held the answers; they were for doers, not contemplative types. As Mehnert found upon sampling just 24 issues of *Molodaia gvardiia*, 'in the nearly 2000 pages there is not even one single one which allows a moment's rest from the tension of political and economic life'. A 'severe struggle [is] made', he continues, 'by the authors, mostly very young, to produce a literature adapted in form and content to the new era.'[37] Writers and readers, it can be seen, were enthralled by the energy and ambition of a revolutionary project.

As I have tried to show in my own work, young activists often engaged with the discursive ideas presented in these periodicals, sometimes extending them in unexpected ways, before they themselves became part of the story. For example, putting collective ideals into practice and enacting calls to 'do away' with the traditional family, an urban commune movement emerged across the 1920s, with youth activists requisitioning living space in order to form exemplary bastions of socialist living.[38] Young commune activists, such as Mai, a student, wrote in to periodicals such as *Krasnyi student* (*Red Student*), proclaiming that she and her friends were 'restructuring the way of life' (*perestroika byta*) in their dormitory-based commune.

We began with 12 members, before growing to 76 persons. ... Each day two duty-communards are allocated to oversee the schedule ... In the commune we aim to overcome the old way of life, and recreate the family-unit for our time.

Picking up on key discursive themes, such as 'restructuring the way of life', Mai and the commune sought to put theory into practice. They extended other discursive ideas, such as the 'scientific organisation of labour', promoting time-discipline, in their case, through a daily schedule that dictated when they would eat, sleep, read, and work. They also keenly embraced daily *fizkultura* (physical culture) sessions, appropriating discursive messages that quite unsubtly associated a healthy body with a healthy mind.[39] And when Aleksandra Kollontai advocated a new approach to love, sex, and relationships in her 'Letters to the Toiling Youth', published in *Molodaia gvardiia*, in 1923, the communes vied to put her advice into practice.[40] Advice literature was soon turned into a new practising socialist lifestyle.

> Each epoch has its own ideal of love; each class strives in its own interests to insert its own content into the moral conception of love. […]

> If in loving relations blind, demanding, all-embracing passion weakens; if the feeling of possession and the egoistical desire to forever fasten the beloved around oneself is washed away; if the self-satiety of the man and criminal renunciation of her own 'I' on the part of the woman disappears: then there will develop other valued aspects of love. … The striving to express love … in togetherness of action, in unity of will, in joint creation.[41]

Reports show communes actively debating sex and love, and promoting comradely relationships based on mutual respect. None claimed to have stumbled upon a ready-made replacement for 'bourgeois love'. In matter of fact, love proved a tricky realm for many communes. Nevertheless, they saw fit to take up the challenge, embedding themselves within the discourse on socialist love.[42]

Soon Soviet periodicals were sending people to stay with such groups and publishing in-depth stories on them. One regular contributor to *Smena* (*Change*), a Komsomol periodical, spent a number of nights in a Moscow commune in the mid-1920s. He reported that such groups appeared determined not only to 'solve the housing problem', but to forge a path to the 'new way of life'. These young activists, it was said, were adapting existing spaces for the collective life. They were presented as the 'new shoots' ready to embrace and construct socialism.[43] Some started to place the communes on a progressive arc from the 'disorder' and 'social decay' depicted in Russian classics, such as *Oblomov* (1859), to the world of order, rationality, and electric light promised by Lenin.[44]

A cyclical relationship was established whereby activists enacted the discourse and promise of the periodicals, and the periodicals reported the achievements and undertakings of the activists. The urban communes became an unsanctioned revolutionary meme – an imitable notion carrying cultural ideas, symbols, or practices – that allowed contemporaries to envision the possibilities of socialism.[45]

Such stories, carefully crosschecked and triangulated with other sources, help to revive a sense of 'the time' from an activist perspective, as well as adding depth to our understanding of how Soviet discourse developed. They also show that the modern socialist discourse of a Soviet periodical was not an unchanging entity. Soviet periodicals did not merely emit flat propaganda or inflict ideas onto a malleable population. Reductive views only work when real life is distilled to the point of abstraction. The Soviet periodical – itself a dynamic and modern object – can offer a glimpse into the dynamism of the Soviet experience.

Inspired by the literary scholars Sean Lantham and Robert Scholes, who in 2006 boldly proclaimed the rise of 'Modern Periodical Studies', an emergent Slavic periodical studies cluster stresses a similar view of this dynamic source base.[46] Taking the lead of Lantham and Scholes, the Slavic, East European and Eurasian Periodical Studies group (SEEEPS), at Princeton, have embraced the idea of assessing Soviet periodicals as 'autonomous objects of study', rather than 'containers of discrete bits of information'.[47] Indeed, Natalia Ermolaev and Phillip Gleisser emphasise that for 'two centuries, not only literary, but political, technological, and economic forces kept the thick journal in a position of influence over readers, critics, and scholars'.[48] The heritage of the 'thick journal' – the nineteenth-century vessel of political, cultural, literary and scientific enlightenment – secured the periodical a place of importance after 1917.

Highlighting the cultural form of Soviet periodicals, moreover, scholars can also more readily appreciate the concepts and categories that came to bear on the Soviet Union. This is particularly true of the intellectual categories, assumptions, and theories of modernity and Russia's modern discourse. Focusing on the periodical as an object, the embrace of modern typeface and typographic experimentation can be just as revealing as the content of this literature. The boom in isotype graphics and pictorial language during the First Five-Year Plan, for instance, gives a sense of the modern mechanical and didactic aspirations that helped make and define this period. The initiator of this new 'language-like technique', Otto Neurath, saw isotype as a means of expressing consistency through the use of graphic elements. The basic element of this technique, pictograms, or simplified pictures of people or things, were designed to function as repeatable units.[49] The Soviet press and periodicals keenly embraced this new 'language-like technique', with oil production measurements displayed through pictorial barrels of oil and the number of nursery places represented through baby pictograms. And, in 1931, the Soviet authorities invited Neurath to Moscow to assist with the establishment of an institute for pictorial statistics.[50] This, and the constant recourse to statistical language and tables in periodicals such as *Za industrializatsiiu* (*Towards Industrialization*) and *Partiinoe stroitel'stvo* (*Party Construction*) for example, gives a sense of a Soviet Union negotiating the influence of those mechanical and rational beings espoused in Russian futurism (and connected discourses).

Conclusion: working with printed sources now

The October Revolution and the wider Bolshevik project was fundamentally concerned with everyday life – viewing it as something that could be changed, as a site for revolutionary action. Soviet newspapers and periodicals offer a means of examining this preoccupation and the resultant impact on the Soviet lived experience. This once underutilised source base can help us understand how meaning was attributed and appropriated in the Soviet Union. As it has recently been pointed out, a wealth of new scholarship has shown renewed interest in the everyday experience of Soviet life.[51] Seen as a crucial component of the modern projects and socialist discourses from which 1917 emerged, the significance of the world of words to everyday life, and everyday life to the world of words, can only be understood when the Soviet press and periodicals are integrated into our research. The promise of modern socialism and the experience of this imagined future is lived out on the pages of the Soviet Union's printed sources.

Together the newspaper and periodical can provide one of the most immediate and accessible lenses on a range of Soviet experiences and discourses. In each case, the same limitations of censorship and editorial accountability remain, but, for instance, different regional publications can offer an insight into the specific experiences of the different peoples, nations, and cultures that made up the multi-ethnic Soviet Union. At the very least, one can begin to see how the notion of a 'friendship of peoples' came to bear in different settings. Aspects of constructed and contested nationalities, and their place within the Union, can be traced through regional print organs such as *Rabotnitsa gazeta* (*Workers' Gazette*) or *Nova droba* (*New Age*), in Ukraine, *Sovet turkmenistany* (*Soviet Turkmenistan*), in what was Turkestan, and *Sabchota abkhazeti* (*Soviet Abkhazia*), in Georgia. This is one of the benefits of Lenin's nationality policy, or the legacy of it, making space for 'autonomised' components of the Soviet Union. Similarly, scholars have used *Rabotnitsa* (*The Women Worker*) and the later *Sovetskaia zhenshchina* (*Soviet Women*) to assess the place of women and gendered perceptions in the Soviet Union. The myriad of experiences that formed the Soviet experiment can be approached through the medium of contemporary print. The centralised and prescriptive nature of Soviet print organs carry obvious limitations for the researcher, but, at the same time, they can still provide a direct route to Soviet understandings of themselves.

Notes

1 Laura Engelstein, *Russia in Flames: War, Revolution, Civil War, 1914–1921* (New York, NY: Oxford University Press, 2017), p. xxi.
2 Ibid., p. xxii.
3 Mark D. Steinberg, *Voices of Revolution, 1917*, documents trans. by Marian Schwartz (New Haven, CT: Yale University Press, 2001), p. 3.
4 Cf. Peter Kenez, *The Birth of a Propaganda State: Soviet Methods of Mass Mobilization* (Cambridge: Cambridge University Press, 1985), esp. p. 153; Martin Malia, *The Soviet Tragedy: A History of Socialism in Russia, 1917–1991* (New York, NY: Free Press, 1994).
5 Boris Kolonitskii, 'Centenary Reflections' [unpublished paper], delivered at the Association for Slavic, East European, and Eurasian Studies (ASEEES) Annual Convention, Chicago, IL, 2017.
6 For a guide to this and other Russian repositories, see Samantha Sherry, Jonathan Waterlow and Andy Willimott (eds.), *Using Archives and Libraries in the Former Soviet Union v.2.0* (BASEES-Open Access, 2013). Also note the online resource ArcheoBiblioBase: <www.iisg.nl/abb/>.
7 Ronald G. Suny, *Red Flag Unfurled: History, Historians, and the Russian Revolution* (London and New York, NY: Verso, 2017), p. 76. A previous version of the historiographical essay consulted here can be found in idem. (ed.), *Cambridge History of Russia*, vol. 3: *The Twentieth Century* (Cambridge: Cambridge University Press, 2006), pp. 5–64.
8 Ibid., p. 80.
9 Ibid., p. 103.

10 See Sheila Fitzpatrick, *Education and Social Mobility in Soviet Russia, 1921–1934* (Cambridge: Cambridge University Press, 1979); Lynne Viola, *The Best Sons of the Fatherland: Workers in the Vanguard of Soviet Collectivization* (Oxford: Oxford University Press, 1987).

11 Lewis H. Siegelbaum, *Stakhanovism and the Politics of Productivity in the USSR, 1935–1941* (Cambridge: Cambridge University Press, 1988); Donald Filtzer, *Soviet Workers and Stalinist Industrialization: The Formation of Modern Soviet Production Relations, 1928–1941* (Armonk, NY: M. E. Sharpe, 1986).

12 Alexander Rabinowitch, *Prelude to Revolution: The Petrograd Bolsheviks and the July 1917 Uprising* (Bloomington, IN: Indiana University Press, 1968).

13 Suny, *Red Flag Unfurled*, p. 114.

14 Ibid., p. 30. A previous version of this essay was published in *American Historical Review*, 107 (2002), pp. 1476–99.

15 Mark D. Steinberg, *The Russian Revolution, 1905–1921* (Oxford: Oxford University Press, 2017), p. 2.

16 Stephen Kotkin, *Magnetic Mountain: Stalinism as a Civilization* (Berkeley, CA: University of California Press, 1995), p. 23.

17 See Jochen Hellbeck, *Revolution on My Mind: Writing a Diary under Stalin* (Cambridge, MA: Harvard University Press, 2006); Igal Halfin, *Terror in My Soul: Communist Autobiographies on Trial* (Cambridge, MA: Harvard University Press, 2003); Igal Halfin, *Intimate Enemies: Demonizing the Bolshevik Opposition, 1918–1928* (Pittsburgh, PA: University of Pittsburgh Press, 2007); Igal Halfin, *From Darkness to Light: Class, Consciousness, and Salvation in Revolutionary Russia* (Pittsburgh, PA: University of Pittsburgh Press, 2000). Latter quotation: Igal Halfin, *Stalinist Confessions. Messianism and Terror at the Leningrad Communist University* (Pittsburgh, PA: University of Pittsburgh Press, 2009), p. 16.

18 Boris Kolonitskii, *Simvoly vlasti i bor'ba za vlast': K izucheniiu politicheskoi kul'tury rossiiskoi revoliutsii 1917 goda* (St Petersburg: Dmitrii Bulanin, 2001).

19 Katerina Clark, *Petersburg: Crucible of Cultural Revolution* (Cambridge, MA: Harvard University Press, 1998).

20 Catriona Kelly, *Refining Russia: Advice Literature, Polite Culture, & Gender from Catherine to Yeltsin* (Oxford: Oxford University Press, 2001).

21 Steinberg, *The Russian Revolution*, p. 1.

22 Ibid.

23 Ibid., p. 2.

24 Ibid.

25 Ibid., p. 3; Citing: Walter Benjamin, 'Paris, Capital of the Nineteeth Century: Exposé [1939]', in Walter Benjamin (ed.), *The Arcades Project*, trans. Howard Eiland and Kevin McLaughlin (Cambridge, MA: Harvard University Press, 1999), p. 14.

26 Ibid., p. 4.

27 'Soldaty idut …' *Ezhednevnaia gazeta-kopeika*, 11 March 1917, p. 1; cited in: ibid., p. 19. With thanks to Mark D. Steinberg for allowing his poetry translations in this and the following note to be reproduced.

28 Stepan Stepanov, 'Razsvelo', 28 March 1917; cited in: ibid., p. 25.

29 *Dekrety Sovetskoi Vlasti* (Moscow: Institute of Marxism-Leninism, 1957), vol. 1, pp. 24–5. Published in *Izvestiia* on 28 October 1917, p. 2.

30 Zenji Asaoka, 'Nikolai Bukharin and the *Rabsel'kor* movement: *Sovetskaia Obshchestvennost'* under the "Dictatorship of the Proletariat"', in *Obshchestvennost' and Civic Agency*, pp. 85–6.

31 Ibid., esp. pp. 90–5.

32 Nikolai Bukharin, *Teoriia istoricheskogo materializma* (Moscow and Petrograd, 1923), p. 229; cited in Zenji Asaoka, 'Nikolai Bukharin and the *Rabsel'kor* movement:

Sovetskaia Obshchestvennost' under the "Dictatorship of the Proletariat"', in Yasuhiro Matsui (ed.), *Obshchestvennost' and Civic Agency in Late Imperial and Soviet Russia: Interface between State and Society* (London: Palgrave, 2015), pp. 85–6.

33 Oleg Kharkhordin, *The Collective and the Individual in Russia: A Study of Practices* (Berkeley, CA: University of California Press, 1999), p. 313.

34 Karl Loewnstein, 'Obshchestvennost' as Key to Understanding Soviet Writers of the 1950s: *Moskovskii Literator*, October 1956–March 1957', *Journal of Contemporary History*, 33 (2009), pp. 473–92 (p. 475).

35 Andy Willimott, 'Revolutionary Participation, Youthful Civic-Mindedness', in James Harris, Peter Whitewood and Lara Douds (eds.), *The Fate of the Bolshevik Revolution: Illiberal Liberation, 1917–1941* (London: Bloomsbury Academic, 2019); Michael David-Fox, 'Review: Obshchestvennye organizatsii Rossii v 1920-e gody', *Kritika*, 3 (2002), p. 181.

36 Klaus Mehnert, *Youth in Soviet Russia*, trans. Michael Davidson (London: Harcourt, Brace, 1933), pp. 88–9.

37 Ibid., p. 110.

38 Andy Willimott, *Living the Revolution: Urban Communes & Soviet Socialism, 1917–1932* (Oxford: Oxford University Press, 2017).

39 Kommunar Mai, 'God raboty kommuny Studentov-vodnikov', *Krasnyi student*, 1 (1925), p. 22.

40 Alexandra Kollontai, 'Letters to the Toiling Youth', *Molodaia gvardiia*, 3 (1923), pp. 11–24; cited William G. Rosenberg (ed.), *Bolshevik Visions: First Phase of the Cultural Revolution in Soviet Russia* (Ann Arbor, MI: University of Michigan Press, 1990), Part 1, pp. 84–94.

41 Ibid., pp. 86, 94.

42 R. Pragera, 'Kommuna desiati', *Smena*, 12 (1928), pp. 10–11; A. Revina, 'Zhizn' desiati', *Smena*, 19 (1929), p. 5.

43 Z. Karenko, 'V kommunakh rabochei molodezhi', *Smena*, 3 (1926), p. 8.

44 'Lenin v commune Vkhutemas', *Molodaia gvardiia*, 2–3 (1924), pp. 107–11.

45 Willimott, *Living the Revolution*, p. 81.

46 Natalia Ermolaev and Phillip Gleisser, 'Periodical Studies: Why and How to Re-Read East European Journals', *ASEEES NewsNet*, 56, 1 (January 2016), pp. 11–12.

47 Sean Lantham and Robert Scholes, 'The Rise of Periodical Studies', *PMLA*, 121 (2006), pp. 517–31.

48 Ermolaev and Gleisser, *ASEEES NewsNet*, p. 11.

49 Christopher Burke, Eric Kindel and Sue Walker (eds.), *Isotype: Design and Contexts, 1925 to 1971* (London: Hyphen Press, 2013), introduction. See also Otto Neurath, *From Hieroglyphics to Isotype: A Visual Autobiography*, eds. Matthew Eve and Christopher Burke (London: Hyphen Press, 2010).

50 *Vsesoiuznyi institut izobrazitel'noi statistiki sovetskogo stroitel'stva i khoziaistva*; IZOSTAT (All-Union Institute of Pictorial Statistics of Soviet Construction and Economy). See Emma Minns, 'Picturing Soviet Progress: Izostat, 1931–34', in *Isotype: Design and Contexts, 1925 to 1971* (London: Hyphen Press, 2013), pp. 257–81.

51 Deirdre Ruscitti Harshman, 'A Space Called Home: Housing and the Management of the Everyday in Russia, 1890–1935', unpublished PhD thesis (University of Illinois at Urbana-Champaign, 2018), pp. 1–2. Ruscitti Harshman, whose own work can be understood as part of the cited scholarship trend, references Willimott, *Living the Revolution*; Steinberg, *The Russian Revolution*; Tsuyoshi Hasegawa, *Crime and Punishment in the Russian Revolution: Mob Justice and Police in Petrograd* (Cambridge, MA: Harvard University Press, 2017); Yuri Slezkine, *The House of Government: A Saga of the Russian Revolution* (Princeton, NJ: Princeton University Press, 2017).

Further reading

Engelstein, Laura, *Russia in Flames: War, Revolution, Civil War, 1914–1921* (New York, NY: Oxford University Press, 2017).

Fitzpatrick, Sheila, and Lynne Viola, *A Researcher's Guide to Sources on Soviet Social History in the 1930s* (London and New York, NY: Routledge, 1990).

Huxtable, Simon, 'A Compass in the Sea of Life: Soviet Journalism, the Public, and the Limits of Reform After Stalin, 1953–1968', unpublished PhD Dissertation (Birkbeck, University of London, 2012).

Kelly, Catriona, *Refining Russia: Advice Literature, Polite Culture, & Gender from Catherine to Yeltsin* (Oxford: Oxford University Press, 2001).

Kenez, Peter, *The Birth of a Propaganda State: Soviet Methods of Mass Mobilization* (Cambridge: Cambridge University Press, 1985).

Kotkin, Stephen, *Magnetic Mountain: Stalinism as a Civilization* (Berkeley, CA: University of California Press, 1995).

Lantham, Sean, and Robert Scholes, 'The Rise of Periodical Studies', *PMLA*, 121 (2006), pp. 517–31.

Lenoe, Matthew E., *Closer to the Masses: Stalinist Culture, Social Revolution, and Soviet Newspapers* (Cambridge, MA: Harvard University Press, 2004).

Rosenberg, William G. (ed.), *Bolshevik Visions: First Phase of the Cultural Revolution in Soviet Russia* (Ann Arbor, MI: University of Michigan Press, 1990).

Ruscitti Harshman, Deirdre, 'A Space Called Home: Housing and the Management of the Everyday in Russia, 1890–1935', unpublished PhD thesis (University of Illinois at Urbana-Champaign, 2018).

Sherry, Samanatha, Jonathan Waterlow and Andy Willimott (eds.), *Using Archives and Libraries in the Former Soviet Union v.2.0* (BASEES-Open Access, 2013).

Steinberg, Mark D. (ed.), *Voices of Revolution, 1917*, documents trans. by Marian Schwartz (New Haven, CT: Yale University Press, 2001).

———, *The Russian Revolution, 1905–1921* (Oxford: Oxford University Press, 2017).

Suny, Ronald G., *Red Flag Unfurled: History, Historians, and the Russian Revolution* (London and New York, NY: Verso, 2017).

Willimott, Andy, *Living the Revolution: Urban Communes & Soviet Socialism, 1917–1932* (Oxford: Oxford University Press, 2017).

10 Visual culture as evidence of the Soviet past

Claire Le Foll

However familiar one is with Soviet history, it is very likely that we will think about it visually through a propaganda poster, a portrait of Stalin, a photograph of the Second World War or an avant-garde painting. Visual culture was crucial to the building of the Soviet state and to the transformation (or indoctrination, some would say) of the population, as in so many other modern and totalitarian states. 'Visual culture formed a central front in the war of ideas'.[1] The Bolsheviks used both old and new forms, written media but also visual means, including cinema, photography or monumental art to destroy the old system and create a new one. From avant-garde to socialist realism, including constructivism and figurative art, Soviet visual culture was a vibrant facet of this new culture in the making. The Russian and non-Russian populations of the Soviet Union were exposed to images and representations in their everyday life, more than ever before: in the pages of the books and magazines they read, in public transport (e.g., in the Moscow metro stations), when queuing for provisions (e.g., on suprematist rationing tickets), in their work place through posters, and, occasionally, in the large exhibitions organized by the state, or during major celebrations and demonstrations. Whether living in big cities or in small villages, the Soviet population could hardly escape this omnipresent visual culture that was meant to be visible not only in museums but also present in objects of everyday life. This is true of the Soviet period, but the same could be said about the Imperial period. Paintings and other representations of the tsars, of their allies and competitors played a prominent role in constructing national identity, no less than the *lubki* and icons which were present in everyday life.[2] It seems obvious, especially for Russian and Soviet history, that the visual consistently remained 'a highly valued ingredient in the construction of identities, power structures, and forms of social communication'.[3] This chapter will take a broad approach to visual culture and will include a variety of genres and objects, and offer insights and a methodology to use them as unique historical evidence for Soviet history.[4]

The different uses of and approaches to visual traces

In spite of this proliferation of images and visuality, Soviet visual culture has been largely neglected in history books. Analysed either as part of Russian art history, or used as illustrations or accompaniments for publications, images are rarely treated as integral parts of Russian and Soviet history.[5] This is not typical of Russian history only and reflects a more general tendency to neglect 'visual culture' in cultural studies and history in general.[6] However, the study of everyday life, material culture, 'public opinion' or mentalities would not be possible without using images as historical evidence. Jacob Burckhardt and Johan Huizinga opened the way with their study of Renaissance Italian and Dutch cultures through painting at the turn of the twentieth century, followed by Aby Warburg in the 1930s, and then culminating with the so-called 'pictorial turn' in the 1970s in France and more vigorously in the 1980s in the English-speaking academic world and in Germany with the *Bildwissenschaft*.[7] A new transdisciplinary field, visual studies, has boomed since then and has explored the theoretical, methodological and practical implications of researching with visual materials.[8] There is a new trend, noticeable in the classrooms and on the institutional websites of history departments, to increase the use of images, but too often they are still used solely to illustrate a slide or alongside 'traditional' written and archival sources.

The aim of this chapter is to encourage students and researchers to use images and other visual artefacts as sources in their own right, as traces of the past that can 'uncover information not recorded in written sources'.[9] Visual sources can be used in three main ways. First, as sources of factual information on daily life and material culture, they 'allow us to "imagine" the past more vividly' and reconstruct the material life of ordinary people, through the history of clothes, technology, cityscapes, domestic interiors, use of objects or bodies.[10] Images can be useful to document the history of certain social groups that are not represented in archives and traditional documents (for instance, children or ordinary women at work). Second, as witnesses to 'the power of visual representations in the religious and political life of past cultures',[11] they serve as points of access to the ideas, attitudes, taste and mentalities of different groups in different periods and places.[12] Being able to decode the meaning of visual sources requires a certain familiarity with the conventions, beliefs, codes and symbols recognized in a given society. Therefore, images help us to understand both mental and political history through the symbolism and values of a time and place. Third and finally, they also allow us to consider the social functions and cultural practices associated with the visual in given societies. The act of watching and witnessing, as well as the credibility entrusted to images at different times and places, reveals a lot about the evolving place of visual culture in society. It is therefore useful to reflect on 'the meanings attributed to vision itself', as well as on the modes of viewing, and the effect of viewing on the viewer. Exploring the act and experience of viewing, in simple words the reception of a given source and its effects on the viewer, requires us to take into consideration a wide range of processes that constitute what Stuart Hall refers to as the 'cultural practices of looking and interpretation'.[13] As 'mute eyewitnesses', visual sources convey a view of the society at a given time and place but can also be re-interpreted indefinitely. They can be difficult to read and interpret, and need careful analysis and source criticism.

Methodology

Images and visual objects can be deceptive. Some appear mysterious and open to various interpretations, while some seem very precise, true reflections of the past and 'reality' alike (e.g., photographs). However, they are representations that require a critical apparatus that includes an analysis of 'the intentions, uses and meanings imputed by the producers and the understandings and practices of viewers and consumers'.[14] The method of critical analysis proposed here will examine how the meaning is shaped at three different stages or 'sites': production, the image itself, and diffusion/reception.[15]

At the production stage, a few factors need to be considered to critically understand the visual object: authorship or makership; technology; subject or genre. The question of authorship for visual sources can be more complex than for written sources. Although the same questions about the author and, in particular, their social and political identities apply as for a written source, they can be seen as less important, as other more important factors such as the patron, cultural context, subject or audience(s) can modify the meaning and the intended message.[16] It is therefore crucial to understand the purpose of the maker in connection with the cultural practices of the time and the economic aspects of the production of a visual object. As producing an image or work of art can involve high costs (in most cases higher than writing), it is important to understand whether the work was commissioned and by whom, with what purpose, where it was to be placed and what function it would serve. These economic factors can have an impact on the content and diffusion of an image but also on the size or style of a work. For instance, most illustrations of books and periodicals in the 1920s in the USSR were two coloured (red and black) because of economic restrictions.

Images can be produced to be sold, but there are many other possible purposes that are not mutually exclusive. These might include a motive to record a period or a disappearing culture, as in the case of the Russian-Jewish ethnographer S. An-sky during his ethnographic expedition to the Jewish towns of Ukraine in 1912–14, in which hundreds of photographs and sketches were made by the artist S. Yudovin. This 'documentary art' is in itself not devoid of intentions, subjectivity and prejudices: An-sky idealized the popular culture that he thought more 'authentic', and therefore more suitable to serve as a source of inspiration for a modern Jewish art. Another purpose is to serve an institution or a power, as exemplified by political or religious images such as portraits of sovereigns, icons or historical paintings. A third is the creation of art for its own sake, and to contribute to or break with an aesthetic movement, to inaugurate a new trend or to create 'pure emotions' (for instance, the French impressionists, or Kazimir Malevich in Russia). The maker's involvement and subjectivity can be explicit in their writing or in some particular images, for example when Diego Velazquez represented himself in *Las Meninas* (1656). However, the 'intentionality' of the author is subject to interpretation and should not be overstated, since, as we will see below, the wider context of reception can completely change the initial intended meaning and the way visual material is understood.

The second aspect that determines how a visual object is seen is a technological one. In some cases the technology chosen by the maker will impact on the object's form, meaning and reception. The different technologies used to produce visual objects can also determine their style, truthfulness, and purpose, whether they were commissioned and also where, by whom and when they might be seen.[17] A drawing is different from an oil painting, not only because it does not require the same material and skill and has fewer economic implications, but also because it will not be valued in the same way or placed in the same places. A sketch directly drawn from life can also be regarded as a more trustworthy reflection of the reality than the painting it inspired. Similarly a photograph is often considered as being more truthful than a painting, but is still constructed by the photographer and informs us about their point of view.[18] Sculptures, whether they involve carving (wood, marble or stone), bronze casting or clay/wax modelling, will have different costs, strength and malleability.

The number of images available is another technological aspect that has wide implications for the diffusion, value and meaning of the images. The revolution of image reproduction increased the quantity of images available, and had an impact on their quality, colour and reception. Although there is debate on whether the massive reproduction of images resulted in the devaluation of the image, it affected the way images were produced (whether they were profitable for example), disseminated and interpreted.[19] This is particularly relevant to Soviet history, as the wider circulation of visual images meant that more people could be reached and that the ideological and political issues at stake were higher, hence resulting in increased control of the visual.

Finally, the author decides to create the visual object according to (or against) specific genre conventions. The genre is a 'way of classifying visual images into certain groups' (e.g., street photograph, portrait, landscape, bas-relief, documentary painting or photography, advertisement, photomontage, icon, religious building).[20] A particular genre will share some visual conventions, a subject and/or a specific set of meaningful objects or symbols. Some visual objects are connected to more than one genre – for instance, the *Mona Lisa* is obviously a portrait but its background relates, in an unusual way at the time, to the genre of the landscape. The emergence, institutionalization and disappearance of genres is very telling about a particular period and the transformations that affected a society. For example, the mid-nineteenth-century transition from portraits and historical paintings to 'genre painting' (scenes of everyday life) in Russia mirrors the interest of a large part of the intelligentsia in the peasants' condition after their emancipation in 1861 and in the ideas of populism. When a new genre emerges or when an artist moves to another genre, it usually means something. The choice made by the Russian painter Ilya Repin to represent scenes of everyday life constituted a rupture with the academic painting that prevailed and that focused on the political elite and historical events. It reflected a revolt of the young generation against the inequality of Russian society under the autocratic regime of the tsars, as exemplified by the social criticism displayed in the *Religious Procession in Kursk Province* (1880–3). So, the genre and subject choice of the visual sources available at a specific time and place affect their meaning.

The image or visual material itself, whether it is a painting, drawing, photograph, sculpture, architecture or object needs to be analysed in relation to its form and content. The style includes the form, composition (or spatial organization) and colouring of an image, while the iconography is an analysis of the subject matter or content. Both aspects can ensue from the production stage: the economic circumstances of an artist can have a constraining effect on this; similarly, a genre can also imply the choice of a specific style or iconography.

First, iconography is the identification, description, and interpretation of the content of images, of their hidden symbols and philosophy.[21] Its aims are to decipher the cultural codes associated with a specific object, situation or person. This iconographic analysis is particularly appropriate and useful to understand Renaissance art or seventeenth-century art as a complex system of symbols and meanings associated with specific ideas and thoughts, usually connected to Greek mythology or Christian/biblical episodes. Russian and Soviet art also has its own iconography, with conventional representations of the monarchy (e.g., the double-headed eagle or the Cap of Monomakh) or Mother Russia (a woman in traditional costume wearing a diadem or crown), that would be replaced with a Soviet vocabulary symbolizing the construction of a proletarian and modern state (e.g., workers and farmers at work; tractors and electrical pylons; portraits of Lenin and Stalin). Anything that departs from usual codes or representations denotes a change of intention, or can be interpreted as such. For instance, when Nicholas II chose to be photographed in intimate settings and family portrayals in an attempt to modernize the image of the tsar, he not only distanced himself from the conventions of the official imperial portrait, but also departed from the iconography and visual symbols of masculinity and strength associated with it, which made him look weak and feminine. It should be noted that although iconographic analysis is not relevant for all periods or visual material, the analysis of an image's content should always start with a description of its different visible elements.

Second, the analysis of style can also help to decode the intended meaning of a visual object. The particular way in which a painting was painted, a photograph was framed, or a building was designed, again can signify a rupture with the past or – on the contrary – continuity. To this extent, the Russian avant-garde, that is the emergence of art groups that defied the conventional rules of perspective in painting, corresponds to deep changes in Russian society at the beginning of the twentieth century and coincides with a desire of the urban middle class to challenge the established authorities. The style analysis can include an identification of: format (size, orientation); centring (long/medium/close shot); forms (outlines; straight/curved/rounded lines); space (volume; flatness/depth; relation between background and foreground; perspective; vanishing point; localization of a building); light (*clair-obscur* [half-light]); touch (brush stroke visible or not, thick or thin), and the composition. The aim of the latter is to direct the viewer's gaze through an arrangement of elements, lines, shapes and colours. It can create the illusion of three-dimensionality if all the lines converge into one vanishing point (Alberti perspective), or guide the eye of the viewer through a more complicated trajectory, in that way creating a narrative within the painting. Colours can also be used to organize an image, to reinforce the impression of perspective, create contrasts between different parts or invent new visual codes (e.g., Chagall and his green human figures). Style and composition are key in the 'sensory experiencing' of images and visual material, which can be difficult to appreciate and convey in words, but which contributes to the 'power of images' and is an integral part of the act and experience of viewing.

Third and finally, the viewer's subjectivity, the dissemination and the context of reception can deeply modify the way an image is understood. The meaning of an image depends not only on the intention of its maker and whether they managed to convey it in the end product, but also on the 'social context' of viewing and on the person(s) looking at it. Rather than the passive receiver of a message in a one-way communication, the viewer is the maker of their own interpretation.[22] The viewers cannot be reduced to a 'broad population' or a homogeneous and constructed group. They have different interpretations of the meaning of an image depending on their social, cultural or psychological background.[23] These interpretations can change over time, and may depend on the conditions and contexts of viewing. Indeed, viewing a given image in an art gallery or in a museum is quite a different experience than seeing it in someone's home or reproduced in a journal. The interpretation of an image is also influenced by the viewer's cultural and social background and their ability to decipher the style and the visual conventions, an ability that is more widespread among middle-class and educated audiences. Furthermore, the emotional and sensory effect of visual objects should not be underestimated. Stuart Hall highlights the fact that as 'visual signs' images have a symbolic power that can touch 'archaic', unconscious and irrational levels of awareness.[24] Images can provoke unconscious process of identification or rejection, for example when representing 'the other' in terms of gender or race. Looking and seeing are therefore cultural and social practices that say a great deal about how, at both individual and social levels, images are subjectively interpreted as 'visual signs'. It is more challenging for historians than for social scientists to document the reception and the interpretation of a visual source, as they usually cannot conduct interviews or observations of the viewers. However, written sources such as diaries, letters or reviews provide valuable insights into the reactions of a variety of audiences. In the case of the Soviet Union, we should keep in mind that the 'frighteningly effective images of propaganda'[25] do not always produce the expected effect, as Anna Shternshis has demonstrated when observing that the viewers of *Seekers of Happiness* (directed by Korsh and Shapiro, 1936) paid no attention to the plot and the ideological message of the film.[26] Audiences can then subvert the visual message but also respond to it, in either their actions or with other images. Social histories of responses to art or analysis of the relation between the spectator and the image are useful to understand why certain images were misunderstood, or to evaluate the breadth of responses that they could generate (from vandalism to other visual uses or subversions).[27]

Visual sources are difficult to interpret. In some ways they are less specific than words, and harder to penetrate. In others, they are more precise and concrete, and can convey a clear message. However, there is no guarantee that this message will be read straightforwardly by the viewers. The meaning of visual sources is therefore elusive and results from a complex relation between the form and content of the image itself, but also the social, economic and political context during the process of creation, diffusion and reception.

The traps of Soviet art and historiography

The study of Soviet visual culture contains its own historiographical and methodological issues. As noted earlier, the Bolsheviks understood from the beginning of their rule the importance of using culture, symbols and language to win the war of ideas and power. This manipulation of cultural symbols and of art – as tools of power – continued throughout the 1930s and beyond. There is a widespread belief, therefore, that culture in the Soviet period was controlled and decided by the highest levels of the state apparatus and party elite. Many documents concerning the relationship between Soviet culture and power show how culture became a tool of 'legitimation' of the state in the hands of Stalin, the Politburo and the Central Committee or local Party leadership.[28] As a consequence of this tight relationship, it can be argued that culture and ideology were conflated and that the former was reduced to serve the Party and build a cult of its leaders.

This vision of a Soviet culture subjugated to political power and deprived of autonomy fits into the 'totalitarian' interpretation of Soviet history. In the sphere of art and visual culture, this position has resulted in a strong focus on visual agitation, the cult of personality and the idea that the Bolsheviks created a 'propaganda state'.[29] This approach to Soviet history presupposes a high degree of state control over the public and private spheres, including art.[30] Exemplified by Igor Golomstock, this paradigm implies that in 'totalitarian' regimes, such as the Soviet Union and Nazi Germany, the state used art as an ideological tool, controlling it and imposing one artistic current, and in doing so suppressing all 'unofficial' forms of art.[31] According to this narrative, the institution of socialist realism after 1930 and the disappearance of the avant-garde was inevitable and a consequence of administrative measures orchestrated by Stalin.[32] Reflecting this long-dominant historiographical tradition and also responding to the recent nostalgia for everything Soviet, a large number of exhibitions and catalogues of Soviet posters have flourished recently, complementing the growing academic literature on propaganda.[33]

On the other hand, other scholars, mostly art historians, have focused on the other extreme of the visual production of the time: the avant-garde. The terms 'Russian avant-garde' or 'left art' designate the artistic groups active in Russia between 1905 and 1930 that broke with 'traditional painting' and the tenets of the Renaissance perspective.[34] Echoing, adapting and furthering Western modernist movements, they corresponded to a number of 'isms' that challenged figurative painting (neoprimitivism, futurism, Cezannism, cubo-futurism, rayonism, constructivism, suprematism). The vitality, originality and intensity of these Russian avant-gardist movements attracted and continue to attract, the fascination and interest of art specialists and amateurs.[35]

With two main centres of interest, analysis of visual culture in the Soviet Union has tended to be reduced to its extremes and opposes the 'constructivist geniuses' to the 'vile conventional realists'.[36] One of the consequences of this polarized vision is that all the artistic groups that did not fit in one or the other category have tended to be ignored or little studied. Furthermore, the transitional period between 1928 and 1932, between the end of the New Economic Policy and the imposition of socialist realism, has been neglected because it undermines the 'totalitarian' narrative.

As exemplified by recent works on Soviet visual culture, the use of visual sources allows us to question this periodization and the dominant categories used by historians of the political sphere.[37] It throws a whole new light on the relations between art and power in challenging the totalitarian model. Situated at the cross-roads of political, intellectual, social and cultural history, visual objects offer a new avenue to understand not only how political power tried to shape the new society but also how society reacted to the official ideology. They give us the opportunity to question the agency and the role of the artists themselves in the transition from 'left art' to figuration and to grasp the scale and the extent of the constraints they were subjected to. A close examination of the vast and varied production of visual sources in the Soviet Union will reveal the complex relations between different groups of artists and between the artists and the state. The state was certainly an ideological warden, but one that did not always clarify what it expected in terms of style or content and requested artists to fix themselves the parameters of official art.[38] Furthermore, the state provided an institutional frame but did not always exert strong central control. It was a source of salaries and funding for visual artists but did not always oversee the detail and modalities of this commissioning system. A study of visual culture will demonstrate the existence of more dissonance, debates and disagreement between different artistic groups than expected, notably around economic and institutional aspects.

Apart from challenging the reigning paradigms, the use of visual culture will also allow us to come up with new questions and insights into the specificity of the visual in the Soviet context. Given the ambiguity of images as conveyors of messages, it is important to reflect on the status of images as compared to other Soviet media, including literature. Were images less controlled and monitored than literature because of their elusiveness? Were images more suitable for embedding subversive messages because of their ambiguities? Were they also a better medium than literature to convey complex and multivalent ideas, and to express the unre-solved or unacknowledged contradictions, anxieties and tensions that Soviet intel-lectuals did not want to confront fully?[39]

Finally, images can also contribute to our understanding of the Soviet Union as a multinational empire and of the disparities between centre and periphery in terms of creation, diffusion and reception of visual objects. Unlike literature, which was supposed to be nationally defined, images played an ambiguous role in the creation of cultures meant to be 'national in form, and socialist in content'. Visual sources can help us to get a sharper understanding of how the centre responded to the national question in visual culture, by reinforcing differences, or, on the contrary, using the 'universal' character of images to homogenize and convey a powerful, all-Soviet message. The circulation of visual symbols, styles and signs between the different republics and nationalities is still not well researched. In the first brief case study, I will give an example of visual cultural transfer, while the second, more extensive case study will help us to understand how socialist realism came into being (Figure 10.1).

This is an illustration in black and white for a children's book by the artist, designer and architect Lazar (El) Lissitzky published in 1923 in Berlin, while he was the Russian cultural ambassador to Weimar Germany, but probably completed

Figure 10.1 El Lissitzky, 'Illustration for *Vaysrusishe Folkmayses*', translated into Yiddish by Leyb Kvitko (Berlin: Jewish section in the Commissariat for public instruction, 1923), collection of the RMN-Grand Palais (musée d'art et d'histoire du judaïsme), Paris.

https://mahj.org/en/decouvrir-collections-betsalel/vaysrusishe-folkmayses-68631 (accessed 19 February 2019) in 1919. After beginning his career as an illustrator of Yiddish children books, Lissitzky joined Malevich's suprematist group in Vitebsk in 1919 and then Moscow in 1921.[40] In 1923 he had emigrated to Berlin and was briefly returning to his earlier interest in Jewish art. The image represents a fish bringing the child to the shore and illustrates the tale 'Ivan Belaruski'. It is part of the collection *Vaysrusishe Folkmayses*, a Yiddish translation by the poet Leyb Kvitko of Belarusian folktales. Although including elements of Slavic iconography (Baba Yaga for example), his drawings were heavily influenced by Jewish iconography and style. Lissitzky had been one of the most prominent members of the Jewish artistic renaissance between 1916 and 1919. As part of his search of a Jewish style in art, he looked for inspiration in folk art on Jewish tombstones or the painted walls of synagogues. In 1916 he went with the artist I. Ryback on an ethnographic expedition in Belorussia to look for traces of Jewish popular art. The paintings covering the walls of the Mogilev synagogue had a powerful effect on them, as demonstrated by the moving account published by Lissitzky in Berlin in 1923.[41] He reused the animals, decorations and visual motifs found in the Mogilev synagogue in his illustrations of Jewish books. More surprisingly he also used them in his illustrations for Ukrainian and Belarusian folktales, probably completed at the end of his 'Jewish period'.[42] In the given example, the fish is very similar to one present on the ceiling of the Mogilev synagogue.[43] Its rolling position reminds us of traditional representations of the Leviathan in Jewish communal registers.[44] These illustrations are very similar in their style to those of his 1916–19 period, and show not only the aesthetic search of Lissitzky and other artists for a national Jewish style, but also their interest in children's literature which they considered a tool to shape the aesthetic tastes and minds of the next generation. They saw the essential characteristics of such illustrations as the use of primitive art, simplification of forms, flatness, poetic and dream-like images to stimulate the children's imagination, and use of dark or grey colours[45]. This image is also telling about the emergence of other national cultures at the time and the co-fertilization and mutual exchanges that were taking place in the peripheries of Russia and Poland between Jewish, Belarusian, Ukrainian or Baltic cultural activists. Lissitzky's particularly expressive images were inspirational for other Jewish and non-Jewish artists and aimed to create a simple, imaginative, but also modern and national visual language (Figure 10.2).[46]

At first glance, this oil painting created in 1932 by Aleksandr Deineka, a painter classified as 'an outstanding figure of Soviet socialist realism', can appear as a typical example of the genre, defined as "realist" by its form and "socialist" by its content.[47] I will argue that this particular painting and Deineka are more ambivalent and are typical of the transition from the 1920s to the 1930s.[48] Deineka himself had a complex trajectory.[49] He survived until the late 1960s and was an active and officially sanctioned artist in the Soviet art system, which in itself demonstrates his successful adaptation to socialist realism. However, he started his artistic career in contact with the avant-garde. After studying in the Kharkov School of Art until 1917, he coordinated agitprop in Kursk during the Civil War, contributing to the production of Russian Telegraph Agency (ROSTA) windows, 'stuffing the purest

Figure 10.2 A. Deineka, *Who Will Beat Whom?*, 1932, oil on canvas, 120 × 159 cm, collection of the State Tretyakov Gallery, Moscow.

http://artpoisk.info/artist/deyneka_aleksandr_aleksandrovich_1899/kto_kogo_001/ (accessed 19 February 2019)

cubism into the potholes of Kursk'.[50] In 1921 he enrolled in the graphics section of the Moscow Vkhutemas (Higher Arts and Technical Studios), where he studied with some masters of the avant-garde. At the dawn of the New Economic Policy (NEP), Deineka felt, as did many other Vkhutemas students, that he had a mission to produce a new form of socialist art. In 1925 he became one of the founding members of the OST (Society of Easel Painters), a group that distanced itself both from the constructivists and from the Association of Artists of Revolutionary Russia that defended realism. During the following years, Deineka invented his own interpretation of modernity in art. Instead of documenting and representing the reality of the socialist construction, he conveyed the movement, energy, emotions and battles that embracing modernity meant for the new men and women (workers in factories and sportsmen in his case). Many of his and other OST painters formal inventions of the 1920s are still noticeable in *Who Will Beat Whom?*: the simplification of forms to avoid documentary realism; the photographic framing (with some parts of the body, skies or building cut out); the montage of different actions; the unfinished state of the right part of the painting that invites the viewer to imagine the future; the use of an allegoric and ambiguous feminine figure at the far right that is reminiscent of the woman in white in *Building New Factories* (1926).

However, things had changed since 1926. The Cultural Revolution of 1928–31 that coincided with the first Five-Year Plan and Stalin's rise to power, boosted a new generation of Party activists.[51] The promotion and education of the youth, necessary to modernize and industrialize the country, went along with a class struggle against the 'old intelligentsia', Western influence and bourgeois specialists. In art, the will to impose a proletarian hegemony did not come from the political leaders, but from young artists who were Party members and who infiltrated the two main artistic organisations.[52] Their attempt to subject those considered 'fellow travellers' and 'bourgeois' class-enemy artists to the control of the 'true proletarian artists' took the form of violent attacks in the press and administrative measures to marginalize them. The OST, divided over its response to these attacks, split in 1931. During this period, Deineka, as others, found refuge in illustration and poster production (e.g., *We are Mechanizing the Donbass*, 1930). In 1932, when Deineka painted *Who Will Beat Whom?*, a brief period of relative relaxation had started. All the artistic groups had been dissolved, the Union of Soviet Artists had been created, and the formula socialist realism was adopted shortly afterwards by the Party to unify literary and artistic life. However, the definition of what socialist realism meant in art was not provided by the Party, which preferred to cultivate vagueness and ambiguity. Each artist tried to come up with their own definition.[53] *Who Will Beat Whom?* can be regarded as Deineka's intuitive interpretation of how the winds would turn.

He painted it for the huge exhibition *15 Years of Soviet Art* (June 1933) that has been regarded in retrospect as the turning point in Soviet artistic life. *Who Will Beat Whom?* was a commissioned painting. However, two qualifying remarks are necessary here. The organizational committee of the exhibition and the panels that evaluated the paintings to be bought, was made up of artists from different tendencies, including prominent former OST painters such as Sterenberg, Labas and Deineka himself. This confirms that at this stage the state was not controlling the process of selection of paintings. Secondly, the process of artistic commissioning for this exhibition was untypical as it did not give any clear guidance on which themes or styles were sought. The authors of the accepted works were then awarded a financial grant but were still the owners of their paintings. It was therefore a quite flexible system, mostly controlled by the artists themselves.

The painting itself was a reflection of both Deineka's pictural search and of the polarization of the period 1928–32. There is no evidence of direct influence of the conferences and discussions on socialist realism on the painting, but one can notice a slight departure from his previous work. The painting tells the story of the socialist construction: it starts at the top with the storming of the Winter Palace, and continues on the left, with the Civil War and then the NEP with the inscription 1924. This scene represents the transition from old, backward times (symbolized by the church and wooden houses) to a bright, new world, symbolized by the new buildings. The arms of the agitator indicates the direction to the viewer, towards the right, while the 'old times' remain behind. His arm brings our gaze to the centre of the painting, that symbolizes the present and the period of the Five-Year Plan: a cultivated field with tractors, a modern factory on top, and modernity symbolized by transport, electrification, and the building of new houses for collective life.[54] On the right, the group of walkers painted against a white background symbolizes the bright future to be built by the proletariat, personified by the woman, hair in the wind, holding a blue paper with the date 1932. The spatial organization, as well as the stark contrast between the dark left side and the bright right side, contribute to tell this story in a composition that is reminiscent of the icon, with episodes of the life of the main hero (the proletariat) told in compartments around the main figure which is also represented as bigger than the others (here, the couple on the right). This painting is, then, more complex than it seems. Far from being the product of a state-controlled commission, it reveals the individual process of Deineka finding his way of adjusting his own aesthetics and iconography to the emerging socialist realism by giving his own depiction of how 'life is becoming'.[55] He chose to compromise and adopt a middle-of-the-road position while other OST painters such as Sternberg or Labas chose not to submit. This painting also demonstrates the level of agency of the artists themselves in the implementation and definition of socialist realism which contrasts starkly with the tighter control that writers were subjected to.

Conclusion

These two case studies have allowed us to look at Soviet history and culture from a different angle, revealing the versatility of images and the complexity of the historical, social and national processes to which they belonged. They might serve as evidence for the 'predisposition for Russians to turn to the visual to summon a new reality into being'.[56] This tendency to use the experience of viewing as an engine of transformation ('seeing into being') makes the use of visual material even more crucial to understand Russian history at large.

Notes

1 José Alaniz, *Komiks: Comic Art in Russia* (Jackson, MS: University Press of Mississippi, 2010), p. 32.
2 *Lubok* (plural *lubki*): a cheap popular print.
3 Valerie A. Kivelson and Joan Neuberger (eds.), *Picturing Russia. Explorations in Visual Culture* (New Haven, CT and London: Yale University Press, 2008), p. 5.
4 To the exclusion of films and moving images, that are the subject of Jeremy Hicks's chapter.
5 With rare exceptions, including Kivelson and Neuberger, *Picturing*. See below for further discussion of the Soviet historiography.
6 Jessica Evans and Stuart Hall (eds.), *Visual Culture: The Reader* (London: Sage Publications, 1999), pp. 1–3; Peter Burke, *Eyewitnessing: The Uses of Images as Historical Evidence* (London: Reaktion, 2001), pp. 9–10.
7 Burke, *Eyewitnessing*, pp. 12–13; Iveta Slavkova, 'Œuvre, expérience visuelle, «tournant pictorial». Débats méthodologiques sur les approches de l'image', *Histoire @ Politique*, Vol. 33. The term *Bildwissenschaft* has no equivalent in the English language; it is usually taken to mean the revival of art history in Germany as a study field of images beyond the merely visual from the 1970s.
8 To name just a few: William J. T. Mitchell, *Picture Theory. Essays in Verbal and Visual Representation* (Chicago, IL: Chicago University Press, 1994); Gillian Rose, *Visual Methodologies: An Introduction to Researching with Visual Materials*, 3rd ed. (London: Sage, 2012); Nicholas Mirzoeff, *The Visual Culture Reader* (London: Routledge, 1998); Nicholas Mirzoeff, *An Introduction to Visual Culture*, 2nd ed. (London: Routledge, 2009); James Elkins, 'An Introduction to the Visual Studies that is not in this Book', in James Elkins and Kristi McGuire (ed.), *Theorizing Visual Studies: Writing Through the Discipline* (New York, NY: Routledge, 2013); Daniel Arasse, *On n'y voit rien: Descriptions* (Paris: Denoel, 2000).

9 Kivelson and Neuberger, *Picturing Russia*, p. 2.

10 Burke, *Eyewitnessing*, p. 13. For a plea for using objects and material culture in history, see Leora Auslander, 'Beyond Words', *American Historical Review*, 110 (2005), pp. 1015–45.

11 Burke, *Eyewitnessing*, p. 13.

12 Ibid., p. 81.

13 Evans and Hall, *Visual Culture*, p. 310.

14 Kivelson and Neuberger, *Picturing*, p. 2.

15 Rose, *Visual Methodologies*, pp. 19–40.

16 Some of these questions include: who were they? Were they famous? Were they independent or did they serve an institution? Were they integrated in artistic networks? Where is this work situated in their production? If they were anonymous, why did they adopt a strategy of self-effacement? Or, on the contrary, what kind of message did they want to express? Do we have textual evidence about them and their work?

17 To name a few technologies: oil painting, aquarelle, lithography, sculpture (wood, marble, ivory, clay, bronze), photograph (digital, black and white), applied arts (e.g., rationing tickets, decorated plates, textile), monumental art (e.g., mural painting), building (cement, metal, glass), posters or popular prints, and so on.

18 Burke, *Eyewitnessing*, Chapter 1 on photograph and portraits; Rose, *Visual Methodologies*, pp. 21–2.

19 It was Walter Benjamin's argument (text reproduced in Evans and Hall, *Visual Culture*, pp. 72–79), see discussion in Burke, *Eyewitnessing*, p. 17; Kivelson and Neuberger, *Picturing*, pp. 10–11.

20 Rose, *Visual Methodologies*, p. 23.

21 See Burke, *Eyewitnessing*, Chapter 2; Roelof van Straten, *An Introduction to Iconography* (Yverdon, Switzerland: Gordon and Breach, 1994).

22 Evans and Hall, *Visual Culture*, p. 310; Burke, *Eyewitnessing*, p. 178.

23 Evans and Hall, *Visual Culture*, p. 311; see also Rose, *Visual Methodologies*, Chapter 10 on audience studies.

24 Evans and Hall, *Visual Culture*, p. 313.

25 Kivelson and Neuberger, *Picturing*, pp. 8–9.

26 Anna Shternshis, *Soviet and Kosher. Jewish Popular Culture in the Soviet Union 1923–1939* (Bloomington, IN: Indiana University Press, 2006), pp. 166–70.

27 See David Freedberg, *The Power of Images* (Chicago, IL: University of Chicago Press, 1989); Michael Fried, *Absorption and Theatricality* (Chicago, IL: University of Chicago Press, 1981).

28 Katerina Clark and Evgeny Dobrenko (eds.), *Soviet Culture and Power: A History in Documents* (New Haven, CT: Yale University Press, 2007), p. xii.

29 Peter Kenez, *The Birth of the Propaganda State: Soviet Methods of Mass Mobilization, 1917–1929* (Cambridge: Cambridge University Press, 1985).

30 The editors of *Picturing Russia* also recognize the 'overwhelming role of reigning authorities in producing, shaping and controlling images' at all times in Russian history, although this impression may be misleading and reflect only the predisposition of the scholar to study political power: pp. 7–8.

31 Igor Golomstock, *Totalitarian Art: In the Soviet Union, The Third Reich, Fascist Italy and the People's Republic of China* (London: Collins Harvill, 1990).

32 Just one recent example: Christopher Le Brun, *Foreword to Revolution. Russian Art 1917–1932* (London: Royal Academy of Arts, 2017), p. 7: 'In 1932 Joseph Stalin issued a decree that all art should express Soviet ideology'.

33 David King, *Red Star Over Russia. A Visual History of the Soviet Union from 1917 to the Death of Stalin* (London: Tate Publishing, 2010), catalogue of the exhibition at the Tate Modern, 8 Nov 2017–18 Feb 2018; David Brandenberger. *Propaganda State in Crisis: Soviet Ideology, Indoctrination, and Terror under Stalin, 1927–1941* (New Haven, CT: Yale University Press, 2011); Victoria Bonnell, *Iconography of Power: Soviet Political*

Posters under Lenin and Stalin (Berkeley, CA: University of California Press, 1997); Sarah Davies, *Popular Opinion in Stalin's Russia: Terror, Propaganda, and Dissent, 1934–1941* (Cambridge: Cambridge University Press, 1997); Maria Lafont (ed.), *Soviet Posters: The Sergo Grigorian Collection* (London: Prestel, 2007); *Russian Constructivist Posters of the 1920s and 1930s*, catalogue of the exhibition (Paris: Pyramid Editions, 2010).

34 Cécile Pichon-Bonin, *Peinture et politique en URSS: L'itinéraire des membres de la Société des artistes de chevalet (1917–1941)* (Dijon: Les presses du réel, 2013), p. 10.

35 The exhibitions that celebrated the centenary of the 1917 revolutions gave a large place to the avant-garde: *Revolution. Russian Art 1917–1932* at the Royal Academy of Arts, London; *Chagall, Lissitzky, Malévitch, l'avant-garde russe à Vitebsk, 1918–1922*, at Centre Pompidou, Paris; *A Revolutionary Impulse: The Rise of the Russian Avant-Garde*, Museum of Modern Art, New York; *'Soothsayers of Oncoming': Russian Avant-garde in the 1910s and 1920s*, Ekaterinburg Museum of Fine Arts. These add to the already considerable amount of literature on the Russian avant-garde. To name just a few: Pamela Jill Kachurin, *Making Modernism Soviet: The Russian Avant-Garde in the Early Soviet Era, 1918–1928* (Evanston, IL: Northwestern University Press, 2013); John E. Bowlt (ed.), *Russian Art of the Avant-Garde: Theory and Criticism, 1902–1934* (London: Thames and Hudson, 2017); Dennis G. Ioffe and Frederick H. White, *The Russian Avant-Garde and Radical Modernism: An Introductory Reader* (Boston, MA: Academic Studies, 2014); Julia Vaingurt, *Wonderlands of the Avant-Garde: Technology and the Arts in Russia of the 1920s* (Evanston, IL: Northwestern University Press, 2013).

36 For criticism of this binary divide see Manuel Fontán Del Junco, 'Aleksandr Deineka: The Mimesis of Utopia (1913–1953)', in *Aleksandr Deineka (1899–1969). An Avant-Garde for the Proletariat* (Madrid: Fundacion Juan March, 2011), pp. 32–33; Oliver Johnson, 'Alternative Histories of Soviet Visual Culture', *Kritika: Explorations in Russian and Eurasian History*, 11 (2010), pp. 581–608 (p. 595). See also Susan E. Reid, 'Socialist Realism in the Stalinist Terror: The Industry of Socialism Art Exhibition, 1935–1941', *Russian Review*, 60 (2001), pp. 153–84; Christina Kiaer, *Imagine No Possessions: The Socialist Objects of Russian Constructivism* (Cambridge, MA: MIT Press, 2005); idem., 'Was Socialist Realism Forced Labour? The Case of Aleksandr Deineka in the 1930s', *Oxford Art Journal*, 28 (2005), pp. 321–45.

37 See review article by Johnson, 'Alternative …' as cited above.

38 Ibid., p. 601.

39 Kivelson and Neuberger, *Picturing*, pp. 8–9.

40 Suprematism is an artistic movement focusing on basic geometric forms (circles, squares, rectangles and lines), and drawing on a limited range of colours. It was developed in Russia in the 1910s and its earliest years are most associated with Kazimir Malevich.

41 El Lissitzky, 'Vegn der mohilever shul. Zikhroynes', *Milgroym*, 3, Berlin, 1923.

42 See Ruth Apter-Gabriel's analysis of the crown in another illustration for the Belarusian folktales and of the snake and flying ship in the Ukrainian ones: Ruth Apter-Gabriel, 'Un passé qui renaît, un futur qui s'évanouit. Les sources de l'art populaire dans le nouvel art juif russe', in Nathalie Hazan-Brunet (ed.), *Futur antérieur: L'avant-garde et le livre yiddish* (Paris: Skira Flammarion, 2009), pp. 57, 66, 142.

43 Visible on Yudovin's photograph of the cupola (southern segment) to the left of the ship. See photograph no. 34 in *Photographs for the 'Album of Jewish Artistic Antiquities'*, vol. 2 (Petersburg: Petersburg Judaica, 2007), p. 9.

44 There were a few examples of such *pinkasim* in An-sky's ethnographic collection that Lissitzky might have seen in Vitebsk in 1919. See copies in Aleksandr Kantsedikas and Irina Serheyeva (eds.), *The Jewish Artistic Heritage Album by Semyon An-sky* (Moscow: Mosty kultury, 2001), nos. 47 and 74; or *Futur antérieur*, cat 8.

45 See Y. Dobrushin's article on Jewish primitive art and art books for children published in *Bikher Velt*, nos. 4–5, Warsaw, 1919; as well as Isaachar Ber Rybak's illustrations of *Mayselekh far kleyninke kinderlekh* (1922).

46 See how Lissitzky's cover for *Elfandl* might have inspired Lebedev for the Russian translation: Kersing Hoge, 'The Design of Books and Lives: Yiddish Children's Book Art by Artists from the Kiev Kultur-Lige', in Mikhail Krutikov, Gennady Estraikh and Kersing Hoge (eds.), *Children and Yiddish Literature from Early Modernity to Post-Modernity* (London: Routledge, 2016), pp. 63–8.

47 *Aleksandr Deineka*, p. 2.

48 I would like to thank Cécile Pichon-Bonin for her advice and comment and point to her important and ground-breaking work on the OST (Society of Easel Painters) and the transition between avant-garde and socialist realism. I owe a lot to her compelling analysis of this painting in particular: Cécile Pichon-Bonin, *Peinture*, pp. 261–6. See also Manuel Fontan del Juncon, 'Aleksandr Deineka', in *Aleksandr Deineka*, pp. 36–54 on Deineka's ambivalence or ambiguity.

49 See Christina Kiaer, 'Aleksandr Deineka: A One-Man Biography of Soviet Art', in Aleksandr Deineka, pp. 58–67.

50 Quoted by Kiaer, 'Aleksandr Deineka', p. 59.

51 On the Cultural Revolution in general see Sheila Fitzpatrick (ed.), *Cultural Revolution in Russia, 1923–1931* (Bloomington, IN: Indiana University Press, 1978).

52 Pichon-Bonin, *Peinture*, p. 160.

53 Ibid., p. 257.

54 Note the overhead shot of the new block of collective flats, which is reminiscent of paintings of other OST artists in the 1920s (Shifrin, *Strastnoi Avenue*, 1926; Rodchenko's photographs).

55 Sheila Fitzpatrick, *The Cultural Front: Power and Culture in Revolutionary Russia* (Ithaca, NY: Cornell University Press, 1992), p. 236.

56 Kivelson and Neuberger, *Picturing*, p. 6.

Further reading

Alaniz, José, *Komiks: Comic Art in Russia* (Jackson, MS: University Press of Mississippi, 2010).

Bonnell, Victoria, *Iconography of Power: Soviet Political Posters under Lenin and Stalin* (Berkeley, CA: University of California Press, 1997).

Bowlt, John E. (ed.), *Russian Art of the Avant-Garde: Theory and Criticism 1902–1934* (London: Thames and Hudson, 2017).

Bown, Matthew Cullen, *Art under Stalin* (Oxford: Phaidon, 1991).

Burke, Peter, *Eyewitnessing: The Uses of Images as Historical Evidence* (London: Reaktion, 2001).

Evans, Jessica, and Stuart Hall (eds.), *Visual Culture: The Reader* (London: Sage Publications, 1999).

Johnson, Oliver, 'Alternative Histories of Soviet Visual Culture', *Kritika: Explorations in Russian and Eurasian History*, 11 (2010), pp. 581–608.

Kiaer, Christina, *Imagine No Possessions: The Socialist Objects of Russian Constructivism* (Cambridge, MA: MIT Press, 2005).

King, David, *Red Star over Russia. A Visual History of the Soviet Union from 1917 to the Death of Stalin* (London: Tate Publishing, 2010).

Kivelson, Valerie A., and Joan Neuberger (eds.), *Picturing Russia. Explorations in Visual Culture* (New Haven, CT and London: Yale University Press, 2008).

Lodder, Christina, Maria Kokkori and Maria Mileeva, *Utopian Reality: Reconstructing Culture in Revolutionary Russia and Beyond* (Leiden, Boston: Brill, 2013).

Mirzoeff, Nicholas, *An Introduction to Visual Culture*, 2nd ed. (London: Routledge, 2009).

Reid, Susan E., 'Socialist Realism in the Stalinist Terror: The Industry of Socialism Art Exhibition, 1935–1941', *Russian Review*, 60 (2001), pp. 153–84.

Shneer, David (ed.), *Through Soviet Jewish Eyes: Photography, War and the Holocaust* (New Brunswick, NJ: Rutgers University Press, 2011).

Stites, Richard, *Revolutionary Dreams: Utopian Vision and Experimental Life in the Russian Revolution* (Oxford: Oxford University Press, 1989).

Struk, Janina, *Photographing the Holocaust: Interpretations of the Evidence* (London: I. B. Tauris, 2004).

Lincoln, W. Bruce, *Between Heaven and Hell: The Story of a Thousand Years of Artistic Life in Russia* (New York, NY: Viking, 1998).

White, Stephen, *The Bolshevik Poster* (New Haven, CT: Yale University Press, 1988).

11 Film and TV as a source in Soviet history

Challenges and possibilities

Jeremy Hicks

The Soviet Union has sometimes been described as a 'propaganda state' that made unprecedentedly extensive and systematic use of mass culture to legitimize its authority.[1] Cinema played a key role in this strategy, reflected in the industry's nationalization on 27 August 1919, as well as in the famous quote attributed to Lenin in 1922, 'of all arts, cinema is for us the most important', and through to Stalin's 1924 statement that '[t]he cinema is a most valuable means of mass agitation. The task is to take this matter in hand' reiterated in 1935: 'in the hands of Soviet power cinema constitutes an enormous and invaluable force … [w]ith unique opportunities for spiritual influence over the masses … '[2] In the years between these two statements, Stalinist society succeeded in transforming cinema from the experiments of the first decade of Soviet power into a medium 'for the millions', and it became a key tool in its propaganda strategies, promoting various interpretations and reinterpretations of history, the hero cult, the Stalin cult and other themes. Then, during the Second World War (known as the Great Patriotic War in the Soviet Union and the Russian Federation), cinema became a key tool to exhort the Soviet population to make every effort to resist and defeat the Nazi invasion, and at the same time film was a significant means of appealing for international aid and support. Cinema remained a key dimension of the Soviet system's appeal to its population following Stalin's death, as Khrushchev framed his 1956 denunciation of Stalin around references to cinema, and reorganized the industry to respond to and realize the post-Stalin era's emphasis upon persuasion rather than coercion. Cinema remained a significant facet of Soviet society through the rule of Brezhnev, right until the end of the Soviet era, playing, for example, a central role in the articulation and inculcation of what has been called 'the cult of victory' in the war.[3] However, from the late 1950s onwards, film existed in tandem with its close relative, the medium of television, sharing many of the aesthetic trends and material resources of cinema. Both media were key in the transformations of the *Glasnost* era, and were themselves revolutionized once more by it, and by the collapse of the Soviet Union it precipitated.

Methodological reflections

While in theory, historians see all material from the past as useful, film and television have been of little interest until the last twenty years, and have been overwhelmingly treated with a special strain of the condescension extended by historians to popular culture in general and visual sources in particular.[4] Productive uses of film in historical scholarship have a longer pedigree in French culture, starting with the work of Marc Ferro, a historian who was pioneering in championing the serious study of film in history, arguing that it is the ambiguity of film language, its need for interpretation, that makes it suspicious for historians.[5] More recently, this includes the work of Pierre Sorlin, whose discussion of the genre of historical films emphasizes them as more revealing of the present rather than the past.[6] Building on their work in an English-language book already in a third edition, Robert Rosenstone acknowledges historical film's factual inaccuracy, but argues that this misses the point, making the case instead for the specific strengths of film as a means for the evocation of and commentary on the past in which these two modes are conflated. Specifically, with his analysis of depictions of Sergei Eisenstein's *October* (*Oktiabr'*, 1927), Rosenstone sees it as an attempt to convey the ecstasy of revolutionary change, creating symbols, such as the storming of the Winter Palace, standing for longer processes.[7] While valuable, Rosenstone's approach is dependent on published sources by or about Eisenstein that have been translated into English, and makes no use of archives. Moreover, its focus is on film as a form of historical representation and interpretation rather than a historical source, a trace of the historical period that generated it. In this respect, it bears similarities with the tendencies of Hayden White or of memory studies, in which the focus is on the narrative construction of the past and the message conveyed about it rather than what actually happened.[8] In many respects this resembles the first sample analysis below.

These important contributions notwithstanding, there has been an overwhelming tendency to reference film (as with art previously) decoratively, to provide a bit of colour, possibly to lighten up the front cover. On the other hand, very detailed close readings, where the filmic text, and especially the subtleties of the style itself become more important than an overall narrative or interaction with the context, will tend to take us more towards film studies or possibly cultural studies, beyond the disciplinary borders of cultural history.

Nevertheless, in works of history, too often, films are not interrogated as systematically as a historian would with other, written, sources. Films have their own stylistic and generic conventions that are part of their meaning, and the historian needs to reckon with these in order to make nuanced arguments about them. At the same time, the historian's traditional skill in working with written documents remains key. Taken seriously, a historical analysis of film is not just about commenting upon the final, released version, but can also touch on any of the following: script variants, the literary source, internal studio and industry correspondence or discussions as well as published policy statements, mentions of a film in memoirs and other writings by the filmmakers, actors, industry figures or audience members, reviews and many other sources. To generate the richest analysis, it is a question of relating the two dimensions, the interpretation of the visual to the written sources, and such a synoptic perspective helps to guard against any danger of excessively subjective readings. Done well, the results of such an analysis can be compelling.

Such an approach to the cultural history of film is one that can be practised with regard to the film industry anywhere, not just in the Soviet Union. However, applying it to the Soviet Union raises some specific issues of method. In part, this is because Soviet cultural elites themselves took a particular interest in popular culture, as the famous statements attributed to Lenin and Stalin show.[9] For them, cinema was not simply to be a source of entertainment and business, but one of edification and education. This slightly alters the habitual approach to it, even if those funding film had to reach compromise with the filmmakers on the one hand, who often had their own aesthetic agendas, and with the preferences of audiences oriented towards entertainment on the other.[10] This didactic stance was evident with regard to film, in particular, and it became a serious art around the world following the enormous success of *Battleship Potemkin* (*Brononosets Potemkin*, directed by Sergei Eisenstein, 1925) – its moral and political seriousness were no less a part of this reason than its aesthetic ambition.[11] However, as Anna Lawton has commented, while both *Battleship Potemkin* and the wider 1920s film movement we have come to know as Soviet montage successfully combined aesthetic innovation with revolutionary politics, they failed in their didactic purpose, because their films were not popular with the masses.[12] These films, with their explicitly political subject matter and stunning artistic qualities, have often been the focus of film historical work on the Soviet period, including that of Rosenstone, but to an extent this perpetuates the division between high and low culture, which has a long pedigree in the study of art history and history in general,[13] including Russian history. *Battleship Potemkin* thus is, in a sense, a product of elite culture, similar to the arts of painting and sculpture, in that it is largely produced and consumed by an elite. Moreover, the focus upon aesthetically rich films is often connected to the notion, popular in film studies, of *auteurism*, the idea that films can be seen as expressing the personal vision of their director, as part of a body of authorial work.[14] In turn, such an approach places prominent individuals at the centre of its analysis and may tend to generate a reading that not only privileges aesthetic merits over others, but also follows a narrative of heroic individual versus the state, problematic for its tendency to see a clandestine liberal subject in thwarted Soviet artists.[15] As discussed below, more recent approaches to Soviet subjectivity have been more nuanced.

The study of popular culture, which has been the focus of many historians especially since the 1960s,[16] permits a different social focus. It also shifts our attention towards a very different set of Soviet films: those truly popular with the public that are as well understood through their position within less hallowed genres such as comedies, melodramas, and musicals. One version of this has already been pioneered by Katerina Clark in her famous study of the socialist realist novel, where the focus is on how various examples of the Soviet novel echo a single master-plot, and rework a central dialectic between spontaneity and conscious-ness.[17] This focus has been made relevant to the post-Stalin era too, by Sergei Yurchak's recent emphasis on the repetitious and ritualized nature of Soviet dis-course.[18] Both perspectives may productively inform the analysis of Soviet cinema, tracing, for example, the variations over time in a given narrative or genre of Soviet cinema, such as representations of the Civil War. The indicative analysis, below, of treatments of death and martyrdom in Soviet cinema from the revolution to 1945, albeit not devoted to the most popular genres, is an example of this kind of approach, and it is one that also has the benefit for students, of not necessarily requiring knowledge of the Russian language, since enough of the relevant films can be found on DVD or various websites with English subtitles, and there are also English-language discussions or summaries of others.

While this kind of analysis of Soviet cinema is productive, what it tends to downplay above all is the element of subjectivity in cinema. This blind spot is all the more frustrating when we consider historians' recent orientation towards the diary as a form recording Soviet subjectivity that was personal, but not individ-ualist, breaking down the public–private distinction.[19] Film was a medium that required enormous economic investment, and was thus dominated by big studios in the context of Hollywood, or by the state in the context of the Soviet Union. This tended to mitigate against diary-like expressions of a subjective vision. This is where the *auteur* theory, for all its aestheticizing bias, may still prove useful, as it is an attempt to locate and describe a subjectivity emerging from a film-maker's *oeuvre* that was not captured by the description of a film in terms of its genre or theme. But we may see this illusive subjectivity emerge in other, more subtle ways too. This will be the focus of the second indicative analysis, below, of wartime Soviet documentary film with regard to Nazi atrocity and the Holo-caust, focusing on the films of Aleksandr (Oleksandr) Dovzhenko. Through such analyses, we see that Soviet film made for propagandist purposes could end up conveying something else, be it a certain subjectivity, or inviting an alternative interpretation of events than that promoted by the Soviet government, serving as involuntary testimony, what Marc Bloch referred to, when the source was a 'witness in spite of itself' which is particularly relevant to documentary film, but applicable to fiction films too, as they tell us things they did not intend to about the attitudes of their time.[20]

Here we need to be attentive to the interplay between the said and the unsaid, the visual and the verbal, what the film shows, and what it deliberately chooses not to show. In the case of Soviet film, to get at these decisions usually requires use of other sources to work out what else was there on the day it was recorded. So, while a film may have been commissioned for propaganda purposes, it can be possible to reveal the decision-making process and uncover alternatives through unpublished discussions, edited and censored variants. This makes the use of archives a very powerful tool for such analysis, but is dependent upon Russian language sources. What emerges is not quite a diary-like individual sensibility, nor is it a monolithi-cally propagandist one either.

In each case here, we are faced with the need to move on and away from the limitations of the totalitarian paradigm, in which film is largely seen as a form of public thought control, from which the individual seeks refuge in a private, usually literary world. In seeking to understand how Soviet citizens actually thought, we can use film as valuable indexical traces of the mentality of this past world. It is merely a question of finding a productive methodological and conceptual framework with which to approach the topic.

Death and martyrdom in Soviet cinema

In her ground-breaking study *Night of Stone*, Catherine Merridale considered the enormous scale of death, suffering and loss suffered by Russia and Russians in the twentieth century by looking at the ritual practises associated with the commemoration of the dead. A particular focus of Merridale's book are the revolutionaries' attempts to create a new secular red funeral culture, where religion was displaced, where the grave became 'a tribune for affirmation of the cause', meaning a focus on a response of action, the fight for a new Russia, asserting that the sacrifice was not vain, which left little space for mourning and marking a real sense of loss.[21] Merridale's reach is wide but her central materials tend to be from oral history. Consequently, the agenda of *Night of Stone* may be extended by applying them to other contexts, examining attitudes to death in the context of the first decades of Soviet film which rationalize and instrumentalize death and violence from its very earliest and most influential examples, presenting it as a worthwhile and meaningful sacrifice.

Soviet film began, however, by dismissing its ideological rivals' claims to transcendence, with *The Unsealing of the Remains of Sergii of Radonezh* (*Vskrytie moshchei Sergiia Radonezha*). Made in 1919, the year of Soviet cinema's origin and a few months before its nationalization, it has the honour of being claimed by both Dziga Vertov and Lev Kuleshov, the two key pioneers of Soviet cinema,[22] and was an attempt to demonstrate the falsity of the Church's claims that the remains of the important Orthodox Christian Saint Sergius of Radonezh were 'incorrupt', that is, had resisted decay. The rather crudely made film, comprising long takes with no close-ups, shows the skeleton being taken out of its resting place and exposed as rotten. The film's final image is of a decidedly dead and decayed pile of bones. The point here was to demonstrate the hollow and unconvincing nature of Orthodox Christianity's claims to the miraculous, its pretensions to have conquered time and overcome death.

The overcoming of death was likewise a theme in the filming, in 1918, of Lenin following the unsuccessful assassination attempt on him of 30 August. Despite his initial reluctance, he agreed to be filmed in the grounds of the Kremlin near to the famous Tsar-canon, to dispel rumours of his death. This was echoed, as Victoria Bonnell has shown, in references to Lenin that were couched in religious terms and a marked increase in depictions of him as a short-hand for the Bolshevik cause.[23] These cultic tendencies reached a new pitch following Lenin's death, as his funeral was organized as a huge public event. As Nina Tumarkin argues, while the grief expressed in this officially sanctioned outpouring was for the death of Lenin, nevertheless the sources of the emotions laid bare were also rooted in and related to the deaths that had occurred in the whole series of war, revolution and civil war experienced by Russian and Soviet society in the previous years.[24] Lenin's funeral recuperated and instrumentalized these disparate emotions, bending them to the overarching Soviet political narrative. Dziga Vertov's film of the funeral, his 1925 *Leninist kinopravda* (*Kinopravda 21*), gave the iconography of Lenin's funeral a compelling and enduring expression, showing the event as galvanizing the Party Central Committee and the Soviet population, who apparently express their grief spontaneously. In cinematic terms the emphasis is on the unceasing movement of the masses past the open coffin. Lenin's death has become a point of mobilization for the country as grief is moulded into a political response. The funeral sequence ends with the promise to complete Lenin's cause and teachings. The third and final reel of the film shows mass enrolments in the party, showing the progress made by the country, but ends with an exhortation to follow Lenin's course into the future. The funeral is used as a means of mobilization, to create a sense of the Soviet state as a mystical, symbolic unity between ruler and ruled, and at the same time to pass on that legitimacy to Lenin's successors in the central committee, named in the film. Thus, after showing the masses filing past the coffin, the film shows, Lenin's family (his widow and sister, Mariia Il´ichna) before showing Felix Dzerzhinskii (head of the *Cheka*), Mikhail Frunze (the legendary military leader), Leonid Krasin (who was a key figure in the organization of the funeral), and then Stalin (whose name was in bigger letters than the others), followed by the other members of the Central Committee. The implication is that, while they mourn too, the political, security and military legacies of Lenin are safe in these hands. Vertov remade this same sequence in 1934, for *Three Songs of Lenin* (*Tri pesni o Lenine*) making Stalin far more prominent.

The pattern whereby Bolshevik death is understood as a meaningful sacrifice, while established in documentary film, is repeated even more effectively in feature films, with Eisenstein's *Battleship Potemkin* the most effective example in its use of a funeral as the central dramatic point in a process of wider, mass mobilization. The funeral, or rather public display of Vakulinchuk's dead body in the city of Odessa, mobilizes huge crowds and serves as the catalyst for the spreading of the bacillus of revolt from the battleship to the town. We see here the same parallel editing evident in Vertov stressing a contrast between the stasis of the dead body and the relentless movement of the masses, suggesting a transfer of energy from mourning the dead revolutionary to the wider revolutionary movement, a still/moving contrast and triumph over death that cinema, in its inherent nature as a series of still images animated to simulate motion, is uniquely suited to convey.

Eisenstein of course stressed the contrasts between his own use of the funeral scene and Vertov's, seeing his 'mathematically constructed invention [as] defeat[ing] untouched truth'.[25] Contemporary critics such as Khrisanf Khersonskii stressed the similarities, arguing that *Battleship Potemkin* built on what was best in Vertov.[26] Vertov, needless to say, saw it differently, arguing that Eisenstein's

Potemkin not only owed a huge debt to *Leninist kinopravda*, but that this dramatic reinvention was a deviation, a parasitic growth that drew its power from the real depictions of life in newsreel and documentary.[27] Nevertheless, Eisenstein, by showing not only the funeral but the death of Vakulinchuk (and others), created an intoxicating formula that suggested a path for subsequent Soviet film's depictions of the mobilizing power of the death of a martyr: death is not defeat, it is only a temporary set-back and can be assimilated into an overarching narrative.

This pattern, established in the 1920s, continued into 1930s cinema, and the era of sound, making effective use of the greater scope for song, dialogue and character development. Grigorii Kozintsev and Leonid Trauberg's narrative of the conversion to Bolshevism of a typical, even rowdily anarchic, member of the working class in *Maxim's Youth* (*Iunost' Maksima*, 1934), made the funeral the key moment of their protagonist's transformation from passive bystander to active revolutionary. Maxim is wavering, with some sympathy for the revolutionaries, but is also being approached to become a police informer. When his friend Andrei dies due to poor safety conditions at the factory, and this is followed by the death of another worker, the workers insist on burying Andrei according to their own, workers' rite: the singing of the song that had been central to the traditions of the red funeral since the 1890s: 'You Fell as a Victim', a title that might also be translated as 'You Fell as a Sacrifice'.[28] The first verse of which went:

> You fell as a victim in the fatal fight
> Of unselfish love for the people [*narod*]
> You gave up all that you could for them,
> For their honour, their life and their freedom!

Through close-up, reaction shots, the key sequence shows Maxim's thought processes as he becomes a revolutionary during the course of this funeral: first watching, listening and then marching, singing, before leaping on to a lamppost to make a rallying speech and ultimately being arrested, the ultimate moment of graduation to the life of a professional revolutionary. Continuing the dead person's work through activism and resistance confers immortality, promising a triumph over death (Figure 11.1).

This attitude, the Bolshevik sense that death would be recuperated by ultimate victory, was both vindicated and challenged by the unprecedented violence of the Second World War and the Nazi invasion of the Soviet Union. The devastation unleashed by the Nazis upon the Soviet population threatened the physical existence not only of so many citizens, but also of the Soviet state itself and its ideological underpinning. Uniquely the Soviet Union was both occupied and had a functioning cinema industry: the resulting cinema was extraordinarily candid in its depiction of Nazi brutality against the Soviet civilian population, but represented those deaths through the established logic of sacrifice and redemption. The narrative of partisan resistance to Nazi occupation was an effective way of conveying conscious, meaningful sacrifice. One of the most famous partisan films told the story of Zoia Kosmodemianskaia, an 18-year-old Moscow schoolgirl

Figure 11.1 Leonid Trauberg and Grigorii Kozintsev, *The Youth of Maxim*, Lenfil´m 1934.

who was killed by the Germans after being captured on a mission behind enemy lines in November 1941. Following a number of newspaper treatments of her story, including the publication of captured German photographs of her hanging, and Soviet ones of her mutilated corpse,[29] Lev Arnshtam made a 1944 film account. The film begins with Zoia being tortured, being repeatedly asked who she is. Her answer, shown in a stylistically bold flashback, starts with newsreel footage of Lenin's funeral, which coincided with her birth. Zoia's willingness to fight and sacrifice herself for the Soviets must be understood, implies the film, through the prism of Lenin's funeral – his martyrdom inspires hers, and that of others (Figure 11.2).

Yet this narrative was challenged by the brutal realities of the war. It was simply not possible to assimilate all this death and suffering into the existing paradigm of the red funeral and of meaningful sacrificial death, because it was simply too hard to believe that so many people's deaths were a reasonable price to pay, part of a utopian logic, a vision of history as redemptive and progressive. Moreover, those killed, such as the Soviet Union's secularized ethnic Jews, over 1.5 million of whom were killed by the Germans in 1941–42 in the mass shootings of the first stage of what later became called the Holocaust, were not dying for their beliefs, but rather being murdered for their inherited cultural and ethnic identity.[30] The mass murder of Soviet Jews was thus particularly hard to assimilate to the Soviet

Figure 11.2 Lev Arnshtam, *Zoia*, Soiuzdetfil′m, 1944.

logic of the funeral and of meaningful martyrdom. This tension was addressed in some wartime films, none more centrally than in Mark Donskoi's 1945 film, *The Unvanquished* (*Nepokorennye*), released shortly after the end of the war. Its central scene depicts a traditional red funeral for a worker killed consciously defying the Germans, but it is interrupted as the mourners see a crowd of Jews being herded to their death. The main character, Ukrainian worker Taras, recognizes the family doctor Aron Davidovich Fishman, to whom he bows. The Jews are then taken to a ravine and massacred in a hail of German bullets.

What we see here is not martyrdom recuperated by the ultimate victory, but a tragic loss that cannot be assimilated into the established narrative. Here we are close to Freud's notion of trauma, in the sense of unassimilable, untellable, experience. It was this sense that the war meant enormous losses that could not easily be contained within the existing narrative of the red funeral, and of meaningful martyrdom, that caused it to be so difficult a theme in the late Stalin years, when very few war films were made. When, following Stalin's death, Soviet film made the war a central topic, these depictions treated the Jewish experience of it as marginal.

In generating historical analyses such as this account of the theme of death and martyrdom, it is important to place the events depicted in film alongside other sources, such as influential English-language histories of the Soviet Union. Cinema needs to be treated here with circumspection as probably the most influential source, but also probably the least reliable, and most likely to have been manipulated. This kind of analysis requires little or even no command of the Russian language, and can even be conducted without trips to Russian archives. In this sense, it could even be suitable for an undergraduate research project. Nevertheless, the range of visual and written sources could be expanded markedly if untranslated Russian sources in all media are also considered, and if the researcher were to identify and draw on new findings from the Russian archives, be they film or paper, such as, in this case, the internal studio discussion of *The Unvanquished*.[31] The following indicative analysis is intended to demonstrate the possibilities of such language-based analysis with slightly later material.

Wartime film

The picture of wartime Soviet film is one that gives itself less easily to the kind of analysis conducted above, in large part because, where there were controversial issues, the final film and published materials on it do not permit us to get a detailed picture of the areas of sensitivity, of the various discussions and options explored by the filmmakers prior to their final decisions.

The example of how civilian deaths during the Second World War were represented in the documentary films of Ukrainian director Dovzhenko illustrate the kinds of Russian and Ukrainian language materials available to researchers, and the kinds of insights they can generate into the tensions between the Soviet attitudes to Nazi atrocities, the Holocaust, Ukrainian nationalism and the personal vision of the filmmaker. Dovzhenko was a prominent filmmaker who had shot to international fame with his montage-style works *Arsenal* (1928), and *Earth* (*Zemlia*, 1930), and who became involved in the Soviet war effort, first as a journalist and writer at the front, and then as a co-director, with his wife Iuliia Solntseva, of a cycle of films about the Nazi occupation and Soviet liberation of Ukraine. This was (and indeed still is) a highly sensitive subject, since, while the Nazi occupation of Ukraine was brutal towards the whole population of that Soviet republic, Jews were targeted disproportionately and murdered for their ethnicity. The Ukrainian population were starved to death, violently repressed if they resisted Nazi rule, and used as slave labour. But Soviet rule in Ukraine had also been brutal, leading to mass starvation during the collectivization of agriculture (sometimes referred to as the Holodomor) and elements within the wide spectrum of Ukrainian nationalists saw the Nazis' expulsion of the Soviets as an opportunity to advance their own project of independence for a Ukrainian nation state through collaboration.[32]

In this context, Dovzhenko began work in 1942 on a screenplay, *Ukraine in Flames* (*Ukraina v ogne*), and a documentary film about the liberation of Kharkov, which ultimately was released in October 1943 as *The Battle for Our Soviet Ukraine* (*Bitva za nashu sovetskuiu Ukrainu*). This film depicts not only the heroic victory of the wider Red Army, but emphasizes the Ukrainians involved in the battle, and, most importantly, emphasizes the victims of the Nazis as Ukrainian. This approach is a distinct one in that, while Soviet films' depictions of the violence the Nazis inflicted on the Soviet population were not unusual, they did not tend to focus on a singular ethnicity, such as the Ukrainians. To make matters more complex, one of the key scenes in the film depicts Drobitskii iar, just outside Kharkov, where the Nazis killed thousands of civilians, but overwhelmingly these were Jews. The film says nothing of this.

What makes the case of Dovzhenko still more fascinating is the fact that, by the time of the war, he had more personal authority than most directors involved in wartime documentary cinema, and was thus able to make a film closer to an authorial vision than any other wartime Soviet filmmaker. Rather than simply compiling the footage they received, he and Solntseva gave specific instructions as to the kinds of images they required, so their film is in part an expression of their own vision of these historical events, their own artistic interpretation.

Both the extent of Dovzhenko's personal vision and the issues around the depiction of atrocities can only really emerge fully through an engagement with archival sources. Thus, while one can access the film in a subtitled version online, or in a dubbed version at London's National Film and Television Archive (part of the British Film Institute), and there is also an English translation of Dovzhenko's wartime diary, and a number of English-language books and articles about Dovzhenko, the context of the film's production can only really be grasped through use of Russian and Ukrainian published sources and the Russian and Ukrainian archives.

One attempt to do this can be found in my own 2012 book, *First Films of the Holocaust*, which makes use of a 2004 Ukrainian edition of Dovzhenko's diary that is fuller than the 1973 English translation, as well as Russian- and Ukrainian-language secondary sources, including memoirs and two collections of documents from a number of different archives, published by Valerii Fomin.[33] This draws on the studio archives of the Central Studio of Documentary Film at Russian State Archive for Literature and Art (RGALI). In those sources, we see the correspondence between Dovzhenko and Solntseva in Moscow, and the cameramen and bosses of film groups at the front, who were being instructed by the directors as to what to shoot. The archives also hold the Central House of Cinema collection, where we can read an internal studio discussion about the film. A recent publication by a team of French scholars[34] has expanded the source base, drawing on secret police informers' accounts of Dovzhenko's private conversations from the recently opened Ukrainian security police archives (GDA SBU), the Russian equivalents of which remain closed to researchers. These materials give a sense of Dovzhenko's ironic attitude towards the realities of Soviet life such as queuing and bureaucracy. They also make use of a fuller still more recent version of the wartime diary, which illustrates his antisemitic attitudes to his obstructive colleagues in the Soviet documentary studio, as he uses the word 'zhidok' with regard to a hypothetical typical adversary.[35] More insightful with regard specifically to the films, however, are the materials published from Dovzhenko's personal archive, also in RGALI. These show that Dovzhenko made the film while working as a member of the Soviet war crimes investigation committee (*Chrezvychainaia gosudarstvennaia komissiia po voostanovleniiu i rassledovaniiu zlodeianii nemetsko-fashistskikh zakhvatchikov i ich soobshchnikov i prichinnogo imi ucherba grazhdanam, kolkhozam, obshchestvennym organizatsiiam, gosudarstvennym prepriiatiiam i uchrezhdeniiam SSSR*), and that he also had to fight hard to ensure that he was in control of the material, where he could ensure its frank depiction of Nazi atrocity and emphasis on the suffering of ethnic Ukrainians.[36]

This same collection of documents enables a deeper understanding of the film that followed, and was eventually released as *Victory in Right-Bank Ukraine and the Expulsion of the German Invaders from the Boundaries of Soviet Ukrainian Lands* (*Pobeda na Pravoberezhnoi Ukraine i izgnanie Nemetskikh zakhvatchikov za predely Ukrainskikh Sovetskikh zemel'*, 1945). In particular they show how Solntseva and Dovzhenko intended a greater emphasis on Babii iar, the ravine near Kiev where the Nazis had murdered over 100,000 people, most of whom were Jewish. A letter on 9 February 1944 from Solntseva to the cameramen in Kiev shows that this was to be achieved through sound interviews with the Soviet POWs who had been forced to dig up and burn the corpses of those killed there, and with the US journalists who visited the site, who were to discuss the difficulty of getting anyone back in the US to publish or even believe these atrocity stories. The letter also calls for sound testimony of eyewitnesses to supplement the fairly inexpressive long shots of Babii iar. The final film included no sound interviews in this episode, even if some of the footage can be found in the documentary film archive, Russian State Archive of Film and Photo Documents (RGAKFD, Krasnogorsk), where outtakes and other unused materials, termed *kinoletiopis'*, are preserved. The reasons why they were not included are unclear from the documentary evidence, but probably because it would have drawn undue attention to the tragic scene of suffering and loss, which would have contrasted with the Soviet media's stress in 1945 on victory and heroism far more. While Dovzhenko and Solntseva's plans for this film were not realized in their entirety, the film still displayed the poetic vision characteristic of Dovzhenko's work. As fellow director Esfir' Shub put it at a discussion of the film at the Central Studio of Documentary Film artistic council (a mechanism for internal feedback), the film demonstrated Dovzhenko's 'authorial style'.[37] While it would be going too far to claim that a diary-like subjectivity was expressed in either film, this was not formulaic propaganda, but something between an individual and collective vision, along the lines described by Hellbeck.

However, Dovzhenko's determination to express his own personal vision of the conflict as a Ukrainian was one that led to his screenplay for *Ukraine in Flames* being censored after Stalin criticized it for its nationalist tendencies. Dovzhenko's reactions to this are illuminated in a report by a certain Medvedev, head of the Ukrainian NKGB (as the NKVD was then named). Drawing on materials from five informers, the report details Dovzhenko's refutation of Stalin's critique of him, where he defends his depiction in *Ukraine in Flames* of Ukrainian nationalists as collaborating due to the brutal treatment they had received under collectivization, saying his conscience as an artist did not permit him to soften his criticisms.[38] The same report details his fears that Khrushchev, then head of the Communist Party of Ukraine and previously Dovzhenko's patron, is now leading a Russification of Ukraine, in which all that is Ukrainian will now be condemned as nationalist.

The use of Russian and Ukrainian archive materials, be they directly from the archives, or in published collections, thus add a richer sense of the interaction between the filmmaker's intended plans and the obstacles to them, the tensions between the state's need for propaganda, and Dovzhenko's attempts to express his own vision of Ukraine's wartime fate. This was, as we can see from the final film, not one that corresponds to our contemporary Western understanding of the Nazi war of annihilation on the Eastern front in terms of the centrality of the Holocaust, the murder of the Jewish population, but it was nevertheless one that deviated from the dominant emphasis of Soviet wartime propaganda upon an undifferentiated Soviet victimhood, and on heroism and victory rather than loss and tragedy. This is in part a problem connected to the way that the Soviet film industry was based around the granting of a certain creative freedom to directors, as Belobudrovskaia has argued, with the idea that the filmmakers needed this space in order to be able to reach out to and inspire the people to build socialism.[39] This meant that the Soviet film industry, despite the rhetoric, was never simply a propaganda machine nor a Hollywood-style factory, churning out predictable and standardized products according to the plan. This is an insight that can be much more substantially demonstrated by looking at a range of archival documents, especially those of the studios.

One of the aspects of Soviet cinema the above indicative analyses do not demonstrate particularly is the sense of cinema as a form of popular culture. In part this is because the dimension of cinema that I have chosen to focus on here is the didactic, explicitly political one, rather than that primarily of entertainment. While it is possible to trace the popular through listings, ticket sales, reviews and memoirs, some of the best materials are internal studies, generated by the industry, of audience behaviour and reactions. This is much easier to do with feature films and the most popular genres. This kind of audience behaviour study became very widespread with the advent of TV, which sought to be a mass medium that engaged the public in the post-Stalin era by reimagining the Soviet ideological project for the format of popular culture. As Christine Evans shows, Soviet Central TV made extensive use of letters and sociological surveys to gauge audience reactions.[40] They acted on the results, the records of which can be found in the Gostel′radio archive in the Russian State Archive (GARF), and expanded the television coverage of Victory Day following information that the new programmes introduced in the run-up and for 9 May 1965 were highly popular, especially one of the very first Soviet TV drama series *Drawing Fire on Ourselves* (*Vyzyvaia ogon′ na sebia*) in February 1965, and *A Minute's Silence,* shown on 9 May. The popularity of the latter ensured it became a yearly fixture of the Victory Day commemorations, and the TV drama series became a staple of Soviet media depictions of history to the final days of the Soviet state and beyond.[41] Many of the programmes are now available to watch on YouTube and Yandex video, albeit without subtitles.

With the example of coverage of Victory Day, once again, use of unpublished archival documents enables a sense of the ways the use of moving images to legitimize the Soviet project entailed compromises with factors specific to the medium. Although there were always a number of factors, the compromise in the case of cinema was primarily with directorial talent, and in that of television the focus was on audience taste as well the need for a more direct, immediate style that at least appeared to be live.

After his rise to power in 1985, Mikhail Gorbachev began to enlist the sense of the liveness of Soviet television as an ally in his fight with party and government opponents. As well as permitting a relatively freer and more critical media environment, symbolized by the 1987 premiere of the current affairs programme *Vzgliad* (*Viewpoint*), in part this was also about Gorbachev exploiting the power of visual media, where his own youthful appearance and presence would potentially work in his favour against older opponents.[42] However, the Soviet media system collapsed through the tensions inherent in the top-down control of an enormous weight of new information, and the need to appear spontaneous. Yet, while this collapse also entailed a crisis in domestic TV productions, with the 1990s seeing a preponderance of imported drama series, the coming to power of Vladimir Putin in the new millennium saw Russian TV return to many of the models of history drama series and documentaries that were elaborated by the Soviet media in the 1960s and 1970s.[43]

The Soviet commitment to didactic and propagandist forms of culture meant that Soviet films, fiction and documentary constitute a unique and privileged historical source on the one hand for what they show, and for their attempts to convey a certain vision of history and culture on the other. With the help of a wider range of sources than the films alone, however, we can also get a greater sense of how what they show was the result of debate, deliberation and discussion, the interplay of a variety of factors; we can also see what they do not show, and what this tells us about those who made them, commissioned them and watched them. The vision of Soviet culture thus afforded is less one of a certain body of precious artefacts, a canon of artistic works that must be reckoned with, but rather a nexus in a web of meanings binding a society, embodying and bonding shared values. That society has since collapsed, even if its legacy endures in contemporary Russia and beyond. Analysing Soviet film as part of cultural history is a way of reconstructing the mental, emotional and conceptual world of that Soviet past that will not pass.

Notes

1 See David Brandenberger, *Propaganda State in Crisis: Soviet Ideology, Indoctrination and Terror under Stalin, 1927–1941* (New Haven, CT and London: Yale University Press, 2011), p. 9; Peter Kenez, *The Birth of the Propaganda State: Soviet Methods of Mass Mobilization, 1917–1929* (Cambridge: Cambridge University Press, 1985).

2 Joseph Stalin, 'Organizational Report of the Central Committee. 13th Party Congress, 24 May 1924', In *Works*, vol. 6 (Moscow: Foreign Languages Publishing House, 1953), p. 227. See also Joseph Stalin, 'Congratulations to Soviet Cinema on its Fifteenth Anniversary', 11 January 1935, In Richard Taylor and Ian Christie (eds.), *The Film Factory: Russian and Soviet Cinema in Documents 1896–1939* (London: Routledge, 1994), p. 348.

3 The term 'victory cult' is from Nina Tumarkin, *The Living and the Dead: The Rise and Fall of the Cult of World War II in Russia* (New York, NY: Basic Books, 1994).

4 Peter Burke, *Eyewitnessing: The Uses of Images as Historical Evidence* (London: Reaktion, 2007), p. 10.

5 Marc Ferro, *Cinéma et histoire*, new revised ed. (Paris: Gallimard, 1993, 1977), translated into English as Marc Ferro, *Cinema and History*, trans. Naomi Greene (Detroit, MI: Wayne State University Press, 1988).

6 Pierre Sorlin, *The Film in History: Restaging the Past* (Oxford: Basil Blackwell, 1980).

7 Robert A. Rosenstone, *History on Film/Film on History*, 3rd ed. (London: Routledge, 2017), pp. 47–61.

8 Astrid Erll, 'Cultural Memory Studies: An Introduction', in Astrid Erll, Ansgar Nünning and in collaboration with Sara B. Young (eds.), *A Companion to Cultural Memory Studies* (Berlin and New York, NY: De Gruyter, 2010), pp. 1–15; Hayden White, *Metahistory: The Historical Imagination in Nineteenth-Century Europe* (Baltimore, MD, and London: Johns Hopkins University Press, 1973).

9 Denise J. Youngblood, *Movies for the Masses: Popular Cinema and Soviet Society in the 1920s* (Cambridge: Cambridge University Press, 1992), pp. 35–8.

10 Ibid., p. 39.

11 Inaugurating a 'new understanding of cinema' the film was transformative not just in Europe, where it stunned German and then other audiences, but even in the US, where Chaplin described it as 'the best film of all time'. Bulgakova, *Sergei Eisenstein: A Biography*, trans. Anne Dwyer (Berlin and San Francisco, CA: Potemkin Press, 2001), pp. 65–6; Richard Taylor, *The Battleship Potemkin* (London and New York, NY: I. B. Tauris, 2000), pp. 65–127. Also see Jeremy Hicks, 'Lost in Translation? Did Sound Stop Soviet Films Finding Foreign Audiences?', in Stephen Hutchings (ed.), *Screening Intercultural Dialogue: Russia and its Other(s) on Film* (London: Routledge-Curzon, 2008), pp. 113–29.

12 Anna Lawton, *The Red Screen: Politics, Society, Art in Soviet Cinema* (London and New York, NY: Routledge, 1992), p. 3.

13 John Tosh, *The Pursuit of History: Aims, Methods and New Directions in the Study of Modern History*, 5th ed. (Harlow: Pearson, 2010), p. 247.

14 John Caughie, 'Introduction', in John Caughie (ed.), *Theories of Authorship* (London: Routledge, 1981), pp. 9–16.

15 Anna Krylova, 'The Tenacious Liberal Subject in Soviet Studies', *Kritika*, 1 (2000), pp. 119–46. See the indicatively titled Herbert Marshall, *Masters of the Soviet Cinema: Crippled Creative Biographies* (London: Routledge and Kegan Paul, 1983).

16 Peter Burke, *What Is Cultural History?* 2nd ed. (Cambridge: Polity, 2008), pp. 27–9.

17 Katerina Clark, *The Soviet Novel: History as Ritual*, 3rd ed. (Indiana, IN: Indiana University Press, 2000).

18 Alexei Yurchak, *Everything Was Forever, Until It Was No More* (Princeton, NJ and Oxford: Princeton University Press, 2006).

19 Jochen Hellbeck, *Revolution on My Mind: Writing a Diary under Stalin* (Cambridge, MA: Harvard University Press, 2006), p. 4.

20 Marc Bloch, *The Historian's Craft*, trans. by Peter Putnam, with an introduction by Joseph R. Strayer (Manchester: Manchester University Press, 1954), p. 61.

21 Catherine Merridale, *Night of Stone: Death and Memory in Twentieth Century Russia* (New York, NY: Viking, 2001), p. 84.

22 Yuri Tsivian (ed.), *Lines of Resistance: Dziga Vertov and the Twenties*, trans. by Julian Graffy (Pordenone: Giornate del cinema muto, 2004), p. 406.

23 Victoria E. Bonnell, *Iconography of Power: Soviet Political Posters under Lenin and Stalin* (Berkeley, CA: University of California Press, 1997), pp. 141–2.

24 Nina Tumarkin, *Lenin Lives! The Lenin Cult in Soviet Russia*, 2nd ed. (Cambridge, MA: Harvard University Press, 1997), p. 142.

25 Tsivian (ed.), *Lines of Resistance*, p. 144.

26 Ibid., p. 138.

27 Ibid., p. 134; Dziga Vertov, *Iz Naslediia. Stat'i i vystupleniia*, vol. 2 (Moscow: Eisenstein Centre, 2008), p. 115.

28 At meetings called to mark Lenin's death, it was one of two songs that were almost invariably sung, along with *The Internationale*, anthem of the Communist movement, then 'national' anthem of the USSR until 1943.

29 There were 20 different publications on Zoia up to 1945 mostly as small pocket-sized brochures. See Rosalinde Sartorti, 'On the Making of Heroes, Heroines, and Saints', in Richard Stites (ed.), *Culture and Entertainment in Wartime Russia* (Bloomington and Indianapolis, IN: Indiana University Press, 1995), pp. 176–93 (p. 184).

30 Yitzhak Arad, *The Holocaust in the Soviet Union* (Lincoln, NE: University of Nebraska Press, 2009).

31 See Jeremy Hicks, *First Films of the Holocaust: Soviet Cinema and the Genocide of the Jews, 1938–1946* (Pittsburgh, PA: University of Pittsburgh Press, 2012), pp. 134–56.

32 Karel Berkhoff, *Harvest of Despair: Life and Death in Ukraine under Nazi Rule* (Chapel Hill, NC: University of North Carolina Press, 2007).

33 Valerii Fomin (ed.), *Kino na voine: dokumenty i svidetel'stva* (Moscow: Materik, 2005); Valerii Fomin (ed.), *Tsena kadra. Kazhdyi vtoroi—ranen, kazhdyi chetvertyi ubit. Sovetskaia frontovaia kinokhronika 1941–1945 gg. Dokumenty i svidetel'stva* (Moscow: Kanon, 2010).

34 Vanessa Voisin, Valérie Pozner and Irina Cherneva (eds.), *Perezhit' voinu. Kinoindustriia v SSSR, 1939–1949 gody* (Moscow: Politicheskaia entsiklopediia, 2018).

35 Aleksandr Dovzhenko, *Dnevnikovye zapisi, 1939–1956* (Khar'kov: Foloi, 2013); Voisin, Pozner and Cherneva (eds.), *Perezhit' voinu*, p. 442.

36 Voisin, Pozner and Cherneva (eds.), *Perezhit' voinu*, p. 452.

37 Ibid., p. 488.

38 Ibid., p. 480.

39 Maria Belodubrovskaia, *Not According to Plan: Filmmaking under Stalin* (Ithaca, NY and London: Cornell University Press, 2017).

40 Christine E. Evans, *Between Truth and Time: A History of Soviet Central Television* (New Haven, CT and London: Yale University Press, 2016), p. 16.

41 Jeremy Hicks, *The Victory Banner: Film, Ritual and Repetition in Russia's Memory of World War Two* (Pittsburgh, PA: University of Pittsburgh Press, 2020).

42 Joseph Gibbs, *Gorbachev's Glasnost. The Soviet Media in the First Phase of Perestroika* (College Station, TX: Texas A&M University Press, 1999), p. 16; Ellen Mickiewicz, *Changing Channels: Television and the Struggle for Power in Russia* (New York, NY, and Oxford: Oxford University Press, 1997), p. 69.

43 Birgit Beumers, 'The Serialization of Culture, or the Culture of Serialization,' in Birgit Beumers, Stephen Hutchings and Natalia Rulyova (eds.), *The Post-Soviet Russian Media: Conflicting Signals* (London and New York, NY: Routledge, 2009), pp. 159–77.

Further reading

Belodubrovskaia, Maria, *Not According to Plan: Filmmaking under Stalin* (Ithaca, NY and London: Cornell University Press, 2017).

Evans, Christine E., *Between Truth and Time: A History of Soviet Central Television* (New Haven, CT and London: Yale University Press, 2016).

Ferro, Marc, *Cinéma et histoire*, New, revised ed. (Paris: Gallimard 1993, 1977).

Hicks, Jeremy, *First Films of the Holocaust: Soviet Cinema and the Genocide of the Jews, 1938–1946* (Pittsburgh, PA: University of Pittsburgh Press, 2012).

Prokhorov, Alexander and Elena Prokhorova, *Film and Television Genres of the Late Soviet Era* (New York, NY: Bloomsbury Academic, 2017).

Rosenstone, Robert A., *History on Film/Film on History*, 3rd ed. (London: Routledge, 2017).

Taylor, Richard, and Ian Christie (eds.), *The Film Factory: Russian and Soviet Cinema in Documents 1896–1939* (London: Routledge, 1994).

12 The diary as source in Russian and Soviet history

Dan Healey

Introduction

After the collapse of communist rule, Western scholars of Russia looked forward to reading in personal diaries about what Soviet citizens 'really thought' of a regime that allowed so little space for the private world. Diaries written during the Soviet years appeared to promise access to the 'inner man and woman' and to confirm once and for all the thoughts, dreams and aspirations of the Soviet people. Surely the Soviet diarist would turn out to be a desk-drawer dissident, criticizing the communist order and preserving a personal authenticity that chimed with Western liberal notions of the free individual personality?

The answer to this question turned out to be rather ambiguous, and a debate over 'Soviet subjectivity' continues to draw upon diaries as fruitful sources that uncover a range of allegiances and conceptions of the self. Many had a 'revolution on their mind' and explored the revolution's meaning for themselves in their journals, but numerous others refused to 'speak Bolshevik' in these pages ostensibly written for their own private use. At some level, the diaries mirrored the wide diversity of Soviet experience, and no simple binary of loyal subject versus desk-drawer dissident can adequately capture the range of voices now available in private journals of twentieth-century Russia. Meanwhile, studies of pre-revolutionary subjectivity now demonstrate a deepening of diary culture to some non-privileged social groups that accompanied expanding literacy in the decades before the 1917 Revolutions.

In part, historians' approaches to these 'new' sources reflected diverging post-Soviet orientations in the wider historiography. These diverging approaches are discussed in the following pages. For some, the common-sense understanding of the diary, as an historical source created on a daily basis by a Western-style rational ('liberal') individual engaged in private reflection on public events, licensed an empirical mining of information from diaries for their self-evidently factual content. This approach remains a dominant methodology for certain kinds of conventional historical investigation. However, as an approach to the 'reality' established in diaries, the method has encountered significant challenges from historians working to explore the historical development of the Russian self, using new tools borrowed from literary and cultural analysis.

This chapter examines Russian and Soviet diaries as historians are currently using them, and some of the debates surrounding the questions they raise. The genre of the diary will be discussed briefly, and a discussion then follows of the theoretical arguments made by some scholars for a more critical approach to diaries and the notion of the Soviet individual. Various applications of these new models will be explored. Finally, reading from the 1955–6 diary of Gulag prisoner, singer, and homosexual Vadim Kozin, the possibilities opened up by these emerging new approaches are demonstrated.

Diary as genre

The modern diary is commonly understood to be a work of intimate writing, composed on a periodic, usually daily, basis. And yet this is a description that needs unpacking. The diary's intimate nature seems axiomatic, however, the personal reflections of the author might focus on virtually any aspect he or she cares to explore. Authors might fill their diaries with thoughts about public, commercial, official, scientific, private, personal, or spiritual issues, for example, and the diary might not necessarily devote itself to a single clear-cut theme or set of questions. Diarists, in other words, choose the aspects of life they wish to explore, and some find more relish in detailing and commenting on meteorological, social or public facts than in delving into the meaning of life and one's place in it. Historically, diary-like writing in Russia as it emerged in the eighteenth and early nineteenth centuries could be fragmentary, evolving from log books, and shifting from dry factual notations to introspective sketches or social observation with little apparent system or discipline.[1] A focus in the Russian diary on the intimate self seems to have arrived in the early nineteenth century with Freemasonry as a significant source of encouragement for introspection and self-development.[2] The evolution of diary-keeping and publication in Russia in the nineteenth century allowed Russians to imagine an increasingly rich variety of subjects suitable for personal journals, and gave them models to imitate or manipulate.[3] The journals of elite thinkers and leading personalities became, starting in the nineteenth century, *public* documents, published with an eye to shaping Russian collective memory and claiming historical, literary, and professional notoriety. Historians and literary scholars have long found the diary a troublesome genre, at once deceptively (and seductively) intimate, and at the same time enervating in its capacious malleability.[4] The range of subjects a diarist explores, and the mode of their exploration, reveals at the very least how the individual author understands the genre of diary-writing, and then something of the literary and cultural tools available to that diarist.

It is undeniable that the diary was, until the 1920s at least in the historical Russian setting, largely an 'elite' genre. Until the twentieth century the majority of the population of the Russian lands was illiterate, and few diaries of serfs, peasants, and lower townsmen were written and have survived. Historians have usually told the stories of the lower classes of Russia using newspapers, crime records, and similarly sidelong-glancing materials, not produced by subalterns themselves.[5] The majority of diaries that were published and celebrated in modernizing Russia until the 1917 Revolution were the journals of aristocratic, intelligentsia, or literary figures. And yet significant exceptions to this rule give glimpses of exceptional personalities from the lower orders: the diaries of eighteenth-century merchant I. A. Tolchenov; the diaristic memoir of a peasant who rose to become a censor for Nicholas I, Aleksandr Nikitenko; and the Moscow townsman who had sex with male servants and friends, Pavel Valsil'evich Medvedev, to offer but three examples.[6] As David Ransel explains, the value of the diary of an individual from the non-elite is considerable for the historian who seeks 'to bring to life an individual as part of a community' through the study of everyday life and routine practices, illuminating a social world otherwise invisible to us.[7]

The temporal features of keeping a diary are of particular value to the historian. 'The diary', writes Kirill Kibrin, 'is the most "historical" of genres' and this is perhaps particularly true for Russian diarists acting as witnesses to their turbulent history.[8] Few other sources promise to offer the reactions of individuals to events in the immediate flow of their historical development. Nor are such reactions coloured by longer retrospective re-evaluation or re-casting with the knowledge of what happened next. The diary seems to present opportunities for the historian to tap experience as it was lived in a way that letters, memoir, and autobiography cannot deliver with the same freshness.[9] What is more, when temporal immediacy is combined with the diaristic form and the intimacy of most modern diaries, we hope to glimpse the individual's uncertain, first-hand, attempts to make sense of events before they are 'fixed' by wider opinion and the influence of social or political narratives. The diary offers a chance to sense how the contingency of historical events was experienced and interpreted by individuals. A striking example can be found in the diaries of the writer Zinaida Gippius. She shared a flat with her husband Dmitrii Merezhkovskii next to Petrograd's Tauride Palace, birthplace of the Provisional Government in February 1917. Her entries for the days of the fall of the Tsar in February give hour-by-hour accounts of events.[10] She was able to record the passing crowds of demonstrators, the coming and going of government ministers known to her personally, and their visits to her flat, most notably many visits from Duma politician and sometime leader of the Provisional Government Alexander Kerensky. Her assessment of this critical politician peaked and troughed as his fortunes careened during 1917:

> Kerenskii is the genuine man in the genuine place. 'The right man on the right place' as the wise English say. Or – 'the right man on the right moment'? And what if it is only 'for one moment'? Let's not begin to guess. In any case he has the right to speak about the war, for [continuing] the war – namely because he has been against the war (as such). He was a 'defeatist' – in the silly terminology of 'those who believe in victory'.

> (20 May 1917, Old Style [OS])[11]

Later on 5 November (OS), relating her perspective on Kerenskii on the eve of his defeat at the hands of the Bolsheviks, Gippius wrote:

> Yes, a fatal man; weak…a hero. Courageous… a traitor. Feminine… a revolutionary. A hysterical commander-in-chief. Soft-hearted, passionate, afraid of bloodshed – a murderer. And very, very much, in everything – unlucky.[12]

Gippius's diary offers a study in the evolution of political disappointment over the course of 1917.

The story of Gippius's diary also raises questions about such journals' textual integrity and provenance. For the historian of Russia, personal documents like diaries are a vulnerable genre, perhaps more so than official documents.[13] The physical survival and coherence of Gippius's journals was ruptured for several years by revolution. Her 'Dark Blue Book' recording the principal events of the Provisional Government's rule in 1917 was left behind in Petrograd when she quit Russia in 1919. She gave it up for lost. It was only returned to her by a friend who visited Paris from Russia in 1927.[14] She had also kept a 'Black Notebook' which chronicled her life in Petrograd from August to December 1919, and a 'Grey Notepad' which, while diaristic in form, lacked dating of entries, but covered the same months before emigration. Gippius managed to take both of these fragmentary documents abroad with her in 1919 and published them in emigration in 1921; she only published the 1917 diary in 1928. Gippius was far from alone in only just managing to preserve her diary. Many Soviet diarists, particularly those of politically, socially, or ethnically mistrusted groups, experienced difficulties in preserving their journals from official scrutiny, 'arrest', or destruction. Sensing that keeping a diary was already becoming risky early in the 1920s, Moscow history professor Iurii Vladimirovich Got'e made arrangements to preserve it by giving it to an American aid worker, who also happened to be gathering documents for the Hoover Institution, in 1922. It languished there, miscatalogued and forgotten, until 1982.[15] It seems to have been standard operational practice for the Soviet security services to seek out diaries during arrests, and such documentation was examined for anti-Soviet statements, as the 1930s diary of Nina Lugovskaia, teenage child of a dissident socialist, illustrates.[16] Once inside the Gulag of the Stalin era, prisoners were not usually permitted access to writing materials and as a result, did not produce diaries. Similarly, due to illiteracy and desperate living conditions, few of the victims of 'dekulakization' or national operations to resettle untrusted ethnic and national groups kept diaries. Both groups of victims of harsh Soviet policies have told their stories through memoirs and oral histories instead.[17] Virtually no diaries have emerged from employees of the NKVD, with a recently translated diary of a Gulag guard being a noteworthy exception.[18]

When considering the diary as a genre, the historian of Russia seeking personal sources should bear in mind the great variety of styles of diary-keeping, with diverse subject material and perspectives on personal, social, cultural, and political events. The personal and introspective mode commonly assumed to be the signature form of the modern diary is only one version of the genre. Historians also need to consider the likely audiences that diaries may address: has the diarist got one eye on posterity, on his or her descendants, or on an unknown sympathetic reader? Does he or she expect the journal to be published one day? Or is the document genuinely only for private study and contemplation? The historian must bear in mind the temporal advantages and limitations of diaries as sources: the immediacy and candidness of impressions may be the great attraction of a diary, and yet the individual's perspective will almost certainly constrain the historian's viewpoint and require corroboration with alternative sources. Finally, the tribulations that personal documents of all kinds have suffered in modern Russia need to be understood. Keeping a diary in the world's first socialist state was unlike doing so in a liberal-democratic or fascist state, and certain types of diaries may simply never have been written, or if they were, they may have failed to survive the extreme conditions of the regime.

Theories and their application

This section examines two general types of theoretical approaches to the diary as a source in Russian history. The first type I designate 'empirical' and the second, a critical 'subjectivity studies' approach. The 'subjectivity studies' approach is more recent, emerging only since the end of the Soviet Union, and it is gaining in popularity among young historians interested in reconstructing comparative histories of the Soviet self.

Many historians, and among them, literary historians (*filologi* in Russian), approach the diary in an empirical spirit. As scholars principally using their material as a source of 'real' facts, they mine diaries as repositories of what people thought, said, and did, usually, to produce a factual account of an event, era, or question. This does not mean that historians adopting this approach should overlook the features of the diary as genre, including their pitfalls, as outlined in the previous section. Conventional historical evidentiary rules apply: confirming key facts against alternative sources, consideration of the likely motives of the author, asking who the audience for a given diary was meant to be, checking facts of provenance and textual integrity. There are many reasons for resorting to diaries for factual evidence, in the Russian historical context. Given the opaque and personalized nature of the tsarist governmental machine, for example, diaries of state officials and members of the Romanov family can be helpful sources explaining events and motives. Examples of historians using diaries in this fashion are manifold, and some are sophisticated in their use of the behind-the-scenes glimpses they afford. Simon Dixon's exploration of the restoration of the Russian Patriarchate before and during 1917 relies upon the diaries of prelates and secular social observers to uncover both the personal rivalries and religious thinking that underpinned the decision to give Russia's Orthodox Church, facing a crisis of the collapse of the state that had bolstered it, a single paramount leader.[19] A similarly 'factual' approach is used by literary scholars in Russian studies who try to reconstruct the lives and creative careers of poets, novelists, and artists. Studies of the early twentieth-century poet, diarist, and composer Mikhail Alekseevich

Kuzmin, for example, rely upon cross-checking between Kuzmin's voluminous diary entries and other evidence – often, from the diaries of fellow artists – for confirmation of events and facts, in order to reconstruct the life of a poet who left very little autobiographical material.[20] The resort to diaries for 'facts' is well established in the practice of Russian history, and examples of the application of empirical method abound.

More recently, a debate about the nature of the 'New Soviet Person' has emerged in part as a result of the access to new sources, including diaries, since the collapse of the Soviet Union. A key feature of this debate about 'subjectivities' in Stalinist or wider Soviet life has been historians' turn to diaries to explore and illustrate certain features of Soviet selfhood. For historians, influenced by Michel Foucault and his Soviet-historian proponent, Stephen Kotkin, 'subjectivity' is a conceptual form of selfhood seen in its historical and cultural context.[21] The interiorized human personality is not presumed to be universal and timeless, but to have significant variation according to historical and local contexts. 'Modern subjects' come into being as humans respond to their surroundings and fashion themselves in reaction – and some diaries can help us to observe that self-fashioning process.

Historians using this approach seek not to mine diaries for concrete biographical or historical 'facts', but rather to read them critically as exercises in self-fashioning by their authors. As key proponent of this method, Jochen Hellbeck explains, '[s]ome Soviet revolutionaries considered the diary, along with other forms of autobiographical practice, as a medium of self-reflection and transformation' and even if other ideologists worried that keeping a diary was 'an inherently "bourgeois" activity', in the Soviet Union of the late 1920s and 1930s, personal journals served as a vital means for self-fashioning in a 'socialist' state where few blueprints for personal transformation existed.[22] Diarists studied by Hellbeck strove 'to inscribe their life into a larger narrative of the revolutionary cause', and in so doing, fostered their own personal versions of 'an illiberal, socialist subjectivity'.[23] Hellbeck's chroniclers of their lives engaged with Stalinist ideology, sought to understand their role in realizing it, and struggled with the contradictions between their experience of state violence and the high aspirations of anti-capitalist morality.

Of course, one can argue that such Soviet subjects were essentially 'singing along' to the tune of the regime, changing themselves (not the world around them), and even truncating features of their personality or intellectual capacities to fit a mould.[24] At stake here are Western scholars' conceptions of the Stalinist or Soviet 'subject' or individual under the Soviet regime. Were Soviet citizens of the 1930s and after 'brainwashed', 'indoctrinated', and atomized by communist ideology? How far did the 'totalitarian' regime penetrate and shape the mentality, the psychology, of the average individual under Soviet rule? Were communists successful in producing the 'New Soviet Person'? According to Anna Krylova, such questions animated discussions about 'totalitarianism' as a lens for analysing the post-1945 Soviet Union, which in the Cold War became the liberal capitalist West's principal adversary.[25] In various guises, political scientists and later in the 1970s and 1980s, 'revisionist' historians, projected an imagined 'liberal subject' hiding behind the façade of Stalinist and later Soviet collectivist society. The Soviet 'subject' was consistently conceived of as a coherent and rational personality, resistant to Soviet ideology, or if they were compliant, they behaved that way because of cynical calculation. It was inadmissible both in Cold-War totalitarian perspectives, and 'revisionist' ones, to imagine Soviet citizens as true believers in the ideology of the regime. Even after the collapse of communism, with access to new sources, Krylova charges that post-Soviet scholarship failed to accept, until recently, that ordinary people might choose to write themselves into history by internalizing the ideology and its values.[26]

Historians have sought out diaries as a means of understanding how some Soviet 'subjects' worked in their journals to become 'New Soviet Persons', or in some cases how they struggled to internalize the ideological values as they understood them. Key examples of the application of this method are Hellbeck's extended study of a selection of diaries and especially his focus on the diary of Stepan Pod-lubnyi, a kulak's son attempting to remake himself as a good Komsomol activist in Moscow in the 1930s.[27] The value of Hellbeck's account is in the deep and close reading of these journals as records of soul-searching, testing of boundaries, and confrontations of the self with ideological challenges on the path of self-transformation. By taking these subjects' struggles to write themselves into Stalinist ideology seriously, the historian reveals their voices and challenges the narratives of the resistant hidden 'liberal subject', and its cousin the cynical mouther of Soviet slogans. (At very least, this taking ideology seriously adds new voices to the variety of diarists we now know about; not all diarists were engaged with the Soviet project, as even Hellbeck allows.)[28] Hellbeck makes only a token effort to understand gendered subjectivity in the diaries he examines; however, Krylova's study of Soviet women in combat uses the female soldiers' own writings, including diaries, to examine how they reconciled femininity and combat duty.[29] Her work on the poet Vera Inber, whose diaries demonstrate a desire to remake herself fully Soviet despite an 'unlucky' biography, also takes this approach.[30]

The temporal focus of this approach is no longer confined to the diaries of the Stalin era. Another recent use of diaries in combination with correspondence, autobiography, and memoirs, to explore Bolshevik subjectivity in the earliest phases of the Soviet regime, albeit, without explicit identification of the author with the 'subjectivity school', can be found in the magisterial study of the House of Government by Yuri Slezkine.[31] Here the diaries of Old Bolsheviks are plumbed not merely for factual information, but to illustrate the self-fashioning travails of the socialist official coming-to-power, confronting dilemmas of responsibility, and realities that upset long-cherished ideals. One of the few studies to use a large number (125) of Soviet diaries is Alexis Peri's examination of journal-keeping during the Siege of Leningrad. She sees these subjects not merely constructing a selfhood but striving, through their diaries during the crisis of blockade, 'to preserve traces of themselves in the face of annihilation'. Diaries were 'tied to survival'.[32] Post-Stalin diaries of the 1950s–1960s are also explored in the work of Anatolii Pinskii, who sees the diary as a genre that answered reforming writers' aspirations for a renewed Soviet subjectivity embodying the independent-minded citizen, under the new conditions of the Khrushchev 'Thaw'.[33]

Homosexual and Soviet: reading the diary of Vadim Kozin

The 1955–6 journal of the Stalin-era gypsy romance crooner Vadim Kozin (1905–94) offers the historian an excellent illustration of the possibilities that a critical reading of a diary, inspired by the new 'subjectivity studies' approach, can provide.[34] Born in St Petersburg into a middle-class family with a 'gypsy romance' singer heritage, Kozin had little formal education but by the 1930s was emerging as a significant singer in the Leningrad light entertainment scene. He left the city for Moscow in 1936 and enjoyed national popularity as recorder and performer of apolitical pop songs. He also conducted a string of affairs with young men, apparently, under the watchful eye of the secret police, even after the Stalin ban on male homosexuality of 1934. He was arrested in 1944 on charges of propaganda against Soviet power in wartime, sex offenses with minors, and male homosexuality. In 1945 he was sent to Magadan, capital of the Kolyma labour camp system in the Far East, where he was a prisoner for five years. On release, he sang for the Magadan Musical-Dramatic Theatre and toured with it in Siberia as a top-billing star. A second arrest on sodomy charges in 1959 resulted in a brief prison sentence and put Kozin's career on ice. He remained in Magadan until his death, continuing to write songs, perform locally, and read voraciously. He also cultivated a young journalist, Boris Savchenko, who took an interest in the singer's Stalin-era career; Savchenko would become his biographer, and the editor of his diary.[35]

Many facts about Kozin's diary are unclear, and this lack of clarity raises concerns for the historian about textual authenticity and completeness. Savchenko reports that he helped Kozin to retrieve the 1955–6 diary from the local Magadan archives of the KGB in the early 1990s; it had been held there after it was taken to assist the police in formulating the charges against the singer in 1959. Savchenko writes 'and from him it came into my hands' after Kozin's death in 1994. 'Of course, with the intention that it would be published posthumously.'[36] The biographer's long-standing professional relationship with Kozin apparently made him in the singer's eyes the ideal literary executor, at least, of the diary. Some distant family members unsuccessfully contested this decision after the 2005 publication of Kozin's journal.[37] The text of the 1955–6 diary remains in Savchenko's possession. Moreover, in 2015 in an interview with a British journalist, Savchenko claimed that Kozin kept journals for many years, but that the manuscripts are scattered: supposedly, more unpublished portions are in the biographer's possession, others were given by Kozin to friends, and some may remain in KGB archives.[38] We do not know how long Kozin kept a diary, how much of it survives, and what changes in its character over time we might observe had we access to the full body of this work.

Who did Kozin write his diary (or diaries) for? At least as reported by Savchenko, the singer had an eye on posterity and wished to see his journal published in post-Soviet Russia, but for what motives or readership is less clear. From the part of the diary available to us, we read this entry from 1956 about his imagined future audience:

> Whoever reads these pages should not think that these are the lines of a schizophrenic, or someone suffering from graphomania. Some lines are the minutes

and hours of inexpressible misery and suffering, remorse for a life incorrectly lived. If I had departed even just a little from my truthfulness, and was even just a temporary hypocrite, my life would have been totally different. But I want to be myself. Let he who obtains these notes be an honest man, and someday somehow speak up in my defence, when after my death they throw stones at me.[39]

Kozin was already imagining the diaries – as he wrote them in the 1950s – as a means of self-justification and a way of striking back against those critics of 'a life incorrectly lived'. In fairness to Savchenko, he genuinely seems to have seen this injunction as a duty he owed to the singer. Moreover, if in fact Kozin did give portions of his diary to friends, perhaps, to lovers, he clearly wanted to share his lively reflections on life with these people, and evidently he was unperturbed by the possibility of wider circulation (by *samizdat* – unofficial self-publication typical of the late Soviet era) or eventual publication.

What conception of the genre of the diary does Kozin's journal reveal? He clearly wrote in the diary in more than one register and about a broad range of subject matter. This is a diary kept while on a working tour and there are surprisingly few days without at least a short, dated entry, sometimes indicating the name of a hotel, the berth he occupied in a railway carriage and the time of day when he wrote. A significant proportion of Kozin's journal is devoted to professional matters: the stages and venues the Magadan Musical-Dramatic Theatre ensemble play in, the programmes of music he sings (most of which have been edited out by Savchenko), the make and condition of the pianos in Siberian houses of culture, the intrigues backstage, and his tart assessments of his colleagues and their mixed abilities. There is a considerable amount of attention devoted to living conditions in the succession of Siberian towns and cities he sees, particularly through his avid consumer's gaze. Kozin describes the shortages of banal products (butter, oil, soap) and he writes in detail about his search for specific items such as a piano, a tape-recorder, and rare books. (The diary's extensive lists of books purchased and sent to Magadan was excised by Savchenko.)

Yet this is not a dull diary of lists, endless performance notes, and petty intrigue between forgotten artistes. Kozin also used the diary to muse upon the condition of the arts in his time, to reflect on the nature of homosexuality, to observe the progress of de-Stalinization, and to record the Soviet Union's changing international relations with friends and foes. I have written elsewhere about the singer's caution when discussing homosexual affairs, his incoherent and often contradictory conceptions of same-sex love as expressed in the diary, and his search for appropriate and dignified terms to set out in his journal the experience of same-sex desire.[40] Having been denied, as a son of a merchant, a higher education, Kozin's reference points for articulating the world he observes were largely acquired in the school of hard knocks, through a life devoted to books and the stage, and particularly from his evolving sense of his origins in the pre-Stalin-era world of St Petersburg/Leningrad's *cafés-chantants* and music halls. It is a world of sharp elbows, sharp opinions, and firm prejudices. He says little about Russian literature and its landmarks of male or female homosexual prose and poetry (so nothing here about Mikhail Kuzmin's notorious 1906 gay Bildungsroman, *Wings*). His is not an understanding of Russia's queer-related culture as exalted and aestheticized, except where the music of Tchaikovsky is concerned.[41] He encounters queers he adores and abhors while on tour – his own sexual desire threatens to run out of control, but he strives, with one or two exceptions, to silence his urges on the page. ('A wonderful person, I am convinced of this ... I was not mistaken about him. It was right that my diary was silent about him'. Kozin wrote this the day after an extraordinarily indiscreet and purple entry celebrated this man as the object of his overwhelming passion.)[42] The diary becomes a place where Kozin contemplates the contempt and mistrust (in our contemporary terms, the homophobia) he suffers at the hands of colleagues who know why and how he was sentenced to the Gulag. Kozin's diary is an extremely rare document of the excruciating dilemma of the *visible* homosexual in post-Stalin Russia.[43]

At the same time, an aspect of Kozin's subjectivity vividly evident in the diary is his identification with conservative, even Stalinist, Soviet values. Like Hellbeck's diarists of the 1920s–1930s, seeking to find their place in the Stalinist-socialist project, Kozin observes Soviet life and expresses his opinions on it. In contrast to the Khrushchev-era reformist writers Pinskii examines, with their imagined 'independent' thinking citizens developing their critical faculties through their diaries, Kozin's response to political reform is conservative and suspicious. In an encounter with travelling companions aboard a ship in July 1956, he recognizes that '[b]efore me were open supporters of Stalin, convinced and unshakeable, believing in the correctness of his policies'. He records that he gave them his address and invited them to visit him in Magadan, 'not to be shy, but they should know that they would receive a warm welcome'. For Kozin de-Stalinization risks making the Soviet Union look foolish in the international arena.[44] Far from working on his 'self' via the diary to fashion a currently 'correct' Soviet consciousness, fifty-year-old Kozin confidently expresses his strong views on the actions of the regime. He does not strive to refashion himself as a post-Stalin critical subject; he already has 'independent' views and they are not the ones Pinskii's reforming writers wish to cultivate.

Kozin's sense of 'Sovietness' can be glimpsed from his views on public decency and moral standards. Kozin's opinions about sexual hints in radio plays are strikingly conservative: more than once he comments that immodesty is taking over the Soviet airwaves:

> What cookie-cutter plays one hears these days on the radio! The players perform in stereotypes, with standard intonations, laughter, [...] It all turns out woeful and sickening. And then those fucking actresses [*eti bliadi artistki*], playing the parts of young Soviet girls, speak and giggle with voices that only used to be heard from prostitutes. Especially when they laugh. [...] The love of a young lad is played with all the chastity of a tart's grimace.[45]

A little later in Cheliabinsk, Kozin meets a male fan, an engineer, with whom he passes time in a restaurant. The fan's modesty and good manners impress the singer to exclaim, 'That's the image of a good Soviet young man!'[46] For Kozin, public modesty, decency, and refined manners remain important 'Soviet' attributes, even if he honours them in the breach with obscenities in his journal.[47]

Kozin contrasts Soviet decency with foreign corruption, glimpsed in imported films. In Krasnoiarsk he sees an Argentinian movie, *The Age of Love* (Julio Saraceni, 1954) and observes that after he had the chance to reflect on the story 'for the Soviet viewer it is just the usual bourgeois nonsense. The film is made under the influence of Hollywood, everything ends happily.' Kozin describes the love-plots of the film with a degree of distaste, and then adds, 'The dancers were very hard to distinguish from American ones, the very same "girls" with short legs. And by the way even the heroine of the film knows how to shake and show off her legs.'[48] Later in Kuibyshev he sees *Le Rouge et le Noir* (Claude Autant-Lara, 1954) and is even more dismissive. 'The love intrigue overwhelms the social significance of the story.' He continues,

> And because the French are such great masters of the consolations of love, they've shown all that off in this picture. For the great mass of our audiences this film, with its totally intentional, purely French erotica, so incomprehensible to the Soviet people, aggravates the nerves and becomes a kind of forbidden fruit and test of strength. I heard how one man behind me openly expressed his feelings. Naively thinking that if it's shown without cuts in the cinema it must all be permitted, the man openly expressed his full agreement with the actions of the hero: 'What a guy! And her too! She herself wants it!' The man had no shame. Such open erotica suits the Russian muzhik down to the ground. I also saw the following scene. A mother brought her nine-year-old daughter to the cinema. The ticket-vendor, a middle-aged woman, refused to let her in. The mother asked why. 'Because we don't let children see this picture. Even the adults act up when they see it. Surely as a mother you don't want your daughter watching such filth?'[49]

Kozin in the same entry imagines the utter corruption of Soviet morals if the 'Geneva Convention' mandated more exchanges of films with the West; 'We'll end up with Sodom and Gomorrah.' Is this just loyal political posturing for a reading policeman who might one day seize the diary? Hardly. Kozin knew intimately the challenges of negotiating the permissible in stage repertoire under Stalin. The singer had devoted his professional career to 'gypsy romance' songs, with their sentimental stories of love affairs and their relatively chaste allusions to relations between the sexes, themes that put his apolitical repertoire at the ideological margins of Soviet music. There were dangers in concentrating one's career on popular tunes apparently lacking a patriotic message during the Stalin era, and through his arrest and imprisonment, Kozin had felt a taste of official disapproval, although the reasons for his sudden fall from grace remain unclear.[50] In his post-Stalin diary, the singer firmly argued that Soviet decency was a key public value, one that he had upheld in his career. In his view it was now under threat from elemental forces (the erotic instincts of the 'Russian muzik') within the USSR, and malign ones from outside in the form of foreign films and culture.

Conclusion

Kozin does not use his diary as a 'workshop' to construct a loyal, politically alert, subjectivity. He did, however, use the practice of daily writing to construct an understanding of the dilemmas of the queer self in Soviet conditions and he also used it to observe and assess those conditions. This is not the kind of 'subjectivity' that most historians in the 'subjectivity school' have been looking for, and yet, historians should not expect to find uniformity in self-fashioning in Russian diaries. Much of the recent work on diaries as constructive of specific subjectivities (the 'New Soviet Person', the worker 'speaking Bolshevik', the 'illiberal socialist subject') relies upon careful case selection to isolate diaries that reflect these particularly loyal 'Soviet' voices. The 'subjectivities studies' scholarship is valuable because it restores these voices to our repertoire of Soviet subjects and the diaries that reflected and constructed them. Nevertheless, if we imagine the vast diversity of diaries at the historian's disposal, we can easily conclude that no single diary could be 'representative' of Soviet subjectivity, and no collection of diaries written by particular types of citizens could reflect the broad swathe of responses to life in the USSR.[51] The subjectivity school assists us in understanding significant voices which we have tended to dismiss as improbable. The methods of diary reading proposed by Hellbeck and Krylova, among others, can be deployed far beyond this specific range of 'illiberal socialist subjects', to argue for the construction of varied and unusual forms of subjectivity. Queer diarists – currently seen as very rare in Russian studies, despite some monumental editorial efforts to preserve and publish leading examples – form just one category of the unorthodox voices available for close reading and critical interpretation.[52] As Irina Paperno notes, there is no single appropriate method for scholars reading diaries to follow. Rather, she observes that 'the scholars' self-conscious and reflective readings of specific diaries, both together with and apart from other private documents', yields unique insights.[53] It is the historian in the conscious work of selecting diaries, their close reading, and critical interpretation, who crafts arguments about how selves are fashioned, and why. Such selection, reading, and interpretation need not be limited to the search for the 'illiberal socialist subject', but can be applied to just about any set of diaries the historian sees fit to examine.[54]

Notes

1 David L. Ransel, 'The Diary of a Merchant: Insights into Eighteenth-Century Plebeian Life', *Russian Review*, 63 (2004), pp. 594–608 (pp. 597–8).
2 Andrew Kahn, M. N. Lipovetskii, 'Irina Reyfman and Stephanie Sandler, *A History of Russian Literature* (Oxford: Oxford University Press, 2018), pp. 385–94.
3 Ibid., pp. 392–7, 426.

4 Irina Paperno, 'What Can Be Done with Diaries?', *Russian Review*, 63 (2004), pp. 561–73.

5 Ilya Gerasimov, *Plebeian Modernity: Social Practices, Illegality, and the Urban Poor in Russia, 1906–1916* (Rochester, NY: University of Rochester Press, 2018), pp. 25–33.

6 On Tolchenov see Ransel, 'The Diary of a Merchant'; on Nikitenko see A. Nikitenko and Helen Saltz Jacobson, *Up from Serfdom: My Childhood and Youth in Russia, 1804–1824* (New Haven, CT and London: Yale University Press, 2001); on Medvedev see Dan Healey, *Homosexual Desire in Revolutionary Russia: The Regulation of Sexual and Gender Dissent* (Chicago, IL: University of Chicago Press, 2001), pp. 23–5, and A. I. Kupriianov, 'Pagubnaia Strast' Moskovskogo Kuptsa', in Iu. L. Bessmertnyi and M. A. Boitsov (eds.), *Kazus: Individual'noe i unikal'noe v istorii* (Moscow: RGGU RAN, 1997).

7 Ransel, 'The Diary of a Merchant', p. 600.

8 Kirill Kibrin, 'Pokhvala Dnevniku', *Novoe literaturnoe obozrenie*, 61 (2003), no page numbers.

9 Although the intertextuality of journals and correspondence within family groups, for example, as informing each other and as performing related social functions should not be discounted; see e.g., John Randolph, '"That Historical Family": The Bakunin Archive and the Intimate Theater of History in Imperial Russia, 1780–1925', *Russian Review*, 63 (2004), pp. 574–93.

10 Z. N. Gippius, *Peterburgskie Dnevniki (1914–1919)* (New York and Moscow: Tsentr PRO, SP SAKSESS, 1990), pp. 82–9 (27, 28 February 1917 Old Style). For a similar hourly account, see Catherine Sayn-Wittgenstein, *La Fin De Ma Russie: Journal 1914–1919* (Paris: Phebus libretto, 2007), pp. 115–18 (27 February Old Style).

11 Gippius, *Peterburgskie Dnevniki*, p. 133. All translations are my own unless noted. Citations in single quotation marks are in English in the original; in double quotation marks are in scare quotes in the original.

12 Ibid., p. 211.

13 On this point see Sheila Fitzpatrick, 'Impact of the Opening of Soviet Archives on Western Scholarship on Soviet Social History', *Russian Review*, 74 (2015), pp. 393–5.

14 N. Berberova, 'Predislovie', in *Gippius, Peterburgskie Dnevniki (1914–1919)*, p. 13. See also Gippius's own account of the return of the journal, Gippius, *Peterburgskie Dnevniki (1914–1919)*, pp. 19–21.

15 Iu. V. Got'e and Terence Emmons,*Time of Troubles: The Diary of Iurii Vladimirovich Got'e – Moscow – July 8, 1917 to July 23, 1922* (Princeton, NY: Princeton University Press, 1988), pp. 4–5.

16 See Nina Lugovskaia and Andrew Bromfield, *I Want to Live: The Diary of a Young Girl in Stalin's Russia* (London: Doubleday, 2006). Homosexuals arrested after 1934 lost their diaries in secret police raids; see Healey, *Homosexual Desire in Revolutionary Russia*, pp. 211, 225.

17 See, e.g., Leona Toker, *Return from the Archipelago: Narratives of Gulag Survivors* (Bloomington & Indianapolis, IN: Indiana University Press, 2000); Lynne Viola, *The Unknown Gulag: The Lost World of Stalin's Special Settlements* (New York, NY, and Oxford: Oxford University Press, 2007).

18 Ivan Chistiakov and A. L. Tait, *The Diary of a Gulag Prison Guard* (London: Granta, 2016).

19 Simon Dixon, 'Orthodoxy and Revolution: The Restoration of the Russian Patriarchate in 1917 (Prothero Lecture)', *Transactions of the RHS*, 28 (2018), pp. 149–74.

20 The field of Kuzmin studies is vast, but in English an excellent starting point is John E. Malmstad and Nikolay Bogomolov, *Mikhail Kuzmin: A Life in Art* (Cambridge, MA & London: Harvard University Press, 1999). For another example of the application of an empirical approach in literary biography, see Michael Makin, *Nikolai Klyuev: Time and Text, Place and Poet* (Evanston, IL: Northwestern University Press, 2010).

21 See Stephen Kotkin, *Magnetic Mountain: Stalinism as a Civilization* (Berkeley and Los Angeles, CA: University of California Press, 1995). For working definitions of 'subjectivity' see Jochen Hellbeck, *Revolution on My Mind: Writing a Diary under Stalin* (Cambridge, MA and London: Harvard University Press, 2006), pp. 9, 11–12; idem., 'The Diary between Literature and History: A Historian's Critical Response', *Russian Review*, 63 (2004), pp. 621–9; also note Eric Naiman, 'On Soviet Subjects and the Scholars Who Make Them', *Russian Review*, 60 (2001), pp. 307–15.
22 Hellbeck, *Revolution on My Mind*, p. 8.
23 Ibid., p. 9.
24 Naiman, 'On Soviet Subjects and the Scholars Who Make Them', pp. 311–12, 315.
25 Anna Krylova, 'The Tenacious Liberal Subject in Soviet Studies', *Kritika: Explorations in Russian and Eurasian History*, 1 (2000), pp. 119–46.
26 Ibid., pp. 141–4. This final point is made principally through a reading of Kotkin, *Magnetic Mountain*.
27 Jochen Hellbeck, *Revolution on My Mind*, pp. 165–222; idem., 'Fashioning the Stalinist Soul: The Diary of Stepan Podlubnyi (1931–1939)', *Jahrbücher für Geschichte Osteuropas*, 44 (1996), pp. 344–73.
28 Diaries that express anti-Soviet views are not hard to find, such as those of collective farmer Ignat Frolov, dekulakised Andrei Arzhilovsky, and artist Liubov' Shaporina in the collection of translated journals Garros, Veronique, Natalia Korenevskaya and Thomas Lahusen (eds.), *Intimacy and Terror: Soviet Diaries of the 1930s* (New York, NY: New Press, 1995).
29 In a single chapter devoted to his sole female diarist, Zinaida Denisevskaia (Hellbeck, *Revolution on My Mind*, pp. 115–64), a subsection (pp. 118–26) deals with her gender and the problem of the language of (hetero)sexuality available to the diarist. Hellbeck does not problematize male gender but sees it as natural, unworthy of investigation. For a study of subjectivity that does examine gender systematically, see Anna Krylova, *Soviet Women in Combat: A History of Violence on the Eastern Front* (Cambridge and New York, NY: Cambridge University Press, 2010). Neither scholar problematizes the heterosexuality of their subjects.
30 Anna Krylova, 'In Their Own Words? Soviet Women Writers and the Search for Self', in Adele Marie Barker and Jehanne M. Gheith (eds.), *A History of Women's Writing in Russia* (Cambridge: Cambridge University Press, 2002).
31 Yuri Slezkine, *The House of Government: A Saga of the Russian Revolution* (Princeton, NJ and Oxford: Princeton University Press, 2017). Chapters 7 'The Great Disappointment' and 10 'The New Tenants' are particularly focused on the personal and intimate lives of the inhabitants of the House of Government, exploring their deep investments in the politics of socialism including the sexual and gender politics that accompanied the Revolution.
32 Alexis Peri, *The War Within: Diaries from the Siege of Leningrad* (Cambridge, MA and London: Harvard University Press, 2017), p. 11.
33 Anatolii Pinskii, 'Dnevnikovaia forma i sub"ektivnost' v Khrushchevskuiu epokhu', Anatolii Pinskii (ed.), In *Posle Stalina: Pozdnesovetskaia Sub"ektivnost' (1953–1985): Sbornik Statei* (Sankt-Peterburg: Izdatel'stvo Evropeiskogo universiteta v Sankt-Peterburge, 2018).
34 For more on Kozin's biography see Dan Healey, *Russian Homophobia from Stalin to Sochi* (London and New York, NY: Bloomsbury Academic, 2018), pp. 75–80.
35 Boris Savchenko, *Vadim Kozin: Sud'ba Artista* (Moscow: Iskusstvo, 1993); for a franker version of the biography, based in part on Kozin's diary, see idem., *Vadim Kozin* (Smolensk: Rusich, 2001); for the diary, see Vadim Kozin, *Prokliatoe Iskusstvo* (Moscow: Vagrius, 2005).
36 Kozin, *Prokliatoe Iskusstvo*, p. 27. It appears that Savchenko had privileged access to Kozin's 1959 criminal investigation file, which was also produced by the local KGB. On

this file see also Mikhail Krushinskii, 'Solovei Za Reshetkoi: Vadim Kozin, Delo No. 85 I 94-K', *Rodina*, 9, 10 (2001), pp. 88–92; 10: pp. 88–93. I am indebted to Uladzimir Valodzin for obtaining copies of this publication.

37 Igor Dorogoi, 'K Voprosu O Sud'be Dnevnikov Vadima Kozina', *Kolymskii trakt* (16 March 2005).

38 Personal communication, Monica Whitlock, 23 February 2015. I am grateful to Monica for fruitful conversations about Kozin, and for her generosity in sharing the insights of her research.

39 Kozin, *Prokliatoe Iskusstvo*, pp. 338–9 (26 September 1956).

40 Healey, *Russian Homophobia from Stalin to Sochi*, pp. 73–89.

41 On Tchaikovsky, see Kozin, *Prokliatoe Iskusstvo*, pp. 98 (11 August 1955), 300 (3 August 1956), discussed in Healey, *Russian Homophobia from Stalin to Sochi*, p. 85. The Russian literary exaltation of homosexuality is described in Brian James Baer, *Other Russias: Homosexuality and the Crisis of Post-Soviet Identity* (New York, NY: Palgrave Macmillan, 2009).

42 Kozin, *Prokliatoe Iskusstvo*, p. 315 (19 August 1956), discussed in Healey, *Russian Homophobia from Stalin to Sochi*, pp. 86–7.

43 For specific examples and further discussion see Healey, *Russian Homophobia from Stalin to Sochi*, pp. 80–3, 87–9.

44 Kozin, *Prokliatoe Iskusstvo*, p. 280 (15 July 1956).

45 Ibid., p. 91 (31 July 1955).

46 Ibid., p. 144 (24 September 1955).

47 Kozin tended to reserve obscenity for his descriptions of his work colleagues and their low morals and parlous artistry; here he extends the favour to radioplay actors. Kozin did not normally resort to swearing when discussing other standard topics of his journal.

48 Kozin, *Prokliatoe Iskusstvo*, p. 84 (27 July 1955). On the film, distributed in the USSR under the title 'Vozrast liubvi', see <https://imdb.com/title/tt0198439/> (accessed 1 January 2019).

49 Kozin, *Prokliatoe Iskusstvo*, p. 185 (16 November 1955). On the film see <https://imdb.com/title/tt0047432/?ref_=nv_sr_2> (accessed 1 January 2019).

50 Savchenko, *Vadim Kozin*, pp. 78–9. Despite publication of a range of 1959–60 files on the singer, we are no clearer on why Kozin suddenly fell foul of his patrons in the Party: see Krushinskii, 'Solovei Za Reshetkoi'.

51 For a similar argument, see Peri, *The War Within*, pp. 15, 235–9.

52 Some examples of queer Russian diaries: P. I. Chaikovskii, *Dnevniki 1873–1891* (Moscow-Petrograd: Gos. iz-vo Muzykal'nyi sektor, 1923), [reprint 1993]; M. A. Kuzmin, *Dnevnik 1905–1907* edited by N. A. Bogomolov and S. V. Shumikhin (St. Petersburg: Ivan Limbakh, 2000); M. A. Kuzmin, *Dnevnik 1908–1915*, edited by N.A. Bogomolov and S. V. Shumikhin (St Petersburg: Ivan Limbakh, 2005); M. A. Kuzmin, *Dnevnik 1934 Goda* (St Petersburg: Iz-vo Ivana Limbakha, 1998); Konstantin Andreevich Somov and Pavel S. Golubev, *Dnevnik: 1917–1923* (Moscow: Dmitrii Sechin, 2017); Konstantin Andreevich Somov and Pavel S. Golubev, *Dnevnik: 1923–1925* (Moscow: Dmitrii Sechin, 2017). For a rare queer woman's diary, see Anna Barkova, *Vosem' Glav Bezumiia: Proza, Dnevniki* (Moscow: Fond Sergeia Dubova, 2009).

53 Paperno, 'What Can Be Done with Diaries?', p. 573.

54 Naiman, 'On Soviet Subjects and the Scholars Who Make Them', p. 312.

Further reading

Chistiakov, Ivan, and A. L. Tait, *The Diary of a Gulag Prison Guard* (London: Granta, 2016).

Garros, Veronique, Natalia Korenevskaya and Thomas Lahusen (eds.), *Intimacy and Terror: Soviet Diaries of the 1930s* (New York, NY: New Press, 1995).

Got'e, Iu. V., and Terence Emmons, *Time of Troubles: The Diary of Iurii Vladimirovich Got'e – Moscow – July 8, 1917 to July 23, 1922* (Princeton, NJ: Princeton University Press, 1988).

Hellbeck, Jochen, 'The Diary between Literature and History: A Historian's Critical Response', *Russian Review*, 63 (2004), pp. 621–9.

_____, *Revolution on My Mind: Writing a Diary under Stalin* (Cambridge, MA and London: Harvard University Press, 2006).

Krylova, Anna, 'The Tenacious Liberal Subject in Soviet Studies', *Kritika: Explorations in Russian and Eurasian History*, 1 (2000), pp. 119–46.

_____, *Soviet Women in Combat: A History of Violence on the Eastern Front* (Cambridge and New York, NY: Cambridge University Press, 2010).

Lugovskaia, Nina, and Andrew Bromfield, *I Want to Live: The Diary of a Young Girl in Stalin's Russia* (London: Doubleday, 2006).

Naiman, Eric, 'On Soviet Subjects and the Scholars Who Make Them', *Russian Review*, 60 (2001), pp. 307–15.

Nikitenko, A., and Helen Saltz Jacobson, *Up from Serfdom: My Childhood and Youth in Russia, 1804–1824* (New Haven, CT and London: Yale University Press, 2001).

Paperno, Irina, 'What Can Be Done with Diaries?', *Russian Review*, 63 (2004), pp. 561–73.

_____, *Stories of the Soviet Experience: Memoirs, Diaries, Dreams* (Ithaca, NY: Cornell University Press, 2009).

Peri, Alexis, *The War Within: Diaries from the Siege of Leningrad* (Cambridge, MA: Harvard University Press, 2017).

Raleigh, Donald J. (ed.), *A Russian Civil War Diary: Alexis Babine in Saratov, 1917–1922* (Durham, NC and London: Duke University Press, 1988).

Randolph, John, '"That Historical Family": The Bakunin Archive and the Intimate Theater of History in Imperial Russia, 1780–1925', *Russian Review*, 63 (2004), pp. 574–93.

Wolfson, Boris, 'Escape from Literature: Constructing the Soviet Self in Yuri Olesha's Diary of the 1930s', *Russian Review*, 63 (2004), pp. 609–20.

13 Soviet memoir literature

Personal narratives of a historical epoch[1]

Claire Shaw

In the field of Soviet history, perhaps no source has been as perennially controversial as memoir literature. While retrospective accounts of life during the Soviet experiment abound, the reliability of the evidence they provide is frequently called into question. In his recent monograph on the history of the Gulag, Steven Barnes devotes a full two paragraphs of his introduction setting out the pros and cons of these sources, balancing the value of memoirs in revealing 'the subjective experience of the camps at a given moment in time' against issues such as the accuracy of memory, the problem of partiality, and the blurring of lines between individual and collective narratives of the past.[2] Memoirs, he suggests, can provide us with evidence of everyday experiences 'on the ground' that supplement, and often challenge, official sources. Yet memoirs also need to be handled with care, alive to the biases and motivations of their authors. For the historian of the USSR, therefore, memoir literature represents a source that is as productive as it is problematic.

This chapter examines memoir literature as a source for Soviet historians, setting out the debates over its utility, and suggesting approaches to its use. As many historians – not just of Russia – have pointed out, memoirs represent an unreliable source, in which the instability of memory forestalls any search for objective truth about the past. For historians of the USSR, in particular, memoirs raise important questions about whether subjective narratives can ever be trusted in a 'totalitarian' regime. At the same time, however, the Soviet Union's emphasis on the significance of collective memory, and the political importance of personal life narratives, mean that memoirs represent a particularly rich source of information about how the past was understood, and how personal preoccupations and memories intersected with broader narratives of socialism and historical progress. In addition, the potential of memoirs to unlock individual experiences of past events, experiences which often foreground the emotional and the sensory, make memoirs a particularly productive source for the historian.

In order to tease out these issues, this chapter will consider the 1966 memoir of Agrippina Kalugina, a deaf woman who witnessed – and participated in – the revolutionary struggle to construct a Soviet deaf community. While on the surface, Kalugina's memoir represents a typical Soviet narrative of progress and transformation, it also reveals important issues of community, gender, and sensory experience, exposing tensions between individual and collective narratives of the past. By examining Kalugina's work, this chapter will demonstrate ways in which memoir literature can reveal the history of socialism as it was lived, experienced and remembered.

'Truth' and the challenges of memoir literature

Debates over the utility of memoir literature are not confined to the history of the USSR, although the Soviet field has shaped and extended these debates in significant ways. For the purposes of this chapter, I define memoir literature in broad terms as a retrospective, personal narrative of a particular moment in history. The distinction between autobiography and memoir is slippery (and this chapter draws on scholarly literature relating to both terms), but the difference between the two is generally understood to lie in the subject matter. While, as Philippe Lejeune points out, an autobiography takes as its subject the 'individual life, story of a personality', a memoir places the focus on the historical moment, as inhabited by its author.[3]

This distinction between individual life and historical moment is not clear cut, however. As Nancy K. Miller points out, 'by its roots, [the term] memoir encompasses both acts of memory and acts of recording – personal reminiscences and documentation'. As such, 'memoir is fashionably postmodern, since it hesitates to define the boundaries between private and public, subject and object'.[4] Yet this definition raises important questions about how, as historians, we should deal with sources that are partial, fragmentary, and deeply personal, even as they purport to reveal to their readers the 'truth' about a moment in history (a common advertising slogan for the contemporary political memoir). Many historiographical discussions of memoir literature start, therefore, by considering the relationship of the memoirist's reminiscences to an objective 'truth' about the historical past.

This attempt to unpack the truth of memoirs (and other 'ego documents') stumbles immediately on the contested role of the author. The place of the author within a memoir – as both the subject and object of enquiry – has the result of making transparent the text's subjective nature. Mostly written in the first person, memoirs place the 'I' of the memoirist centre stage, filtering historical events through the memoirist's own experiences, and interpreting those experiences through the prism of the memoirist's own understanding of the world, an understanding that is inevitably shaped by identity frameworks such as nationality, political and religious beliefs, gender and racial identity. As such, memoirs produce a narrative which privileges the narrow, subjective experience over 'big picture' historical enquiry.

Historians are therefore particularly attentive to how this subjective view shapes narratives of the past, often seeking in their analyses to separate out the partial from the reliable. In particular, the motivation of the author is frequently called into question. As Mary Fulbrook explains, there are many reasons that might compel a memoirist to put pen to paper:

> People produce accounts of their own lives for very different reasons: to update significant others; to think through, preserve, or pour out experiences; to explain past actions and attitudes, or defend themselves against accusations; to transmit what they think is important across generations; to bear witness to appalling times; to make money, or seek posthumous fame; to ventilate frustrations, explore dilemmas, and shape self-representations; and for countless other purposes.[5]

These reasons for writing inevitably have a bearing on what is written, and how. The desire to sell a 'tell-all' book creates pressure to sensationalize, or to frame the narrative in particular ways. Political memoirs, even the most candid, tend to spin events to the benefit of their authors. The need to bear witness to trauma for those who cannot frames the story that is told. Context and external pressures also play a part; as Fulbrook recounts, while many victims of war crimes in post-war Germany felt compelled to testify to the suffering they had endured, the context of war crimes investigations and post-war welfare and restitution policies pushed victims to 'provide a particular account of [their] own past' that enabled them both to participate in the legal reckoning with perpetrators of Nazi crimes, and to access sources of financial support.[6]

The question of motivation reveals another concern for historians: the temporal gap between the author-narrator and author-subject. Most memoirs are written a considerable time after the events they describe; as such, they are inevitably shaped by an awareness of what came after, both in the author's own life, and in history. As Sidonie Smith and Julia Watson explain, memoirs create meaning by 'engaging the past' as a way to 'reflect on identity in the present'.[7] The past of a memoir is constructed in such a way to speak to the concerns of those reading it; its narrative, although it might be embedded in historical events, mobilizes hindsight and context to resonate with its imagined readers. The memoir's focus is also shaped by that hindsight, with the author's older self often explaining and justifying the actions of the younger from a perspective of greater knowledge and understanding. As a result, a memoir can be read as operating on two temporal levels, each informing the other.

Indeed, the overlapping temporal narratives present in a memoir often have the effect of revealing the fallibility of memory itself. Joan Tumblety explains that recent research in a variety of disciplines, including the neurosciences, has shown that memory is not a stable archive of information to be consulted at will, but a construction:

> we do not have memory as much as remembrances, or even performances of remembering, where what is remembered is shaped fundamentally both by the meaning of the initial experience to the individual in question, and by the psychological – and inextricably social – circumstances of recall.[8]

As such, memories are shaped on a number of levels, from the psychophysiological to the social.

The understanding that individual memory can be unreliable has inevitably influenced the ways in which historians approach memoir literature. Historians now recognize that violent and traumatic events – the very stuff of gripping history – can often produce unstable and fragmented memories. As Cathy Caruth points out, one of the central problems of traumatic memory is its inability to be assimilated into a stable narrative of the past; instead, the information is either suppressed, or endlessly repeats itself.[9] According to Sarah Young, the 'compulsive and involuntary return of the repressed [memory]' stands at odds with 'the deliberate recollection necessary for the production of testimony, memoir, or autobiography'.[10] Yet even for those memoirists recalling less traumatic events, it is not unusual for facts to be misremembered: the colour of a dress, the date of an event, the presence of a particular individual at an important historical moment. The ability of individuals to remember the past with accuracy and coherence cannot be taken for granted.

At the same time, those working with memoirs have also paid attention to the impact of broader social frameworks on the shaping of individual memories. As Maurice Halbwachs argues, 'no memory is possible outside frameworks used by people living in society to determine and retrieve their recollection'.[11] In other words, individual memories are shaped and conditioned by practices of collective commemoration – such as national ceremonies to remember soldiers killed in war – which privilege certain events and play down others, creating national and international memory 'scripts'. While it would be wrong to suggest that individual memories are simply overtaken or reprogrammed by such scripts – collective memories are shaped by the convergence of individual experiences, and individual memories gain meaning and resonance in their interplay with group acts of remembering – the melding together of individual and group memory requires careful consideration by the historian. To return to Fulbrook's account of Holocaust memoirs, we can see that accounts written in the post-war context conformed to established tropes about the horrors of the Holocaust, but often did so in a way that ignored the fragmentary and problematic nature of traumatic memories.[12]

For many historians, these theoretical discussions about the capacities and limits of individual memory raise fundamental questions about whether memory – and by extension the memoir – can ever be trusted. As Caruth explains, debates over traumatic memory have a tendency to return to a concern with 'false recovered memories', and thus dismiss all traumatic memories as somehow tainted.[13] Similarly, John Popkin points to several controversies in recent decades over memoirs that have been shown to be either wholly fabricated or a complex blend of fact and fiction. As Popkin explains, such controversies, while extremely few, have the result of tainting the reception of 'indubitably genuine eyewitness accounts'.[14] Put simply, memoirists can lie – either inadvertently or by design – and that knowledge has made some historians wary of trusting memoir literature as a source.

If the reliability of life narratives as evidence of historical events is questioned even in democratic regimes, where individuals' 'freedom' to recount the past as they see it is not in dispute, then the stakes for such narratives are seen to be considerably higher in the Soviet Union. As Sarah Davies asks:

> How do we recover the thoughts and values, hopes and beliefs of 'ordinary people'? So often their voices have been silenced by the rich and powerful. In Stalin's Russia, this silencing was particularly insidious. Not only were people literally silenced – shot, or incarcerated in concentration camps for expressing unorthodox views – but also the entire Soviet media eliminated virtually all reference to heretical opinion.[15]

In light of this perceived 'totalitarian' repression of popular opinion, historians – particularly those writing during the lifetime of the USSR – have tended to divide Soviet memoirs into two groups: 'official', published works by Soviet loyalists, which conformed to Soviet propagandistic tropes and narratives, and 'unofficial' works by dissidents, either circulated underground in typescript form (a phenomenon known as *samizdat*, or 'self-publishing') or published abroad (*tamizdat*, or 'over-there-publishing'). In the context of Western scholarship, the former were considered to be a politicized distortion of history, and the latter a sensational revelation of the 'truth' about Soviet socialism.

This debate reveals a broader conceptual concern regarding the 'truth' of Soviet personal narratives. As Anna Krylova has explained, much of the historical scholarship on the USSR has tended to posit a divide between a Soviet individual's public self, which parroted the language of the state for reasons of fear or personal advancement, and their private, 'liberal' self, which sought ways to resist the imperatives of the Soviet project. This assumption of a 'tenacious liberal subject' shaped attitudes to sources, encouraging historians to read 'between the lines' of public utterances to uncover examples of individual resistance to the overbearing Soviet state.[16] In relation to memory and memoirs, Polly Jones explains, this has led to the persistent interpretation that 'Soviet public memory consistently falsified and silenced popular memories, and so produced private (and oppositional) countermemories'. In other words, '"real" memory had been silenced, even killed, throughout the Soviet period'.[17]

More recent histories have sought to collapse this binary between official and unofficial, public and private, looking at ways in which the collective narratives of Soviet ideology shaped Soviet subjectivities. The opening of the archives in 1991 was central to this shift, with newly discovered sources revealing that, in the words of Jochen Hellbeck, 'personal narratives were so filled with the values and categories of the Soviet revolution that they seemed to obliterate any distinction between a private and a public domain'.[18] Yet Soviet scholarship continues to question the truthfulness of publicly articulated narratives of the self. On the one hand, scholars such as Jones have argued convincingly that 'public memory (or, equally, public forgetting) is usually shaped by interplay and contestation between different narratives of the past and different framings of memory', thus allowing for the expression of genuine popular feeling in dialogue with broader ideological narratives.[19] On the other, Stephen Kotkin's suggestion that Soviet citizens simply learned to 'speak Bolshevik' in their public utterances – 'It was not necessary to believe. It was necessary, however, to participate as if one believed' – continues to dominate the scholarship.[20]

Unpacking Soviet memoirs

On the basis of the above discussion, the student of Soviet history might be forgiven for giving memoirs a wide berth, choosing instead to work with more ostensibly 'reliable' – in other words, private and unofficial – documents. Indeed, as Barnes points out, there are many historians who advocate just that. J. Arch Getty, in his *Origins of the Great Purges*, points to memoirs' self-consciously 'literary' form, arguing that, for the historian, memoirs 'provide more heat than light': 'For no other period or topic have historians been so eager to write and accept history-by-anecdote'.[21] While memoirs can 'tell us what the camps were like', he suggests, they cannot uncover 'why they existed'.[22] Similarly, Orlando Figes suggests that oral history represents a more reliable method, in that 'it can be cross-examined and tested against other evidence to disentangle true memories from received or imagined ones.'[23] In both cases, the narrowly subjective take of the memoir, and its interpenetration with collective memory, is seen to delegitimize the form. And yet, as Barnes argues, historians – including Figes and Getty – continue to make 'careful use of published and unpublished memoirs' in their historical work.[24] Indeed, recent years have seen a rash of histories that make sustained use of memoirs as a source.

The boom in the use of memoirs does not suggest that historians have found new ways to prove the 'truth' of memoir accounts. Instead, they are asking new questions of these sources, finding ways to incorporate and value precisely these kinds of subjective, multi-layered narratives of the Soviet past. This turn to memoirs reflects broader shifts in historical methodologies, which owe much to the influence of poststructuralism and the 'literary turn'. As David Carlson argues in his discussion of approaches to autobiography, viewing these works as narratives in their own right – that is, paying attention to the role of the author's conception of their own agency, their faulty and selective memory, their motivations and imagined audience – unlocks important information about understandings of the 'self' in a particular historical context. As such, he asserts, the fact that these narratives 'may fall short as sources of objective "truth" does not undercut their value as historical sources'.[25]

In the first instance, memoirs can be viewed as particularly useful sources to access history 'from below', shifting the focus from the grand narratives of Soviet political history to the minutiae of everyday experiences. This is certainly true for historians of the Gulag, who have made the case for the unique value of memoirs to understanding the dynamics of camp life. As Anne Applebaum argues, 'the subtler aspects of camp life – the relationships that prisoners had with one another, with the Gulag administration, and with people on the outside – can be clearly understood only through such accounts'.[26] Barnes, in turn, concludes that, in a challenge to Getty, 'it is precisely for that "what the camps were like" that memoirs are used'.[27] Indeed, the vividness and relevance of memoirs in helping us to understand the everyday experiences of Soviet people – even in the most 'historic' of contexts – are sometimes seen as an implicit challenge to historians' own narrative abilities: as Sheila Fitzpatrick argues, 'Memoirs have a capacity for re-creating lived experience that is hard to equal in a scholarly work'.[28]

Memoirs not only reflect these lived experiences, but also reveal important information about how memoirists understood and felt about them. As Joyce Appleby, the historian of the American Revolution, suggests, while ego narratives might not be the best source of factual information, they remain 'an unparalleled source of clues about sensibilities – the most evanescent of cultural phenomena – as well as of the values and interpretations that constructed reality for a given generation'.[29] While this information might seem peripheral to the bigger picture of historical causation, the significance of 'feelings' to understanding Russian history has been recently explored by Mark Steinberg, among others, who argues that 'emotions are [...] a social practice organized by stories and images, an experience inseparable from the culturally situated language and gestures in which it is conveyed'.[30] For the history of emotions, memoirs represent a powerful source of information about individual and collective moods and the meanings ascribed to them.

The same can be argued for sensory experience. The feel of history – its sound, sight, taste, touch and smell – is revealed through first-person narratives in a way not possible in more official sources, enabling us to grasp Mark M. Smith's argument that 'the senses are not universal, but, rather, a product of place and, especially, time, so how people perceived and understood smell, sound, touch, taste and sight changed historically'.[31] As I have argued elsewhere, the ways in which senses were understood in the Soviet context – and the treatment of disabled groups who lacked one sense, and therefore privileged others – enables us to develop new perspectives on history and to understand bigger issues such as identity, selfhood, and belonging.[32] Writing from a subjective position, therefore, allows memoirists to pay attention to experience itself – including physical feeling, emotion, and sensory perception – and to demonstrate how these experiences were understood.

The opening up of grassroots perspective and the turn to emotional and affective frames of experience, have been used to great effect in recent histories to uncover marginal or minority historical experiences in Russia and the USSR. This includes gender; as Anne Gorsuch explains, 'the private lives of women have been generally less accessible to our eyes and our understanding than the more public lives of (some) men', and therefore the recent outpouring of memoir literature has been particularly revealing of female experience.[33] This opening up of women's experiences, as Gorsuch is at pains to point out, raises yet further questions: 'What were the "categories" within which Soviet women saw themselves? What was the relationship between women, the Soviet experience, and women's own sense of self as described in these life stories? Was women's sense of self a gendered sense?'[34] Indeed, as Gorsuch argues, while 'gender mattered to these women', they often 'did not deploy categories of gender in their presentations of self'.[35]

Again, debates over the categories used to express individual experiences and the self-conscious construction of the 'I' in these narratives, is not seen as a reason to discount the memoir in its entirety; rather, it is an invitation to ask further, more searching questions to understand how individual experience shapes history and vice versa. If it is this interplay between self-experience and historical events that makes a memoir truly valuable, therefore, then it is important to understand the nature of the memoir self. In his exploration of approaches to ego documents, Paul John Eakin argues that the 'I' of autobiography is 'neither singular or first', but instead represents a 'relational identity', defined in dialogue with others and in relation to culturally available models of identity that frame how we understand our lives.[36] Moving away from an 'autonomous' approach to selfhood – which posits that all individuals have the same ability, across time and space, to understand and choose their own actions – he writes instead of 'situated selves, products of a particular time and place; the identity-shaping environments in these autobiographies are nested one within the other – self, family, community set in a physical and cultural geography, in an unfolding history'.[37]

While Eakin is at pains to stress that not all ego narratives share what he calls this 'breadth of vision', his description is particularly apt in the Soviet case, in which the line between self and history is frequently blurred; a direct result of the educational and cultural policies brought in following the revolution which encouraged Soviet citizens to view themselves as active participants in an unprecedentedly 'historical' epoch, in which a socialist state – the inevitable culmination of humankind's development – would be finally achieved. As many historians have noted, constructing the historical myth of the building of socialism required the active and engaged participation of Soviet individuals themselves, who, in the words of Frederick Corney, became 'implicated' in the foundation narrative of October and its aftermath.[38] As a result, Sheila Fitzpatrick explains, Soviet citizens tended to write about their lives in a testimonial style, eschewing the personal in favour of the political, and viewing life events 'with the wide open eyes of a historian'.[39]

This life writing was in itself a widespread cultural phenomenon. As Fitzpatrick has shown, all Soviet citizens in the 1930s were required to maintain an official, narrative autobiography, which covered details such as social origin and employment history, alongside personal experiences, formative life moments, and family connections. These autobiographies were expected to demonstrate an exemplary life history and 'coming to consciousness' as a Bolshevik in order for their writers to advance in work or the Communist Party; the stakes for such narratives were therefore particularly high.[40] Jochen Hellbeck similarly writes of a 'flood of personal documents from the first decades of Soviet power', whose writers 'revealed an urge to write themselves into their social and political order. They sought to realize themselves as historical subjects defined by their active adherence to a revolutionary common cause'.[41] This practice of 'writing oneself into history' was also evident in the 'memoir boom' that emerged with Khrushchev's Thaw, which saw

Soviet individuals writing, for public consumption, about their experiences of such historical moments as the Terror, the Revolution, and the Second World War.[42] As Denis Kozlov argues, such writings – even those that challenged the legitimacy of the Soviet project – showed that 'autobiographical and historical reflections' were 'inseparable from each other'.[43]

The historian making use of Soviet memoir literature thus needs to grapple with, as Hellbeck puts it, 'what it means to write *I* in the age of a larger *We*'.[44] Narratives of the revolution and building socialism, conceptions of class and party-mindedness, and the subsuming of individual desires in the face of collective imperatives – all staples of Socialist Realist literature – shaped the ways in which Soviet memoirists thought and wrote about themselves and their country's history. As such, these memoirs unlock important information on how Soviet citizens conceived of themselves and their place in the world. At the same time, they destabilize Lejeune's distinction between autobiography and memoir; in the Soviet Union, all individual lives were, by definition, about history.

Yet despite Soviet citizens' training to write about themselves using particular categories and narrative tropes, Soviet memoirs still reveal a variety of subjectivities and experiences and allow us to understand the complicated agency of Soviet individuals – an agency which challenges the frequent dismissal of Soviet ego documents as simply 'performance' or a facet of collective memory. To go back to Eakin, even as the 'unfolding history' of the USSR shaped individual life narratives, 'self, family, community' determined the ways in which individuals responded to that history.[45] As recent histories have shown, pre-revolutionary experiences, membership of minority communities, or problematic family ties provided powerful alternative identity structures, and determined the ways in which individuals responded to events on the ground and were able to access and participate in what Brigid O'Keeffe has termed 'Sovietism'.[46] As argued above, emotions, senses, and gendered experiences open up space for a plurality of experiences and understandings within the Soviet ideological framework. Memoirs can therefore enable us to access alternative experiences of Soviet socialism and complicate the relationship between Soviet people and ideology.

Even as they raise fundamental questions about memory and the nature of subjective narrative, therefore, memoirs have the capacity to reveal new perspectives on Russian and Soviet history, including marginalized and everyday experiences, emotional and sensory perceptions, and the shifting interplay between self and society, individual and history, across time. That is not to say that these memoirs should be used uncritically. The questions raised by critics of memoir literature are not insignificant: the subjective position, motivations, and memory of the author should certainly be questioned, and the information given should be compared to other sources to ensure its veracity. Yet to dismiss the memoir entirely on this basis would be to lose a source of significant potential. As Jochen Hellbeck asserts, 'against a widespread proclivity to read Stalin-era subjectivity between the lines and focus on cracks and silences, reading should begin with the very lines'.[47]

Case study: Agrippina Kalugina's *Life in Silence*

Reading Russian and Soviet memoirs, as the above discussion suggests, involves assessing the factual information a memoir contains, analysing questions of intention and style, and thinking through issues of subjectivity, sensibility, and personal (and collective) experience. It also involves balancing the potential pitfalls of the subjective narrative with the rewards it can bring. When faced with a memoir, therefore, the historian must ask a series of questions. These can include: who wrote this memoir, and when? What was the historical context, both of the events depicted, and the time in which the memoir was written? What was the intended audience of the memoir when it was written? In what ways does the author address the audience and how does this shape the narrative? Do the events depicted in the narrative accord with our wider understanding of the historical record? Are there gaps, repetitions, or distortions? How might we understand them? Does the author rely on particular narrative tropes, such as the Soviet transformation narrative? How are the events of the memoir experienced? Do we see any privileging of emotional, sensory, or gendered understandings? How does the author understand her own identity, her relationship to certain individuals and communities, and to history? Can we see this account as representative, either of a particular community, or of the wider Russian/Soviet experience?[48]

The remainder of this chapter will demonstrate these problems and possibilities in relation to one particular text: Agrippina Nikanorovna Kalugina's 1966 memoir of the deaf community during the Russian revolution, *Life in Silence* (*Zhizn' v tishine*). Kalugina was born in 1904. She lost her hearing as a complication of scarlet fever at the age of seven and received her education at the Arnol'do-Tretiakov School for Deaf-Mutes in Moscow; following the revolution, she became a member of the nascent All-Russian Society of Deaf-Mutes (*Vserossiiskoe obshchestvo glukhonemykh*, or VOG) and an activist in the Komsomol (the Communist Union of Youth). Kalugina worked as a journalist for the deaf newspaper *Life of Deaf Mutes* (*Zhizn' glukhonemykh*) until the Second World War. In 1966 – in the midst of the Soviet 'memoir boom' – she completed her memoir. Extracts from the manuscript were published in the deaf magazines *In a United Rank* (*V edinom stroiu*) and *World of the Deaf* (*Mir glukhikh*); they were praised by the deaf poet Ivan Isaev for their 'vivid, memorable descriptions of […] those who began the unification of the deaf of Russia into a single Society'.[49] *Life in Silence* was finally published in full in Russian in 2012, in a volume of deaf memoirs edited by Viktor Palennyi and Iaroslav Pichugin.

To a certain degree, *Life in Silence* reveals the problematic nature of memoirs as a source. Written from the vantage point of the 1960s, a period referred to as the 'golden age' of the Soviet deaf community, Kalugina's memoirs construct a positive narrative of the inevitable emergence of this community, defined by its distinctive forms of visual and sign language culture, and at the same time closely entwined with Soviet institutional structures and ideological understandings of the self and society. The memoir recounts the evolution of VOG, from a grassroots club system to a nationwide organization charged with the political and cultural transformation, material support and labour placement of deaf people, demonstrating the reach of revolutionary ideals of individual and social transformation into the deaf community. As Kalugina exclaims, 'what truly wide horizons were opened up for deaf people in our Soviet era'![50]

This desire to portray a teleological narrative of progress and the overcoming of obstacles sometimes smooths over – or indeed misremembers – points of tension. Her description of a speech given by Anatolii Vasilievich Lunacharskii, the Commissar of Enlightenment, to the II Congress of VOG in January 1929, is a case in point. Kalugina remembers Lunacharskii speaking to deaf people 'simply, from the heart, as a human being', and commenting that, despite their hearing loss, deaf people 'keenly hear the voice of life, the voice of reason'.[51] A comparison with the archival text of Lunacharskii's speech, however, reveals a much more complicated picture; the speech, which relied heavily on the theories of the educational psychologist Lev Vygotskii, suggested that, unless deaf people learned to speak, they would 'fall from the living cloth of society.'[52] Lunacharskii went on to argue that deafness was, in many ways, symbolic of anti-Sovietness: 'He who thinks only of himself is deaf. He who does not unite in a single thought and action with his brother people is deaf.'[53] Kalugina's warm memory of the acceptance of deaf people by Soviet state representatives does not always accord with the more complicated, and often prejudicial, reality.

These points of tension, while problematic, illuminate the ways in which a strong foundation narrative of the Soviet deaf community had developed over time, giving a positive, revolutionary gloss to a period that was, in reality, chaotic, punctuated by obstacles, failures and misunderstandings on the part of the authorities. That the deaf community developed such a foundation narrative is unsurprising; this way of thinking about history – as a struggle for liberation, and as a definitive triumph against the odds – was widespread in the Soviet Union. Kalugina was certainly not alone in viewing the successes of the Soviet deaf community as the ultimate fulfilment of the revolution's promise: as a textbook on deafness published in 1957 pointed out, 'After the Great October Socialist Revolution opened the wide expanse of their creative abilities and initiative, deaf-mutes, who were once considered inferior [*nepolnotsennye*], superfluous members of society, felt that they were full citizens of the great Soviet Motherland and in no way inferior to those who can hear. [...] they march in step with the hearing and make their contribution to the general task: the building of communism in our country.'[54] This type of language – of liberation and equality, engendered by the revolution – echoes through Kalugina's narrative, and inevitably shapes its conclusions.

While Kalugina's memoirs evidently seek to write the deaf community into the triumphant history of the Soviet experience, that does not mean that the information contained within them is untrue. The picture Kalugina paints of the emergence of a powerful deaf community corresponds to archival reports and her account of the accomplishments of revolutionary deaf activists adds richness to the historical record, providing vital information to the historian. Indeed, Kalugina's narrative provides a unique insight into 1917 and its aftermath from the perspective of the deaf community. While key historical events – such as the Civil War and the death of Lenin – punctuate the narrative, the changes these events provoked in the lives of deaf people represents the central theme of the memoir. Kalugina describes the new path, 'wide and clear, [which] opened to us deaf people after the October revolution. I wanted to do something bigger, more significant, to fight for a new truth and remake my life'.[55] Following a brief stint working as a typist at the People's Commissariat of Health, Kalugina found this purpose in VOG, particularly the club on Moscow's Ulanskii Pereulok. The memoir vividly describes her initiation into club life, her ease in the company of other deaf people, and her eager participation in the 'plays, lectures and games' run by club members. Yet the memoir is clear that these activities were not merely diverting. Kalugina explains that VOG's purpose was deeply political, describing speeches by the deaf agitator Dmitrii Pavlovich Voronov, 'a participant in the 1905 revolution' and lectures advocating for 'the solidarity of deaf-mutes in fight for the Russian proletariat, for the eight-hour working day, and for the raising of wages'.[56]

Alongside this detailed information on the grassroots deaf community, Kalugina's memoir provides a particularly vivid picture of the sensory experience of being deaf, before and after the revolution. The memoir opens with her account of her rapid hearing loss:

Only yesterday, I lived in a world full of sounds: people talked, laughed and sang, sparrows chirped, dogs barked, pedestrians walked, some with booming steps, some with light ones, the church bells rang, the wheels of the tram, which had only recently replaced the horse-drawn carriage, knocked against the rails.

I lay in a large hospital bed. The sunny, spring day streamed through the window, but everywhere there was a strange, inexplicable silence.[57]

Kalugina recounts the events of the memoir with a particular focus on the visual: she describes in detail the physiognomy of each important individual, the style of their sign-language gestures, and the layout of rooms. Sight and the (absence of) hearing are not the only senses present in the memoir; one memorable section describes the hunger of the Civil War years, and the taste of makhorka tobacco and dried apples.[58] Yet the memoir dwells on the experience of silence, described by Kalugina as 'absolute, complete […] my normal state'.[59] As she explains, however, she does not consider this to be a 'loss': 'spent in the world of silence, my life has been full of a variety of events, vivid impressions, and unforgettable meetings with interesting people'.[60] Silence is a facet of her deaf identity, one which, in the context of the wider deaf community, has given her access to vital life experiences.

While silence represents a significant interpretative category for Kalugina's narrative, gender is significantly less so. Kalugina's account gives its readers insight into gendered spaces and relationships, including the female dormitories at the Arnol'do-Tretiakov School, and Kalugina's group of female friends, whom she refers to as the 'troika'. Yet the memoir does not reflect on her identity as a woman or consider the degree to which her experience might be gendered. If there is discussion of marginality or discrimination, this relates solely to her identity as deaf, which is seen to throw up particular obstacles that she – and the deaf community as a whole – must work to successfully overcome. For example, she recounts a conversation with a physics teacher at the Higher School of Trades Union Activity, who confesses that 'with all my strength I opposed working with you. Teaching deaf people seemed to me to be extraordinarily hard. […] But now I confess that I was both deeply and happily wrong.'[61]

In many ways, Kalugina's memoir represents a standard Soviet autobiographical narrative, tracing her coming-into-being as an educated, politically conscious worker, in step with the transformation of the USSR as a whole. The conclusion to the memoir makes this link abundantly clear; Kalugina explains that, 'merging with the whole Soviet people in a united aspiration to transform life, [to make] a better future, we – people from the world of silence – find in this a calling, and our life's happiness'.[62] Kalugina's struggle to 'overcome' imperfection, and to remake herself in the mould of the New Soviet Person, echoes the collective 'script' identified by Jochen Hellbeck as the desire of Soviet people to 'write themselves into their social and political order'.[63] Indeed, the memoir frequently shifts the focus from Kalugina's own life to the life of the country as a whole, making clear that the latter is the true subject of this work.

At the same time, however, to return to Eakin, the memoir reveals a multifaceted, 'relational' identity, in which Kalugina's deafness remains as important, if not more so, than her Sovietness. Even as Kalugina links her life experiences to the transformation of the Soviet Union as a whole, she places this alongside the landmarks in the development of the deaf community, and her own coming-into-being as a deaf woman, including the moment of hearing loss, her mastering of sign language, her entry into the deaf community and her understanding that being 'with the deaf-mutes and for the deaf-mutes' is the driving purpose of her life.[64] Yet the memoir makes the case that these two identities – the Soviet and the deaf – are not mutually exclusive, but hybrid and intertwined. Kalugina explains that her deafness, and her place in the 'world of silence', means that she is more devoted to the Soviet project than she might have been, if she 'had not, in childhood, through a chance exposure to scarlet fever, lost my hearing'.[65] 'Soviet power', she argues, 'the most humane in the world, opened up and showed to us the wide path of life'.[66]

Kalugina's narrative is richly detailed, vividly written and full of the kind of personal commentary that lends colour and sensibility to historical analysis. As such, it is not surprising that I have continued to return to her memoir – testing and triangulating her assertions against other sources – in my own research into the deaf community, using it to build a strong understanding of the grassroots experience of the Soviet project amongst deaf people. True, her account is not fully representative of all deaf people's experiences: Kalugina's position of relative privilege in the VOG apparatus shapes her attitude to deafness and Soviet power. Similarly, its conformity to a 'foundation narrative' of the Soviet deaf community inevitably shapes and directs its conclusions. Yet, in its foregrounding of sensory experiences, and its exploration of the similarities and tensions between deaf and Soviet narratives of living the revolution, this memoir provides vital insight into what it meant to be deaf at this critical, revolutionary moment in history.

Conclusion

This chapter has shown that memoirs continue to be a controversial source, tainted – in the eyes of many historians – by their subjective and partial nature and the fallibility of individual memory. In the Soviet context, the problems of memoirs are amplified by wider concerns about the totalitarian suppression of personal experiences. Yet, as the continued use of memoirs attests, subjective narratives of past events are a vital source of information about the past. Memoirs do not simply recount what happened, but rather reveal how events were experienced and understood, exposing the relationship between, in the words of David Carlson, 'creative human minds and the social institutions that surround them'.[67] In the Soviet Union in particular, where individual lives were seen to have world-historical implications, memoirs have the capacity to transform our understanding of life during the Soviet experiment.

Notes

1 I am extremely grateful to Chris Read and George Gilbert for their comments on this chapter.
2 Steven A. Barnes, *Death and Redemption: The Gulag and the Shaping of Soviet Society* (Princeton, NJ: Princeton University Press, 2011), p. 4.
3 Philippe Lejeune, *On Autobiography*, ed. by Paul John Eakin (Minneapolis, MN: University of Minnesota Press, 1989).
4 Nancy K. Miller, *Bequest and Betrayal: Memoirs of a Parent's Death* (Bloomington, IN: Indiana University Press, 2000).
5 Mary Fulbrook, 'Life Writing and Writing Lives: Ego Documents in Historical Perspective', in Dahlke, Birgit, Dennis Tate and Roger Woods (eds.), *German Life Writing in the Twentieth Century* (Rochester, NY: Camden House, 2010), pp. 25–38.
6 Ibid., p. 31.
7 Sidonie Smith and Julia Watson, *Reading Autobiography: A Guide for Interpreting Life Narratives*, 2nd ed. (Minneapolis, MN: University of Minnesota Press, 2010), p. 1.
8 Joan Tumblety, 'Introduction: Working with Memory as Source and Subject', in Joan Tumblety (ed.), *Memory and History: Understanding Memory as Source and Subject* (London: Routledge, 2013), pp. 1–16.
9 Cathy Caruth, 'Introduction', in Cathy Caruth (ed.), *Trauma: Explorations in Memory* (Baltimore, MD: Johns Hopkins University Press, 1995), pp. 3–12.
10 Sarah J. Young, 'Recalling the Dead: Repetition, Identity, and the Witness in Varlam Shalamov's Kolymskie Rasskazy', *Slavic Review*, 70 (2011), pp. 353–72 (p. 355).
11 Maurice Halbwachs, *On Collective Memory*, trans. by Lewis A. Coser (Chicago, IL: University of Chicago Press, 1992), p. 43.
12 Fulbrook, 'Life Writing', p. 31.
13 Caruth, *Trauma*, p. ix.
14 Jeremy D. Popkin, *History, Historians, and Autobiography* (Chicago, IL: University of Chicago Press, 2005), p. 21.
15 Sarah Davies, *Popular Opinion in Stalin's Russia: Terror, Propaganda and Dissent, 1934–1941* (Cambridge and New York, NY: Cambridge University Press, 1997), p. 1.
16 See Anna Krylova, 'The Tenacious Liberal Subject in Soviet Studies', *Kritika: Explorations in Russian and Eurasian History*, 1 (2008), pp. 119–46.
17 Polly Jones, *Myth, Memory, Trauma: Rethinking the Stalinist Past in the Soviet Union, 1953–70*, reprint edition (New Haven, CT: Yale University Press, 2016), p. 10.

18 Jochen Hellbeck, *Revolution on My Mind: Writing a Diary under Stalin* (Cambridge, MA: Harvard University Press, 2009), p. 11.

19 Jones, *Myth*, p. 10.

20 Stephen Kotkin, *Magnetic Mountain: Stalinism as a Civilization* (Berkeley, CA: University of California Press, 1997), p. 220.

21 J. Arch Getty, *Origins of the Great Purges: The Soviet Communist Party Reconsidered, 1933–1938*, new ed. (Cambridge: Cambridge University Press, 2008), pp. 4–5.

22 Ibid., p. 213.

23 Orlando Figes, *The Whisperers: Private Life in Stalin's Russia* (London: Penguin, 2008), pp. 636–7.

24 Barnes, *Gulag*, p. 260, note 8.

25 David Carlson, 'Autobiography', in Miriam Dobson and Benjamin Ziemann (eds.), *Reading Primary Sources: The Interpretation of Texts from Nineteenth- and Twentieth-Century History* (London and New York: Routledge, 2008), pp. 175–91 (p. 178).

26 Anne Applebaum, 'Introduction', in Anne Applebaum (ed.), *Gulag Voices: An Anthology*, trans. by Jane Ann Miller and Anne Applebaum (New Haven, CT: Yale University Press, 2011), pp. vii–xv.

27 Barnes, *Gulag*, p. 260, note 8.

28 Sheila Fitzpatrick, 'Lives and Times', in Sheila Fitzpatrick and Yuri Slezkine (eds.), *In the Shadow of Revolution: Life Stories of Russian Women from 1917 to the Second World War* (Princeton, NJ: Princeton University Press, 2000), pp. 3–17 (p. 3).

29 Joyce Appleby, *Inheriting the Revolution: The First Generation of Americans*, new ed. (Cambridge, MA: Harvard University Press, 2001), p. viii.

30 Mark D. Steinberg, 'Melancholy and Modernity: Emotions and Social Life in Russia between the Revolutions', *Journal of Social History*, 41 (2008), pp. 813–41 (p. 815).

31 Mark M. Smith, *Sensing the Past: Seeing, Hearing, Smelling, Tasting, and Touching in History* (Berkeley, CA: University of California Press, 2008), p. 3.

32 See Claire L. Shaw, *Deaf in the USSR: Marginality, Community, and Soviet Identity, 1917–1991* (Ithaca, NY: Cornell University Press, 2017).

33 Anne E. Gorsuch, 'Women's Autobiographical Narratives: Soviet Presentations of Self', *Kritika: Explorations in Russian and Eurasian History*, 2 (2001), pp. 835–47 (p. 836).

34 Ibid.

35 Ibid., p. 838.

36 Paul John Eakin, *How Our Lives Become Stories: Making Selves* (Ithaca, NY: Cornell University Press, 1999), p. 43.

37 Ibid., p. 85.

38 Frederick C. Corney, *Telling October: Memory and the Making of the Bolshevik Revolution* (Ithaca, NY: Cornell University Press, 2004), p. 1.

39 Tatiana Varsher, cited in Sheila Fitzpatrick, 'Lives and Times', in Sheila Fitzpatrick and Yuri Slezkine (eds.), *In the Shadow of Revolution: Life Stories of Russian Women from 1917 to the Second World War* (Princeton, NJ: Princeton University Press, 2000), pp. 3–17 (p. 3).

40 Sheila Fitzpatrick, *Tear Off the Masks!: Identity and Imposture in Twentieth-Century Russia* (Princeton, NJ: Princeton University Press, 2005), p. 104.

41 Hellbeck, *Revolution*, pp. 4–5.

42 On the memoir boom, see Anna Krylova, *Soviet Women in Combat: A History of Violence on the Eastern Front* (Cambridge: Cambridge University Press, 2011), p. 11; Jones, *Myth*.

43 Denis Kozlov, *The Readers of Novyi Mir: Coming to Terms with the Stalinist Past* (Cambridge, MA: Harvard University Press, 2013), p. 2.

44 Hellbeck, *Revolution*, p. xi.

45 Eakin, *How Our Lives Become Stories*, p. 85.

46 Brigid O'Keeffe, *New Soviet Gypsies: Nationality, Performance, and Selfhood in the Early Soviet Union* (Toronto: University of Toronto Press, 2013), p. 6.

47 Hellbeck, *Revolution*, p. 11.
48 These questions draw on similar questions posed in Carlson, 'Autobiography', p. 183; Gorsuch, 'Women's Autobiographical Narratives', p. 836.
49 A. Kalugina, 'Zhizn' v tishine: dokumental'nia povest' o liudiakh vserossiiskogo obshchestva glukhikh', in V. A. Palennyi and Ia. B. Pichugin (eds.), *Vspolokhi tishiny* (Moscow: Vserossiiskoe obshchestvo glukhikh, 2012), pp. 5–102 (p. 68).
50 Ibid., p. 68.
51 Ibid., p. 66.
52 See Shaw, *Deaf in the USSR*, p 71.
53 Ibid.
54 V. G. Dmitriev, *Glukhie i glukhonemye v Sovetskom Soiuze* (Moscow: Sovetskaia Rossiia, 1958), p. 35.
55 Kalugina, *Zhizn'*, p. 19.
56 Ibid., p. 26.
57 Ibid., p. 5.
58 Ibid., p. 20.
59 Ibid., p. 100.
60 Ibid., p. 11.
61 Ibid., p. 89.
62 Ibid., p. 101.
63 Hellbeck, *Revolution*, p. 5.
64 Kalugina, *Zhizn'*, p. 85.
65 Ibid., p. 100.
66 Ibid., p. 101.
67 Carlson, 'Autobiography', p. 189.

Further reading

Applebaum, Anne (ed.), *Gulag Voices: An Anthology*, trans. by Jane Ann Miller and Anne Applebaum (New Haven, CT: Yale University Press, 2011).
Barnes, Steven A., *Death and Redemption: The Gulag and the Shaping of Soviet Society* (Princeton, NJ: Princeton University Press, 2011).
Carlson, David, 'Autobiography', in Miriam Dobson and Benjamin Ziemann (eds.), *Reading Primary Sources: The Interpretation of Texts from Nineteenth and Twentieth Century History* (London and New York, NY: Routledge, 2008), pp. 175–91.
Caruth, Cathy (ed.), *Trauma: Explorations in Memory* (Baltimore, MD: Johns Hopkins University Press, 1995).
Eakin, Paul John, *How Our Lives Become Stories: Making Selves* (Ithaca, NY: Cornell University Press, 1999).
Fitzpatrick, Sheila and Yuri Slezkine (eds.), *In the Shadow of Revolution: Life Stories of Russian Women from 1917 to the Second World War* (Princeton, NJ: Princeton University Press, 2000).
Gorsuch, Anne E., 'Women's Autobiographical Narratives: Soviet Presentations of Self', *Kritika: Explorations in Russian and Eurasian History*, 2 (2001), pp. 835–47.
Halbwachs, Maurice, *On Collective Memory*, trans. by Lewis A. Coser (Chicago, IL: University of Chicago Press, 1992).
Hellbeck, Jochen, *Revolution on My Mind: Writing a Diary under Stalin* (Cambridge, MA: Harvard University Press, 2009).
Jones, Polly, *Myth, Memory, Trauma: Rethinking the Stalinist Past in the Soviet Union, 1953–70*, Reprint ed. (New Haven, CT: Yale University Press, 2016).

Kotkin, Stephen, *Magnetic Mountain: Stalinism as a Civilization* (Berkeley, CA: University of California Press, 1997).

Krylova, Anna, 'The Tenacious Liberal Subject in Soviet Studies', *Kritika: Explorations in Russian and Eurasian History*, 1 (2000), pp. 119–46.

Lejeune, Philippe, *On Autobiography*, ed. by Paul John Eakin (Minneapolis, MN: University of Minnesota Press, 1989).

Olick, Jeffrey K., Vered Vinitzky-Seroussi and Daniel Levy (eds.), *The Collective Memory Reader* (New York: Oxford University Press, 2011).

Popkin, Jeremy D., *History, Historians, and Autobiography* (Chicago, IL: University of Chicago Press, 2005).

Smith, Sidonie, and Julia Watson, *Reading Autobiography: A Guide for Interpreting Life Narratives*, 2nd ed. (Minneapolis, MN: University of Minnesota Press, 2010).

Tumblety, Joan (ed.), *Memory and History: Understanding Memory as Source and Subject* (London: Routledge, 2013).

14 Prisoner memoirs as a source in Russian and Soviet history

Mark Vincent

Introduction

Prisoner memoirs have a long and storied life in Russian and Soviet history, stretching from the work of Archpriest Avvakum, sentenced to exile for his opposition to church reforms in the 1650s, to the more recent writings of Maria Aloykhika of female punk activists *Pussy Riot*, and many more in between.[1] Although influenced by the writings of Fyodor Dostoevsky and members of the Decembrist Uprising of 1825, all imprisoned in the nineteenth century, the development of this genre in its fully-fledged form is often attributed to the (albeit temporary) publication of former Gulag inmate Alexander Solzhenitsyn's novella *One Day in the Life of Ivan Denisovich* in the November 1962 issue of the literary journal *Novyi mir* (*New World*).[2] This development of the memoir corpus was given further impetus by the publication of Solzhenitsyn's genre-defining *The Gulag Archipelago* (1974–6). Popularising the term 'Gulag', his six-volume 'experiment in literary investigation' provided such a powerful insight into the horrors of camp life that it led to left-leaning intellectuals across Europe renouncing their communist ideals.[3] Solzhenitsyn brought together the accounts of several prisoners in a ground-breaking work compiled from a number of oral history interviews and collated underground (*samizdat*) manuscripts. The scale of this literary corpus raises several important questions. What might readers have expected from the emergence of 'unabridged' literature previously only available through *samizdat* and *tamizdat* accounts?[4] What insights could they provide that were not available through other sources? How might they conform to predetermined narratives? What are the particular *issues which arise from using them?*

This chapter examines how memoirs from Russian and Soviet penality have been used by historians and the various difficulties which surround them. Firstly, the genre of memoirs will be outlined briefly, followed by a discussion of the arguments made by scholars regarding their use. The various problematic aspects of these sources will be assessed, alongside suggestions about how to work around this. Finally, a reading of the 1998 memoir *Man is Wolf to Man*, written by former prisoner Janusz Bardach alongside Australian researcher and author Kathleen Gleeson, will demonstrate some of the aspects of their use which cannot be found through any other source material.

Prisoner memoirs as a genre

A cursory browse through the physical or online collections of booksellers reveals that historical publishing remains inundated with memoirs from former prisoners, spanning from the horrors of Nazi concentration camps to the Chinese Laogai. At first glance, the definition of memoir appears to be a straightforward one, with the *Oxford English Dictionary* suggesting that it is 'a record of history or events written from personal knowledge or the experience of the writer or based on special sources of information.'[5] This description of what constitutes a 'memoir' (sometimes referred to as 'egodocument') needs to be assessed clearly and carefully, as it frequently overlaps with semi-autobiographical texts which are based on the authors' personal experience, but names, dates and places are quite often changed. In our temporal context this can be seen through the pre-revolutionary writers such as Dostoevsky, who added a fictionalised narrator to *The House of the Dead*, and Petr Iakubovich, who changed the penal setting of his two volume *In the World of the Outcasts*.[6] Although edited and translated, particularly important for non-Russian speakers, these texts remain personal reflections of the authors' own personal ideology along with what they, willingly or otherwise, choose to explore from their experience of camp life. As will be discussed later, this could mean that they retain class-based prejudices and/or phobias toward other prisoners. Other blind spots could also be a result of the trauma of their individual experience and often intensely harrowing surroundings.

Despite their individual nuances, Leona Toker's study *Return from the Archipelago: Narratives of Gulag Survivors* discusses how memoirs of incarceration in the camp system all display common morphological features, displaying a set of commonplace themes specific to their genre.[7] Toker describes the tensions between the ethical and aesthetic impulses of the authors, the connection between individual and communal concerns, the inclusion of specific morphological variables, and a modal scheme that can be described in terms of 'Lent': an institutionalised and circumscribed period of voluntary asceticism revealed in Gulag memoirs concerning the relationship between 'physical' and 'moral' survival. What this shows is that there are many similarities in subject matter, the writer's motivation for the narrative act and book structure, although in some cases the likelihood is these have been dictated by publishers. Many of these works, like Puritan spiritual autobiographies, slave narratives, or the writings of disillusioned or exiled Communists, are written either by non-professional writers and often represent the author's first literary endeavour.[8] Certain universalities of the Gulag experience reveal several reoccurring themes, of which Toker claims at least seven out of the nine appear in each individual narrative: the arrest; dignity; stages; escape; moments of reprieve; Room 101; chance; the zone and larger zone, and, finally, end-of-term fatigue.[9] One particular example of this, the prevalent threat of arrest and subsequent imprisonment, becomes a leitmotif so powerful that it also features in memoirs written by former camp employees.[10]

While all display common morphological features and a pre-defined format specific to their genre, each of these has its own individual importance, containing slight variations in style, tone and point of view.[11] In the view of Susan Crane, this demonstrates the importance of writing the individual back into collective history and expanding historical discourse to conceptualise each of us as both writers and historical actors.[12] This also shows a concern to testify and preserve the memory of incarceration and a duty to those who have passed on or are still imprisoned, which not all prisoners share (the impulse or ability to articulate).[13] As a result, the nature of memoir allows what authors choose to reveal. This can reflect their personal ideology and worldview, not only during the period in question but also following their release. As former prisoners, memoir writers were victims of the state apparatus and therefore inclined towards a negative outlook, although it is important to note that not all memoirists were opponents of the regime before their arrest or became dissidents following their release.[14] Conversely, during the amateur memoir-writing boom of the late 1980s, many victims identified so strongly with the ideological position presented by survivors of the Soviet camp system that they suspended their independent memories and allowed books to speak for them as, despite documentation clearly representing the contrary, a number of ex-prisoners remained insistent on witnessing scenes depicted in works by well-known memoirists.[15]

Regardless of how compelling or evocative a memoir is, it remains one person's recollection, reflecting what they were most interested in telling and what they had modified during the art of collection.[16] Memoirs are rarely written at the same time as the events they describe, raising difficult but important questions regarding the malleability of memory and its reconstruction of events, especially given the advancing age of many. Janusz Bardach, whose memoir will be explored in the final section, was just twenty-two years old when he entered the camp system and did not keep a diary, but looked to recall events in 1990s America. Although he was exceptional in many ways, later becoming a world-renowned plastic surgeon and Emeritus Professor in Iowa, these are still important considerations.[17] This lapse in time displays similarity to former Gulag employee Fyodor Mochulsky, who sat down to write his reminiscences of Pechorlag where he was posted between 1940–6 over twenty years later at the end of the 1980s.[18] Like in oral history projects, this highlights that one of the biggest difficulties of obtaining accurate testimony is that the majority of former Gulag prisoners have now either passed or have entered old age.[19]

This details how the search for truth can remain perpetually elusive.[20] It is possible for an author to dupe their audience, but it is equally plausible for them to deceive themselves by telling a false story, even if recalled with the utmost sincerity. Advances in cognitive neuroscience show that people with traumatic memories have a tendency to block out parts of their own pasts, organising their memory in a series of fragmented, disjointed episodes rather than a linear chronology. Kathleen McGowan describes how our memories are highly dynamic and vulnerable, stating that 'we alter our memories by just remembering them' and that, without realising, 'we continually rewrite the stories of our lives.'[21] Although in theory, some memoirists could re-remember and re-record the same events differently in later life, both perceptions could have been right for that particular time and place.[22]

Discussing this problem, literary theorist John Cuddon has stated that 'Everyone tends to remember what he wants to remember. Disagreeable facts are sometimes glossed over or repressed, truth may be distorted for the sake of convenience or harmony, and the occlusions of time may obscure as much as they reveal.'[23] The memoirist Alexander Dolgun, a US consul clerk imprisoned in the Gulag between 1948–56, describes his lapses in memory by stating in his introduction to his memoir that 'most of my story is what I remember, but some of it is what must have been.'[24] This echoes Bruno Bettelheim's stance when writing his own autobiography, that anyone who undertakes such a task 'binds himself to lying, to concealment, to flummery.'[25] Moreover, it is also important to consider that these experiences are also subject to the process of being gleaned, contextualised and disseminated, often with the help of mediators, editors and translators.

Exclusive use of memoirs, therefore, is problematic. They might be partial, unreliable, unclear in terms of whether they provide accounts of individual or collective memory, or focus disproportionately on the concerns of the author(s) at the time they write. Gabor Rittersporn has highlighted these issues, describing Solzhenitsyn's *The Gulag Archipelago* as being written under 'particularly difficult circumstances', such as being hidden in note form and completing chapters in various locations. Rittersporn suggests, quite correctly, that historians should be hesitant when tacitly adopting memoirs as a frame of reference and accepting their validity *a priori*.[26] Despite not having the full manuscript in front of him over either the ten-year period when writing it, or even the year revising and correcting his manuscript, Steven Barnes has shown that by cross-referencing the work with other sources it has proven to be a remarkably reliable account of both camp conditions and important events such as the 1954 Kengir uprising.[27]

Some of these problems are further apparent in the debate surrounding the authenticity of Slawomir Rawicz's 1956 memoir *The Long Walk*, in which the original memoir, and indeed the secondary claimant, was later shown to be incorrect. Rawicz's memoir was published in 1956, selling half a million copies and translated into 25 languages. Its authenticity has been questioned by another former prisoner, Wiltold Glinksi, who claims he was one of the original participants. Archival evidence, however, has contradicted both Glinksi and Rawicz's versions of events.[28]

Although a memoir cannot always provide us with a verifiable history, it does help fill out the archival record with a visual immediacy, thus allowing scholars to connect to the human experience of the camps and show that official documents only partially record the 'truth'.[29] Nevertheless, significant numbers, convergent and comparative accounts of similar events, verification with records and relatively objective accounts and placing the narrator in the correct sociohistorical context, can contribute to transforming unconditionally accepted testimony into conditionally accepted evidence.[30] Thus, even those who criticise the use of memory-based sources have refrained from dismissing their use entirely. Encouraging a critical approach that looks to filter out the aspects of morality which led to memoir accounts being deemed as virtually 'untouchable' by early Gulag scholars,

J. Arch Getty suggests that memoirs 'can tell us what the camps were like, but not why they existed.'[31]

While memoirs often reveal details about camp society not found in archival documents, they typically represent a self-styled group comprised largely from amongst the intelligentsia and have a tendency to contain silences regarding taboo topics which transgress social boundaries. Despite this, reliance upon memoirists remains crucial as other prisoners were less likely to articulate their experiences in the form of written records.[32] To this end, survivor memoirs remain essential as they can help record informal activities that either do not interest party bureaucrats or are conspicuously absent from the official record. Although questions over the nature of the system remain important, exemplified in recent debates between Golfo Alexopolous and Daniel Healey, it is vital to continue reconstructing precisely 'what camps were like' and explore the Gulag as a lived experience.[33] It is the investigation of prisoner society which has led me to develop a theory-based approach influenced by the work of the sociologist Erving Goffman.

Theories and their application: reconstructing the 'underlife' of the Gulag

This section examines not only the depth of the literary corpus but also some of the theories which have been discussed regarding their use. Firstly, it will provide a brief and inconclusive look at the development of the genre (alongside the major events in Soviet historiography) before looking at one of the most major theoretical developments in recent years: the contributions of Adi Kuntsman. Following this, it will demonstrate how similar theoretical approaches can be constructed to suit the particular interests of the historian. Recognition of the potential biases, blind spots and censorship has been widely recognised by historians, who continue to advocate that they can provide what official documentation cannot.[34]

Following Solzhenitsyn's fashioning of the archipelago metaphor during his interviews with another former prisoner Dmitrii Likhachev, the original acronym 'GULag' has moved far beyond its bureaucratic use indicating 'Main Camp Administration' (*Glavnoe upravlenie lagerei*).[35] The penal system encompassed a wide range of institutions including regular prisons which were primarily used before sentencing, corrective labour camps, the much-understudied corrective labour colonies, post-Second World War hard labour camps (*Katorga*), and Special Camps and Special Settlements which were intended to assist the Stalinist regime's protracted war against the peasantry.[36] Also added to this were scientific camps (*Sharashki*), as discussed in Solzhenitsyn's *The First Circle*, and filtration and POW camps which linked the penal apparatus to the Second World War. As Judith Pallot has eloquently suggested, rather than be seen as an aberration, the process of penal transportation (*etap*) itself should also be considered an integral part of the cycle of punishment.[37]

Although many of these early texts were initially overlooked, the development of prisoner memoirs from those who escaped the showcase Solovetskii penal archipelago in the 1920s ensures that contemporary researchers face the complete opposite problem from the first wave of Gulag scholars who relied almost exclusively on a relatively small collection of survivor accounts. Memoirs authored by former prisoners who had successfully taken flight from the transit point to Solovetskii's Great Isle on the Karelian mainland include fellow former White Guards Iurii Bezsonov and Sozerko Mal'sagoff.[38] Both writers were part of the same group's escape and both had their recollections published in 1926. Although quickly followed by similar texts from other Solovki prisoners, these accounts found little audience in the West, being confined mainly to small circles of Russian émigrés, as the Soviet regime remained partially insulated from the development of more widespread external criticism because of propaganda footage which accompanied large-scale infrastructure projects aided by prisoner labour. Images from sites such as the White Sea-Baltic Canal flickered across newsreels at the same time as the frantic scenes from Wall Street led to widespread panic amongst the major global powers.

Although the publication of Gulag memoirs disappeared during the Second World War, the post-war period saw a revival of publications from several Polish prisoners who had been released from incarceration following an amnesty initiated by Stalin. Most prominently this included Gustaw Herling, imprisoned for a year while attempting to cross the border into neutral Lithuania, who took his title *A World Apart* from a passage in Dostoevsky's *The House of the Dead*. Herling's memoir which emerged in the early 1950s had been preceded by an anonymous collection entitled *The Dark Side of the Moon*, whilst several extracts from the wave of Russian emigres who found themselves in western Europe following the conflict were used by David Dallin and Boris Nikolaevsky in their remarkable academic exposé of the camp system, becoming full-length titles of their own right in the years which followed.[39] The most notable included Margaret Buber-Neumann's *Under Two Dictators* and Elena Lipper's *Eleven Years in Soviet Prison Camps*, both published within a year of each other during 1950–1. Removed from her former lifestyle as a Comintern member and wife of a leading German communist, Buber-Neumann's experience of, firstly, Karandga (present-day Kazakhstan) and then the notorious Ravensbruck concentration camp, where she was transferred following the Molotov-Ribbentrop Pact in 1939, provided a startling reminder of the fragility felt by many during the period.

Lipper, on the other hand, provided an extremely harrowing account of the potential dangers faced by female prisoners as she recalled a gang rape taking place on her penal transportation to Magadan. From the numerous publications surrounding Khrushchev's denouncement of Stalinist repression at the Twentieth Party Congress in 1956, German prisoner Joseph Schlomer's *Vorkuta* revealed further insights into camp society and the relationship between inmates and camp employees.[40] The publication of Solzhenitsyn's *One Day in the Life of Ivan Denisovich* led to an influx of manuscripts based around various terror and camp themes, as the early to mid-1960s saw these writings appear in official Soviet publications.[41] This apparent 'thaw', however, was short-lived as publications relating to the labour camps were driven underground through the 'self-published' circulation across the Soviet Union by hand known as *samizdat*, and eventually made its way to western publishers (whereby it became known as *tamizdat*). This pathway to the reading public can be seen through Eugenia Ginzburg's *Journey into the Whirlwind*, which traced her initial 1937 imprisonment and time in Kolyma, which was eventually released in the Soviet Union during Gorbachev's reconstruction (*glasnost'*) during the mid-1980s.

Ground-breaking publications during an earlier period were Aleksandr Gorbatov's *Years and Wars* (1964) and the recollections in Anatoly Marchenko's *My Testimony* (1967) which became noteworthy as the first published account of the Gulag after Stalin.[42] Suffice to say, these works helped fuel the already-burgeoning dissident movement and led to the 1960s becoming the period when 'Gulag memoirs' became a clearly defined and organised genre. Solzhenitsyn's *Gulag Archipelago* (1973) paved the way for a number of new texts, including American citizens Alexander Dolgun (whose recollections had previously appeared in *The Gulag Archipelago* as 'Alexander D') and Victor Herman, whose works sat amongst those of communists from other countries, such as Michael Solomon and Karlo Stanjer.[43] Dmitrii Likhachev's memoir, *Reflections on the Russian Soul,* traced his story right back to his incarceration on the Solovetskii archipelago in the late 1920s. The late 1980s saw further development of the genre, exemplified by the appearance of the Memorial Society following its founding conference in January 1989.[44] This boom saw the works of Shalamov, Solzhenitsyn and Ginzburg receive publication in Russia alongside accounts in the literary press.

Crafted around the structure of Solzhenitsyn's magnus opus, Anne Applebaum's Pulitzer Prize-winning *Gulag: A History* (2003) helped introduce memoirists to a new millennial audience. A wealth of newly published material by historians such as Steven Barnes and Lynne Viola which followed – although focusing on other aspects – continued to draw from memoir sources. Partial extracts appeared in the collection *Gulag Voices* (2011), alongside publications which look solely at the experience of female prisoners, such as *Till My Tale Is Told* (1999) and Veronika Shapovalov's collection *Remembering the Darkness* which followed two years later.[45] In terms of online resources, the database created in collaboration between the Moscow branch of the Memorial Society and the *Fondazione Giangiacomo Feltrini* based in Milan lists around six hundred published memoirs. Alongside this, various other branches of Memorial have their own collections of unpublished memoirs.[46] The Sakharov Centre's Memoir Database also maintains a particularly impressive collection, while Sarah J. Young has compiled an extensive bibliography of both Russian and English-language sources for a metadata project.[47]

The recent English-language publication of Tamara Petkevich's *Diary of a Gulag Actress* (2010), German prisoner Ilse Johansen's memoir of her incarceration at the end of the Second World War, alongside the publication of materials such as *Gulag Letters* (2017) – compiled from the writings of Latvian poet and novelist Arsenii Formakov – suggest the interest of reading public is far from exhausted. In particular, the 2010 publication of former camp employee Fyodor Mochulsky led to a lengthy online debate amongst scholars which has only recently begun to filter into published material.[48] While the recollections of the specialist about his time at a remote camp near Vorkuta contains similar structural features to other memoirs, it also provides an insight into the reality behind official documents in so far as which orders were deemed important and which were ignored. It also helps to elucidate what camp staff really thought of their work and the prisoners, opening the possibility for discussion regarding the wider field of perpetrator studies.[49] Demonstrating the interplay between prisoners and camp employees, Mochulsky's recollections have been seen to draw comparisons with Primo Levi's conceptualisation of the 'Grey Zone' which questions the overly-simplistic binary divide between victims and perpetrators.[50] The recently discovered diary of Gulag prison guard Ivan Chistiakov would seemingly add to this ongoing discussion about how to fill in the blanks about groups outside of the intelligentsia.

As Adi Kunstman outlines, much of the 'dissident literature' has looked to place the politics of sexuality, particularly in connection to same-sex relations, outside the boundaries of the civilised world. By marrying the topic of homosexuality directly with criminal inmates' concepts of disgust and pollution, memoir literature has depicted such actions as sadistic and barbaric, often using bestial metaphors to help sustain this point. Kuntsman uses the writings of Shalamov and Ginzburg alongside less well-known accounts from the Socialist Revolutionary prisoner Ekaterina Olitskaia, yet to be translated into English.[51] Similar to this binary between the 'heterosexual' political prisoners from among the intelligentsia and 'homosexual' prisoners from the criminal underworld, are recollections from the late Imperial penal system. As Sarah Badcock has described, these memoirs looked to create a strict divide between female inmates as being either victims or whores.[52] Even without considering the issue of their sexuality, although on many occasions it would feed into this, male criminal recidivists would often be described using the same bestial or demonic epithets as recalled by Kuntsman.[53]

As will be demonstrated further, Bardach's recollections help reconstruct what Erving Goffman has described as the 'underlife' of public institutions.[54] Goffman's definition of what constitutes the underlife rests on the topic of 'secondary adjustments' which are learned and collectively sustained in that particular environment.[55] In the Gulag this system of signs and behavioural rules included the persistence of informal practices such as *blat* and *tufta*. According to some of the earliest reports *blat* (the importance of informal connections) was endemic throughout the camp system, just as it was in wider Russian and Soviet society. Similarly, *tufta* (the falsification of work norms) was also widely reported by memoirists and has been viewed as a form of everyday resistance to the regime.[56] Many more informal practices existed alongside these, such as the systematic refusal to perform work duties known as *otrisalovka* which included instances of prisoners mutilating themselves.[57] More of what Goffman terms 'secondary adjustments' to life in the Gulag can be seen through the prevalence of prisoner 'make-do's' whereby tattoos, playing cards and even narcotics were adapted out of available materials. Although a partial insight into these practices can be gleaned through official documentation, which generally only recorded when disciplinary measures had been put into place, the outlook on everyday life in the camps appears very different when seen through the eyes of an ex-prisoner.

Janusz Bardach's *Man is Wolf to Man*

The 1998 memoir of Janusz Bardach (b. 1919, d. 2002) offers the historian an excellent illustration of the insights memory-based sources can provide. Raised in Volodymyr-Volynskyi (now Ukraine but then part of Poland), the young Bardach was ordered to enlist in the Red Army after his hometown had been annexed in the summer of 1941.[58] Around a year later, Bardach would find himself court-martialled following an incident in which he was responsible for getting a tank he was driving stuck during a river crossing and was subsequently sentenced to be executed. Indeed, the memoir opens with Bardach digging his empty grave in the Belorussian forest before the apparent benevolence of an NKVD official (Polzun), who recognised his family name from his birthplace (Odessa), thus allowing him a stay of execution. After his sentence was commuted to ten years in the Gulag, Bardach travelled from the Belorussian front to the notorious Kolyma camp complex in the Russian Far East. During this time Bardach passed through several remote transit camps, including those in Burepolom and Buchta Nakhodka, and travelled in both a cattle car and steamer ship. Bardach's eventual destination would be the camp complex at Kolyma where he remained until release in August 1945. After graduating from the Moscow Medical Stomatological Institute, Bardach would then move back to his native Poland in 1954. After becoming increasingly targeted by antisemitism, he would take up a position at the University of Iowa in 1972. After becoming a world-renowned plastic surgeon, he retired as an emeritus professor, holding the position until his death at 83 in August 2002.

Many aspects of Bardach's memoir remain unclear. For example, in his recollection of rolling the tank and the subsequent *ad hoc* trial, Bardach cannot give clear details about where this took place and the officials involved (except the arrival of Efim Polzun, the Odessan NKVD operative sent to supervise). Yet, we do know that over the course of the war 158,000 soldiers were executed by military tribunal.[59] Given that statistic it is indeed remarkable that Bardach survived, leaving the memoirist ruminating on the potential consequences on Polzun for changing the sentence.[60] Similarly, another great unknown is why did Bardach look to preserve his testimony? No clear motivations for this appear, other than an indication in the preface to his second book titled *Surviving Freedom* suggesting a desire to give 'a glimpse into life and death in that abysmal and peregrine world'.[61] Kathleen Gleeson's recollections of her time with Bardach, written in a heartfelt and endearing postscript, suggest his veracity for life, intellectual stimulation and awareness of his own fortune could be other reasons behind this desire to document his experiences.

What features of genre, then, does Bardach's memoir reveal in terms of Toker's suggested features described above? The structure of the book can be considered using Toker's terminology, noted here in italics. Other than its brief opening vignette in which he is found digging his own grave, the memoir follows a standard chronological approach before moving through his early life into *the arrest*. Likewise, the memoir remains geographically structured into different *stages* with chapters dedicated to his time in the transit camp 'Burepolom' and on the 'Siberian

Figure 14.1 Danzig Baldaev, *Man is Wolf to Man.*

Reproduced with permission of FUEL publishing from Danzig Baldaev, *Russian Criminal Tattoo Encyclopaedia*, vol. 1 (London: FUEL Publishing, 2004), p. 294.

Trail'. As with the seemingly impossible situation facing him after the military tribunal, where he fantasises about taking out the soldiers surrounding him, Bardach's plans of *escape* from the cattle car were realised when he slipped out by prising open a loose board. However, Bardach was be hunted down in a nearby forest and savagely beaten by the guards as a result.[62] As already suggested Bardach also keenly reminisces of the *chance* encounter with the NKVD operative Polzun and shows *end-of-term fatigue* by discussing only briefly how he felt upon return to his hometown of Volodymyr-Volynskyi and life after release (saved for his second book, *Surviving Freedom*).

Although conforming to these categories there are other aspects unique to Bardach's text, exemplified by the title of the book and its signature episode. Using the sorrowful Latin epithet *Homo homini lupus*, a universal sobriquet for the barbarism and senseless violence inflicted upon each other by mankind, Bardach explains that in a more personal sense it had been passed on to him by his mother when he was a young boy. While also representing the dark extremities of the Gulag (and a saying which evidently became commonplace in the camps), Bardach's reinterpretation of the proverb was directly linked to his own experience of the Burepolom transit camp (in the present-day Nizhnii Novgorod region) during his transfer to Kolyma.[63] Alongside hygiene and overcrowding issues, the prolonged experience of penal transportation, punctuated by 'temporary' accommodation in inadequately maintained transit stations such as Burepolom, were characterised by a lack of surveillance from the authorities and the resulting hegemony this offered to some inmates. Although clarifying that his use of the phrase also signified the wilder displays of inmate-on-inmate violence, sexual assaults and fatalities already witnessed on his carceral journey, Bardach depicted a specific visit to the bath-house where he was to observe both consensual acts, masturbation and violent homosexual rape:

> A young man lay on his stomach, and another man lay on top of him, embracing him around the chest and moving his hips back and forth. His back was tattooed with shackles, chains and the popular Soviet slogan 'Work is an act of honour, courage, and heroism.' On both sides were trumpeting angels. He breathed heavily, while the young man underneath moaned and cried out. The spectators shouted. I caught sight of the young man's grimacing face.[64]

Bardach description of the tattoos of the authoritative inmate demonstrates how some prisoners would use their own body to subvert Soviet propaganda slogans.[65] Recalling that the prisoner's dominant role suggested that he was the 'active' partner in the same-sex act, Bardach later lamented that at 22 he was too young to resist any such assault and was granted a week in the sick bay to recover from injuries he had sustained.[66] This oblique reference to the personal experience of rape displayed similarity to how other memoirists subtly alluded to similar incidents. In particular, this includes Elena Glinka's short essay *Kolyma Tram*, which detailed a gang rape which took place in the small Siberian fishing village of Bugurchan during the transfer of a women's prisoner brigade to Kolyma in the early 1950s. Although written in the third person, it has widely been recognised that Glinka inserted herself into the story as 'student from Leningrad'.[67] Given the trauma of the events this is completely understandable and offers an insight into Toker's suggestion of the personal experiences that could be included in *Room 101*.

While the near-universal 'disgust' toward inmate same-sex relations was largely removed from Bardach's testimony, his recollections of Gulag hierarchy and how that was intertwined with violent and consensual homosexual relations was far from the only revealing aspect of criminal subculture revealed by his testimony. Survivor memoirs have regularly been lauded for their ability to highlight aspects of Gulag prisoner society often hidden or obscured from official bureaucratic documents, such as the issue of prostitution or forced sexual relations (so-called *sozhitel'stvo*).[68] As Dan Healey has shown, officials were extremely reluctant to report any instance of rape and sexual abuse toward prisoners.[69] As his journey toward Kolyma continued, Bardach witnessed gang rape on board a transport ship to the transfer port of Magadan, recalling how a group of prisoners broke through a hole in the iron grille into the women's hold. After they had sexually assaulted both male and female convicts, the guards eventually looked to quell the revolt by blasting the aggressors with water. Despite the removal of a number of dead and injured prisoners, no one received a formal reprimand for the assault.[70] Bardach's account confirms reports of the traumatic experience of *etap* which had been recognised as early as the 1920s.[71]

Eugenia Ginzburg's infamous recollections of her prisoner transportation on board a ship to Magadan, a handful of years before Bardach, described how the 'ladies' (a common term for female political prisoners) were terrorised and bullied by criminal recidivists who looked to steal their food and clothing.[72]A number of memoirist recollections of conditions in the ships' hold have been collated by Martin Bollinger in his work *Stalin's Slave Ships*. What Bollinger's analysis fails to take into account are questions of agency and surveillance and also Judith Pallot's considerations regarding seeing transportation as an integral part of the penal arc.[73] Although Bollinger's account is thoroughly researched in regard to the details of the Gulag fleet itself, the current analysis instead stresses the importance of adopting theoretical approaches to explain questions such as: why did mass rape happen on such a large scale during transportation? What was the response from the authorities toward this and what can this tell us about their feelings toward inmates? How did these events, which often happened at an early point on the carceral journey, feed into the agency of prisoners once they reached their destination? What can we learn by studying the language used by memoirists toward the perpetrators?

Another revealing aspect of Bardach's memoir is his relationship with criminal prisoners. His first interaction at a remand prison near Gomel (in present-day Belarus) shortly after his 1942 arrest saw him physically threatened in an incredibly graphic manner, along with having his boots stolen.[74] Travelling in a cattle car heading – as the prisoners speculate – towards labour camps in the Komi Republic, Bardach found himself befriending an *urka* (professional criminal) named Fima, who he identified as being a *bezprizornik,* an orphaned or otherwise abandoned child, who often formed *ad hoc* street gangs and made their way into adult criminal spheres:

> The next morning he (Fima) invited me to meet the other *urkas* on one of the upper bed boards. There were over twenty of them, all elaborately tattooed on their torsos, backs and arms. The emblems of naked women, striking snakes, soaring eagles, vodka bottles, machetes, and playing cards identified these men as members of the underworld. Although I had difficulty understanding their jargon, they were more congenial than the military prisoners and I began to spend most of my days with them.[75]

Offering the most space and comfort, the upper bed boards were often fought over by prisoners. As with curtained-off areas in the communal barracks, these spaces wold be dominated by criminal recidivists who used the partial secrecy it offered to congregate there. Bardach's description of the inmate tattoos in this image conforms to the popular view of heavily inked recidivists terrorising the rest of the inmate population. Although their enlarged status in popular culture would suggest otherwise, before the more widespread development of a codified system of tattoos as displayed by the mafia organisation 'Thieves in Law' (*vory v zakone*), tattoos were only one of many reasons behind the ink on inmates' bodies. Whether made in the camps through makeshift needles sometimes made from notebook wire (referred to by Goffman as 'make-do's') or outside penality, these multifarious tattoos formed an important part of the Gulag's semiotic code. Similarly, far from being a 'secret language', prisoner slang contained many layers but was often made to make prisoners more visible alongside providing a short-hand which defined everything important in camp society. Bardach's views toward military prisoners displayed in this extract may have come from his own personal experience, as he was treated with xenophobia and suspicion on account of his Polish nationality on a daily basis'.[76] Given the numbers of military personnel incarcerated during this period, prisoners with wartime experience began to form a clearly defined group of their own in the camps, one which was able to stand up physically to the criminal recidivists.

Obtaining a vantage point gained by very few memoirists during his time in the Sverdlovsk (Ekaterinburg) transit camp, Bardach managed to get close enough to describe the internal hierarchy and behavioural rituals of a group of recidivist prisoners. After losing his boots and pants in a card game through the slight-of-hand of the dealer Vanya, Bardach's ability to take his defeat in what was considered to be a respectful manner caught the attention of a muscular man who had a ring of snakes tattooed around his neck and ran down toward his chest. This authoritative prisoner indicated to another member of the group, a lower-ranked prisoner named Misha, to give Bardach a portion of bread and lard and make room for him on the upper bed boards:

> Why was this man – the apparent leader of the group – acting so friendly toward me? I felt unsettled, but Misha gave me the bread and lard, and I ate greedily. *Urkas* usually didn't break bread with outsiders. Meals were an important *urka* ritual, and I had heard that allowing someone to eat from the same bowl, or sharing a piece of *paika*, was a rite of initiation into the group. In the barracks and prisons, they kept to themselves, staying close to one another, eating together, playing cards, and telling jokes.

> There was an established hierarchy. The *pakhan* was the pack leader; his orders meant more than the orders given by the guards. Obviously, the bald man with the moustache was the *pakhan* but why he'd invited me to eat with them was beyond me.[77]

The bald, moustachioed *Pakhan* was nicknamed 'Riaboj' ('Pockmarked') and, as he would later reveal to Bardach, had a professional reputation as a bank-robber with an expertise in safe-cracking.[78] Pockmarked was particularly inquisitive about Bardach's upbringing in Poland, and became fascinated with his descriptions of restaurants in Warsaw. Bardach would subsequently fabricate a story about a young dancer from the city, which was so popular that a number of other *urkas* crowded around to listen. The *pakhan* was so impressed with his oratory skills that he informed Bardach that from then on he would be his personal guest at every meal, ordering the inmate who had stolen his boots and pants to return them. Subsequently, Pockmarked regularly demanded Bardach's presence as his 'story-teller', a position which was also occupied by a number of other memoirists.[79] After lifting plots from the Westerns of Karl May (who himself had spent time in prison), it was revealed that Bardach would be leaving for another camp, whereupon Pockmarked passed on advice and informed the memoirist that he could 'use' his name. As Bardach himself acknowledged, this was potentially an important 'ticket to security in the *urka* world', and a mark of respect between the two.[80]

As with other systems of penality, scarce provisions meant that food and drink became exceptionally important in the wartime Gulag. Mealtimes provided opportunities for inmates to build solidarity, though conversely some prisoners were forbidden to eat out of communal bowls.[81] In a similar fashion to prison tattoos, card playing contributed towards the inmates' semiotic code, moving beyond an opportunity to obtain items from other prisoners into a device to enforce camp hierarchies. Although the overwhelming majority of games were won through cheating, this nevertheless became an important signalling function to indicate agency amongst prisoners, especially for taking advantage of new arrivals. The established hierarchy as recounted by Bardach took the same basic structure as that recalled by other memoirists. At the top of the food chain sat the *pakhan* (represented here by Pockmarked), who would not only give out orders but play an active role in enforcing the rules of behaviour. Providing the *pakhan* with a lackey or lieutenant for the purposes of delegation was the role of *Shestyorka* ('Sixers'), whose name derived from the lowest card in a Russian deck, another feature showing the prominence of gambling in both camp life and wider criminal subculture. In turn the *shestyorka* would benefit from the support – or take advantage of – the keenness of the lower-ranked *Shobla yobla* ('Rabble') who were looking to advance their own position.

Bardach's insights into these informal prisoner hierarchies are especially important as virtually no memoirs exist from criminal recidivists, giving little indication of camp life from their perspective. Mikhail Demin's *The Day Is Born of Darkness* is often cited as an example of this, but a close reading of his text and exploration of his background reveals that, though he provides a remarkable perspective, he is in fact of Bolshevik aristocracy (the novelist Yuri Trifonov was his cousin).[82] Although descriptions of *urki* did not always depict them as an indistinguishable mass of people – often the case in accounts of late Imperial penality – they had a profound impact upon how they have been viewed in collective memory.[83] Whilst appreciating the commemorative function of memoirs for the families of memoirists and others imprisoned for their political beliefs, it is vital that we continue to utilise memoirs as part of a wider mosaic of sources, especially considering many prisoners did not create texts of their incarceration.

Conclusion

Although the discussion about the starting point of the Gulag and its legacy on the current penal system is set to continue, there is little doubt about the impact that the institution has had on generations of prisoners and their families.[84] Given the potential falsities of archival documentation, excellent recent work such as Alan Barneberg's microhistory on Vorkuta's transformation from Gulag site into Company Town and Jeffrey Hardy's writings such as the Gulag after Stalin continues to lean on an extensive corpus of memoirs in order to provide insight into daily life.[85] Similarly, Andrea Gullotta's recent publication on Solovki provides great detail about some of the memoirists of the 1920s, whilst Wilson Bell's study of the role of the Stalinist Gulag during the Second World War also utilises memoir literature.[86]

As cited here in the analysis of Bardach's recollections of homosexual relations, the strong methodological underpinnings as demonstrated in Daniel Healey's *Russian Homophobia from Stalin to Sochi* provide important insights into how historians can critically assess memoirs and read them against the grain.[87]

As shown by Badach's memoir, it is vital that we avoid simplifying the images of prisoners or treating them as a homogenous mass. To this end, much can be learnt from Lynne Viola's comments on the search for the Soviet 'perpetrator', an echo of comments by Primo Levi.[88] Perceptions of other social groups alternated even amongst memoirists cited in this chapter. After she had arrived at Kolyma, Ginzburg found relations with the 'criminals' (whom she had recalled as terrorising prisoners during transportation) to be more cordial than during her time working in the camp medical ward, whilst Bardach, whose descriptions are generally more complimentary, was stabbed by an *urka* whilst waiting to board a steamer at Vladivostok.[89] Both descriptions are of equal importance, yet collective memory and camp historiography still tends to draw on the former.[90] This is not, however, to exonerate anyone from some of the murderous, sexual actions discussed earlier in this chapter, which can also be supported by archival documents.

As Steven Barnes has commented, Bardach is by no means in the minority in his ability to evade the common criminal-political prisoner divide. A cursory look through his biography and camp experience illustrates problems in constructing a binary divide between political prisoners and common criminals. Although his intellectual and family background appears to qualify him for political status, his sentence for wartime military treason leaves him outside the margins of such a fixed boundary.[91] Furthermore, Bardach's oratorical skills became an important entry requirement in terms of gaining the protection of a criminal authority, thereby increasing his chances of survival. This shows that the rigid system of classification often attributed to prisoners by camp authorities was not always replicated at ground level. If we are to create a more accurate picture of inmate 'social life' and 'camp culture' we must continue to look beyond this binary.[92]

Given the vast number of memoirs available to the historian, no single text can represent the experience of Stalinist crime and punishment. With the population of the camp system ebbing and flowing alongside the process of external events, it remains extremely important to continue challenging current teleological boundaries.[93] More work needs to be done to challenge reductive labels and class-based prejudices, creating methodologies which will open our interpretative lens even further. These could include work on camp staff, alongside various nationalities and social 'outcasts' who were targeted at different times alongside those sentenced, like Bardach, during the Second World War. The prisoner divisions during and immediately after this time became extremely pronounced, often spilling over into direct confrontation as seen by rifts that emerged in the criminal underworld.[94] Although a good understanding of the memoir genre remains crucial, the application of theories and development of arguments relating to these texts lies entirely in the hands of the researcher. In an echo of the individuality of the memoir itself, each historian must strive to apply new techniques in order to expand our interpretative framework even further.

Notes

1 Protopope Avvakum, Petrovich, *The life of the Archpriest Avvakum: By Himself*, trans. by Jane Harrison and Hope Mirrlees (London: Leonard & Virginia Wolf at the Hogarth Press, 1924); Maria Alyokhina, *Riot Days* (London: Penguin, 2018).
2 Miriam Dobson, 'Contesting the Paradigms of De-Stalinisation: Readers' Responses to One Day in the Life of Ivan Denisovich', *Slavic Review*, 64 (2003), pp. 580–600.
3 Wilson Bell, 'Gulag Historiography: An Introduction', *Gulag Studies*, 2–3 (2009–10), pp. 6–7.
4 *Tamizdat* refers to literature smuggled abroad for publication.
5 Fyodor Vasilevich Mochulsky, *Gulag Boss: A Soviet Memoir*, trans. and ed. by Deborah Kaple (Oxford: Oxford University Press, 2011), p. 173.
6 Fyodor Dostoevsky, *The House of the Dead*, trans. by Constance Garnett (New York, NY: Macmillan, 1915); Petr F. Iakubovich, *In the World of the Outcasts: Notes of a Former Penal Laborer*, trans. by Andrew Gentes (New York, NY: Anthem Press, 2014). The same argument could be made for Sergei Dovlatov's *The Zone* which was based on his experience of being a prison guard in the 1960s. Sergei Dovlatov, *The Zone*, trans. by A. Frydman (London: Oneworld, 2011).
7 Leona Toker, *Return from the Archipelago: Narratives of Gulag Survivors* (Bloomington, IN: Indiana University Press, 2000), p. 74.
8 Ibid., p. 74.
9 Ibid., pp. 82–94.
10 Mochulsky, *Gulag Boss*, p. 71.
11 Ibid., pp. 173–4.
12 Susan A. Crane, 'Writing the Individual Back into Collective Memory', *American Historical Review*, 102 (1997), pp. 1372–85 (p. 1384).
13 Toker, *Return from the Archipelago*, p. 74.
14 Nanci Adler, *Keeping Faith with the Party: Communist Believers Return from the Gulag* (Bloomington, IN: Indiana University Press, 2012), p. 5.
15 Orlando Figes, *The Whisperers: Private Life in Stalin's Russia* (London: Allen Lane, 2007), p. 635.
16 Adler, *Keeping Faith with the Party*, pp. 6–8.
17 Janusz Bardach and Kathleen Gleeson, *Surviving Freedom: After the Gulag* (Berkeley and Los Angeles, CA: University of California Press, 2003), p. 249.
18 Mochulsky, *Gulag Boss*, p. xx.
19 John Tosh, *The Pursuit of History* (London: Routledge, 2002), p. 295.
20 Mochulsky, *Gulag Boss*, pp. 174–5.
21 Kat McGowan, 'How Much of Your Memory Is True', *Discover Magazine* (July–August 2009). <http://discovermagazine.com/2009/jul-aug/03-how-much-of-your-memory-is-true> (accessed 19 March 2019).
22 Adler, *Keeping Faith with the Party*, p. 8.
23 J. A. Cuddon cited in Mochulsky, *Gulag Boss*, p. 176.
24 Figes, *The Whisperers*, p. 633.
25 Bruno Bettelheim, *Recollections and Reflections* (London: Penguin, 1989), p. ix.
26 Gabor Rittersporn, *Stalinist Simplifications and Soviet Complications: Social Tensions and Political Conflicts in the USSR* (Switzerland: Harwood Academic Publishers, 1991), pp. 230–1.
27 Steven Barnes, *Death and Redemption: The Gulag and the Shaping of Soviet Society* (Princeton, NJ: Princeton University Press, 2011), p. 9; David Brandenberger has made similar observations about using oral history sources collected in the Harvard Interview Project (HIP) on the Soviet Social System, a large-scale sociological study in which recently emigrated Soviet citizens during the early years of the Cold War were interviewed: David Brandenberger, 'A Background Guide to Working with the HPSSS Online'. <https://library.harvard.edu/collections/hpsss/working_with_hpsss.pdf> (accessed 19 March 2019).

28 For more information see Hugh Levinson, 'Walking the Talk?', *BBC News*, 30 October 2006. <http://news.bbc.co.uk/1/hi/6098218.stm> (accessed 19 March 2019).

29 Toker, *Return from the* Archipelago, p. 74.

30 Adler, *Keeping Faith with the Party*, pp. 6–8.

31 J. A. Getty cited in Barnes, *Death and Redemption*, p. 260.

32 Andrew Gentes has also noted this in reference to prisoners in late Imperial prisoners: Andrew Gentes, '"Beat the Devil!": Prison Society and Anarchy in Tsarist Siberia', *Ab Imperio*, 2 (2009), pp. 201–24 (p. 206).

33 Golfo Alexopolous, 'Destructive Labour Camps: Rethinking Solzhenitsyn's Play on Words', in Michael David-Fox (ed.), *The Soviet Gulag: Evidence, Interpretation, and Comparison* (Pittsburgh, PA: University of Pittsburgh Press, 2016), pp. 42–64; Daniel Healey, 'Lives in the Balance: Weak and Disabled Prisoners and the Biopolitics of the Gulag', in David-Fox (ed.), *The Soviet Gulag*, pp. 65–86; Barnes, *Death and Redemption*, p. 260.

34 Alan Barenberg, Wilson Bell, Seam Kinner, Steven Maddox and Lynne Viola, 'New Directions in Gulag Studies: A Roundtable Discussion', *Canadian Slavonic Papers*, 59 (2017), pp. 376–95.

35 For more on Solzhenitsyn and Likhachev's relationship see Vladislav Zubok, *The Idea of Russia: The Life and Work of Dmitry Likhachev* (London: I. B. Tauris, 2017), pp. 108–9.

36 Lynne Viola, *The Unknown Gulag: The Lost World of Stalin's Special Settlements* (Oxford: Oxford University Press, 2007), p. 6.

37 Judith Pallot, 'The Gulag as a Crucible of Russia's Twenty-First Century System of Punishment', in Michael David-Fox (ed.), *The Soviet Gulag* (Oxford: Oxford University, 2013), pp. 299–300.

38 Andrea Gullotta, *Intellectual Life and Literature at Solovki 1923–30: The Paris of the Northern Concentration Camps* (Oxford: Legenda Press, 2018), pp. 21–2.

39 See, in particular, the chapter 'Eye-Witness Reports' including extracts from Colonel Malakhov, Leonid Shchekach, Julis Margolin and Margaret Buber-Neumman: David Dallin and Boris Nicholaevsky, *Forced Labour in Soviet Russia* (London: Hollis & Carter, 1948), pp. 20–40.

40 Joseph Scholmer, *Vorkuta*, trans. by Robert Kee (New York, NY: Holt, 1955).

41 Stephen Cohen, *The Victims Return: Survivors of the Gulag after Stalin* (Exeter: Publishing Works, 2010), p. 12.

42 Polly Jones, *Myth, Memory, Trauma: Rethinking the Stalinist Past in the Soviet Union, 1953–70* (New Haven, CT: Yale University Press, 2013), p. 161; Anotoly Jones Marchenko, *My Testimony*, trans. by Michael Scammell (London: Sceptre, 1987).

43 Karlo Stanjer, *Seven Thousand Days in Siberia*, trans. Joel Agee (Edinburgh: Canongate, 1988).

44 See Nanci Adler's chapter on how the Memorial Society developed after its founding conference: Nanci Adler, *Victims of Soviet Terror: The Story of the Memorial Movement* (London: Praeger, 1993), pp. 83–102.

45 The Anne Applebaum edited 2011 collection is not to be confused with the oral history volume of the same name: Jehanne Gheith and Katherine Jolluck, *Gulag Voices: Oral Histories of Soviet Incarceration and Exile* (New York, NY: Palgrave, 2011); Simeon Vilensky (ed.), *Till My Tale Is Told: Women's Memoirs of the Gulag*, trans. John Crowfoot (Bloomington, IN: Indiana University Press, 1999); Veronica Shapovalov (ed.), *Remembering the Darkness: Women in Soviet Prisons* (Oxford: Rowman and Littlefield, 2001).

46 Barnes, *Death and Redemption*, pp. 259–60. A comprehensive list can also be found in Wilson Bell, 'Selected Bibliography of Historical Works on the Gulag', *Gulag Studies*, 1 (2008), pp. 143–60.

47 See the Sakharov Center website, Vospominaniia o GULAGe. <www.sakharov-center. ru/asfcd/auth/> (accessed 19 March 2019). Sarah J. Young's bibliography can be found

on her website, 'Gulag Bibliography', Russian Literature, History and Culture. <http://sarahjyoung.com/site/gulag-bibliography/> (accessed 19 March 2019). For more about the metadata project see Sarah J. Young, 'Gulag narratives: a bibliography and metadata project (version 1)', Russian Literature, History and Culture. <http://sarahjyoung.com/site/2016/09/05/gulag-narratives-a-bibliography-and-metadata-project-version-1/> (accessed 19 March 2019).

48 Steven A. Barnes, 'Gulag Boss – A Blog Conversation', Russian History Blog. <http://russianhistoryblog.org/2011/10/gulag-boss-a-blog-conversation/> (accessed 19 March 2019).

49 Lynne Viola, 'The Question of the Perpetrator in Soviet History', *Slavic Review*, 72 (2013), pp. 1–23.

50 Primo Levi, *The Drowned and the Saved*, trans. Raymond Rosenthal (London: Joseph, 1989), pp. 186–7.

51 Adi Kuntsman, '"With a Shade of Disgust": Affective Politics of Sexuality and Class in Memoirs of the Stalinist Gulag', *Slavic Review*, 68 (2009), pp. 308–28.

52 Sarah Badcock, *A Prison without Walls? Eastern Siberian Exile in the Last Days of Tsarism* (Oxford: Oxford University Press, 2016), p. 55.

53 For a particularly vivid example of this see Gustaw Herling's recollections of a 'gorilla' demanding he hand over his coat after the other prisoner had staked it during a card game: Gustaw Herling, *A World Apart: The Journal of a Gulag Survivor*, trans. by Andrzej Ciolkosz (New York, NY: Arbour House, 1951), p. 18.

54 Erving Goffman, *Asylums: Essays on the Social Situation of Mental Patients and Other Inmates* (London: Penguin, 1961).

55 Ibid., p. 180.

56 Wilson Bell, *Stalin's Gulag at War: Forced Labour, Mass Death, and Soviet Victory in the Second World War* (Toronto: University of Toronto Press, 2018), p. 94.

57 Federico Varese, *The Russian Mafia: Private Protection in a New Market Economy* (Oxford: Oxford University Press, 2001), p. 152.

58 Bardach citation and Steven Barnes's comments are found in Barnes, *Death and Redemption*, p. 144.

59 Steven Lovell, *The Shadow of War: Russia and the USSR, 1941 to the Present* (West Sussex: Wiley-Blackwell, 2007), p. 40.

60 Bardach, *Man is Wolf to Man*, p. 91.

61 Janusz Bardach with Kathleen Gleeson, *Surviving Freedom: After the Gulag* (California, CA: University of California Press, 2003), p. xiii.

62 Bardach, *Man Is Wolf to Man*, pp. 106–21.

63 Danzig Baldaev, *Russian Criminal Tattoo Encyclopaedia*, vol. 1 (London: FUEL Publishing, 2004), p. 294.

64 Bardach, *Man Is Wolf to Man*, p. 125.

65 An imitation of Dmitrii Moor's famous Civil War enlistment poster 'Have you Volunteered?' can be found in: Baldaev, *Russian Criminal Tattoo Encyclopaedia*, p. 242.

66 Bardach, *Man is Wolf to Man*, p. 125.

67 Anne Applebaum (ed.), *Gulag Voices: An Anthology* (New Haven, CT: Yale University Press, 2011), p. 42.

68 Wilson Bell, 'Sex, Pregnancy, and Power in the Late Stalinist Gulag', *Journal of the History of Sexuality*, 24 (2015), pp. 198–224 (p. 211).

69 Daniel Healey, *Russian Homophobia from Stalin to Sochi* (London: Bloomsbury, 2017), p. 36.

70 Bardach, *Man Is Wolf to Man*, pp. 191–4.

71 These accounts include Sozerko Mal'sagoff, *An Island Hell: A Soviet Prison in the Far North*, trans. by F. H. Lyon (London: A. M. Philpot, 1926), pp. 132–8; Elena Glinka, 'The Hold', Veronica Shapovalov (ed.), *Remembering the Darkness: Women in Soviet Prisons* (Boston, MA: Rowman & Littlefield, 2001), pp. 301–10; Elena Lipper,

'The God That Failed in Siberia', in Agniesza Critchlow and Donald Critchlow (eds.), *Enemies of the State: Personal Stories from the Gulag* (Chicago, IL: Ivan R. Dee, 2003), pp. 17–41.

72 Eugenia Ginzburg, *Within the Whirlwind*, trans. by Ian Boland (New York, NY: Harcourt Brace Jovanovich, 1981), p. 266.

73 Martin Bollinger, *Stalin's Slave Ships: Kolyma, the Gulag Fleet, and the Role of the West* (London: Praeger, 2003), pp. 45–53.

74 Bardach, *Man Is Wolf to Man*, pp. 93–5.

75 Ibid., pp. 105–6.

76 Bardach comments regarding his nationality cited in Barnes, *Death and Redemption*, p. 144.

77 Bardach, *Man Is Wolf to Man*, p. 151.

78 Ibid., p. 151.

79 See also the experience of the American Alexander Dolgun and former Spartak Moscow footballer Nikolai Starostin in Alexander Dolgun with Patrick Watson, *Alexander Dolgun's Story: An American in the Gulag* (New York, NY: Alfred A. Knopf, 1975), p. 145; Jim Riordan, 'The Strange Case of Nikloi Starostin, Football and Lavrentii Beria', *Europe-Asia Studies*, 46 (1994), pp. 681–90 (p. 685).

80 Similar to situation in Imperial penality where the murderer Pazul'skii wrote a 'letter of recommendation' for journalist Vlas Doroshevich, which meant that he could visit prisons in Rykovsk and Ono. Andrew Gentes, *A Translation of Vlas Doroshevich's 'Sakhalin'* (London: Anthem Press, 2009), p. xxvi.

81 Healey, *Homophobia*, pp. 45–7.

82 See Sarah Young's intriguing blog post on assessing criminal tattoos as a historical source. 'Assessing sources: Russian criminal tattoos', Russian Literature, History and Culture. <http://sarahjyoung.com/site/2017/03/06/assessing-sources-russian-criminal-tattoos/> (accessed 19 March 2019).

83 Kuntsman, 'With a Shade of Disgust'.

84 Pallot, 'The Gulag', in David-Fox (ed.), *The Soviet Gulag*.

85 Alan Barenburg, *Gulag Town, Company Town: Forced Labour and Its Legacy in Vorkuta* (New Haven, CT: Yale University Press, 2014), p. 12; Jeffrey S. Hardy, *The Gulag after Stalin: Redefining Punishment in Khruschev's Soviet Union, 1953–1964* (New York, NY: Cornell University Press, 2016), p. 2.

86 Bell, *Stalin's Gulag at War*, p. 80; Gullotta, *Intellectual Life and Literature at Solovki*.

87 Healey, *Homophobia*.

88 Viola, 'The Question of the Perpetrator', pp. 1–23.

89 Bardach, *Man Is Wolf to Man*, p. 178; Eugenia Ginzburg, *Journey into the Whirlwind*, trans. by Paul Stevenson and Max Hayward (London: Harcourt Brace and Company, 1967), p. 277.

90 For instance, the ten-page section dedicated to the *urki* in Anne Applebaum's *Gulag: A History* quotes from a number of memoirists, describing 'the terror, the robbery and the rape that thieves inflicted on the other inhabitants of the camps': Applebaum, *Gulag*, pp. 261–70.

91 Steven A. Barnes, 'A Life in the Gulag: Janusz Bardach and the Complexities of a Gulag "Society"', H-Russia, August, 1999. < https://networks.h-net.org/node/10000/reviews/10166/barnes-bardach-and-gleeson-man-wolf-man-surviving-gulag> (accessed 19 March 2019).

92 Bell, 'Selected Bibliography', pp. 143–60.

93 Wilson Bell has made pertinent and insightful comments regarding how we should look to break down the existing definition of what constitutes the 'Stalinist Gulag' by looking specifically at different periods of the camps. See his discussion 'The Gulag at War', Sean's Russia Blog. <https://seansrussiablog.org/2019/03/01/the-gulag-at-war/> (accessed 19 March 2019). See also Barenberg, *Vorkuta*, pp. 5–6, and 'Introduction',

in Matthias Neumann and Andy Willimott (eds.), *Rethinking the Russian Revolution as Historical Divide* (New York, NY: Routledge, 2018), pp. 1–19.

94 See discussion of the 'Bitches War' and impact of an influx of battle-hardened combat veterans during this period in Gavin Slade, *Reorganizing Crime: Mafia and Anti-Mafia in Post-Soviet Georgia* (Oxford: Oxford University Press, 2013), p. 15.

Further Reading

Applebaum, Anne, *Gulag: A History* (New York, NY: Penguin, 2004).

Bardach, Janusz, and Kathleen Gleeson, *Man Is Wolf to Man: Surviving Stalin's Gulag* (London: Simon and Schuster, 1998).

Bardach, Janusz, with Kathleen Gleeson, *Surviving Freedom: After the Gulag* (California, CA: University of California Press, 2003).

Barenburg, Alan, *Gulag Town, Company Town: Forced Labour and Its Legacy in Vorkuta* (New Haven, CT: Yale University Press, 2014).

Barnes, Steven, *Death and Redemption: The Gulag and the Shaping of Soviet Society* (Princeton, NJ: Princeton University Press, 2011).

Bell, Wilson, *Stalin's Gulag at War: Forced Labour, Mass Death, and Soviet Victory in the Second World War* (Toronto: University of Toronto Press, 2018).

Ginzburg, Eugenia, *Journey into the Whirlwind*, trans. by Paul Stevenson and Max Hayward (London: Harcourt Brace and Company, 1967).

_____, *Within the Whirlwind*, trans. by Ian Boland (New York, NY: Harcourt Brace Jovanovich, 1981).

Goffman, Erving, *Asylums: Essays on the Social Situation of Mental Patients and Other Inmates* (Harmondsworth: Penguin, 1968).

Gullotta, Andrea, *Intellectual Life and Literature at Solovki 1923–30: The Paris of the Northern Concentration Camps* (Oxford: Legenda Press, 2018).

Hardy, Jeffrey, *The Gulag after Stalin: Redefining Punishment in Khrushchev's Soviet Union, 1953–64* (Ithaca, NY and London: Cornell University Press, 2016).

Healey, Daniel, *Russian Homophobia from Stalin to Sochi* (London: Bloomsbury, 2017).

Jones, Polly, *Myth, Memory, Trauma: Rethinking the Stalinist Past in the Soviet Union, 1953–70* (New Haven, CT: Yale University Press, 2013).

Kuntsman, Adi, "With a Shade of Disgust': Affective Politics of Sexuality and Class in Memoirs of the Stalinist Gulag', *Slavic Review*, 68 (2009), pp. 308–28.

Mochulsky, Fyodor, *Gulag Boss: A Soviet Memoir*, trans. and ed. Deborah Kaple (New York, NY, and Oxford: Oxford University Press, 2011).

Toker, Leona, *Return from the Archipelago: Narratives of Gulag Survivors* (Bloomington, IN: Indiana University Press, 2000).

Vilensky, Simeon, John Crowfoot and Majorie Faquharson (eds.), *Till My Tale Is Told: Women's Memoirs of the Gulag* (Bloomington, IN: Indiana University Press, 1999).

Viola, Lynne, 'The Question of the Perpetrator in Soviet History', *Slavic Review*, 72 (2013), pp. 1–23.

15 Soviet letters

Courtney Doucette

Introduction

Letter writing assumed a central role in the Bolsheviks' vision of the state even before the October Revolution. An early statute approved at the Second Party Congress in 1903 stated:

> Every member of the Party and any person who has any business with the Party has the right to demand that his statements be delivered to the Central Committee or the editorial board of the Central Organ or to a Party congress.[1]

Here "his statements" referred to citizens' letters as well as oral communications that could be written down with help from others. This statute is important for two reasons. One, it shows that the Bolsheviks saw letter-writing as an important part of the citizen–state relationship. Two, it suggests that petitioning the government in the form of a letter constituted an essential right for citizens. Though simple in content, this statute laid the foundations for a profoundly extensive tradition of public letter-writing in the Soviet Union. In the course of the twentieth century, letter-writing gained a uniquely prominent place in Russia, perhaps becoming even more central to the relationship between citizens and the state and citizens' everyday lives than in any other part of the world.

Historians have long used letters as a source for investigating the thoughts and experiences of citizens across the social spectrum. In Soviet times, when archives were largely closed and foreign scholars had only guarded access to Soviet people themselves, letters were often seen as the best evidence available for showing what Soviet people were thinking. In time, letters also came to be valued as a source for assessing forms of governance and the relationship between citizens and the state. Letters also illuminate something much more immediate to the letters themselves: namely, the practice of public letter-writing in the Soviet Union—a practice so extensive that it was regulated by laws, became an essential component of the periodical press, and required hundreds of thousands of people to staff letter departments charged with processing all the missives drawn up by Soviet citizens. Focusing in particular on public letters rather than private ones, this chapter will introduce the history of the letter in the Soviet Union with special attention to the imperial traditions, institutions, and legal practices that shaped it. It will then give an overview of the historiographical discussions of letters, address methodological approaches to working with letters, and provide a sample reading of a *perestroika*-era letter sent from V. Pristavkin to the newspaper *Komsomol'skaia pravda* (*Komsomol Truth*) in 1990.

A history of public letters in Russia

What, exactly, is a letter? This source, it seems, should be easy to identify: it is a written communication from one person to another, usually with a salutation to the recipient at the beginning and a closing from the author at the end. Yet the kinds of documents that fit this description are numerous. There are private letters between family and friends or authors and recipients who know each other. There are also public letters from citizens to leaders at all levels of the political hierarchy, to other well-known public figures who are not part of the government, to institutions and ministries that could address any number of grievances or requests, and, most numerous of all, to diverse media, including the printed press, radio stations, and television networks. There are also letters that do not fit neatly into the private/public divide, such as business correspondence. The number of authors also shapes a letter. Some missives bear the signature of one author and others hundreds or even thousands of signatures. Still others have no signature at all, which, in the Soviet Union, put them into the distinct category of the *anonymka*, or anonymous letter. In terms of the recipient, some letters addressed just one; others a group of an entire institution; and yet others the public at large, such as open letters made famous by Soviet dissidents.[2]

The many forms and purposes that public letters assumed reflects the long history of letter-writing in Russia. As Margareta Mommsen demonstrates, the public letter originated in Imperial Russia with the petition.[3] Subjects of all ranks, including peasants and serfs, always had the right to petition authorities all the way up to the Tsar himself. The notable exception to this rule was during the reign of Catherine the Great (r. 1762–96), when only nobles had the right to directly petition the ruler.[4] In 1801, Alexander I reinstated the right, but limited it to appeals regarding private concerns, such as excesses or failures of a commission, landlord, or official. Any petitions that strayed from these concerns were thrown out.[5] Literacy rates in the Russian empire were notoriously low, measured at 6 per cent of the total population in the 1860s, and rising to no more than 21 per cent by the end of the nineteenth century.[6] Yet even illiterate peasants had the opportunity to petition the Tsar with the aid of village scribes.

Another form of public letters that dates back to Imperial Russia is the letter to the editor, born of press reform under Alexander II during the period of Great Reforms. Newspapers started to publish letters as a form of staged debate between readers and also to further the didactic message of the publication. Printed letters also bolstered the appearance of *glasnost'*, or openness, a term that first appeared with some prominence in the 1860s and reemerged under Gorbachev in the 1980s.[7]

The tradition of public letter-writing took on new proportions after the October Revolution of 1917. Since the turn of the century, the Bolsheviks emphasized the usefulness of public letters, encouraging their publication in Social Democratic newspapers such as *Iskra* (*Spark*) and *Pravda* (*Truth*) and even creating statutes, as noted above, to ensure letters were taken seriously.[8] Even as the First World War had not quite ended and the Civil War touched off, Bolshevik leaders set out across Russia, giving speeches and collecting written and oral complaints and comments. They examined citizens' communications with representatives of relevant commissariats along the way.[9] By the end of the Civil War, work with citizens' letters had become a central part of Soviet newspaper work and remained so throughout the period of the New Economic Policy and the Stalin era.[10] Careful attention to citizens' letters constituted one vector within Bolsheviks' multivalent propaganda initiative that contributed to a Red victory in the Civil War.

Bolsheviks' attention to letter-writing, even in times of bloodshed and famine, raises a question: why did the Party invest so much attention in public letters even when facing seemingly more pressing matters? As Matthew Lenoe points out, the letter served so many purposes for the Bolsheviks that it was hardly ever a trivial matter. 'From the point of view of state authorities', he writes, 'reader letters were instruments of political education, cultural enlightenment, surveillance of local government officials, and intelligence collection'.[11] In short, the survival of the fledging state depended on the regime's work with letters.

The state's call for Soviet citizens to write letters and the state's extensive work with those letters, called into existence numerous institutions to process mail. These institutions show how deeply pervasive letter-writing became in Soviet culture. Each letter signified one (or more) citizen's initiative to communicate, as well as a whole segment of society mobilized to then process and react to the letter. One institution that existed for the entirety of the Soviet period was the letter department. Every public institution included a letter department charged with responding to letters, achieving resolutions to the problems letter writers raised and producing summaries and/or intelligence reports on incoming mail. By the late Soviet period, such departments had sizeable staffs. *Pravda* boasted the largest letter department with seventy workers, and *Komsomol'skaia pravda* (*Komsomol Truth*), a popular Soviet daily that at its peak in 1990 circulated more than 23 million copies per day, employed roughly fifty individuals, including forty rank-and-file workers, nine correspondents, and one editor.[12]

In the early Soviet period, the celebration of public letters was undoubtedly connected to surveillance efforts and in this way the Soviets resembled their Imperial predecessors and other governments across Europe at the time.[13] During the First World War and the Civil War, Soviet authorities regularly perlustrated private letters in part to censor information soldiers communicated to relatives on the home front. Perlustration also allowed authorities to draw up intelligence reports based on citizens' letters (*svodki*) that helped track developments on the front and assess the mood of the battle front and home front.[14] Letter departments at newspapers and governmental institutions also contributed to surveillance efforts by drawing up summaries of letters (*obzory*) to submit to state organs, which had become an established tradition by 1919.[15] Letter departments submitted overviews of mail to local and federal offices on a monthly and sometimes weekly basis. The state organs to which a newspaper submitted reports depended on the location and organizational affiliation of the paper.

The contribution of letter departments to the surveillance apparatus is important, though summaries of public letters—and the departments that processed them— served additional purposes as well. They communicated useful information about public opinion and the wishes of the broader population to the state. State organs often acted on this information too, granting a citizen's wish for a refrigerator or cow, looking into the poor conditions at a hospital, adding certain language to Party documents circulated by newspaper, or any number of other specific requests. Moreover, letter writers often counted on public institutions, including the press, to share their letters with appropriate state organs. Readers often saw the press as an important link to the government, and even as the surveillance system must have supported state repression, many citizens believed the connection between the state and the press could meaningfully resolve problems expressed in letters.

Soviet law required every public institution, including newspapers and govern- ment agencies, to respond to every piece of mail received, though internal discus- sions in letter departments confirm that not every letter received a response and that many responses were at best perfunctory. Nonetheless, the work of letter depart- ments was taxing and required great commitment on the part of employees. When a piece of mail entered the letter department, a staff member read the letter and attached a card to it that noted where the letter came from, select information about the author, and a brief description of the contents of the letter. The letter was then sent to the editor of the relevant department, the journalist to whose article they responded, or to the appropriate government ministry. The recipient was tasked with acting on the letter or at least replying to it.[16]

Following the death of Stalin in 1953, as Soviet leaders replaced terror as a tool of shoring up state power with other initiatives, ranging from mass housing campaigns to increased educational opportunities, public letters remained integral to the functioning of the Soviet state and society. A decree of August 29, 1967, described letters as

> one of the main forms of strengthening and broadening the link between party and people, of the participation of the population in the conduct of state affairs, a means for the expression of public opinion, [and] a source of information on the life of the country.[17]

The decree aimed to improve work with letters and introduced the requirement that letters be dealt with within a month of receipt. The following year, a decree of the Presidium of the Supreme Soviet articulated further guidelines for processing citizens' letters.[18] Stephen White argues that both decrees indicated a newfound significance of public letters in the Brezhnev era, yet in light of their profound sig- nificance in the 1920s and 1930s, it seems that the difference is a matter of degrees. The Soviet Constitution of 1977 differed from its 1936 predecessor in raising the ability to complain to state bodies to the level of a right. Articles 49 and 58 guaranteed a citizen's right to complain free of persecution and obliged the appropriate officials to examine and respond to citizens' complaints in a timely fashion.[19] At the same time, these articles simply enshrined in the Constitution statements articulated in earlier decrees.

Perestroika (Reconstruction), which commenced with Gorbachev's election in March 1985, heralded a unique period in the history of public letter-writing. At the Central Committee Plenum in April 1985, the new leader called on Party committees 'to ensure all channels of communication with the masses, to track the kind of attention devoted to public opinion, critical remarks, suggestions and letters from citizens'.[20] Letter-writing constituted part of a broader effort to activate the population and recover the socialist origins of the Soviet project—goals at the heart of *perestroika*. There was nothing new about the existence of letters under Gorbachev and yet this period witnessed unprecedented popularity of public letter-writing, indicated above all by the impressive ascent in the quantity of mail received. In the 1920s, the Central Council of the People's Commissars had received roughly 10,000 letters a year.[21] In the 1970s, the Central Committee received on average 516,000 letters a year.[22] But in 1986, the Central Committee counted 954,294 letters, nearly twice as many as six years earlier.[23] During *perestroika*, the quantity of mail to governmental organizations was dwarfed only by letters to the press, which also experienced a staggering rise in the number of letters received. Some of the most celebrated early figures include April 1924 when the newspaper *Krestianskaia gazeta* (*Peasant Newspaper*) received 4,876 letters in the course of a single week. In 1974, *Pravda* received 456,000 letters, while in 1975 *Izvestiia* (*News*) recorded 467,858 letters and *Trud* (*Work*) counted 548,174 letters received.[24] In contrast, in 1985 *Komsomol'skaia pravda* recorded 643,000 letters, and a staggering one million in the first nine and a half months of 1986.[25] That amounted to 3,922 letters per day. For the *perestroika* period, and perhaps the entire Soviet period, the amount of mail received by Soviet newspapers remained unparalleled in Western presses.[26]

The increase in mail correlates to greater public celebration of letters, fuelled in part by the devotion of more space on the printed newspaper page to readers' letters. Certain periodicals achieved unprecedented popularity in part for their letter section, including the weekly glossy *Ogoniok* (*Spark*) and the weekly *Sobesednik* (*Companion*), a companion publication to *Komsomol'skaia pravda*.[27] Newspaper correspondent Yuri Shchekochikhin described his work with readers' letters and in the newspaper reception room in *Hello, I Am Listening*, the popular scenario of which became the premise of a play and a film.[28] Groups devoted to discussing letters printed in newspapers abounded. Sensing the heightened significance of letters to the editor in particular, history students at Irkutsk State University created an archive for letters that periodicals no longer had space to preserve.[29]

The increased quantity of mail also points to a larger and more literate population than ever before. Literacy rates, which reached 40 per cent on the eve of the First World War, bolted upwards after the Bolshevik's 1919 decree on liquidating illiteracy. They reached 56.6 per cent in 1926 and 75 per cent of the total population by 1937.[30] In the 1950s, the USSR ranked among the only countries to boast a nearly 100 per cent literacy rate. The highly literate Soviet population also had greater access to newspapers during *perestroika* than ever before. The government permitted higher print runs and gave newspapers greater discretion over circulation, allowing production to come closer to demand. The more Soviet citizens had access to the paper, the more people could read and respond to articles and also read published letters.[31]

It appears that over the course of Soviet history, letter writers became increasingly diverse. In a study of the background of authors of letters to the press in the 1930s, Lenoe suggests that the practice of writing to the press was dominated by Communists, Komsomol members, and Soviet officialdom.[32] Letters to other state organs, however, might paint a different picture. After all, one need not have been a Party member or even sympathizer to attempt to mobilize state aid or influence governmental policy. By the late Soviet period, letters to state institutions and newspapers alike had become ubiquitous. As the writer Nadezhda Mandelstam remembered in her 1970 memoir, 'Which one of us had never written letters to the supreme powers[?]'[33] By the late Soviet period, letters from Party members to the press and other public outlets did not outnumber those from authors without Party affiliation.

For those who read Russian and those who do not, letters make rich sources for historical research. There are countless published anthologies of letters in Russian. Periodicals also offer a record of printed letters and are increasingly available in searchable digital format. Some newspapers published English-language editions, such as *Moscow News*. There are also translated volumes of letters, particularly for the *perestroika* period, which reflect heightened international attention to the practice of letter-writing at this time. Letters appear in nearly every archival collection. Even when letters do not turn up in an archive, other sources might provide a paper trail of letters that once existed, including publications, summaries of letters, intelligence reports, and discussions of letters recorded in meeting transcripts. Some internal archives also still preserve the extensive notecard filing system with basic information and summaries of every letter the institution received. These sources remain as important as letters themselves in understanding popular opinion, the relationship between citizens and the state and letter-writing as an institution in the Soviet Union.

Historiography of letters and letter-writing

The historiography of letter-writing reflects some of the broader developments in the field of Soviet studies that we see so well with other primary sources. Like diaries, for instance, letters have long appealed to scholars of twentieth-century Russia for their potential to reveal the inner thoughts of ordinary people, the expression of which have been assumed to be a rare commodity for as long as Russia has been perceived as a totalitarian state. As scholars began to challenge the totalitarian paradigm, many came to suggest that letters convey less about the individuals who wrote them than they do about the inner-workings of the state, the state's approach to governing a diverse nation, and the relationship between citizens and the state.

In short, how scholars have approached letters as sources reflects their broader assumptions about Russia and the Soviet Union.

The earliest scholarship on public letters dates back to the aftermath of the Second World War. Sociologists Alex Inkeles and Kent Geiger conducted a broad study of published letters to the editor with the goal of understanding the nature of public criticism in the USSR and the extent to which it was possible to voice subversive opinions in public. While they noted the Marxist-Leninist tradition of criticism and self-criticism—a tradition that remains essential to keep in mind when working with Soviet letters, especially critical letters—they nonetheless attributed the proliferation of critical letters not to ideology but to strategies of state survival. 'Letters to the editor may be said to serve as a channel for airing personal grievances', they wrote.

> To the degree that this serves to release tensions generated by the realities of everyday Soviet life, the *samokritika* (self-criticism) letters may be said to serve an important function in facilitating the rule of a regime which finds it extraordinarily dangerous to permit the relatively free expression of affect concerning many aspects of the function of the existing social system.

In other words, they saw critical letters as a safety valve intended to release steam and prevent an explosion of popular hatred that could undermine the regime.[34]

Inkeles and Geiger also analysed the sociological background of the authors and recipients of letters to investigate the relationship between author and recipient and the place of critical letters within the broader hierarchy of state figures. They demonstrated that public criticism commonly targeted mid-level bureaucrats but never the highest-ranking ones. This discrepancy reinforced the sense that those political figures, e.g., Stalin and his closest associates, made no mistakes and were beyond criticism.[35] Inkeles and Geiger's questions and conclusions appealed to Cold-War Western scholars. Their work elaborated the burgeoning interpretation of the Soviet Union as a premier example of totalitarianism—an interpretation that carried the field of Soviet studies through the end of the Cold War.

As long as the Cold War prevailed and scholars perceived the USSR as a textbook example of totalitarianism, studies of letter-writing offered only moderately different conclusions. An exception is political scientist Stephen White, who looked not just to letters, but the laws and formal institutions that governed the practice of letter-writing.[36] His study is instructive in how shifting the source base, even while relying on published sources, can produce new insights. White concluded that letters were no mere safety valve; rather, they provided citizens a tool for influencing state policy.[37] He applied this point to the Brezhnev era, not the Stalin period. Turning away from the period of the archetypal totalitarian leader was also key in shifting the interpretation of what letters revealed. Like earlier scholars, however, White implied that Soviet letter writers were primarily opposed to the state. It was impossible for him to imagine otherwise. Despite the ways his work reinforced the totalitarian paradigm, it raised the important question about institutions and laws that guided letter writing, which remain important to consider when using letters as historical sources, because they show how elaborate was the tradition that produced the documents we now have access to today.

The questions and conclusions that guided the discourse on letter-writing took a swift turn in the 1980s and 1990s with the archival revolution. As Gorbachev and then Yeltsin opened the doors of the archives, historians beheld the mountains of unpublished letters stored within. Sheila Fitzpatrick played a leading role in interpreting these sources. She worked extensively in the monolithic collection of letters to *Krestianskaia gazeta* at the Russian State Economic Archive (RGAE).[38] The chronological focus of the discussion returned to the Stalin period, especially the 1930s, though broad considerations of letter-writing as a practice produced studies of petitions and other pre-revolutionary precursors to the public letter.[39] Using the tools of cultural history, Fitzpatrick distinguished the variety of genres of letters that surfaced in the archive, including complaints, denunciations, petitions, requests for assistance, confessional letters, letters of opinion, and threatening letters. At least two journals devoted special issues to the subject of denunciations in particular.[40]

In the subfield of letter-writing, like the broader field of Soviet history, the archival turn provoked a fundamental reconsideration of the totalitarian school of Soviet studies. Fitzpatrick rethought the place of letters in Stalinist society. She rejected Inkeles and Geiger's 'safety valve' conclusion. With qualifications, she also challenged the broader conception of Stalin's Soviet Union as one with no public sphere whatsoever. 'The writing and reading of these letters to the authorities', she wrote in 'Supplicants and Citizens', 'is as close to a public sphere as one is likely to get during the Stalin period'.[41] In a way, her point suggested that letters were about far more than individual complaints and concerns. This sentiment echoed in the findings of Matthew Lenoe. 'Although it is possible to find in these letters indirect evidence about private political opinions, resistance to Stalinism, and individual manipulation of the Soviet state', he wrote, 'they have much greater value as direct windows on the everyday functioning of Soviet society, the instruments of power, and the ways in which agents of the Soviet state acted to shape the public identity of their subjects'.[42] These insights shifted the interpretation of letters from evidence of how fed up Soviet citizens were with the state – and by extension how poorly the state worked – to how letters constituted a central part of *how* the state functioned.

Another question that emerged from the archival turn concerned who, politically speaking, letter-writers were. Early literature suggested that authors could only be resisters. How could anyone, social scientists implicitly suggested, actually believe in the Soviet project? This view became so entrenched in the discussion of letters that historians like Lenoe, as demonstrated in the previous quotation, simply rejected the interpretation of letters as evidence of resistance, privileging instead what letters tell us about state power. In contrast, Juliane Fürst turned the question of resistance on its head. Her study of letters to *Komsomol'skaia pravda* in the late Stalin period argued that far from *resisting* the state, letter-writers aimed to *participate* in the life of the state. 'Without a basic conviction that their letters contributed to personal betterment and the good of the collective', she wrote, 'authors would not have picked up their pens'.[43]

The archival revolution that transformed historians' work with letters coincided with Gorbachev's *perestroika* and the explosion in political and popular attention to letters in the Soviet Union. The archival revolution and the letter revolution were not entirely unconnected: the explosion of letters under Gorbachev fuelled scholars' excitement about letters from earlier periods. Yet in other ways, the two movements remained disjointed. Anthologies of public letters published in the West appealed to an audience thirsty for insight into the minds of individual Soviet citizens.[44] As Studs Terkel described one volume, it offered the 'words and reflections of the Soviet people themselves'.[45] This view reflected the rapidly aging totalitarian paradigm of Soviet studies, especially the assumptions that Soviet people had long been denied the opportunity to speak their minds and that public discourse had only become possible under Gorbachev. This view of *perestroika*-era letters also implied that letter-writing was new under Gorbachev when, in fact, the practice had existed for centuries.

The shortcomings of literature on the heyday of letters in the Gorbachev era offers a sound reminder of the importance of contextualizing public letters when using them as historical sources. It is not that letters do not reveal the 'words and reflections' of their authors; but when richly contextualized, they reveal far more than that.

Interpreting public letters

Letters are time-consuming and tenacious sources to work with. Unlike Party speeches, they employ highly colloquial, idiosyncratic language and are largely handwritten. Both language and script make it challenging to interpret the documents, let alone decipher them. When confronted with a stack of letters, it is difficult to know which ones to focus on and the only way to find out is to begin reading through the pile. The reading process can be slow going, but can be made faster by having a list of questions ready before digging in.

When sitting before a single letter or a stack of letters alike, first, it is worth considering why the document(s) exist. Why did these letters end up in the archive? Or why did these particular letters reach publication? Newspapers were required to save letters for no more than three years, and so an original letter in a periodical archive was likely saved for a reason. The filing away of letters often has to do with the recipient: that person might have taken the time to respond to it and saved the letter to prove the effort exerted, or they might have felt a particular draw to letters on a certain topic. For published letters, editors always had options: they had thousands of letters to choose from. Why did they pick these letters in particular? What message do editors convey in the selection of letters published?

As you delve into the letters themselves, identify what you want to get out of the document. What questions do you hope to answer? How you would like to write about the sources? Is the goal to document the experience of 'the people' in a specific time or place? Is it to understand how a particular institution functioned? Is it to assess the inner workings of economic production? Is it to find evidence of shortcomings of a particular enterprise? Not every question requires countless letters for an answer.

If your questions are not clear before you start reading, develop them as you go. In either case, it is helpful to start with a shortlist of points to record in your notes to ensure your notes have the information you might need later, or at least lead you back to a specific place in a weighty stack of letters. These points might mirror the rubrics that letter department workers used for each letter received: Who was the author? When was the letter written? What were the letter's geographic origins and destination? Who was the recipient? What was the author's relationship to the recipient? What is the general content of the letter?

On additional readings of the letter, dig deeper into each question, especially who the author is. What is their name? Gender? Age? Profession? Educational background? What biographical information do they share about themselves? What are their political affiliations and persuasions? There is still a strong trend in work with letters as historical sources to mine them for voices critical of the state and, implicitly, to see the author as a resister. Avoid jumping to this conclusion. An author might bitterly complain about their surroundings without being anti-Soviet. Look for clues in the letter itself to determine the author's political outlook.

As much as a letter might document the voice of an individual author or a group of authors, it remains a communication between at least two bodies. It is thus as important to consider the recipient as the author. Who is the recipient? Why did the author pick this recipient in particular? Who is the intended audience beyond the recipient? Did the author hope this letter will be forwarded to other bodies? Or published? How might the recipient shape the author's tone and vocabulary and even the message? How might they present details of their own life in certain ways because of their audience or aims?

Letters reflect and elaborate broader social discourses, even if addressed to a specific person or institution. It can also be helpful to try to figure out what discourses might be relevant. Newspapers offer an excellent source for doing so. Triangulating between multiple kinds of sources can make a reading of any single letter much more robust.

Case study: V. Pristavkin to *Komsomol'skaia pravda*

The questions above offer a starting point for unpacking a letter. We can try them out on a sample letter from V. Pristavkin to the popular daily *Komsomol'skaia pravda*. Pristavkin wrote:

> Hello.
>
> A year ago *perestroika* was not so noticeable; now you feel it loud and clear. Yesterday I returned from work (having in the cupboard at home a loaf of bread and a piece of frozen meat; I used up the sugar a month ago when making a jar of jam), and went out to buy something for dinner. Here's what they had: ketchup, Turkish tea, flour for 31 kop[ecks], bay leaves, matches, salt,

coffee beans, and that was it, and there was a list of distribution norms [of what should have been there] on the shelf next to it. So *perestroika* is everywhere visible. Nobody can convince me that *perestroika* is for nothing. It's for something alright. It's a different matter that all this may be temporary, that they will [eventually] feed us not only a line, but noodles as well.

All the while, for everything happening in the country, the good and the bad, the responsibility falls on *perestroika* and the people making it a reality. But while fairly crediting it [*perestroika*] for *glasnost* and democratization, don't chalk the rest of our foul life up to the times of stagnation or the Tatar-Mongol occupation. People now often ask if it's worth going to the West. I'll say about myself, I would not leave and the feeling of love for my Homeland is not the reason; I simply am a sentimental person and I value the cattails along the Moscow river; and who needs me there, [a person who] collected antediluvian machines (as a child) and fixes old boiler equipment (now).

So goes life, without even the opportunity to work with a feeling of satisfaction, with beautiful and useful instruments, on quality, modern equipment, [and to] depend on one's own hands and head rather than the boss. I of course want to believe that perhaps children await a different, interesting, free work and life, but this is not what previous experience amounts to. But for now it is not the person that matters. Even criminals (though there are real people among them) get more attention than the so-called common man, ordinary people. They try to understand criminals, to justify their crimes by the circumstances of our lives, fight for their humane conditions in places of exile and so on. All of this is probably necessary (except for rapists and murderers, [they are] not people).

But without choking on conversations, the most important thing is to help and give the opportunity to live a dignified life to the simple, average person, maybe then there will be less abominations in our life.

Respectfully, V. Pristavkin

31.07.90[46]

Pristavkin's letter appears in a collection of several thousand letters to *Komsomol'skaia pravda* written between 1988 and 1994. The collection is housed at the Russian State Archive for Socio-Political History (RGASPI) in Moscow. This letter is filed together with 95 other letters under the subject heading: 'Citizens' letters to the editor of the newspaper '*Komsomol'skaia pravda*' about the situation in the country, p[art] 1'. While the heading is vague, most letters focus on economic conditions. There are more questions than answers about why this letter exists today. Archivists who created the finding aids could not explain why these particular letters ended up in the archive. The editor of *Komsomol'skaia pravda*'s letter department explained in an interview that the letters were taken without forewarning by staff of the youth archive in the mid-1990s, but could not explain why these particular letters made it to the archive or why these letters were saved more than three years by the newspaper.[47]

I encountered this collection when conducting archival research on the history of *perestroika* and citizens' engagement of reform. I consulted this folder in particular for a more targeted evaluation of citizens' response to the acute economic crisis that plagued the last years of *perestroika*. At the outset, I wanted to know: did citizens continue to engage the reform program even as shortages increasingly plagued the Soviet Union after 1989? Pristavkin's letter appeared to offer particularly rich insight into this question.

On first reading, we can play the role of letter department staff member. The source is penned by V. Pristavkin on July 31, 1990. The letter does not indicate where the author is from, but the return address and postal stamps on the envelope attached to the letter state Dnepropetrovsk, a central Ukrainian city on the Dnieper River. The recipients included the staff of the mailroom at *Komsomol'skaia pravda*. There is no documentation that indicates the nature of the response to the letter or that it received a response at all. As far as I could establish, the letter was not published. The author relates to the recipient as a reader of the newspaper. The letter describes food shortages in Pristavkin's city and tries to square the absence of goods from stores with the promises of reform.

On second reading, the letter reveals far more about the author, even while some basic information remains obscure. As indicated by the consonant ending on the last name, the author, Pristavkin, is a man. The letter does not indicate his age. There is nothing directly about his education either, but correct spelling and precise use of language suggest he had some education, probably higher education. His language shows his sense of humour and feel for idiomatic expressions. The last line of the first paragraph (translated here as 'they will [eventually] feed us not only a line, but noodles as well') plays on the Russian idiom 'Don't hang a noodle on my ear!' The sentence shows his ability to play with language. He calls himself 'sentimental'. He mentions his love of nature and his quirky pastime of collecting old machines. He does not explicitly state his profession, though he might repair boilers.

This letter is particularly interesting in terms of the author's political background. He notes that he is not particularly patriotic, which sets him apart from the rapidly expanding ranks of Russian and Ukrainian nationalists. He also notes he has no ambition to emigrate, distinguishing him from the many who left the Soviet Union in the late 1980s. The sparse list of groceries he found in his cupboards and the random assortment of goods he found at the store suggest dissatisfaction with the course of *perestroika*.

It seems reasonable to assume that even if Pristavkin does not want to leave the USSR, he is a critic of the state. Additional probing of the document, however, might challenge this conclusion. The recipient of the document is *Komsomol'skaia pravda*. The author does not indicate if he is a regular reader of the paper, as many letter writers did, but his middle-of-the-road politics resonate with the newspaper's political agenda. In this case, the recipient of the letter provides a clear indication of where to look to assess the broader social discourses that this letter engaged: the newspaper he addressed. From July through December 1990, the newspaper was filled with coverage of the economic crisis and plans for decentralizing the Soviet economy, including Stanislav Shatalin's 500 Days Program.

In this case, a closer look at reportage on the economic situation transforms how we read Pristavkin's letter. On September 29, 1990, the front page of the newspaper published a diary from 'Citizen K' that documented goods she could and could not buy in her region. In remarks surrounding the excerpted diary, editors noted the influx of letters about shortages. They also invited readers to become sociologists or investigative journalists, documenting the ebb and flow of goods where they lived in 'kitchen diaries' or letters. 'From Parliament, the government, [and] Shatalin's group, we await change', it noted. 'From citizens male and female, [we await] letters. Keep diaries in the kitchen and send them to us. This will be the thermometer under the armpit of reform'.[48] Even though this particular example of the newspaper calling on citizens to document shortage appeared after Pristavkin wrote to *Komsomol'skaia pravda*, it remains relevant to his letter. It is one of several instances in which the newspaper called on readers to relate to shortages in this way and reflects a broader expectation of how citizens could engage reform.

Reading Pristavkin's letter alongside this publication casts it in a new light. First, it helps make sense of the extensive lists in the first paragraph. Here the author is documenting items that exist in his cupboards and on the store shelves. Notably, he does not say what does *not* exist, but what *does* appear on the shelves. Second, it chips away at the interpretation of the author as purely a critic of reform. It now appears that he is interested in participating in reform in precisely the ways offered by the newspaper: by documenting shortage.

This point is important to the question I started with: did citizens continue to engage the reform program even as shortages increasingly plagued the Soviet Union after 1989? Pristavkin's letter seems to suggest they did. A close reading of this particular letter also illuminates the specific forms engagement assumed in a period of acute shortages. This finding raises questions about the relationship between Soviet citizens and the state in times of shortage and the link between economic crisis and the Soviet collapse. But it is important not to over-extend the conclusions of a single source. Answering these broad questions requires a look into more public letters and other sources.

Conclusion

Public letters offer a unique record of the voices of ordinary Soviets – citizens who did not occupy particularly elevated positions of power and whose experiences shape the historical narrative of twentieth-century Russia far less than well-known leaders. But no source, including letters, offers unmitigated access to those voices. Public letters are not simply a record of static opinions or understandings of the self. They offer articulations of opinions and even understandings of the self that are worked out in part in the process of writing the letter. Moreover, letters aim to do more than express the thoughts of the author. On the most basic level, they are communications between two parties. Expressing the thoughts of the author is just one of many aims a letter-writer might seek to accomplish; they might also hope to educate, to effect change, to express frustration, or to find a sympathetic reader. To mine letters for their full historical value, it is important to contextualize the document within the tradition of letter-writing, the laws that guided the practice, and the institutions designed to process citizens' mail. Also situate letters in broader public discourses, even if letters were by and large closed communications. Doing so reveals how public letters shed light on far more than individual thoughts and experiences and provide a source for understanding individual lives within the broader constellation of society and state.

Notes

1 'Iz organizatsionnogo ustava RSDRP, priniatogo na II s"ezde partii' (1903), in B. P. Iakovlev (ed.), *V.I. Lenin, KPSS. O rabote s pis'mami trudiashchikhsia* (Moscow: Politizdat, 1984), p. 129.

2 On the distinction between public and private letters, see Sheila Fitzpatrick, 'Supplicants and Citizens: Public Letter Writing in Soviet Russia in the 1930s', *Slavic Review*, 55 (1995), pp. 78–105 (pp. 78–9).

3 Margareta Mommsen, *Hilf mir; Mein Recht zu finden. Russische Bittschiften von Iwan dem Schrecklichen bis Gorbachow* (Frankfurt am Main: Popyläen Verlag, 1987).

4 Isabel de Madariaga, *Catherine the Great: A Short History* (New Haven, CT: Yale University Press, 1990), p. 122.

5 Andrew Verner, 'Discursive Strategies in the 1905 Revolution: Peasant Petitions from Vladimir Province', *Russian Review*, 54 (1995), pp. 65–90 (p. 66). On petitions in the Imperial period, also see Gregory L. Freeze, *From Supplication to Revolution: A Documentary Social History of Imperial Russia* (Oxford: Oxford University Press, 1988); and Emily Pyle, 'Peasant Strategies for Obtaining State Aid: A Study of Petitions During World War I', *Russian History/Histoire Russe*, 24 (1997), pp. 41–64.

6 Jeffrey Brooks, *When Russia Learned to Read* (Princeton, NJ: Princeton University Press, 1985), p. 4.

7 On letters to the editor in the late Imperial period, see James Krukones, *To the People: The Russian Government and the Newspaper Sel'skii vestnick ('Village Herald'), 1881–1917* (New York, NY: Garland, 1987).

8 Matthew Lenoe, 'Letter-Writing and the State: Reader Correspondence with Newspapers as a Source for Early Soviet History', *Cahiers du Monde russe*, 40 (1999), pp. 139–69 (p. 141).

9 Stephen White, 'Political Communications in the USSR: Letters to Party, State and Press', *Political Studies*, 31 (1983), pp. 43–60 (p. 44).

10 Lenoe, 'Letter-Writing and the State', p. 143.

11 Ibid., pp. 143–4.

12 Jim Riordan et al. (eds.), *Dear Comrade Editor: Readers' Letters to the Soviet Press under Perestroika* (Bloomington, IN: Indiana University Press, 1992), p. 3; and M. A. Kechkina, Interview with author, June 12, 2014.

13 Peter Holquist, 'Information Is the Alpha and Omega of Our Work': Bolshevik Surveillance in Its Pan-European Context, *Journal of Modern History*, 69 (1997), pp. 415–450 (p. 418); Vladlen S. Izmozik, 'Voices from the Twenties: Private Correspondence Intercepted by the OGPU', *Russian Review*, 55 (1996), pp. 287–308; and Lenoe, 'Letter-Writing and the State', pp. 151–8.

14 William Rosenberg, 'Reading Soldiers' Moods: Russian Military Censorship and the Configuration of Feeling in World War I', *American Historical Review*, 119 (2014), pp. 714–40.

15 Lenoe, 'Letter-Writing and the State', p. 143.
16 Riordan, Dear Comrade Editor, p. 3.
17 Quoted in Stephen White, 'Political Communications in the USSR: Letters to Party, State and Press', *Political Studies*, 31 (1983), p. 45.
18 Ibid.
19 For an English translation of the Constitution, see 'The Soviet Constitution of 1977', https://en.wikisource.org/wiki/Constitution_of_the_Soviet_Union_(1977,_Unamended) (accessed 24 July 2018).
20 *Materialy plenuma TsK KPSS 23 aprelia 1985 goda* (Moscow: Izdatel'stvo politicheskoi literatury, 1985), pp. 20–1.
21 White, 'Political Communications', p. 44.
22 This figure is based on numbers in ibid., p. 47.
23 Russian State Archive of Contemporary History (RGANI), f. 100, op. 1, d. 285, l. 2.
24 White, 'Political Communications', p. 52. By the 1970s, the total number of letters to all Soviet national papers taken together reached approximately 60 to 70 million a year. Ibid., p. 51.
25 A. Murtazaev, '1 000 000 pisem s nachala nyneshnego goda poluchila redaktsiia', *Komsomol'skaia pravda*, 211 (16 September 1986), p. 1.
26 Riordan et al. (eds.), *Dear Comrade Editor*, pp. 3, 8.
27 On letters in *Ogoniok*, see editor-in-chief Vitaly Korotich's introductory remarks to two anthologies of letters to the magazine: Vitaly Korotich (ed.), *The Best of Ogonyok: The New Journalism of Glasnost* (London: Heinemann, 1991); and Vitalii Korotich (ed.), *Pis'ma v 'Ogonio'* (Moscow: Izdatel'stvo 'Pravda,' 1990).
28 Iurii Shchekochikhin, *Allo, my vas Slyshim: Iz khroniki nashego vremeni* (Moscow: Molodaia gvardiia, 1987).
29 For a description of their efforts and a selection of the archive, see Mikhail Rozhanskii, et al. (eds.), *Pis'ma ob istorii i dlia istorii, 1988–1990 gody* (Irkutsk: Tsentr nezavisimykh sotsial'nykh issledovanii i obrazovaniia, 2014).
30 Sheila Fitzpatrick, *Stalin's Peasants: Resistance and Survival in the Russian Village after Collectivization* (New York, NY: Oxford University Press, 1994), pp. 225–6 and p. 363, note 78.
31 Riordan et al. (eds.), *Dear Comrade Editor*, pp. 4–7.
32 Lenoe, 'Letter-Writing and the State', p. 151.
33 Quoted in Fitzpatrick, 'Supplicants and Citizens', p. 78.
34 Alex Inkeles and Kent Geiger, 'Critical Letters to the Editors of the Soviet Press: Areas and Modes of Complaint', *American Sociological Review*, 17 (1952), pp. 694–703 (p. 703).
35 Idem., 'Critical Letters to the Editors of the Soviet Press: Social Characteristics and Interrelations of Critics and the Criticized', *American Sociological Review*, 18 (1953), pp. 12–22 (pp. 21–2).
36 White, 'Political Communications in the USSR', pp. 44–6.
37 Ibid., p. 43.
38 See Fitzpatrick's *Stalin's Peasants*, and 'Readers' Letters to *Krest'ianskaia gazeta*, 1938', *Russian History/Histoire Russe*, 24 (1997), pp. 149–170.
39 See Richard Hellie, 'The Origins of Denunciation in Muscovy', *Russian History/Histoire Russe*, 24 (1997), pp. 11–26; Mommsen, *Hilf mir, mein Recht zu finden*; Josh Sanborn, 'Conscription, Correspondence, and Politics in Late Imperial Russia', *Russian History/Histoire Russe*, 24 (1997), pp. 27–40; and Andrew Verner, 'Discursive Strategies in the 1905 Revolution: Peasant Petitions from Vladimir Province', *Russian Review*, 54 (1988), pp. 65–90.
40 Sheila Fitzpatrick (ed.), 'Petitions and Denunciations in Russia from Muscovy to the Stalin Era', Special Issue, *Russian History/Histoire Russe*, 24, (1997); idem. (ed.),

'Practices of Denunciation in Modern European History, 1789–1989', Special Issue, *Journal of Modern History*, 68 (1996).
41 Fitzpatrick, 'Supplicants and Citizens', p. 80.
42 Lenoe, 'Letter-Writing and the State', p. 140.
43 Juliane Fürst, 'In Search of Soviet Salvation: Young People Write to the Stalinist Authorities', *Contemporary European History*, 15 (2006), pp. 327–45 (p. 332).
44 See Christopher Cert et al. (eds.), *Small Small Fires: Letters from the Soviet People to Ogonyok Magazine, 1987–1990* (New York, NY: Summit Books, 1990); Vitalii Korotich (ed.), *The Best of Ogonyok: The New Journalism of Glasnost* (London: William Heinemann, 1990); Ron McKay (ed.), *Letters to Gorbachev: Life in Russia Through the Postbag of Argumenty i Fakty* (New York, NY: Viking Penguin, 1991); and Riordan et al., *Dear Comrade Editor*.
45 Quoted in Cerf et al., *Small Fires*, front cover.
46 RGASPI, f. M-98, op. 2, d. 30, ll. 253–255.
47 M. A. Kechkina, Interview with author, June 12, 2014.
48 *Komsomol'skaia pravda*, September 29, 1990, p. 1.

Further reading

Alexopoulos, Golfo, *Stalin's Outcasts: Aliens, Citizens, and the Soviet State, 1926–1936* (Ithaca, NY: Cornell University Press, 2003).
Fitzpatrick, Sheila, 'Supplicants and Citizens: Public Letter Writing in Soviet Russia in the 1930s', *Slavic Review*, 55 (1995), pp. 78–105.
_____, 'Signals from Below: Soviet Letters of Denunciation of the 1930s', *Journal of Modern History*, 68 (1996), pp. 831–66.
_____, (ed.), 'Practices of Denunciation in Modern European History, 1789–1989', Special Issue, *Journal of Modern History*, 68 (1996).
_____, (ed.), 'Petitions and Denunciations in Russia From Muscovy to the Stalin Era', Special Issue, *Russian History/Histoire Russe*, 24 (1997).
Fürst, Julianne, 'In Search of Salvation: Young People Write to the Soviet Authorities', *Contemporary European History*, 15 (2006), pp. 327–45.
Inkeles, Alex, and Kent Geiger, 'Critical Letters to the Editors of the Soviet Press: Areas and Modes of Complaint', *American Sociological Review*, 17 (1952), pp. 694–703.
_____, and Kent Geiger, 'Critical Letters to the Editors of the Soviet Press: Social Characteristics and Interrelations of the Critics and the Criticized', *American Sociological Review*, 18 (1953), pp. 12–22.
Kozlov, Denis, *The Readers of Novyi Mir: Coming to Terms with the Stalinist Past* (Cambridge, MA: Harvard University Press, 2013).
Lampert, Christopher, *Whistleblowing in the Soviet Union: Complaints and Abuses under State Socialism* (London: Macmillan, 1985).
Lenoe, Matthew E., 'Letter-Writing and the State: Reader Correspondence with Newspapers as a Source for Early Soviet History', *Cahiers du Monde russe*, 40 (1999), pp. 139–69.
Todd, William Mills, *The Familiar Letter as a Literary Genre in the Age of Pushkin* (Princeton, NJ: Princeton University Press, 1976).
White, Stephen, 'Political Communications in the USSR: Letters to Party, State and Press', *Political Studies*, 31 (1983), pp. 43–60.

Index

References to endnotes are preceded by an (n) and have only been included if they substantially expand on discussion in the text.

The main entries for source materials that are the subject of a chapter are in **bold**.

Made in the USA
Las Vegas, NV
28 August 2023

76728359R00157